A

HISTORY OF HERKIMER COUNTY,

INCLUDING

THE UPPER MOHAWK VALLEY,

FROM THE

EARLIEST PERIOD TO THE PRESENT TIME:

WITH A

BRIEF NOTICE OF THE IROQUOIS INDIANS, THE EARLY GERMAN TRIBES, THE PALATINE IMMIGRATIONS INTO THE COLONY OF NEW YORK, AND BIOGRAPHICAL SKETCHES OF THE PALATINE FAMILIES, THE PATENTEES OF BURNETSFIELD IN THE YEAR 1725.

ALSO

BIOGRAPHICAL NOTICES OF THE MOST PROMINENT PUBLIC MEN OF THE COUNTY:

WITH

IMPORTANT STATISTICAL INFORMATION.

BY NATHANIEL S. BENTON.

ALBANY:
J. MUNSELL, 78 STATE STREET.
1856.

TO THE PEOPLE OF HERKIMER COUNTY

I dedicate this humble and unpretending volume. If the manuscript sheets, which have been prepared with some labor, and a scrupulous regard to the best authenticated facts, shall assume the form of a readable book, it will be through their generous appreciation of the writer's efforts.

And, if my labors to condense and illustrate the annals of what has hitherto been and now is an interesting portion of one of the largest and most populous states of the American Union, in the destinies of which the citizens of Herkimer county have hitherto so largely participated, shall merit and receive the approval of those so well qualified to form just conceptions of their value and importance, I shall have no hope or ambition left unsatisfied.

THE AUTHOR.

CONTENTS.

ERRATA.

The reader is requested to note the following corrections:

Page 25, line 3, after the word *of* there should be a —.
" 25, 5th line from top, for *Theidelburgh* read *Heidelburgh.*
" 31, last line, for *navigated* read *immigrated.*
" 40, 3d line from bottom, for *interest* read *influence.*
" 121, 2d par., line 6, for *affairs* read *offences.*
" 124, 2d par. line 7, for *retaining* read *exerting.*
" 161, 162 and 193, Col. Gansevoort's name is misprinted.
" 204, 5th par. line 2, read law of attainder.
" 246, 14th line from bottom, for *portion* read *fraction.*
" 271, 12th line from bottom, for *states* read *state.*
" 320, 2d par. line 11, for *county* read *country.*
" 361, 3d par. 1st line, for *cause* read *care.*
" 369, 2d par. for *Edward* read *Edmund.*
" 377, 2d par. 12th line, for *Merray* read *Merry.*
" 407, note, for *John Spinner* read *John P. Spinner.*
" 437, first line, for *Klacks* read *Klocks.*

The letter J frequently occurs in proper names for I; the reader familiar with the names will be able to make the correction.

NEW GRÆFENBERG WATER CURE ESTABLISHMENT. See page 400.

INTRODUCTORY CHAPTER.

It is now one hundred and thirty-three years since the German emigrants from the Lower Palatinate of the Rhine, to escape from the iron workings of a colonial vassalage more stern, cruel and crushing, than European serfdom in its baldest and most naked form, planted themselves in the upper Mohawk valley, under the benevolent auspices of Governor William Burnet. They came to seek for themselves and their posterity homes and abiding places, where they could enjoy the fruits of their labor and eat the bread of toil, unmolested by imperial hirelings and intrusive task-masters, and to worship the God of the living and the dead in accordance with a lowly and approving conscience: it is now nearly ninety-eight years since that portion of these people, who had seated themselves on the north side of the Mohawk, at "the German flats," now Herkimer, were unexpectedly assailed by a numerous body of French and Indians, many of them killed, their dwellings and well stored barns plundered and burned, their stock of various kinds also killed or driven off, and finally the survivors carried into captivity: it is now seventy-eight years since the Oriskany battle was fought, or, I might with propriety say, the Oriskany massacre was perpetrated, which disastrous event converted the whole valley into a house of mourning: seventy-two years since peace restored hope, quiet and safety to the desponding husbandman; small consolation to the mourning widow and the homeless orphan: sixty-four years since the county was organized, when peace with all its concomitant blessings had resumed its sway: and no one had yet been found bold or patient enough, to undertake the labor of writing out the annals of Herkimer county.

It was too late by forty years to collect and arrange the early traditional history of the valley, when the writer turned his attention to a subject he had often discussed with others, and with them regretted that the matter had been so long postponed or neglected. I have pursued my original plan and object, projected two years ago, as rapidly as other pursuits and urgent calls in other directions would allow. I have not acomplished in extenso all I designed, and it would be invidious in me to state wherein and why, I have failed. The reader familiar with the history of this state, will at once perceive, I have consulted without stint the Annals of Tryon County, Stone's Life of Brant, Schoharie County and the Border Wars of New York, the Documentary History of New York, Documents relating to the Colonial History of this state, Journals of the New York Provincial Congress, Schoolcraft's Reports on the Iroquois, Hammond's Political History of New York, and Munsell's Typographical Miscellany.

One of the strongest inducements that led me to undertake the task which I have now completed, was to correct as far as I could, some of the grave, and it seemed to me manifest errors or mistakes, which found their way into published works of supposed authenticity, in regard to General Nicholas Herkimer and his family. No author ever spoke of him, to my knowledge, as a brilliantly great man, and no one can with justice or propriety deny that he was a brave and good man; firmly devoted to the provincial cause and American freedom. If a cloud appeared in the distance to hang over him, growing out of the fact that some members of the family were hostile to the movements of the colonists, could it be any fault of his, unless he had the ability to control them, and failed to exert it? But let it be remembered that other members of the same family who survived the General, devoted themselves in the future progress of the war, with zeal and courage in defense of the country.

Another motive prompted me to the undertaking. Herkimer county was one of the first erected after the revolution, and while the surrounding counties, and some of them carved from the territory it once embraced, were esteemed worthy of elaborate historical notice which had been liberally patronized by the populations of those counties, it seemed strange indeed that she should so long have remained neglected and forgotten, like the illustrious individual whose name she bears, and no one of her sons, native or adopted, would venture to place her in a just position. All that portion of the book compiled from public works and documents, such as the origin of the titles to lands, the description and boundaries of the county and the towns, and the statistical and other information derived from the recent census, may be relied upon as strictly and critically accurate.

Heretofore, several, if I may not say many, of the political men of the county, have held not only reputable, but high positions in the councils of the state, and some of those, who are now dead, have left an enduring impress of their talents and exertions upon the political institutions of the state. The somewhat peculiar political characteristics, which have heretofore marked the action of a considerable majority of the voting population of the county, seemed to me a matter worthy of elaborate consideration. Why two peoples, distinct in their origin, dissimilar in tastes, habits and customs, should harmonize on a great political problem for a period of more than fifty years, and in numbers to carry almost every popular election, presented a question worthy of inquiry and solution. Animated with a strong desire to arrive at a just and proper conclusion in respect to this question, I have given, in the sequel of the book, a full statement of the facts which are believed to have drawn the German and English or New England populations into harmony.

A brief allusion to the aboriginal inhabitants of the country, found roaming over its extended surface and almost impenetrable wilds, at the first advent of the European emigrant, was appropriate to the subject in hand as a necessary starting point from which to trace the authentic events of history, intended to be developed in the subsequent pages of the work. This is not the place to make an effort to reach the origin and follow the progress of a proud and brave, but a barbarous and illiterate people, whose annals can only be traced through a dark cloud of traditional mysticism, highly figurative, unnatural, and entirely improbable, when examined and compared with the providences of God, as given to us and illustrated by the written history of other branches of the human race; it has not therefore been attempted.

Although a history of the upper Mohawk valley does not necessarily embrace that of any other country or state, I have not considered a brief elucidation of German history as out of place, inasmuch as the first European settlements in the valley were made up entirely of a people of purely German origin, whose recent immigration into the colony had given no opportunity of change in habits, manners and customs, if any such change could have been effected in the adult emigrant, even if he had been a whole life time in reaching the land of promise, and had meanwhile sojourned with divers nations and people.

The particulars of this Palatine or German immigration, so far as they can now be given, are interesting, and seemed worthy of extended notice. The events which produced the movement in the heart of an old and polished European nation, and the causes which prompted these people to seek a refuge and home on the western continent, are quite as legitimate a subject of local American history, as the oft-repeated relation of the exodus of the pilgrim fathers from Europe, and their landing at Plymouth rock.

Persecution and religious intolerance drove the Puritans

to seek an asylum from civil and ecclesiastical oppression, and to fix themselves as the planters of a new colony, on a lone and desolate shore, surrounded by an unbroken wilderness, while the same illegitimate emanations from the religion of the cross compelled the German Palatines to plant themselves in an exposed and wilderness frontier, as an out-post and van-guard, to protect and cover the older settlements in their rear from Indian assaults and depredations, and the not much less refined warfare carried on by a neighboring European colony, whose relentless cruelties, unmitigated barbarities and bigoted intolerance, they and their fathers had so often before seen, suffered and tasted.

We are not only able to name the first European settlers, the pioneers of the upper valley, but we can trace the descendants of most of them, as being still inhabitants of the county, while some of those families, from emigration or other causes have become entirely extinct, and the name is no longer known among us. Although there now are numerous descendants of the female branch of the Herkimer family in the county, it is believed there is not, at this time, one inhabitant in it bearing that name. With perhaps two or three exceptions, the chapter of biographies of the Palatine families, will attract but little interest out of or beyond a confined locality. As a whole the subject is worthy the attention and labor bestowed in getting it up. It will be noticed that several individuals of these families have held prominent official stations in the county. From the first settlement of the valley, under the Burnetsfield patent, to the outbreak of the revolution, many German settlers came into the upper valley, some from Schoharie county, and the lower valley, now Montgomery county, others from New York and the shores of the Hudson river, a few from New Jersey, and probably several of the third emigration of the Palatines, who arrived in New York in 1722. I have not been able, as yet, to learn the names of a single family of English descent, settled in the German-flats district, previous to the revolution, except that of Thompson on Cosby's manor. There may have been two or three others. Much care and attention has been given to the biographical sketches of the official personages, who have been residents of and who died in the county. These sketches are not all I intended they should be in the outset nor all I would now wish them to be. I took what I believed proper measures, at an early day, to obtain precise and accurate information in regard to this subject. I did not anticipate any difficulty, and much less a failure. But my motives and objects were misconceived, or not approved of, or some of the parties to whom my circulars were addressed have exhibited an ignorance or indifference painful to think of.

I am compelled, reluctantly, to make an apology for a seeming neglect of the religious institutions of the county. I did hope to have been able to lay before the readers of this unpretending volume, a brief historical outline of the various religious organizations in the county, their foundation, progress and present condition; and took such measures at an early day, as would, I believed, secure this most desirable object. I care not to indulge in a single remark further on this topic. The statistical results, taken from the late state census, which will be found in a subsequent chapter, with some extracts from the journals of two missionaries who visited the county more than fifty years ago, must content the reader on this head. I should have been most happy to have followed them with a record of the names and the results of the labors of those who then and afterwards occupied this ground and ministered to our fathers in spiritual things, and should have done it, if I could have accomplished it by any other means than the course adopted, which entirely failed.

The reader unacquainted with our localities, should not conclude that the people of Herkimer county are indifferent to the grave subject which relates to their future welfare, because they find no elaborate display of churches, missionary and Bible societies organized within the county. As one reason of my failure in this respect, it may have been supposed, I was engaged in a work, the profits of which would amply repay me for the trouble and expense of collecting all the information needful to make the book perfect, interesting and valuable.

The writer, compiler and publisher of a local history, is in a condition somewhat like the Connecticut parson, whose congregation gave him a call and fixed the salary at one hundred dollars a year, one half to be paid in grain and such other necessary articles of living as they might have to spare and he might want. When he called for the payment of the balance of his salary, he was modestly told, he owed the parish fifty dollars for the rent of the parsonage and glebe. A local historian must be willing to perform any amount of labor required to make his book what he knows and wishes it should be, but if he hazards a large outlay, merely for the glory of publishing a book, his ambition will cost him dear.

The author who writes for extended glory or large profit, must bestow his talents and labor on subjects quite different from those I now have in hand. Nevertheless, if I shall be so fortunate as to meet the reasonable expectations of the people of the county, I shall have achieved all that my ambition can crave, or my most sanguine hopes have ever anticipated.

The chapter embracing the history of the several towns in the county will be found interesting, on account of the local historical matters there collected, and the statistical information condensed and arranged which will render the work highly useful as a manual. The brief notices of the early New England settlers are necessary links to conduct the reader through the early history of the county. The annals of the county would not be complete without the condensed view embraced in the chapter comprehending its political history. Whatever may have been and are the author's predilections on the questions discussed in that chapter, he would not feel this a proper occasion to give them any undue prominence, and he is confident a candid public will acquit him of indulging in any partisanship, or the least departure from a liberal and candid recital of facts connected with the party politics of the times. I am aware that local historians have hitherto given but small space in their works to the political histories of the counties. The reasons for this omission do not seem to me quite obvious, nor is it in any respect important now to make them a subject of discussion or inquiry. The intelligent reader will, I think, find himself amply repaid for his time by a perusal of the chapter.

The historical works relating to the Mohawk valley, heretofore published, have necessarily been confined to the prominent and leading events of the old French and the Revolutionary wars. The minor events and leading incidents, which have marked the progress of the country, have attracted but little or no attention, and consequently have no place in the works alluded to. The author's object has been, so far as relates to the upper Mohawk valley, to supply this desideratum. The upper valley being only an outskirt of civilization and a frontier during the whole period of these two wars, would not of course attract the particular attention of writers, not familiar with all its localities, its legends and its traditions, and the character of its population; hence we must not be surprised to observe the little regard bestowed upon the eventful transactions of that locality. The author has endeavored to cover the whole ground, and fill up all chasms.

The attainder by the state government of the adherents to the British crown, and the consequent forfeiture and confiscation of their estates, has been incidentally mentioned by former writers of our history, drawn out by the fact that a large tract of valuable lands in the county had escheated to the state, by the statute attainder of Sir John Johnson. In consequence of the misapprehension of the facts in regard to the extent of this escheat, the author, in connection with the history of the land titles, has deemed it proper not only to elucidate the subject fully and minutely, but to attempt, not an apology merely, but defense, ample and elaborate, of the revolutionary patriots and fathers, who adopted and rigidly enforced the attainder act of 1779. My countrymen have more than once been charged with illiberality and cruelty in exacting the "pound of flesh," after the British king had yielded the point and confirmed the independence of his rebellious colonies. These advocates for republican munificence and generosity, seem to have forgotten the lives immolated on the altar of oppression, and the millions of money expended in defending the country against the aggressive acts of many of these same attainted adherents of loyalty; and that, if stern and inexorable justice was exacted, it was only in observance of a rule of public law sanctioned by the most refined civilization. The emancipated colonists should have been willing to mete out exact and even-handed justice, but they were not in any view which could be taken of this question, in a condition to be generous.

Although this may be quite a proper subject for general history, and elaborate discussion by statesmen, it finds a suitable place in the humbler annals of the upper Mohawk valley, where the forfeitures have been incurred, and the law of reprisal has been enforced. While the advocates of restoration of forfeited estates are zealously engaged in finding condemnatory arguments against the Americans for not yielding the forfeiture, let them bear in mind not only the circumstances that provoked the action of the colonial authorities, but the hostile attitude of the British authorities long after the peace of 1783 was inaugurated. The frontier posts were long held, in despite of the energetic remonstrances of the United States, and in violation of the treaty of peace;

the western Indian tribes were instigated to acts of hostility, and rumored threats of a renewal of the war, and a speedy subjugation of the rebel colonists, did not and could not fail to influence the state governments in their action upon this question.

I take great pleasure in tendering my acknowledgments to the present Secretary of State, of this state, and A. G. Johnson, Esq., his deputy; the Hon. Abijah Beckwith, of Columbia; Hon. F. E. Spinner, of Mohawk; Hon. E. P. Hurlbutt, of Newport; Jonas Cleland, Esq., of Warren; Doct. William Mather, of Fairfield; Lauren Ford, Esq., Little Falls; Samuel Earl, Esq., Herkimer; D. C. Henderson, of Norway; E. T. Cleland, Esq., county clerk; to whom I am indebted for facilities afforded in obtaining useful information, and for timely assistance in collecting materials and furnishing valuable documents. I am under obligations to several other individuals for suggestions and information, for which they have my thanks.

In committing this work to the public, the author admits, it might have been better executed by an abler pen than his, at an earlier period of the country, but he confidently hopes, however, it will be found an interesting and useful addition to our local history.

N. S. BENTON.

Little Falls, 1855.

CHAPTER I.

The Mohawk Indians — The Iroquois — Extent of Country — Confederation — Probable Period when it took Place — Not a Perfect Union — Popular Aspect of the System — Presiding Officer in General Council — War Chief — Tuscaroras — Territory Claimed by the Mohawks — St. Regis Colony — Indians Treated as Owners of the Soil — The Hostility of the Mohawks to the French — Friendship to the English — Sir William Johnson's Influence — They Join the English and Abandon their Country — The Oneidas — Bravery and Cruelty of the Mohawks — Upper Castle in Danube — Fighting Men in 1677 — Same in 1763 — Hereditary Descent in Female Line — Council of Nations — Marriage — Wife's Right of Property — Witchcraft — Hendrik — Little Abraham — Garangula.

The aboriginal inhabitants of the territory whose history is intended to be delineated in the subsequent pages of this work, were the Maquaes, or Mohawk Indians, one of the five confederated tribes or cantons of the Konoshioni or Iroquois, found in that part of the state extending from Albany north to lake Champlain and the river St. Lawrence, south-westerly to the head waters of the Susquehanna and Delaware rivers, and westerly to lakes Ontario and Erie, and even to the valley of the Ohio, when the Dutch made their appearance on the waters of the Hudson, in 1609.

The period when this confederacy was formed is quite as much involved in the mists of tradition as any other remote event of Indian origin. Some fix the epoch a short time prior to the occupation by the Dutch, while others extend it back to A. D. 1414. This confederation seems to have been established for the common purposes of defense and offense in war. It was not a perfect union whereby each tribe or canton surrendered to the council any portion of the internal policy of the tribe. Each was perfectly independent of all control by the other members of the confederacy, except when the united cantons in council had resolved unanimously to go upon the war path, and even then, that question had to be referred to the warriors of each tribe assembled in council, where also a unanimous decision was required. Thus every resolve carried with it the full popular will, and hence the success which always attended the war parties of the Iroquois against the other American tribes. Each tribe was governed by its own civil and war chiefs. In the general council of the confederacy, the Mohawks, Oneidas, Onondagas and Cayugas were each represented by one delegate, and the Senecas by two, the latter being much more numerous than either of the other tribes. The presiding officer in this congress of ambassadors was always assigned to the Onondagas, and the principal war chief was taken from the Mohawks.

The Tuscaroras, who were always admitted as off-shoots of the New York Iroquois tribes, retired from North Carolina in 1714, after being severely chastised by the whites and a party of southern Indians, for several cruel massacres, and joined the Five Nations, and thereafter became one of the members of the confederacy. The Oneidas assigned lands to them within their cantonal limits. Each tribe claimed dominion over territory having general boundaries, and that of the Mohawks embraced all that part of the state included within a line running from the Hudson river to the head waters of the Susquehanna and Delaware, and extending thence to the St. Lawrence near Ogdensburgh, and embracing all the lands between Lake Champlain and the St. Lawrence, as well as those about Lake George. Their northern limits were not fixed in 1771, and they probably claimed as hunting grounds all the lands between the St. Lawrence and St. John's rivers to Montreal. This probability is much strengthened by the fact that an off-shoot of the Mohawks, the St. Regis colony, was seated on the south side of the St. Lawrence as early as 1650, or about that period.

The Dutch and English colonial governments, although they treated the Indians within their respective jurisdictions as subjects, would not make any grants of the ultimate fee until the Indian titles had been extinguished by purchase. The Mohawks were always on terms of amity with the English, but exercised the most bitter hostility against the French in Canada and their Indian allies, even when France and England were at peace. Sir William Johnson's influence over these people was unbounded, and at his death they transferred all their deep-seated savage affections to his family.

Under the influence of the Johnson family, they early attached themselves to the royal cause in the revolutionary war, emigrated to Canada, and but few, if any, ever returned. The Onondagas, Cayugas, and Senecas, were also hostile to the colonists during the whole period of the war. The Oneidas promised to remain neutral, but towards its close, they with some of the Tuscaroras joined the American forces, and performed good service in punishing marauding parties of the enemy. In the preliminary articles and definitive treaty signed at Paris, Great Britain abandoned their sable allies, except those who emigrated to Canada, to the mercy of the Americans.

The Oneidas were driven from their towns by the enemy for their attachment to the cause of the colonists, and were compelled to seek a home for their old men, women and children, near Schenectady.

The Mohawks distinguished themselves on many occasions by acts of bravery and devotion, so striking and peculiar as to elicit from those whom they served, the highest commendations, while their deeds of cruelty in war have been long remembered and deeply execrated by those who were so unfortunate as to be numbered among their enemies.

The Upper Mohawks' castle was erected in the present town of Danube, on a beautiful flat east of the Nowadaga creek, and here a mission was established and a small church built for them before the revolution. The spot on which the first church was erected, has always been consecrated to pious uses, and a small church is now standing on the site of the old mission building, called in the language of the inhabitants of the country the Indian Castle Church. The principal Christian mission establishment of this tribe was at Fort Hunter, near Amsterdam, in Montgomery county.

Wentworth Greenhalgh, in 1677, describes the Maquaes or Mohawks, as possessing four towns, besides one small village one hundred and ten miles west of Albany, and that they had in all about three hundred fighting men.

Sir William Johnson, in 1763, states there were one hundred and sixty men of the Mohawks, that they had two villages on the river which bore that name, and a few emigrants at Schoharie, about sixteen miles from Fort Hunter.

An extended notice of these people is not designed, but it will not be out of place to present a few of their peculiarities. Hereditary descent was confined to the female line, and thus the son of a chief's daughter would inherit a chieftainship to the exclusion of his uncle, and a chief's brother would succeed him, and not his male children, provided there were no descendants through the female line.

Another peculiarity marked these people. The matrons of the tribe, in council, could always propose a cessation of hostilities, and this could be done without compromising the warriors and chiefs. For this purpose a male functionary, the messenger of the matrons, who was a good speaker, was designated to perform an office which was deemed unsuitable to the female. When the proposition to drop the war club was resolved upon, the message was delivered to this officer, and he was bound to enforce it with all the powers of eloquence he possessed.

Marriage among the Iroquois was a mere personal agreement between the parties, requiring no particular sanction and in no respect affected the rights of property, if the wife had any. Whatever goods, effects or valuables of any kind the wife had before marriage, she continued to hold absolutely, and if a separation took place, the wife was entitled to take with her all her property.

These people, like all others in the rude and savage state, were sturdy believers in witchcraft. Their ancient religious system or mode of worship no doubt contributed to strengthen this belief. The worship of a good and an evil spirit, must of necessity have produced such results; and dreams were considered the revelation of inspiration too sacred to be neglected or disregarded, and hence the effects of this belief upon the prosperity and population of these tribes must have been, at times, most disastrous.

This is a brief and by no means a perfect outline of the characteristics of a people who occupied the Mohawk valley when first visited by the Europeans.

After the death of Hendrik, the celebrated Mohawk chief, Little Abraham, his brother, became by the laws of the tribe the war chief of this branch of the Iroquois confederacy, and consequently was the leader of the confederate forces, when upon the war path, unless degraded in accordance with Indian usages. I shall in a subsequent part of this work again allude to Little Abraham's situation, and give the reasons why he was probably superseded as the war chief of the Six Nations, at the commencement of the revolutionary war through the influence of British officials.*

---

* I can not forbear to give, in this place, a speech delivered by Garangula, an Onondaga chief, in the presence of De La Barre, the governor of Canada, in 1684. He speaks as the representative of the five confederate tribes, and no doubt in accordance with the usages of these people, which conferred on the chief of his tribe the office of enunciating or declaring the sentiments and wishes of the general council of the cantons.

This speech is found in Colden's History of the Five Nations, and the historian may not have done any injustice to the native orator—at any rate the point and sarcasm of the language, spoken in the slow and measured cadence of Indian oratory, must have touched his auditor to the quick, and can not but interest the general reader. It shows a noble specimen of native independ-

King Hendrik.

This celebrated sachem of the Mohawk canton of the Iroquois confederacy and distinguished war chief of the Six Nations, was born during the latter part of the 17th century,

---

ence and self-reliance. The sachem, standing in front of the governor who was seated, addressed him as follows:

"Yonnondio, I honor you, and the warriors that are with me honor you—your interpreter has finished your speech. I now begin mine. My words make haste to reach your ears; harken to them, Yonnondio. You must have believed, when you left Quebec, that the sun had burnt up all the forests which render our country inaccessible to the French, or that the lakes had so overflown their banks that they had surrounded our castles, and that it was impossible for us to get out of them; yes, truly, *you must have dreamed so, and the curiosity of seeing so great a wonder has brought you so far.* Now you are undeceived, since that I, and the warriors here present, are come to assure you, that the Cayugas, Senecas, Onondagas, Oneidas and Mohawks, are yet alive. I thank you, in their name, for bringing back into their country the calumet, which your predecessors received from their hands. It was happy for you that you left under ground that murdering hatchet, that has so often been dyed with the blood of the French. Hear! Yonnondio; *I do not sleep!* I have my eyes open, and the sun which enlightens me, discovers to me a great captain at the head of a company of soldiers, who speaks as if he were dreaming. He says that he only came to the lakes to smoke on the great calumet, with the Onondagas. But Garangula says he sees the contrary; that it was to knock them on the head, if sickness had not weakened the arms of the French. I see Yonnondio roving in a camp of sick men, whose hairs the great spirit has saved by inflicting this sickness upon them. Hear, Yonnondio! our women had taken their clubs; our children and old men had carried their bows and arrows into the heart of your camps, if our warriors had not disarmed them, and kept them back, when your messengers came to our castles. *It is done; I have said it.*

"Hear, Yonnondio! we plundered none of the French, but those that carried guns, powder and balls to the Twightwies and Chictagicks, because those arms might have cost us our lives. Herein we follow the example of the Jesuits, who break all the kegs of rum brought to our castles, lest the drunken Indians should knock them on the head. Our warriors have not beavers enough to pay for all those arms they have taken, and our old men are not afraid of war.

"This belt preserves my words.

"We carried the English into our lakes, to trade with the Utawawas and Quatoghies, as the Adirondacks brought the French to our castles, to carry on a trade which the English say is theirs. *We are born free;* we neither

not very near the close of it, however, as he was called "old King Hendrik," at the time of the old French war. He was in the vigor of manhood and at the hight of power

depend on Yonnondio or Corlear; we may go when we please, and carry with us what we please, and buy and sell what we please. If *your allies be your slaves*, use them as such; command them to receive no others but your people.

"This belt preserves my words.

"We knock the Twightwies and Chicagicks on the head, because they had cut down the trees of peace, which were the limits of our country. They have hunted beaver on our lands, they have acted contrary to the customs of the Indians, for they have left none of the beavers alive; they killed both male and female; they brought the Satanas into their country, to take part with them after they had concerted ill designs against us. We have done less than either the English or French, that have usurped the lands of so many Indian nations, and chased them from their own country.

"This belt preserves my words.

"Hear, Yonnondio, what I say is the voice of all the Five Nations. Hear what they answer—open your ears to what they speak. The Senecas, Onondagas, Cayugas, Oneidas and Mohawks, say that when they buried the hatchet at Cadaraqui, in the presence of your predecessors, in the middle of the fort, they planted the tree of peace in the same place, to be there carefully preserved; that in the place of arms and ammunition of war, beavers and merchandise only should enter there.

"Hear, Yonnondio! take care, for the future, that so great a number of soldiers as appear there, do not choke the tree of peace, planted in so small a fort. It will be a great loss, if after it had so easily taken root, you should stop its growth, and prevent its covering your country and ours with its branches. I assure you in the name of the Five Nations, that our warriors shall dance to the calumet of peace under its leaves, and shall remain quiet on their mats, and shall never dig up the hatchet till their brother Yonnondio, or Corlear, shall either jointly or separately endeavor to attack the country which the Great Spirit has given to our ancestors.

"This belt preserves my words, and this other the authority which the Five Nations have given me."

Then addressing himself to the interpreter, he said:

"Take courage, you have spirit, speak, explain my words, forget nothing, tell all that your friends and brethren say to Yonnondio, your governor, by the mouth of Garangula, who loves you and desires you to accept this present of beaver, and take part with me in my feast, to which I invite you. This present of beaver is sent to Yonnondio, on the part of the Five Nations."

The Indian orator in using the name Corlear, in his address, intends to designate the English or colonial governor of New York.

when the upper section of the Mohawk valley was opened for settlement.

From his long association with the Europeans and particularly with Sir William Johnson, whom he highly regarded, and who found but little difficulty in directing the actions of the chief as he thought best, Hendrik had adopted and wore the English costume, and become accustomed to live in

KING HENDRIK.

a house. He resided much of the time at the upper Mohawk castle, in the town of Danube, his dwelling being located upon the elevated ground not far from the Indian Castle Church, commanding an extended view of the surrounding country. He is spoken of as a man of great sagacity and vigor of mind, inflexibly brave and of "unmovable integrity."

The French authorities of Canada, with all their intrigues, were never able to move him and his faithful Mohawks from their allegiance to the British crown. Dr. Dwight says, "a gentleman of very reputable character, who was present at a council held with the Six Nations by the governor of New York and several agents of distinction from New-England [this was in 1754], informed me that his figure and countenance were singularly impressive and commanding; that his eloquence was of the same superior order, and that he appeared as if born to control other men, and possessed an air of majesty unrivaled within his knowledge." He fell at the battle of Lake George, on the 8th of September, 1755, winning glory, a fortune and a title for his friend, Major General William Johnson.

The anecdote illustrated by the following dialogue between Sir William, before he was knighted, and the old king, should be repeated, although quite as unreal as most dreams are.

Scene.—Sir William's parlor; the knight seated in deep thought. Enter King Hendrik giving a searching glance round the room as he approached and saluted his friend.

King Hendrik (addressing Sir William), "I dream."

Sir William. "Well, what did you dream?"

King Hendrik. "I dream you give me one suit of clothes."

Sir William. "Well, I suppose you must have it."

The scene changes, and Sir William and Hendrik meet in their sylvan excursions.

Sir William (addressing Hendrik with a bland smile on his face). "I dreamed last night."

King Hendrik. "Did you? What you dream?"

Sir William. "I dreamed you gave me such a tract of land" (describing the outlines of it).

King Hendrik (pausing). "I suppose you must have it, but" (raising and shaking his finger significantly), "you must not dream again."

The petition of Sir William and thirty-nine other persons for a license to purchase the Indian title to 40,000 acres of land lying between the two Canada creeks, was presented to the governor and council on the 8th of July, 1761, six years after Hendrik's death. This was the first step taken to obtain the title to the royal grant.

Although a stern and rigorous warrior, Hendrik was kind to the white population of the valley, and was highly regarded by them. He well understood the extent of his mission—that he must guard and protect the liege subjects of his sovereign to the extent of his power against the attacks of the hostile French and Indians, and he did not fail to execute it. If he was not the most distinguished for courage and strategy of all the native war chiefs, known to the Europeans, after the settlement by them of the country, history has dealt too favorably with his fame, and he still wears an undeserved crown of immortality.

NOTE.—I have collected the following notices of Hendrik from the "Documents relating to the Colonial History" of this state. July 8, 1697, he is recognized as a chief of the Mohawk canton. In 1698, he is described as a chief, a "convert to the Christian faith, of eight years' standing," and as being of full age. In 1699, he was examined before the mayor, recorder and justices at Albany, in regard to what he had said about Dom. Dellius's going away, and is spoken of as a married man. 1710, he visited England. 1711, October 9th, at a conference with Gov. Hunter, he gave the governor a letter addressed by the chiefs to the Archbishop of Canterbury, and desired him to thank the Queen of Great Britain for the care taken by her to convert the Indians to the Christian religion. September 3d, 1720, Hendrik, the Maquaes, having been suspended four years before from being a sachem in the tribe, was restored and installed as a chief, at the request and in presence of the commissioners of Indian affairs. In 1753, he attended a conference between Sir William Johnson and the Mohawks, and in 1754 he was at the Congress of the Commissioners from the six northern provinces, held at Albany, to consult on Indian affairs. He was the chief speaker at both of these conferences. Judge Harring, now living, who came to Johnstown in 1795, and at an early day was quite familiar with the inhabitants, old and young, then on the stage, says, that Sir William dreamed for the land known as the Kingsborough patent, where he built his own family mansion, and not for the royal grant.

CHAPTER II.

Early History of the German Tribes — This Name first Applied by Julius Cæsar —Their Authentic History commences with the Christian Era — Early Habits and Stature — Confederation of Tribes — Severe Laws of Conversion to Christianity — The Reformation — Luther and Dr. Eck — Lower Palatinate of the Rhine — Religious Wars — Frederick Prince Palatine — Theidelburgh Library — The Palatinate Devastated — Continental Wars of Europe — Manheim — Characteristics of these People — A Legend.

The reader having been introduced to the aboriginal possessors of the soil of Herkimer county, so far as can now be defined, will have the goodness to indulge me a few moments, while I give a brief historical outline of a people of known European origin, who first planted themselves in the upper Mohawk valley. Indeed, the Anglo-Saxon race are of German descent, and whoever claims a Teutonic ancestry, traced through an English channel, will have some of the blood of a Saxon or Dane on which to rest that claim. Our design in this chapter is to set out, as far as needful, the origin of a race who are losing every distinct national characteristic, which they maintained more than one hundred years upon the American continent.

The Germans were believed, by the Romans, to be an aboriginal, pure and unmixed race of people.[1] The primitive language of the inhabitants of Germany is the Teutonic, called High Dutch, and has no affinity with the Celtic tongue. The name Germanum, when applied to the tribes collectively, was first used, it is said, by Julius Cæsar; but German historians assert the aboriginal name of these people is what they bear at this time. It can not be very remarkable that the original collective name of a people inhabiting a particular district of country, so much divided into tribes or septs as was the territory embraced in and now known as Germany, should be familiar to strangers coming from Rome or middle and southern Gaul. A *Teutscher*, or *Deutscher*, according to the method of pronunciation, was a person belonging to the nation. Some would no doubt translate this as meaning Dutchman. The first intercourse the original barbaric tribes of Germany had with a people practiced in historical writing, was in the year 113 before the Christian era, 1968 years ago, when the Cimbrians and Teutonians made an incursion into the Roman territories; but this must have been too transitory to have permitted the Romans to take any particular note of the origin or historical antecedents of their invaders. When Julius Cæsar, about fifty years before the birth of Christ, advanced to the frontiers of what might then be considered Germany proper, and hence was brought into more immediate contact with its people, he is enabled to speak with certainty. Any thing like authentic German history commences with the Christian era, and it ripens with the progress of civilization and learning, and light comes to us through the darkness and gloom of the middle ages.

Historians describe the early German race as having "but one determined and equal form of body. Their chests were wide and strong; their hair yellow, and with young children of a dazzling white. Their skin was also white, their eyes blue, and their glance bold and piercing." Some ancient writers say their usual height was seven feet. It is also said that "from their earliest youth upward they hardened their bodies by all devisable means. New-born infants were dipped in cold water, and the cold bath was continued during their whole lives as the strengthening renovator, by both boys and girls, men and women." It is not intended to give an extended and detailed view of the habits, manners, regulations, and institutions of these people. But it is proper to note some points in their history down to the period of the immigration of the Palatines to this western continent.

It must be apparent to all, that in order to provide against assaults from without, there must have been a confederation of the German tribes at some period. The laws relating to these confederations were very severe, and their principle was, "one for all and all for one, for life and death." The most perfect of these alliances among the tribes took place about the year A. D. 235, in order to form a barrier against the Roman armies. The great migration of the Mongolian Huns from Asia and the irruption of the western tribes into Italy between the years 375 and 476 after Christ, changed materially the aspect of things among the German confederates, and subsequently produced changes in their customs and institutions. It was not until about the close of the eighth century, in the time of Charlemagne, that all the German tribes, or rather nations, were converted to Christianity.

The outbreak of the reformation in 1517 under the conduct of Martin Luther, an Augustinian friar, and professor of theology in the University of Wittenberg, Saxony, is the first great event to which our attention is directed; that being the epoch from which we can trace the causes that drove the Palatines of the Lower Rhine to seek a home in the then province of New York nearly two hundred years afterwards.

It is worthy of note here, that in the celebrated controversy at Leipsic in 1519, which formed an interesting event in the development of the history of those times, two peasants' sons, Martin Luther and Dr. John Mayer of Eck, represented the antagonistic ideas that characterized the times, and whose unity or further division could not fail to produce consequences of the greatest importance in the civilized world. Luther was the descendant of a peasant family living at the foot of the Thuringian forest in Moravia, and Eck was the son of Michael Mayer of Eck, a peasant.

The princes of the Lower Palatinate of the Rhine early

embraced the tenets of the Reformation, vibrating between the doctrines of Luther and Calvin, as suited the inclinations and peculiar notions of the individual reigning princes; and the great body of their people usually changed with their sovereigns. It once or twice occurred, in the course of one hundred and fifty years, that the reigning prince embraced the *old religion*, as it was then called; but this happened only when the Palatinate was bestowed upon some new family or house, or when political motives dictated a return to the Romish doctrines; but the great mass of the people rigidly adhered to the Protestant faith.

The final adjustment of the religious questions in the German empire and the conclusion of the treaty of Westphalia, took place in 1648, but this did not put an end to the religious wars in Europe. During the whole of the seventeenth century, and before and since that period, up to the extinguishment of the title, the emperors of Germany adhered to the Roman Catholic faith, and many of the princes of the empire were devoted to the same tenets; and while multitudes of the peasantry and middle classes embraced the doctrines of the Reformation, there was but small hope of toleration until Gustavus Adolphus, king of Sweden, conquered a peace for them.

There were, perhaps, two motives that induced the people of the Palatinate to look to England for succor, at the commencement of the eighteenth century. Frederick, then Prince Palatine, who had married Elizabeth, daughter of James I, king of England, was in 1619 elected king of the states of Bohemia; but in the year following he was signally defeated at the battle of Weissenberg by the emperor of Germany, driven into exile, and all his estates were confiscated. This was during the thirty years' religious war in Germany. By the treaty of Westphalia the eldest son of the banished Frederick was restored to his patrimonial estates of the Lower Palatinate. This prince was cousin to Anne, daughter of James II, who ascended the British throne in

1702, on the death of William III. The Palatinate was occupied by the imperial armies in 1623, when the magnificent library of Heidelburg was seized and presented to the Pope of Rome. It was restored in 1815. The lower Palatinate was invaded by the French in 1689, many of its towns were burnt and the country devastated, while the defenseless inhabitants, who begged for mercy on their knees, were stripped naked and driven into the fields, then covered with snow, where many of them perished. One historian, in speaking of the cruelties committed by the French on this occasion, states that "the elector beheld from his castle, at Manheim, two cities and twenty-five towns in flames, and where lust and rapine walked hand in hand with fire and sword." Thus for nearly seventy-five years was this fair country, described as one of the most beautiful in Germany, the theater of wars and the scene of rapine, ravages and desolations, until the remnant of its population could no longer find a hiding place in fatherland. The Catholic rulers of France for a time sided with the Protestant league in Germany during the thirty years' war, and soon afterwards cut the throats of their Huguenot subjects at home.

The continental wars of Europe, at the close of the seventeenth and commencement of the eighteenth centuries, seem to have been promoted very much by religious considerations. The see of Rome was determined to "crush out" heresy, and exerted all its spiritual and temporal powers to accomplish it, and well did the Catholic powers and princes of Europe second the papal injunctions, except when great reasons of state intervened to prevent. The majority of Europe adhered to the Romish faith.

From the proximity of the Lower Palatinate to France and the Netherlands, it is very probable that it received accessions of population from both of those countries during the religious wars; and Manheim, a strong and well-built city at that day, was in the year 1576 appointed as the place of retreat for the families of the reformed religion; at that time

driven from the Spanish Netherlands, which considerably enriched this electorate. A historian of the last century describes the people of the Palatinate as "the most civilized and polite of any in Germany; extremely open and hospitable to strangers, and generally well informed."

Although some of the characteristics of these people may have been modified by their intercourse with their southern and more civilized neighbors, commencing nearly fifty years before Julius Cæsar invaded Gaul, it is not supposed that this intercourse was so marked or extensive as to change materially the habits, manners and customs of the inhabitants of the Palatinate from those of their German countrymen, or that they lost any of the primitive High-Dutch tongue.

It is not remarkable that a people so strongly attached to the nomadic life as the early Germans were, and being divided into tribes or septs, should vary in their dialects in the different provinces, all however emanating from the same original language.

This brief outline of the origin and persecutions of a people whose exodus from Europe to America it is designed to notice, will doubtless be excused, if not approved of, in a work so entirely local as the one in hand. A more extended recapitulation of European history in respect to the events to which the writer has aimed to give prominence, seems not to be required or desirable. He has brought forward historical evidence of the facts he presents to the reader's consideration; concurrent historical evidence, and that is the best testimony he can produce after the lapse of more than three hundred years since some of those events happened, and one hundred and fifty years since the latest of those events transpired. The reader who desires to see more on this head, is referred to Kohlrausch's History of Germany.

There is an historical legend connected with German history to this effect, but which is variously related by German historians. Drusus, the Roman general, had made three campaigns into Germany, and while progressing on the fourth, in the 9th year before the Christian era, he was standing alone on the banks of the Elbe, ruminating no doubt on the events and fortunes of war, when a supernatural figure in the form of a gigantic woman of stern and threatening appearance stood before him and addressed him in the following language: "How much further wilt thou advance, insatiable Drusus? It is not appointed for thee to behold all these countries. Depart hence! the term of thy deeds and thy life is at hand."

Drusus retired from his position on the Elbe, whether from fright and dismay at hearing words which in that age might be deemed prophetic, is not certain, and in a few weeks fell from his horse and died in consequence. In a superstitious age an ardent imagination might have conjured up spectres quite as appalling as this, but it is probable this was a device of some of the prophetic women of the country.

NOTE—Approved authors assert that the early German tribes navigated from central Asia into Europe.

CHAPTER III.

1709 TO 1722.

The Immigration of the Palatines — Joshua Kockerthal and his Company — Arrive at New York in 1708–9 — Naturalized in England — Settle in Ulster County — Second Arrival in 1710 — Sickness and Deaths on the Passage — Governor Hunter — Board of Trade and Plantations — Lands on the *Mohaks* River and *Skohare* to be Surveyed — Hunter buys Lands of Livingston — Complaints of the People — Their Children taken from them and Bound Out — John Peter Zenger the Printer — They Volunteer to go to Canada under Col. Nicholson in 1711 — Refuse to Stay Longer on the Manor and Insist on going to *Scohary* — Party Migrate to Schoharie Creek in 1712-13 — Reason why placed on Frontiers — Character of Robert Livingston by a Minister of the Crown — Gov. Burnet's arrival — His Instructions — John Conrad Weiser — Third Arrival of Palatines, 1722 — Burnet to Board of Trade — Indian Deed to Palatines — Their Desire to Remove — Object of the Home Government — Results not foreseen.

The origin or cause of the first immigrations from the Lower Palatinate of the Rhine to America, as we have seen, was religious persecution, and the devastations of the country consequent upon the religious wars of Europe, of which Germany was the battlefield nearly one hundred years. The affinity existing between the sovereigns of England and the Palatinate, and the deep sympathy felt by Protestant Englishmen for their suffering brethren in Germany, produced the application to Queen Anne, in 1708, to send the Palatines to her then colony of New York.

Immigration of the Palatines.

In the first quarter of the eighteenth century, three bodies of these people arrived in New York, having been sent over at the expense of the British government. By an order in council made at Whitehall, England, May 10, 1708, it appears that Joshua Kockerthal, evangelical minister, and several poor Lutherans, had come to England from the Lower Palatinate in Germany, being forty-one persons, ten men, ten women and twenty-one children. They are described as having been reduced to want by the ravages of the French in their country, and are represented as being of good character. This paper states they would have been sent to Jamaica or Antigua, but it was feared the hot climate of those islands would prove injurious to their constitutions. It was finally concluded to send them to the colony of New York, where they could be employed in obtaining naval stores after being seated on the frontiers as a barrier against the French and their Indians; and on the 10th of August following, the provincial governor was directed to provide subsistence for Joshua Kockerthal and fifty-two German Protestants, and "to grant him 500 acres of land for a glebe with liberty to sell a suitable portion thereof for his better maintenance till he shall be able to live by the produce of the remainder."

An order was made in the provincial council at New York, May 26, 1709, to continue the relief promised by the queen until the expiration of twelve months from the date of their arrival, and this relief was to include clothes, mechanical tools and materials to work with. This was the vanguard which was to be planted in advance of the population then in the province as a barrier against the common enemy. This company probably arrived at New York about the close of the year 1708, and did not leave England before the month of August of that year. They were naturalized by the crown before they started. In the year 1714, we find a Lutheran minister, Joshua Kockerthal, settled in Ulster county, and hence it will be inferred that most if not all of the first company which came over, followed their spiritual teacher and remained with him.

The second and more numerous company of Palatines arrived at New York, some of them in the ship Lyon, a short time before June 13, 1710, and in consequence of sickness during the voyage they were directed to remain at quarantine at Nutten island, now called Governor's island, where huts were erected for them and provisions furnished at the public expense. More than three thousand emigrants came over about this time. It was asserted by Governor Hunter that over four hundred and seventy died on the passage, and ten vessels were employed in bringing them to their future and long wished for homes.

It should be noticed here for reasons that will be sufficiently obvious by and by, that this company came over in special charge of Hunter, who had particular directions where to settle them, for in the report of the board of trade and plantations, dated December 5th, 1709, approved January 7th, 1710, on the settlement of an additional number of Palatines in New York, the commissioners assert that these settlements would be a protection against the French of Canada and the Indians scattered over the continent. In pointing out the place most suitable for seating the Palatines, the commissioners designate " a tract of land lying on the Mohaques river, containing about fifty miles in length, and four miles in breadth, and a tract of land lying upon a creek [evidently the Schoharie] which runs into said river, containing between twenty-four and thirty miles in length. This last mentioned land is claimed by the Mohaques, but that claim may be satisfied on very easy terms." They notice the obstruction to water navigation on the river by the Cohoes falls, but think this should be no hindrance, as there would be only a short land-carriage. In the spring of 1710, Hunter directed the survey of lands on the "Mohaks" river, and particularly in the "Skohare to which the Indians had no pretence." But these lands, although very good, he thought unfit for the design in hand, as they lay remote and there were no pines, and after admitting that pine lands were unfit for farming purposes, he says, " I am in terms with some who have lands on the Hudson's river fitt for that purpose which I intend to view next week." In October of the same year he says, "I have been obliged to purchase a tract of land on Hudson's river from Mr. Livingston, consisting of 6000 acres, for £400 of this country money, for planting of the greatest division of the Palatines." He remarks that the soil is good, adjacent to pines which he had also purchased, and convenient to vessels of fifty foot water. He also informs the board of trade he had found an ungranted tract near by on the west side of the river where he had planted the remainder of the Palatines or intended to do so soon.

Mr. Robert Livingston, who sold the 6000 acres to Hunter, obtained a contract from the governor to victual the Palatines, and cheated them in the quantity of flour delivered, by marking the tare of the barrels less than the actual weight of them. The Palatines on Livingston's manor and on the opposite side of the Hudson river, in 1711, numbered about 1800 in all, according to the subsistance accounts rendered to the government by Livingston and his agents, and it is not probable they would make the number less than they should be. There appears to have been much complaint among these people in respect to their treatment by the government officials, and they no doubt felt themselves sorely aggrieved, and did not hesitate to present their case to the home government in strong but respectful language, boldly asserting that the conditions on which they agreed to come to New York had not been kept with them. A very considerable number of their children were taken from them by the governor and bound out to the inhabitants of the colony, and among these were two sons of John Conrad Weiser, who afterwards became somewhat conspicuous among the Schoharie settlers; and also John Peter Zenger, the son of a poor widow, who was bound to William Bradford, a printer in New York. Zenger, it is said, afterwards became the proprietor of a newspaper in that city, and having indulged rather freely in some strictures on the government, his paper was burned by the common hangman, and the patriotic and fearless Palatine was indicted for a libel in 1734. He was however acquitted on the traverse of the indictment, to the great gratification of the people assembled to hear the trial. Zenger was then about thirty years old.

In the year 1711, about three hundred Palatines accompanied Col. Nicholson in the expedition into Canada, and among these volunteers the following names are found: Hen. Hoffman, Warner Dirchest, Fred. Bellinger, Hen. Wederwachs, Frantz Finck, Martin Dillenback, Jacob Webber, William Nellis, George Dachstader, Christian Bauch, Mich. Ittick, Melch. Folts, Niclaus Loux, Hartman Windecker, Hans Hen. Zeller, Jno. Wm. Finck, Jno. Hen. Arendorff, Johan Schneider, Henry Feling, Joh. Jost Petry and Lud. W. Schmit, names familiar in the Mohawk valley, if they did not compose some of the first settlers at the German Flats.

Mr. Clark, the colonial secretary, under the date of May 30, 1711, informed the board of trade that the Palatines would not work at making pitch and tar, nor remain on the lands where they had been seated, on the Hudson river, but were intent on going to *Schohary* and settle on the lands the queen had ordered for them. In 1712 the insubordination had become so great that troops were called into the Palatine settlements to reduce the people to order. But Gov. Hunter failed in compelling an entire submission to his will, for in the fall of that year some of their leading men were sent to the Indians on the Schoharie creek to crave permission to settle among them, and this being granted, a Palatine migration to the Schoharie valley took place in the winter of 1712–13, comprising some forty or fifty families. Others followed, no doubt, soon after. This seems to be the first off-shoot of the first two emigrations in the direction of the Mohawk valley.

While the French retained Canada, it was no doubt a wise

policy on the part of the mother country to strengthen the northern and western frontiers of this colony, and the Palatines having tasted the bitter cup of persecution in their own country, and suffered all the horrors that savage and relentless war could inflict, but death, which to many would have been a blessing, were the fittest people on the European continent to be placed where the home government designed they should be. They had not forgotten the names of the nations, the armies and religionists which had sacked and burned their towns and hamlets and driven them from loved homes and revered fatherland, nor would they soon disremember them.

In a letter written in March, 1711, by a member of the British government to one of his colleagues, the writer says: "I think it unhappy that Colo. Hunter at his first arrival in his government fell into ill hands, for this Livingston has been known many years in that province for a very ill man, he formerly victualled the forces at Albany, in which he was guilty of most notorious frauds by which he greatly improved his estate; he has a mill and a brew-house upon his land, and if he can get the victualling of those Palatines who are conveniently posted for his purpose, he will make a very good addition to his estate, and I am persuaded the hopes he has of such a subsistance to be allowed, were the chief, if not the only inducements that prevailed with him to propose to Colo. Hunter to settle them upon his land." Hunter was no doubt the willing dupe of, or sadly overreached by Livingston, and his folly or imbecility had come to the knowledge of his superiors. His bills were protested and the adjustment of his accounts suspended for further examination and vouchers.

A biographical notice of this Robert Livingston shows him to have been a native of Scotland—that he came to this country in 1674, settled at Albany, and filled several important offices in the course of a long and pretty successful life. That at one time he had some connection with the world-renowned and "most abandoned villain," Capt. Kidd, whom he had introduced to the notice of Lord Bellomont, when colonial governor, and that all three were in some way concerned in fitting out a privateer of which Kidd was to take charge on joint account. Livingston's biographer acquits him and Lord Bellomont of being cognizant of Kidd's felonies on the high seas, but thinks he was possessed of large acquisitiveness. He no doubt acquired a good deal of wealth from his connection with the Palatines, not alone by means of his contract with the government for victualing them, but in appropriating their labor to improving his lands.

Governor Burnet came out in the year 1720, and in consequence of the preceding troubles had with the Palatines and the difficulties attendant on the coercive efforts to retain them on the Hudson river, he was specially instructed to remove such of them as might desire it, to lands more suitable for them. The action of the home government was, no doubt, accelerated by the presentation of a strong memorial from the commissioners of the Palatines at Schoharie, who went to England in 1718 to present the condition, grievances and oppressions of the Germans in the province of New York to the proper authorities there. John Conrad Weiser, a captain of one of the companies in the expedition against Montreal in the year 1711, was at the head of this commission. Their petitions or memorials were presented to the board of trade only sixteen days before the above instructions were given.

The object has been, in this examination, to fix the date of the first settlement of the Palatines at German Flats, and since it is known that these people came over at different times, to ascertain which three bodies of immigrants, or what portions of them finally seated themselves in the wilderness frontier of the upper Mohawk valley.

The third company of Palatine immigrants arrived at New York from Holland in October, 1722, having touched at England on the passage; and the ship in which they came had lost many of its passengers during the voyage. The exodus of the Palatines from Schoharie to Pennsylvania and the lower valley of the Mohawk had not taken place before this period.

On the 21st November, 1722, Gov. Burnet informed the board of trade, &c., that he had expected when he was at Albany, to have fixed the Palatines in their new settlement which he had obtained of the Indians for them at a very easy purchase, but in consequence of the divisions among them, and their complaints about the quality of the lands in the new purchase, he concluded not to show any earnestness in pressing them to go on to the lands. But he says there were about sixty families who desired to have a distinct tract by themselves, and being those who had all along been most hearty for the government, he had given them leave to purchase lands from the Indians between the English settlements near Fort Hunter and part of Canada, on a creek called Canada creek, where they will be more immediately a barrier against the sudden incursions of the French, who made this their road when they last attacked and burned the frontier town called *Schonectady*. The Indian deed for the lands at and west of Little Falls, covered in part by the so called Burnetsfield patent, is dated July 9th, 1722, anterior to the arrival of the third company of Palatine immigrants, and this fact forces the conclusion that the grantees of the patent were composed chiefly, if not entirely of those Palatines who arrived in 1710, and were first seated on the Hudson river; and this view seems to be strengthened by Gov. Burnet's remarks to the board of trade. It is quite certain that but few, if any, of the Schoharie people were among the first settlers of the German Flats, unless they straggled from below. But there is no such name as Erghemar, Herkemer or Herkimer in the lists of those who came over in the two first companies of immigrants, nor apparently any name from which *Herkimer* could be derived or coined without violating all known rules of etymology.

The Erghemar family were not among the Palatines on Hudson river in 1711, nor of those who remained in New York. They probably arrived with the third company of immigrants in 1722, from Holland, where they had sojourned many years.

At what time these people actually settled upon the lands patented to them by the crown, in the spring of 1725, is perhaps problematical, and rests in tradition. They were very urgent to remove to a part of the country where they could pursue their avocations and indulge in their own peculiar customs, unmolested by strangers and uncontrolled by colonial task masters; where the lands they tilled were secured to them by all the sanctions of a public grant emanating from the king. They had long felt and known that "patience and hope made fools of those who fill their hands with them." They and their ancestors, for three quarters of a century nearly, had been afflicted with all the worldly evils and miseries that an intolerant and tyrannical hierarchy, supported by absolute despotic governments, could bring upon them; and they had looked to the future with patient and hopeful emotions for a day of deliverance. After twelve years of trial and privation incident to a new climate and a wilderness country, during which time they saw that strangers, and not their families after them, were to be benefited by their labors, no lands had yet been set out to them, by grant from the crown, well might they exclaim that those who endure patiently present wrongs and take no other means of relief only to hope for it, were unwise and improvident.

The Dutch recaptured New York in 1673, but it was restored to the English by treaty in 1674. At this time and to the close of the seventeenth century, a very great majority of the people of the province were Low Dutch or Hollanders, and the French of Canada exerted much interest with all the Iroquois Indians, through the agency of the Jesuits and the control of the fur trade, except the Maquaes, Mohocks or

Mohawks. The whole country from Albany north to Lake Champlain, and from Schenectady west to Lakes Ontario and Erie was an unbroken wilderness, and it was therefore important that England should strengthen her colony of New York in both directions by planting settlements as barriers against hostile approaches, but she had no people to spare; the continental wars in which she had been long engaged and was then involved, more than decimated her population, and she eagerly embraced the opportunity of sending over the Palatines at the public expense. Gov. Burnet, whose talents, learning and kindness commended him to the well disposed colonists, seconded this policy of his government with zeal and success. Little did the governor or the home government then believe they were planting a barrier of stout hearts and sinewy arms on this frontier, which was soon to aid in obstructing the designs of the mother country in one of her most deliberate and best planned campaigns of the revolution. Nor could these then homeless exiles put aside the curtain of futurity and behold the terrific and tragic scenes which were so effectively and relentlessly enacted upon the soil they had chosen for their homes, and by the power through whose agency they had obtained their promised land.

The precise time when the Palatines made their first lodgment in the county is not ascertained. It was not later than 1725. Some who have speculated upon the subject suppose they came up the Mohawk valley as far as the Little Falls and to the Stone Ridge as early as the year 1720. Their agents, sent to spy out the lands, may have traversed the valley to the western bounds of the territory claimed by the Mohawk Indians as early as 1720, and perhaps before that period; but Gov. Burnet had not fixed them in the new settlement he had obtained for them of the Indians, at a very easy purchase, as late as November, 1722, and he that year permitted some of them to purchase lands of the Indians "on a creek called Canada creek." They secured the carrying place at the lesser falls as well as a long extent of wilderness country above, by their Indian deed; and the license of the colonial government to make the purchase, may have been considered by both parties, an authorization for them to remove before the patent was made out, as it no doubt was a solemn, irrevocable public pledge that the lands would be granted by the crown as soon as they should be surveyed. On this hypothesis it may be conjectured that settlements were made at or near the present site of the Stone Church in the town of German Flats, and at Herkimer village as early as the years 1723–24, if not before. Owning the lands at the carrying place, it is not likely that point was long neglected or unimproved.

Burnetsfield patent, so called in popular parlance, is a curious document, and well worthy of some special notice. It was granted on the 30th of April, 1725. It recites that "whereas our loving subjects, John Joost Patri and Coenradt Rickert, in behalf of themselves and other distressed Palatines, by their humble petition presented the 17th day of January, 1722, to our trusty and well beloved William Burnet, Esq., Captain General and Governor in chief of the province of New York, in council have set forth that in" accordance with the governor's license they had purchased "of the native Indians in the Mohawks country" the tract of land on both sides of the "Mohawks river" commencing at the "first carrying place [Little Falls], being the eastermost bounds called by the natives Astourogon, running along on both sides of the said river westerly unto a place called Gauondagaraon, or the upper end of it," being "about twenty-four English miles along on both sides of the said river." The Indian deed is dated July 9th, 1722. That the council advised the governor to "grant to each of the said persons, man, woman and child, as are desirous to settle within the limits of the said tract of land the quantity of one hundred acres."

The grantees were to hold the lands of the crown in free

and common socage, that being the usual tenure named in the colonial grants at this time, as of the manor of East Greenwich, in the county of Kent, in Great Britain, subject to an annual quit-rent of two shillings and sixpence per hundred acres, and on condition that the grantees, their heirs and assigns, should within three years from the date, plant, settle and effectually cultivate at least three acres of land of every fifty acres" granted to them. This patent also contains the usual reservation of gold and silver mines, timber fit for the royal navy, and the right to enter upon the lands and take and carry away the same.

Of the ninety-two persons named in the patent to whom lands were granted, twenty-two appear to be females, by the description, married, single or widowed. The paper does not disclose the number of families or the heads of families represented by males who settled on the tract, or how many one hundred acre lots went to any one family, husband, wife and children. There are several Pellingers, Starings, Wevers, Smiths, Edicks, Beermans, to whom grants were made. Jurgh Erghemer, Johan Jost, Madalana and Catharina Erghemar are separately named, but Nicholas Herkimer, afterwards the General, was not a patentee.

One design of this work is to rescue the names of those martyrs to posterity from the oblivion of old parchments and musty records, and place them on the historic page, from which, humble as their pretensions may be considered by some, they have been too long excluded. Some of those names will hardly be recognized, at this day, by their descendants.

List of Patentees.

Names of patentees arranged.	No. of lot.	No. of acres in each.	On which side of river located.	Remarks.
B.				
1. Beerman, Mary, ...	11	100	North	At the Little Falls.
2. Beerman, Johannes,*	26	"	"	
3. Same, ...	26	"	"	
4. Bowman, Jacob, ...	27	"	South	
5. Bowman, Johan Adam, ...	14	30	North	All the 30 acre lots were set on what were called the Great Flats, in and near the present village of Herkimer. The 70 acre lots are described in the patent as wood land.
Same, ...	14	70	"	
D.				
6. Dacksteder, Anna, wife of Jurgh Dacksteder, ...	28	100	South	
7. Dacksteder, Jurgh, ...	18	30	North	
Same, ...	18	70	"	
E.				
8. Edich, Elizabeth, ...	5	100	"	
9. Edigh, Johan Michael, ...	33	"	South	
10. Edich, Jacob, ...	21	"	"	
11. Editch, Michael, ...	20	"	"	Mohawk Village.
12. Erghemar, Jurgh, ...	44	"	"	
13. Erghemar, Johan Jost, ...	36	"	"	
14. Eighemar, Madalana, ...	24	70	"	And large island in river.
15. Erghemar, Catharina, ...	5	100	"	
F.				
16. Feller, Nicholas, ...	7	30	North	
Same, ...	7	70	"	
17. Feller, Mary, wife of Nicholas Feller, ...	16	100	South	
18. Felmore, Coenradt, ...	19	"	"	Mohawk Village.
19. Felmore, Christiana, ...	18	"	"	
20. Fols, Jacob, ...	3	"	"	
21. Fols, Melgert, ...	2	30	North	
Same, ...	2	70	"	
22. Fox, Christopher, ...	26	100	South	
H.				
23. Heger, Henry, ...	8	"	North	
24. Helmer, Elizabeth, wife of Lendert Helmer, ...	14	"	"	
25. Helmer, Philip, ...	25	"	"	East side of West Canada Creek.
26. Helmer, Johan Adam, ...	6	30	"	
Same, ...	6	70	"	
27. Helmer, Lendert, ...	21	30	"	
Same, ...	21	70	"	
28. Helmer, Fredrick, ...	1	100	"	
29. Helmer, Anna Margaret, wife of John Adam Helmer, ...	12	"	South	
30. Herter, Apolone, ...	7	"	"	

* Two lots of same number to Johannes Beerman.

Names of patentees arranged.	No. of lot.	No. of acres in each.	On which side of river located.	Remarks.
31. Herter, Lowrens,	37	100	South	
32. Hess, Augustines,	10	"	North	At the Little Falls.
33. Hoss, Johannes,	31	"	South	
K.				
34. Keslaer, Johannes,	45	"	"	
35. Keslaer, Nicholas,	25	"	"	Near Rankin's Lock.
36. Kast, Johan Jurgh, Jr.,	5	30	North	
Same,	5	70	"	
37. Kast, Johan Jurgh,	22	30	"	
Same,	22	70	"	
38. Koons, Mary Catharine, widow	1	30	"	
Same,	11	70	"	
39. Korsing, Rudolph,	29	100	South	
40. Korsing, Belia, wife of Rudolph Korsing,	13	"	"	
41. Koues, Lodowick,	2	"	"	
L.				
42. Lant, Anna Catherine, widow,	13	30	North	
Same,	13	70	"	
M.				
43. Mayor, Hendrik,	11	30	"	
Same,	11	70	"	
44. Mayor, Anna,	29	100	South	Opposite Great Flats.
45. Miller, Johannes,	43	"	"	
O.				
46. Orendros, Conradt,	40	"	"	
47. Orendorf, Hendrik,	39	"	"	
P.				
48. Pears, Catharine,	23	"	"	Opposite Great Flats.
49. Pears, Lodowick,	27	90	North	And ½ of an island.
50. Pell, Frederick,	15	100	"	On east side of West Canada Creek.
51. Pell, Anna Mary,	16	"	"	Same.
52. Pellinger, Johannes,	20	30	"	
Same,	20	70	"	
53. Pellinger, Peter,	23	30	"	
Same,	23	70	"	
54. Pellinger, Margaret, wife of Peter Pellinger,	4	100	"	
55. Pellinger, Frederick,	35	"	South	
56. Pellinger, Margaret, wife of Johannes Pellinger,	22	"	"	Near Mohawk Village.
57. Petri, Johan Joost,	8	30	North	
Same,	8	70	"	
58. Petri, Gurtruydt, wife of Johan Joost Petri,	17	86	"	Stone Ridge, Herkimer Village.
59. Petri, Mark,	15	100	South	
60. Pouradt, Johannes,	46	"	North	Capt. Peter Klock.
61. Poenradt, Gurtruydt, wife of Johannes Poenradt,	9	"	"	

Names of patentees arranged.	No. of lot.	No. of acres in each.	On which side of river located.	Remarks.
R.				
62. Reelle, Godfrey, ...	15	30	North	
Same, ...	15	70	"	
63. Reele, Godfrey, Jr.,*	10	100	South	
64. Reele, Godfrey, ...	10	100	"	Ilion Village.
65. Rickert, Lodowick, ...	19	30	North	
Same, ...	19	70	"	
66. Rickert, Catharine, ...	3	100	"	
67. Rickert, Conradt, ...	34	"	South	
68. Rickert, Mark, ...	6	"	"	
S.				
69. Shoemaker, Rudolph, ...	17	"	"	
70. Shoemaker, Thomas, ...	12	30	North	
Same, ...	12	70	"	
71. Smith, Adam Michael, ...	4	30	"	
Same, ...	4	70	"	
72. Smith, Johan Jurgh, ...	9	30	"	
Same, ...	9	70	"	
73. Smith, Ephraim, ...	9	100	South	Ilion Village.
74. Smith, Marte, ...	4	"	"	
75. Speis, Peter, ...	38	"	"	
76. Speis, Elizabeth, wife of Peter Speis, ...	8	"	"	
77. Spoon, Hendrik, ...	32	"	"	
78. Spoon, Hendrik, Jr., ...	7	"	North	
79. Staring, Mary Eva, wife of John Adam Staring, ...	13	"	"	At the Little Falls.
80. Staring, John Adam, ...	28	94	"	And ⅜ of an island.
81. Staring, Frederick, ...	24	30	"	
Same, ...	24	70	"	
82. Staring, Johannes Velden, ...	6	100	"	
83. Staring, Nicholas, ...	42	"	South	
84. Staring, Joseph, ...	41	"	"	
85. Staring, John Velde, Jr., ...	1	"	"	
T.				
86. Temouth, John Jost, ...	12	"	North	At Little Falls.
87. Temouth, Fredrigh, ...	17	30	"	
Same, ...	17	70	"	
V.				
88. Veldelent, John, ...	3	30	"	
Same, ...	3	70	"	
89. Veldelent, Anna, ...	2	100	"	
W.				
90. Wever, Jacob, ...	10	30	"	
Same, ...	10	70	"	
91. Wever, Nicholas, ...	16	30	"	
Same, ...	16	70	"	
92. Wever, Andries, ...	11	100	South	
93. Wever, Jacob, Jr., ...	15	"	"	
94. Welleven, Nicholas, ...	30	"	"	Ft. Herkimer, Stone Church.

* Same lot to Godfrey Reele and Godfrey Reele, Jr.

NOTE.—The emigration of the Palatines to the province of New York in 1709, was an interesting event in the history of the colony. John Conrad Weiser, a man of note and influence among these people, and who went to England to solicit relief for them, in his memorial to the government, of August 2d, 1720, states their numbers when they left England, near the close of 1709, at about 4000, and that 170C of them died on the passage or at their landing in New York. His son Conrad Weiser, as appears from the Collections of the Historical Society of Pennsylvania, states that the number at leaving was 4000. They came over with Gov. Hunter and under his charge. They were sent out at the expense of the British government, not only for their passage but for their subsistence one year after they arrived. In all published documents, colonial and imperial, their numbers are stated at 3000 and no more.

Mr. Cast, who was placed over them as a superintendent, reported the whole number on both sides of the Hudson river, May 1, 1711, at 1761, and Secretary Clark, to the lords of trade, states there were 1803 in June 1711, still remaining on Livingston manor, and on the west side of the river where they had been planted by Gov. Hunter. And again, the number reported for subsistence in the seven towns on the 24th of June, 1711, is 1874. A six months' voyage across the Atlantic at that early day was a severe task upon human endurance, but a loss of more than 2100 lives in eighteen months, or about 1100 out of the 3000, shows a want of care on their part, or excessive remissness on the part of those who had charge of them.

Gov. Hunter, as late as 1713, reported that all the Palatines were within the province, and for the most part on the lands where he had planted them; and in May following, that "many have gone of their own heads to settle at *Scoharie* and on the frontiers. In October, 1712, the governor told the managers of the Palatines they must of themselves seek employment for the winter, and upon this intimation some hundreds went to *Scoharie*, and that he was the more easy under it because he could not prevent it. In 1715, he says these people were dispersed by his orders.

It is quite evident the Earl of Clarendon, formerly Lord Cornbury, colonial governor, understood his subject when he told Lord Dartmouth that Livingston was an "ill man," who would peculate upon the public by his subsistence contract, and that Hunter should have planted the Palatines on the *Mohacks* river.

Mr. John Cast wrote Gov. Hunter in March, 1711, that five of the Palatines said to him, "We came to America to establish our families — to secure lands for our children on which they will support themselves after we die; and that we can not do here." In December, 1709, the board of trade reported to queen Anne in favor of settling 3000 Palatines on the Hudsons or Mohaques rivers, or on the *Score* creek, each family to have forty acres of land as a reward; to be employed in making naval stores for a limited time, and to be naturalized in the province free of charge; and the attorney-general in England reported a contract which was executed by them and by which they were to have granted to them forty acres of land for each person forever, free from taxes and quit rents for seven years. It was the non-fulfillment of this contract, and planting them on lands where they were employed in improving other men's estates, that caused their disquiet, and what was called unruly conduct.

It was not until 1724, after Governor Burnett's arrival, that the 6000 acres purchased by Gov. Hunter of Mr. Livingston fourteen years before, was secured by patent to the Palatines remaining on Livingston's manor. Justice, though slow, came with a liberal hand at last, for each of the sixty-three families took what they had in possession improved, and the residue of the 6000 acres in common.

Johannus Wilhelm Schess, one of the agents of the Palatines in London, on the 1st November, 1720, presented a petition to the lords commissioners of trade and plantations, in which he asks to have the lands possessed by the Palatines in *Schorie* confirmed to them, and also that grants may be made to those people residing in other parts of the province. He asks to have Weiser's petition, presented the previous August, for a grant of land in Pennsylvania dismissed, as being contrary to the wishes of the people who sent them to England. Weiser stated there were 3000 Germans in the Schoharie valley. Schess rated them at about 1000 souls and 3000 more dispersed in different parts of the province.

As all the colonial governments surrounding New York and New Jersey were at this time proprietary and not royal, these agents understood very well the policy of placing their numbers at a high figure. The whole number reported to be in the province in 1718, exclusive of widows and orphans, was only 1601. It was the object of the crown, as expressed by Gov. Hunter, to retain these people in New York or New Jersey. Apprehending a failure on this head by a further effort to carry out Hunter's plans, the whole policy was changed when Governor Burnet came out. Although several of the Schoharie settlers, and among them Captain Weiser, were parties to the petition to the governor and council in 1721, for a license to purchase the Indian title, and also grantees named in the Indian deed made in 1722, they were not, it seems, parties to the act of confirmation which took place January 17, 1723. Captain Weiser went to England in 1718, and did not return until 1723, and in the spring of that year he, with most of the Germans at Schoharie, went to Pennsylvania. Some of them remained at Schoharie and others came over to the Mohawk river.

Governor Burnet at one time contemplated removing the whole mass of the German population then under his government to the center of the state, for in his letter of October 16, 1721, to the lords of trade, he says: "I did intend to settle the Palatines as far as I could in the middle of our Indians, but finding they could not be brought to that, I have granted their own request, which was to have a license to purchase of the nearest Indians which are on the Mohocks, which I have granted them with this condition, that they be not nearer than a *fall* in the Mohocks river, which is forty miles from Fort Hunter, and four score from Albany, by which the frontier will be so much extended, and those people seem very well pleased and satisfied with what I have done."

The governor's first idea was, in conformity with instructions from the home government, to plant all the Palatines together on one large tract, the Indian title to which he had then obtained at a late purchase, but he found them divided into parties, the *cunningest* among them fomenting divisions in order to induce the most of them to leave the province, and they expressing an unwillingness to take these lands, he abandoned that project also; and in his letter to the lords of trade, of November 21, 1722, "as about sixty families desired to be in a distinct tract from the rest," he gave them leave to purchase from the Indians on the Canada creek, where they would be more immediately a barrier against the sudden incursions of the French.

The act of confirmation, January 17, 1723, as may be seen, required that the names and number of all the persons to be concerned in the grant should be certified to the surveyor-general before the survey was made, and as appears by the patent issued, there were only thirty-nine families and ninety-four persons reported, or who came forward and accepted the bounty of the government.

CHAPTER IV.

1722 TO 1772.

First settlement at the German Flats — License to Purchase of Indians — Some notice of the Patent — Names of Patentees — Period of Rest — Fort at Oswego built in 1726 — Defenses near Rome — Frontier Posts destroyed by the French in 1756 — Palatine Settlement destroyed in 1757 — M. de Belletre's account of it — Not credited by one of his Countrymen — Gov. de Laney — Fort Harenieger — Alleged Apathy of the Inhabitants — Reasons for Doubting — Indian Statements — Deputy Superintendent — Indian Fidelity Questioned — Escape of the Minister — Another Attack in 1758 — Conduct of Teamsters and the Rangers — Woman Scalped — Quiet Restored by the Capture of Fort Frontenau in 1758 and Quebec in 1759 — Colonial Wars — Commerce Restricted — Complaints of Colonists — Lord Camden — Mr. Pitt — Sir William Johnson — Attachment of the Palatines to the Cause of the Colonists.

The settlements at the German Flats enjoyed nearly thirty-five years of rest, and in that time had made rapid progress in clearing their farms, building houses and barns, raising stock and establishing defenses against attacks from any hostile quarter. Governor Burnet had in 1726, although violently opposed by the governor-general of Canada, erected a fort at the mouth of the Oswego river, the good will of the Iroquois had been secured in its defense, and the fur trade with the Indians within the province, which had been chiefly engrossed by the French of Canada, was principally secured to the English. Besides the protection afforded by the fort at Oswego, there were some defenses at or near the present village of Rome; and although other frontier portions of the colony had been afflicted with the scourge of barbarous and exterminating war, these Palatines had enjoyed a long period of repose. In 1756, the English fort at Oswego was captured, and the small fortifications on Wood creek and the upper Mohawk were taken and demolished by the French; and on the 12th of November, 1757, an expedition under the command of M. de Belletre, composed of about three hundred marines, Canadians and Indians, which had traversed the wilderness by the way of Black river, attacked and destroyed the Palatine settlements on the north side of the Mohawk river at or near the present village of Herkimer. A portion of the French narrative of this expedition, with all its exaggerations and expletives, is given verbatim as a specimen of colonial bragging and French grandiloquence of that day:

"On the 11th November, at three o'clock in the afternoon, M. de Belletre, preceded as was his custom by scouts, crossed the river Corlaer [Mohawk] with his detachment, partly swimming, partly in water up to the neck. He encamped at nightfall in the woods a league and a half from the first of the five forts that covered the Palatine settlements.

"The 12th, at three o'clock in the morning, he gave his detachment the order of march and attack so as to surround the said five forts and the entire Palatine village, consisting of sixty houses.

"Though M. de Belletre knew that the English got notice the day preceding, yet that the courage of the Indians may not receive the least check, and to show them that he would not rashly expose them, he liberated an Indian of the Five Nations, whom he had until then detained under suspicion. But this savage could not injure M. de Belletre, because he commenced at the same time to attack the five forts and the Palatines' houses.

"At sight of the first fort he decided to take it by assault. The enemy kept up a most active fire of musketry, but the intrepidity with which M. de Belletre, with all the officers and Canadians of his detachment advanced, coupled with the war whoop of the Indians, terrified the English to the degree that the mayor of the village of the Palatines, who commanded the said fort, opened the doors and asked for quarters.

"M. de Belletre lost no time in repairing to the second, the third, the fourth and fifth, which were not less intimidated than the first, by his intrepidity and the cries of the Indians. They all surrendered at discretion, and were entirely burnt.

"During this time a party of Canadians and Indians ravaged and burnt the said sixty houses of the Palatines, their barns and other out buildings, as well as the water mill.

"In all these expeditions about forty English perished—killed or drowned. The number of prisoners is nearly one hundred and fifty men, women and children, among whom is the mayor of the village, the surgeon and some militia officers. We had not a man killed; but M. de Lorimer, officer, was wounded in the right side by a ball, and three or four savages slightly.

"The damage inflicted on the enemy is estimated according to the representations of the English themselves, to wit:

"In grain, of all sorts, a much larger quantity than the island of Montreal has produced in years of abundance. The same of hogs; 3000 horned cattle; 3000 sheep. All these articles were to be sent in a few days to Corlaer [Schenectady]; 1500 horses, 300 of which were taken by the Indians, and the greater number consumed for the support of the detachment.

"The property in furniture, wearing apparel, merchandise and liquor, might form a capital of 1,500,000 livres [$277,-500]. The mayor of the village alone has lost 400,000 [$74,000]. The French and Indians have acquired as rich a booty as they could carry off. They have in specie more than 100,000 livres [$18,500]. One Indian alone has as much as 30,000 [$5,550]. There was likewise plundered a quantity of wampum, silver bracelets, &c., scarlet cloth and other merchandise, which would form a capital of 80,000

Plan and Profile of Retrenched Work round Harkemeis house at ye German Flats 1756.

more. All this damage could not be done short of forty-eight hours. M. de Belletre made provision to be always able to resist the enemy, who, as has been observed, were to the number of 350 men in the said Fort Kouari [Herkimer], about a quarter of a league from the field of battle."

This is a most extraordinary narrative of a most barbarous transaction, and is so characterized by one of M. de Belletre's own countrymen, Mr. Daine, in his report to the French minister, in which he says the injury inflicted "in horned cattle, sheep and horses has been greatly exaggerated in the relation of M. de Belletre's expedition. It must be diminished at least a good half. It is still more exaggerated in regard to furniture, wearing apparel, merchandise and liquors, which are carried up to fifteen hundred thousand livres, as well as the loss of the Palatine village in Indian corn." And Gov. De Lancy, in mentioning the destruction of "a valuable settlement on the north side of the Mohawk's river, opposite to Fort Hareniger, called the German Flats," says "the loss is estimated at twenty thousand pounds this money," fifty thousand dollars, a pretty large discrepancy from that given by the valorous Frenchman, who seemed somewhat desirous that his achievement should *begin* to compare with the martial deeds of his illustrious countryman, Turrene, when he ravaged the German Palatinate about one hundred years before.

The confidence inspired by a long exemption from hostile visits, proved in this case extremely unfortunate. It is asserted that these people were informed the day before, by friendly Indians, of the contemplated attack of the French and Indians, but being extremely incredulous, they gave no heed to these admonitions. Their settlement was in sight of a fort on the south side of the river, garrisoned by three hundred and fifty men; so says the French account, and it must be taken at considerable discount. But if this was true in all its parts, these people had some grounds to suppose, if they were attacked, that they would be aided by an armed force so near at hand in repelling the assault; their retirement to the fort with their families and effects could not have preserved their houses and crops from destruction. Militia forces from Albany had been ordered the year before to repair to the German Flats; and the fort mentioned in the French account and by Gov. De Lancy is described as a "stockaded work around the church and block-house, with a ditch and a parapet pallisadoed, thrown up by Sir William Johnson a year ago [in 1756] upon an alarm then given."

But there is another witness who must speak in relation to this sad affair. Sir William Johnson having been informed that the Indians had not notified the Palatines of the enemy's approach until the morning the attack was made, sent his deputy agent and Indian interpreter, to inquire of the Oneida and Tuscarora Indians, several of whom he was told were assembled at the German Flats, respecting this affair, and ask them to explain why they had not given more timely notice of the designs and approach of the enemy.

The deputy agent, Mr. Croghan, did not arrive at the scene of desolation until the Indians had left for home; he sent for them to return; the narrative then proceeds:

"The aforesaid Indians returned, and on the 30th November [1757], at Fort Harkeman, *Conaghquieson*, the chief Oneida sachem, made the following speech to Mr. Croghan, having first called in one Rudolph Shumaker, Hanjost Harkeman and several other Germans, who understood the Indian language, and desired them to sit down and hear what he was going to say.

Conaghquieson then proceeded and said:

"Brother: I can't help telling you that we were very much surprised to hear that our brethren, the English, suspect and charge us with not giving them timely notice of the designs of the French, as it is well known we have not neglected to give them every piece of intelligence that came to our knowledge.

"Brother: About fifteen days before the affair happened, we sent the Germans word that some Swegatchi Indians told us the French were determined to destroy the German Flats, and desired them to be on their guard. About six days after that we had a further account from the Swegatchi, that the French were preparing to march.

"I then came down to the German flats, and in a meeting with the Germans, told them what we had heard, and desired them to collect themselves together in a body at their fort, and secure their women, children and effects, and make the best defense they could; and at the same time told them to write what I had said to our brother Warraghiyagey [Meaning Sir William Johnson. The Palatines never sent this intelligence.]. But they paid not the least regard to what I told them, and laughed at me, saying they did not value the enemy. Upon this I returned home and sent one of our people to the lake [meaning the Oneida lake] to find out whether the enemy were coming or not; and after he had staid there two days, the enemy arrived at the carrying place, and sent word to the castle at the lake, that they were there, and told them what they were going to do; but charged them not to let us at the upper castle know any thing of their design. As soon as the man I sent there heard this, he came on to us with the account that night, and as soon as we received it we sent a belt of *wampum* to confirm the truth thereof, to the flats, which came here the day before the enemy made their attack; but the people would not give credit to the account even then, or they might have saved their lives. This is the truth, and those Germans here present know it to be so.

"The aforesaid Germans did acknowledge it to be so, and that they had such intelligence.

"GEORGE CROGHAN."

In testing historical facts, all the circumstances of the relations given must be examined with care, the position of the narrators known, and all probabilities nicely and properly balanced. Hitherto these people, in their intercourse with the colonial officials of the crown, had given no such evidence of inanition and stolidity as is here charged upon them. They did not lack shrewdness and a good degree of intelligence in selecting their lands. This is evident to any one who will take the trouble to examine into it. They had every motive, the preservation of life, and the protection of property, to induce them to be cautious and guarded in all their actions; they would not be likely in one short year to have forgotten that all the frontier posts between them and their habitual foes had been captured, and that an invasion of their own homes had been feared.

De Lancy knew nothing of the facts stated, bearing upon this particular subject, except what he derived from reports or rumors, and M. de Belletre's narrative is a mere bagatelle, discredited by one of his own countrymen; besides, how could he know the English had notice of his coming the day preceding, except from rumor? The statements of the narrative which has been partly transcribed, present the gravest subject of reflection, touching the matter to be disposed of. Sir William Johnson had, at this time, been several years superintendent of Indian affairs under the crown, possessing great shrewdness, much talent and an untiring perseverance in the discharge of his duties; his intercourse with the Indians was marked with uncommon sagacity, and to carry into effect, fully, the policy of his government in respect to the Indians, appeared to be the end and aim of all his actions. He had already achieved a standing with the home government, that could not be easily assailed, and won for himself a title, to his posterity a fortune. His influence over and control of the native Indians within his superintendency, was very great, and it seemed their brother Warraghiyagey had only to express a desire, to have it fulfilled, so far as it depended on their agency. They could not forfeit his confidence in them with impunity;

and they well knew that every approach of the enemy, or even rumor of it, through their country, towards the English settlements, must in accordance with the conventional relations existing between him and them, be immediately communicated to the parties expected to be assailed. This attack on the Palatine 'village was sudden, and no doubt unexpected, to Sir William, and when the news reached him his first thought seems to have been that his Indian outposts had been negligent of their duty, for he despatched his deputy and interpreter to the spot to inquire why they had not given more timely notice of the designs and approach of the enemy, he having been informed that no intelligence had been given by the Indians until the morning the attack was made. The affair was a very grave one, and might create some embarrassments.

The blame of permitting this murderous assault, without making any preparation to meet it, must fall upon Sir William and his sub-agents, the Indians, or the German settlers, and it is not very difficult to see what would be the result of the inquiry, when the judge and witness were interested parties, and it must be more agreeable to the sub-agent to find the Indians blameless, than chargeable with a neglect that must in some degree reflect discredit upon the chief superintendent of Indian affairs. The document, partly copied, was not found in the archives of the state, either here or in England, nor among Sir William's papers, and there is no evidence found, except the paper itself, that the Palatines knew any thing of its contents or were present on the occasion; and what is quite remarkable, no paper has been seen or found wherein Sir William alludes to this invasion, but he was at the German Flats in 1756, in April, 1757, and in 1758. The fact is not improbable that the deputy agent was better pleased to find the fault of being unprepared attributable to the settlers, rather than the Indians, for then there could be no cause for censure, however remote, against the Indian superintendency. The reader has all the facts within the reach of the author, and must form such conclusions as may seem just.

These people were then seated on as fertile a spot as any in the state, had good buildings on their farms, and were generally rich. Their buildings and crops were destroyed by fire, and their horses, cattle, sheep and hogs were many of them killed. Some of the people were slain by the marauders and nearly one hundred carried into captivity. The German minister and a majority of the inhabitants who followed him, saved themselves by going to the fort on the south side of the river, on the morning of the attack. The enemy burned a gristmill, probably on what is now called Starings's creek, and a sawmill within a few miles of the settlement. There were about twenty houses between Fort Kouari [Herkimer] and Fall Hill or Little Falls, on the south side of the river at this time, and eight on the north side, which were abandoned for a time when the settlement at Herkimer was destroyed.

In the following spring, April 30th, 1758, a large party of Indians and a small number of French attacked the Palatine settlement on the south side of the river, near the fort. About thirty of the inhabitants were killed, and one officer, Lieut. Hair of the rangers, was wounded slightly in the breast. The enemy were rather roughly treated when they came in contact with the rangers, having had about fifteen of their number killed and wounded. Captain Herchamer commanded the fort at this time, and on the first intimation of danger, collected within the fort all the inhabitants he could gather, before the attack was made upon the settlements, but there were several families who had fled from Henderson's purchase that spring, and with them two Indian traders by the name of Clock, and several teamsters, taking baggage to the fort, who were not notified in time, or for some other cause, did not retire to the fort before the enemy came upon them, rushed into the houses, killing and scalping all they could find. The teamsters being together in one of the houses attacked, ran up stairs and made a brave defense until the Indians were driven away by the rangers; one of them, however, John Ehel, hearing the Indians threaten to set fire to the house they were in, became frightened, jumped out of the chamber window and was killed. A woman came into the fort the next morning, who had been scalped, her nose nearly cut off, and wounded in her breast and side; and she was even then, in that mutilated condition, supposed likely to recover. She related all that happened to her until scalped, and said there were Onondaga Indians with the enemy. One or two facts are worthy of special notice. The account given of this second disaster to the Palatines, states that Capt. Herkimer or Herchamer, was notified by an Oneida Indian, at 12 o'clock, that the Indians and French were near the fort and would come down on the settlements that day, and at four o'clock the attack was made, giving only four hours to gather in the inhabitants from the different localities in the neighborhood of the fort, and some of the houses were some distance from it. Now, why was not a more timely notice given, and why were any Onondaga Indians found with the enemy making war upon this frontier settlement?

At this period of the history of the Mohawk valley, there were nearly five hundred houses between the East Canada creek and Sir William Johnson's residence near Amsterdam, on both sides of the river, and the road or path usually traveled from Utica as far down as the East Canada creek was on the south side of the river. There was no wagon or carriage track between the two creeks at that early day.

The capture of Fort Frontenac, Kingston, C. W., by the English in 1758, and the surrender of Quebec and Fort Niagara in the following year, with a general pacification with the Indian tribes, again secured to the inhabitants of the German Flats the blessings of peace. Their surviving friends returned from captivity, and with cheerfulness and hope rebuilt their homes, replenished their stocks and prepared their fields for seed time, with a full anticipation of once more reaping the plenteous harvest in quiet.

The gloom of the past now began to fade in the brightening prospects of the future, with this little band of frontier pilgrims, whose more than fifty years of wanderings, since they left their fatherland, had not been unattended by toils, privations, sicknesses, devastations and deaths. And such deaths too as were inflicted on some of their number! Humanity, bowing in reverent submission, weeps in agony at the recital, and asks when retributive justice will be visited upon the perpetrators of such deeds; and when and how these tribulations shall have an end.

The repose and tranquility that succeeded the conquest of Canada by the English, and the general Indian pacification before alluded to, was only the calm that precedes the earthquake. In 1763, Nova Scotia, Canada, Cape Breton and other dependencies were ceded by France to the British crown, and the two Floridas by Spain, and thus Great Britain became mistress of the whole North American continent; a territory equal in extent to that of several European kingdoms. From 1689 to 1760, a period of seventy-one years, the colonies had been involved in four wars, which lasted in all, twenty-seven years, but their population had increased from two hundred thousand to nearly three millions. Agriculture had steadily advanced, and trade and commerce had greatly increased; but in arts and manufactures little progress was made, the introduction of them being opposed by the mother country. Hitherto the commercial enterprise of the colonists had encountered but few checks from the home government, and a direct trade with several of the Spanish and French colonies had been permitted, although contrary to the letter of the British navigation laws. This trade was highly beneficial to the colonists, as it enabled them to exchange their products for gold and silver and other valuable commodities, whereby they were enabled to make their remittances in payment of British manufactures, which their necessities compelled them to have, and could not be supplied from any other country. Shortly after the treaty of Paris in 1763, the spirit with which the colonists prosecuted their commercial affairs, alarmed the mercantile and shipping interests in the mother country, upon whose representations the government imposed restrictions that annihilated this trade, to the serious injury of the northern colonies. Although some modification of former restrictions subsequently took place, they were coupled with regulations and the exaction of duties to raise a revenue in America, which the colonists considered dangerous innovations. The people of the colonies were not relieved and their fears were greatly excited in consequence of the novel principles attempted to be engrafted upon the British constitution by the enactment of laws of this description. The British national debt had become enormous for that period, and it was found necessary to provide means for diminishing the burthen, and the idea of raising a substantial revenue in the colonies from taxes imposed by parliament was conceived, and laws to carry it into effect were passed. The causes that produced collision with the mother country and eventuated in the independence of the American colonies, can not be minutely traced in a work of this character. The colonies insisted they were members of the British empire and could not be taxed without their consent; that representation and taxation were inseparable; and that this was a fundamental principle of the British constitution.

Lord Camden, in a debate in the house of peers on one of these tax bills, uttered the following emphatic and impressive language: "My position," said he, "is this; I repeat it; I will maintain it to my last hour: *Taxation and representation are inseparable.* This position is founded on the laws of nature. It is more, it is an eternal law of nature. For, whatever is a man's own, no other man has a right to take from him without his consent, and whoever does it commits a robbery." And Mr. Pitt said in the house of commons: "You have no right to tax America. I rejoice that America has resisted. Three millions of our fellow subjects so lost to every sense of virtue, as tamely to give up their liberties, would be fit instruments to make slaves of the rest." These sentiments, couched in language so bold and nervous, were not slow in reaching the ears of a deeply interested audience. The distinguished and liberal British statesmen who uttered them, did not, perhaps, imagine they were speeding a ball that was so soon to strike from the British crown one of its brightest jewels.

It may not be out of place here to remark, that Sir William Johnson was highly esteemed, and no doubt justly, by his neighbors of the lower Mohawk valley, and exercised over many of them an unbounded influence. On his death that esteem and regard was transferred to his family, who did not fail to exert their influence among their friends and dependants, in all matters relating to the approaching conflict. Quite a number of the people then living at and near Johnstown, Fort Hunter and other parts of Tryon county, left it with Sir John Johnson and Guy Johnson, and went to Canada; the descendants of some of them may now be found settled on the shores of Lake Ontario, between Niagara and Burlington Heights, Hamilton; and others in different parts of Upper Canada. These were followed by others, disaffected, who left during the revolutionary war.

The Palatines at the German Flats, were seated at some distance from Sir William, and had comparatively but little intercourse with him. They knew him as an officer of the government, and not as a neighbor and friend. They had but few opportunities of intercourse with his family, and consequently were not influenced by them in regard to the difficulties between the colonies and the mother country.

If any efforts were made to detach them from their allegiance to the country, those efforts were not attended with any great success, as only a very few of them are known to have abandoned their homes and followed the fortunes of the Johnson family. They may have had abundant reasons for doubting the disinterestedness of any proffers that were made to them from that quarter, and they chose not to put any further faith in promises which had to their grief and sorrow been so often broken. They had not in seventeen years forgotten the scenes of November, 1757, and April, 1758, when they were left an unprotected and exposed frontier, subject to attack by an enemy whose trophy was the human scalp, and the record of whose warlike achievements was found in the smouldering ruins of destroyed hamlets, slaughtered cattle, and captive women and children; when, if any males were spared, these were preserved to grace the triumph of victory, by running the gauntlet between two lines of infuriated demons, whose privilege and duty it was to inflict torments, and whose greatest solace consisted in viewing the agonies of the tortured victim.

But these people had other and loftier motives to guide their actions and control them in the course they should pursue in the contest, where even brother was to strive with deadly weapons against brother, and the son with the father; a most unnatural conflict, provoked by kingly power. Tradition, if they possessed no other means of information, had unfolded to them all the miseries of serfdom, a concomitant of regal power and the absolute rule of one man. They saw and felt the justice of the sentiment, that man ought not to be burdened without his consent; but exposed as they were, and suffer as they well knew they must, from the blows that would be dealt upon them by their old foes, soon to be leagued with former friends, they embraced with zeal, and with a resolution not to be shaken, the cause of the colonies against the mother country, and held out firmly to the end; thereby proving themselves unfit "instruments to make slaves of the rest" of their fellow subjects.

This is plain, unembellished historic truth, respecting the inhabitants of the country now embraced within the bounds of the county, and of which the descendants of the Palatines composed, by far, the greatest number.

From the close of the French war to the stirring events that shortly preceded the commencement of the revolutionary contest, neither history nor oral tradition has given us any marked or striking incidents worthy of notice. Until 1772, Albany county extended westward without any defined limits, when Tryon county was erected, and the administration of justice must have been characterized by a patriarchal simplicity, often silenced, no doubt, by military rule. The white settlements were mostly confined to the Mohawk valley and its vicinity, although some families were found remote from the principal settlements along the river.

CHAPTER V.

1772 TO 1783.

Events Preceding the Revolution — Tryon County — Territorial Divisions of White Settlements before the War — General Congress in 1774 — Provincial Convention in 1775 — Second General Congress in 1775 — Committees of Safety — Meeting of in Tryon County — Conduct of Guy Johnson — Indian Council at German Flats — Gloomy Prospects — Sir John Johnson — Declaration of Independence — Preparations of the Enemy — Generals Schuyler and Herkimer — Vigilance of the Foe — Fort Schuyler Invested by St. Leger — Herkimer's Proclamation — Tryon County Militia assemble at German Flats — Herkimer Marches to the Relief of Fort Schuyler — Col. Gansevoort — St. Leger's Forces — Insubordinate Conduct of Herkimer's Officers — Battle of Oriskany — Willett's Sortie — Sir John Johnson's Effort to Detach the Inhabitants from the Patriot Cause — Walter N. Butler captured — Arnold arrives at Fort Dayton — His Proclamation — Honjost Schuyler's Mission and Success — Situation of the Valley in the Winter of 1777, 1778 — Andrus — Town destroyed by Brant — Retaliation on Young's Settlement — German Flats destroyed by Brant — The Liberty Pole — William Dygert — Fate of the Palatines — Mills burnt at the Little Falls — Alexander Ellice — Enemy's Visit to Rhiemensnyder's Bush — Mount Family in Jersyfield — Sir John Johnson's Retreat — Destruction of Fort Schuyler — Solomon Woodworth — John Christian Shell — Donald McDonald — Defeat of Ross — Death of W. N. Butler. — Losses and Sufferings of the Enemy — Willett's Return from Pursuing the Enemy — Resolution of British Commons — Failure of the Expedition against Oswego —Close of the War — Conciliatory Proposals of Peace.

Upon the organization of Tryon County, the territory was divided into four large districts of country, although each contained but a comparatively small number of inhabitants. These districts were subdivided into smaller precincts. The Mohawk district was the easternmost, and lay in that part of the county directly under the influence of the Johnson family; the Canajoharie lay above the Mohawk on the south side of the river, and embraced all the territory south and as far west as the Little falls; the Palatine district embraced all the country on the north side of the river between the Little falls and Mohawk district; and the German Flats and Kingsland districts included all the territories and settlements on both sides of the river westward of the Palatine and Canajoharie districts. These comprised the territorial divisions.

In those days, the exciting events that formed the topic of conversation among the colonists, on the seaboard and in the eastern provinces, were slow in reaching the secluded valley of the upper Mohawk. The Johnson family, controlled a district of country lying between it and Albany, and it was not without some hazard, that any one friendly to the colonists could venture to convey intelligence of an unfriendly bearing to the mother country into the upper disircts.

A congress, composed of delegates from most of the colonies, met at Philadelphia, in September, 1774. In April, 1775, a provincial convention met at New York, and chose delegates to the second congress, which convened in May following, at Philadelphia; and, on the 22d May, 1775, a *provincial* congress assembled at New York, at which necessary measures were taken to defend the country. This body delegated their powers, for one month, to a *committee of safety*, consisting of three members from the city, and one from each of the other counties.

It may be superfluous to remark that these organizations were voluntary; but deriving all their authority from the people, these bodies claimed to exercise, and did exercise all necessary power, for the protection of their constituents, on the disruption of the royal governments. Local *committees of safety* were appointed, in all the districts of Tryon county, in accordance with the recommendations of the general and *provincial* congresses. The committees of the Palatine and Canajoharie districts seem to have taken the initiative in these affairs and were active and zealous in their patriotic efforts to present to their countrymen the true grounds of difference between the colonies and the mother country.

The committee of the Palatine district, on 21st of May, 1775, in a letter sent by express to the Albany committee, say: "We have just sent an express to the German Flats, and Kingsland districts, desiring them to unite with us, and give us their assistance; which districts, or at least a great majority of them, we are credibly informed, are very hearty in the present struggle for American liberty." Mr. Campbell, in his Annals of Tryon County, says the first united meeting of the committee, for the whole county, was held on the 2d day of June, 1775, and gives the following names of members from the several districts.

From the Palatine district: Christopher P. Yates, John Frey, Andrew Fink, Andrew Reiber, Peter Waggoner, Daniel McDougal, Jacob Klock, George Ecker, Jun., Harmanus Van Slyck, Christopher W. Fox, Anthony Van Veghten; 11.

From the Canajoharie district: Nicholas Herkimer, Ebenezer Cox, William Seeber, John Moore, Samuel Campbell, Samuel Clyde, Thomas Henry, John Pickard; 8.

From the Kingsland and German Flats districts: Edward Wall, William Petry, John Petry, Augustine Hess, Frederick Orendorf, George Wentz, Michael Ittig, Frederick Fox, George Herkimer, Duncan McDougal, Frederick Helmer, and John Frink; 12.

From the Mohawk district: John Morlett, John Bliven, Abraham Van Horne, Adam Fonda, Frederick Fisher, Sampson Simmons, William Schuyler, Volkert Veeder, James McMaster and Daniel Lane; 10. In all, 41.

The members from the Mohawk district had hitherto been hindered from meeting with the delegates from the other districts, by the Johnsons. Guy Johnson, finding the people of the valley resolute in their determination, and becoming more united, as correct information was circulated among them of the true state of the controversy between the colonies and mother country, had made up his mind to quit the country and retire to Canada. Under the pretence of holding a council with the Indians, he had left Guy Park, with his family and dependants, and stopped at a Mr. Thompson's, on Cosby's Manor, a few miles above German Flats, where this committee addressed to him a spirited, but firm and temperate letter, in which they placed before him their views of the controversy between the two countries; disabused themselves of "false and malicious" charges that had been injuriously circulated against them, and announced their resolution of standing by the country until all grievances were redressed. They besought him, as superintendent of the Indians, "to dissuade them from interfering in the dispute with the mother country and the colonies." This letter was communicated to Johnson by Edward Wall and Gen. Nicholas Herkimer, who waited upon him at Cosby's Manor. The answer to the committee's letter, dated Cosby's Manor, June 6th, 1775, was characteristic of a man who had resolved on what he would do; but, in view of the great interests he had at stake in the country, and the critical position of Sir John Johnson, whom he had left behind, its asperity was very much softened. Col. Johnson went to Fort Stanwix, from the Manor, thence to Ontario and Oswego, and after holding councils with the Indians of the Six Nations, and attaching them firmly to the interests of the English, by his promises and rewards, finally retired to Montreal, where he continued, during the war, to discharge the duties of his agency, with a fidelity to his government that inflicted upon his former neighbors unutterable sorrows and sore desolations.

The whole country was unprepared for the crisis then

fast approaching—destitute of arms, and without munitions of war—no public treasury, nor organized governments—no trained soldiery, or equipped navy; and without officers versed in the science of war. Three millions of people, scattered over a wide extent of country, reaching from Maine to Georgia, and from the Atlantic ocean to the Alleghany mountains, are seen preparing for a contest in arms, with the most powerful and wealthy nation in the civilized world; and who but the descendants of the resolute Anglo-Saxon race could thus resolve and thus achieve a nation's freedom? No one of the twelve colonies afforded so many and influential adherents to the royal cause as New York; and in no other were the severities, that particularly characterized the border warfare of the times, more effectually inflicted, for years in succession, than upon her northern and western frontiers; the inhabitants of the upper and lower Mohawk valleys often drinking deep of the bitter cup.

The colonists, fully aware of their position, and of the exposed condition of the inland border settlements to Indian warfare, took early measures to dissuade the five nations, inhabiting western New York, from taking any part in the approaching contest between them and the mother country. A council was held at German Flats, on the 28th of June, 1775, with the Oneidas and Tuscaroras, who were met by the inhabitants of the district, and a deputation from Albany, which resulted in a pledge of neutrality by most of the Indians present.

About this time, the supplies of provisions intended for Col. Guy Johnson's journey had been stopped at Mr. Thompson's, Cosby's Manor, by the inhabitants of the Kingsland district, and by a note or memorandum of a council held between the inhabitants and Oneidas, July 1st, 1775, in which the reasons for doing so were fully explained, it seems that the Indians were dissatisfied, claimed that the stores were intended for the Five Nations, who might suffer by being deprived of them, and insisted that Col. Johnson's designs were not then known, but when they were found out they would assemble and consider about them. The provisions were sent forward to Johnson, then at Fort Stanwix.

On the 15th and 16th of August, 1775, a preliminary council was held, at German Flats, attended by Messrs. Turbot, Francis, and Volkert P. Douw, on behalf of the Indian commissioners of the northern department, and several sachems of the Six Nations, and among them was Little Abraham of the Mohawks. The object of this meeting was to induce the Six Nations to send deputies to Albany to meet the American commissioners, where it was proposed "to kindle up a great council-fire." The people of the valley were even then suspicious of the Indians, and gave some indications of a resolution which created apprehensions among the Indians that they might be molested on their journey. They mentioned this to Col. Francis, who promised them the road should "be open for them to go to Albany."

The council at Albany commenced on the 23d, and closed on the 31st of August. And although the Indians had been kindly treated, furnished plentifully with provisions, during the three weeks occupied at German Flats and Albany, and on their departure manifesting much good will, being bountifully supplied with presents, still this was the last time the council-fire was opened with the Six Nations until after the close of the war. The result of this conference, although not fully attended by any but the Oneidas and the lower Mohawk clan, was for a time beneficial to the country. The engagements of peace and neutrality, then made, relieved the frontier inhabitants from apprehensions of immediate danger. It was not many months, however, before the great body of the Mohawks, Onondagas, Cayugas and Senecas gave undoubted indications of attachment to the royal cause.

The state of affairs in Tryon county strongly admonished the county committee of safety to prepare for coming events; that body therefore organized the militia of the county into four battalions, one in each district, and transmitted the return, through Nicholas Herkimer, the chairman, on the 26th August, 1775, to the general committee of safety, in session in the city of New York, during the recess of the provincial congress. This return was laid before the general committee, on the 6th of September following, and approved. To conform to the regulations established by the continental congress, the nomination of four additional majors and four quarter-masters, one for each battalion, was called for. The names of only the field officers of the first three battalions are here given.

First battalion, Canajoharie district.—Nicholas Herkheimer, colonel; Ebenezer Cox, lieutenant-colonel; Robert Wells, major; Samuel Clyde, adjutant.

Second battalion, Palatine district.—Jacob Clock, colonel; Peter Waggoner, lieutenant-colonel; Harmanus Van Slyck, major; Anthony V. Vechten, adjutant.

Third battalion, Mohawk district.—Frederick Fisher, colonel; Adam Fonda, lieutenant-colonel; John Bliven, major; Robert Yates, adjutant.

Fourth battalion, German Flats and Kingsland.—Hanyoost Herkheimer, colonel; Peter Bellinger, lieutenant-colonel; Hanyoost Shoemaker, major; John Demooth, adjutant.

1st company.—John Eisenlord, captain; John Keyser, 1st lieutenant; Adam Bellinger, 2d lieutenant; John Smith, ensign.

2d company.—John Petry, captain; Hanyoost Mx. Petry, 1st lieutenant; Hanyoost H. Petry, 2d lieutenant; William Empie, ensign.

3d company.—Daniel Petry, captain; Peter Volts, 1st lieutenant; Marx Raspach, 2d lieutenant; George Helmer, ensign.

4th company.—Frederick Bellinger, captain; Henry Herter, 1st lieutenant; John Demooth, 2d lieutenant; Peter Ja. Weaver, ensign.

5th company.—Peter Bellinger, captain; Jacob Baschawn,

1st lieutenant; Nicholas Staring, 2d lieutenant; John P. Bellinger, ensign.

6th company.—Hanyoost Herkheimer, captain; Frederick Ahrendorf, 1st lieutenant; Tinus Clapsaddle, 2d lieutenant.

7th company.—Rudolph Shoemaker, captain; Deiterick Stale, 1st lieutenant; Frederick Shoemaker, 2d lieutenant.

8th company.—George Herkheimer, captain; Frederick Fox, 1st lieutenant; Archibald Armstrong, 2d lieutenant; Hanyoost Tygert, ensign.

9th company.—William Tygert, captain; Jacob Volts, 1st lieutenant; George Wents, 2d lieutenant; Frederick Frank, ensign.

The county committee, at this time, seeing the necessity of having some tribunal for the determination of petty disputes and controversies, in civil matters, to the amount of twelve and a half dollars, adopted a resolution, investing its members with a sort of civil jurisdiction, and sent it to the provincial congress for approval. The general committee of safety in reply to it say:

"The congress of this colony have hitherto avoided interfering in the administration of justice in civil matters, or arresting the cognizance from the officers of justice. We cannot, therefore, approve of the resolve by you entered into, respecting the trial of civil causes in your county, and find it highly expedient to recommend its repeal."

This was a serious detriment to the inhabitants of this remote part of the colony, where there were only a few officers of justice, and those few being strongly attached to the interests of the crown, felt no inclination to hold the scales of justice even, between a loyalist and a man he deemed a rebel.

It was for a time doubtful, whether some marked demonstration unfavorable to the cause of the twelve provinces, would not be made in the colony of New York. The intrigues of the artful and menaces of power were not vainly exerted and unfelt, and disaffection appeared openly in the provincial congress. The Tryon county committee of safety, were at this time a noble body of men. Enthusiastically devoted to the interests of their constituents, and the cause of the colonists; their zeal was untiring, and they faltered not in the important work before them. Supported by a great majority of the inhabitants of the valley, they exercised all the powers of government, for the time, executive, legislative and judicial, and all their proceedings were cheerfully acquiesced in, except by those attached to the royal cause. Sir John Johnson, was still at Johnstown, surrounded by his adherents, whom he had organized and armed, waiting a favorable moment to strike a bold and effectual blow against treason and disloyalty, which he failed to achieve; and finally fled into Canada in the spring of 1776, when he was commissioned a colonel in the British service, and raised a regiment composed of men who accompanied him, which was known as the Royal Greens.

No event of much interest has been noticed as having transpired within the territory of the present county of Herkimer, during the year 1776. The Declaration of Independence was solemnly adopted on the 4th of July, an event not originally anticipated by the great mass of the colonists; and immediately proclaimed to the world, after a state of war had existed fifteen months; a conflict for a redress of grievances, and not for the dismemberment of an empire. The attitude thus assumed was solemn, and the aspects of the future were ominous of woe to the inhabitants of the western frontiers; but the Palatines of the German Flats who still survived, and their descendants, quailed no before the coming storm. Their delegates in the county committee had the year before assented to the principle of separation, and they were not now backward in the cause, but with their brethren in the lower Mohawk valley, welcomed the act which was to separate them and their country from kingly power. The British ministry were by no means idle. An aggregate of 55,000 men, it was contemplated, should compose the invading forces, at the different approachable points, and with these the colonists were to be crushed at a blow.

Congress directed General Schuyler, who then commanded the northern department, to repair and strengthen Fort Stanwix, afterwards known as Fort Schuyler, an important post, and to erect other fortifications in the Mohawk valley. Colonel Dayton, then stationed at German Flats with a detachment of regular troops, was charged with the works at Fort Stanwix, in which the Tryon county militia participated, but he seems to have made slow progress in completing the defenses, as they were incomplete when invested by St. Leger the following year.

The interview between General Herkimer and Capt. Joseph Brant, a Mohawk sachem, at Unadilla, in July, 1777, will be noticed in another place, that interview partaking more of personal character than of local historical interest. The important event of this year must receive a passing notice.

> "Sad was the year, by proud oppression driven,
> When transatlantic liberty arose;
> Not in the sunshine and the smile of heaven,
> But rapt in whirlwinds and begirt with woes."

The untiring vigilance of the emissaries of the crown began to unfold itself about midsummer of this year. The news of the approach of the British armies and their savage allies on the northern and western frontiers of the state, had been industriously circulated throughout the whole country, and the Mohawk valley was by no means neglected. The people there were alarmed and became depressed and desponding. They had cheerfully seconded all the movements of the colonists, in asserting their rights against the encroachments of the crown, and their situation was one of exposure and hazard. Protected from the inroads of the enemy only by light parties of regulars which could afford but little security against the marauding tories and their savage allies, they were incessantly harrassed by alarms, burthened with service, and worn down by fatigues; who can feel surprise that the patriotic should despond and the weak falter? Or why should a people so beset with foes within and without be suspected of loyalty to the cause to the support of which they had so recently pledged their lives, fortunes and honor? The first outburst of patriotic sentiment had doubtless stifled a lurking aspiration for the success of the royal cause, which now began to show itself in open disaffection to an alarming extent as the crisis approached; but it may with truth be said, that few, very few, if any of the inhabitants of the upper valley of the Mohawk, were found disloyal to the cause, or unwilling to put their shoulders to the wheel at their country's call.

Fort Schuyler was invested by Colonel St. Leger, on the 3d of August, 1777, with a force of seventeen hundred men, composed of British, Hessians, Johnson's Greens, Canadians and Indians. It would be out of place to notice particularly the events of this siege, or the disasters that befell the besiegers.

Notice of the assembling of the hostile forces at Oswego, for the purpose of invasion, contemporaneously with the approach of General Burgoyne by the way of Lake Champlain from the north, had been communicated by the Oneida Indians, to Col. Gansevoort, at Fort Schuyler, and the provincial authorities in Tryon county, and at Albany; and steps were immediately taken to meet the approaching crisis and drive back the invaders. General Herkimer, who commanded the Tryon county militia, issued a spirited and patriotic proclamation to the people of the county, on the 17th of July, 1777, notifying them of the assembling of the enemy at Oswego, and of their destination and objects, and calling on the male population *en masse*, to repair to the field, at a moment's warning, armed and equipped, to meet the invading forces.

Those in health between the ages of 16 and 60, were required to take the field, and those above 60, as well as the invalids, were directed to assemble, armed, at proper places, for the defense of the women and children. The members of the county committee of safety, and the exempts from military duty, were invited to repair to the place to be appointed, to join in repulsing the common enemy.

The whole American force at Fort Schuyler, when invested by the enemy, was seven hundred and fifty men. Col. Gansevoort was joined by Lieutenant Col. Mellon, of Col. Weston's regiment, with two hundred men, and two batteau loads of provisions, and military stores, on the 2d day of August. The deficiency of ammunition for the cannon was very great—being an inadequate supply for a protracted siege at a frontier post.

As soon as the approach of St. Leger to Fort Schuyler was known in Tryon county, General Herkimer ordered the militia of his brigade to rendezvous at Fort Dayton (then called German Flats). This defense was erected in the western part of Herkimer village, and the General soon found himself at the head of about nine hundred men, composed of the three militia regiments commanded by Colonels Klock, Cox, Vischer and some others, with volunteers of officers and men from various parts of the country. The published accounts of the forces collected under General Herkimer on this occasion, do not designate the localities from which the several regiments were drawn; enough is known, however, to warrant the assertion, that the militia of the German Flats and Kingsland district were attached to the regiment commanded by Col. Peter Bellinger, whose lieut. colonel was Frederick Bellinger; major, Enos Klepsattle. The militia of these districts participated in the battle of Oriskany. The alacrity and zeal evinced on this occasion should have entirely eradicated all impressions unfavorable to the patriotic devotion of the inhabitants of the valley, growing out of the expression of despondency in the early part of the year. Surely after this, no one could complain of German disloyalty to the cause of the colonists. General Herkimer left Fort Dayton on the 4th of August, and encamped near the Oriskany on the 5th, crossing the Mohawk river at old Fort Schuyler (now Utica) on the march up. At this point the General expressed his doubts of the expediency of a forward movement, until reinforcements should arrive, or the prearranged signal should be given by Col. Gansevoort from the fort. An express, Adam Helmer with two other men, had been dispatched to the fort, informing the commandant of the General's approach, and to arrange measures of cooperation. The messengers did not reach the fort until ten or eleven o'clock in the morning of the 6th. Three successive discharges of heavy ordinance was the signal agreed on, announcing the arrival of the express; the reports of which, it was assumed, could be heard at Herkimer's encampment, eight miles distant from the fort. Recriminatory and insubordinate language was used on the occasion, and the General was denounced to his face as a tory and coward; who replied, that their safety was in his hands, and he desired to avoid all difficulties that could not be surmounted by bravery and good conduct. On this occasion the General told some of his subordinates, who had been rather noisy and liberal in their accusations of his fidelity and courage, that they would be the first to run on the approach of the enemy; which was soon verified to the very letter.

All previous accounts had fixed St. Leger's forces at 2000 strong, nearly half of which were Indians led by Brant, a brave, active and artful Mohawk sachem. Herkimer knew this, and he no doubt believed, as well he might, that a force superior to his own, could be sent against him, which would select its own battle-field, without in any way interfering with the investment of the fort. But noisy insubordination prevailed, and precipitated the little band of patriots into the jaws of death. Smarting under the repeated accusations heaped upon him, and irritated no doubt, the General gave orders to take up the line of march, which was received with cheers by the men, who proceeded rapidly on their way, two deep, having thrown out the usual advanced and flanking parties.

At 10 o'clock, on the 6th, the main body of troops passed over a causeway on a marshy ravine, the advance having commenced an ascent of the westerly slope, when a well directed fire from the enemy, in front and on both flanks, accompanied with the dismal Indian war-whoop, unfolded to the American general that his division had become involved in an almost inextricable ambuscade. Retreat was impossible, for the causeway over the marsh was already blocked up with teams; and the rear guard, just commencing the descent of the eastern declivity, commanded by one of the officers who in the morning had taunted his general with cowardice, turned and fled on the first fire of the enemy. But flight did not save them from the fate that awaited their comrades on the west side of the ravine; the enemy, knowing well the ground, had gained the rear, and shot down the fugitives as they ran away from their companions. As might well be expected, the suddenness of the attack and the intensity of the enemy's fire, not only produced great disorder among the provincials, but annihilation seemed almost inevitable for a time.

In this disorder, the conflict raged about half an hour, when the Americans forming themselves into circular squads, the more effectually to repel the attacks of the enemy, who were steadily approaching on all sides; and, from this moment, resistance became more effective. The enemy then charged with bayonet, but they were met by brave hearts and strong arms, and thus the battle raged, until the parties were compelled to desist, by a heavy shower of rain, which raged with great fury more than an hour. The enemy sought the best shelter they could find, at a good distance from the provincials, when the latter, under the directions of their general, occupied a favorable piece of ground, and then so formed themselves as to be able to repel an attack from any quarter. The fight was renewed, but the Indians, suffering severely by the deadly fire of the militia, began to give ground, when a detatchment of Johnson's Greens, composed chiefly of loyalists who had fled from Tryon county, were brought into action face to face with many of their former neighbors. Then mutual hate and revenge raged with unspeakable intensity between the combatants, and the conflict now became, if possible, more a death struggle than ever.

In the meantime, while the battle was the most fierce, a firing was heard in the direction of the fort; no unwelcome sound, as may well be supposed, to the handful of surviving provincials, nor very gratifying to the enemy. During the conflict at the Oriskany, a well conducted sortie from the fort, under the command of Col. Willett, was made upon the forces under St. Leger, for the purpose of drawing the enemy's attention to the preservation of their camp in that direction. This was well understood by the provincials, and in it they saw great hopes of deliverance. This was not a fight suited to the taste of savages, who found *their* numbers fast diminishing, nor could such a contest be long maintained with much hope of survivorship, by either party. "*Oonah,*" the retreating cry of the Indians, was heard in the distance, and their flight commenced with a salute of shouts and bullets from the surviving provincials. The Greens and Rangers soon followed the example of their illustrious allies, by a precipitate retreat, abandoning their dead and wounded, and the deeply crimsoned battle-field, in the undisputed possession of the Tryon county militia. Was this a victory, or a defeat of the provincials? By all the laws of war, they are victors who remain masters of the battle-ground. The American report gave the number of provincial militia killed, two hundred, besides the wounded and prisoners. The British accounts state the killed at four hundred, and two hundred prisoners, making in all six hundred, besides the wounded. Now in modern warfare, and in the severest battles, the wounded are more than two to one of the killed, say nothing about prisoners. The British accounts do not claim there was over one thousand militia on the march at this time to raise the siege of Fort Schuyler. Surely four hundred killed, eight hundred wounded and two hundred prisoners, out of one thousand, is making said havoc in the fighting line. But this is not so; and St. Leger, when he gave this statement of killed and prisoners to Gen. Burgoyne, was indulging not a little in the M. de Belletre vein.

The battle was a severe one. The severest, perhaps, for the number engaged, that took place during the whole revolutionary war. And from the character of the combatants, the surprise, and the disadvantages under which the provincials labored during the whole six hours conflict, the proportion of killed to the wounded must have been greatly beyond what ordinarily occurs in the hardest actions, where firearms are used as the principal weapon of assault and defense.

Leaving the personal incidents of this disaster to be noticed in another place, the events of the year, subsequent to the battle of Oriskany, must now be considered. Failing to induce Col. Gansevoort to surrender Fort Schuyler on any of the terms offered by Col. St. Leger, an effort was made by Sir John Johnson, and Cols. Claus and John Butler, to detach the inhabitants of the valley from the patriot cause, and for this purpose emissaries were sent below with incendiary proclamations, to induce the timid, terrified and disaffected people to abandon the cause of the country, and to join the British forces under St. Leger. Col. Weston was at Fort Dayton, with his regiment, during the siege of Fort Schuyler, and learning that a secret meeting of tories was to be held at Mr. Shoemaker's, a loyalist residing a mile or two distant, Weston sent a party of men, who surprised and captured Lieut. Walter N. Butler, of St. Leger's army, and twenty-eight soldiers and Indians, who had come clandestinely to the German Flats on a mission from Sir John and others.

Butler was tried by a court martial as a spy, and received sentence of death, but was reprieved, sent to Albany a prisoner, where he was detained some time, and finally making his escape, afterwards exhibited his kindly feeling to the land of his birth by becoming one of its severest scourges. Humanity has no tears to shed over the subsequent fate of this man, nor can the pretense that he came "on a truce to the inhabitants of the county," be of any avail whatever. He came on a secret mission and in a clandestine manner, and was taken in the very act of attempting to alienate the inhabitants from their allegiance to the country, and his reprieve by the American general was an act of grace, favored by many influential persons, who had previously known him at Albany.

General Arnold arrived at Fort Dayton a short time before the 21st of August, at which point troops were assembling with a view of proceeding to the relief of Fort Schuyler, still beleaguered by St. Leger's forces, and to counteract the effect of the incendiary efforts of Johnson, Claus and John Butler, the American general on the 20th of August, issued a proclamation stating that "whereas a certain Barry St. Leger, a Brigadier-General in the service of George of Great Britain, at the head of a banditti of robbers, murderers and traitors, composed of savages of America and more savage Britons (among whom is the noted Sir John Johnson, John Butler and Daniel Claus), have lately appeared in the frontiers of this state, and threatened ruin and destruction to all the inhabitants of the United States," urging the inhabitants to continue their fidelity to the common cause, offering pardon to all those who may have been misled by the artifice and misrepresentation of the enemy, if they would in ten days come in and lay down their arms, but denouncing "the just vengeance of heaven and of this exasperated country" against all who should persist in their wicked courses. On the 23d of August Gen. Arnold left Fort Dayton, determined to hazard a battle with forces inferior to the enemy before

Fort Schuyler, rather than have the garrison surrender, and had proceeded half a day's march, when he was met by an express from Col. Gansevoort, with the cheering news that the seige had been raised; but the cause of this sudden movement on the part of the enemy was wholly unknown to the gallant Colonel and his brave garrison; not so however with Arnold.

Hanyost Schuyler was the instrument made use of to scatter the besieging forces surrounding Fort Schuyler, and send them helter-skelter back to Canada in double quick time. The home of this strange and singular being, was near the upper Mohawk Indian castle in the present town of Danube, where he resided with his mother and brother Nicholas, and hence in early life had much intercourse with the Indians. He is described as coarse and ignorant, and but little removed from idiocy, and still possessing shrewdness enough to be made the instrument of accomplishing an important object. Hanyost was somewhat tainted with loyalty, and had been captured at Shoemaker's with Walter N. Butler, and others; he was tried by a court martial and sentenced to death. His mother and brother, on hearing this sad news, of course hastened to headquarters to intercede for his life. For a time their efforts were unavailing, but finally it was proposed he should repair to St. Leger's camp with a friendly Oneida Indian, and so manage to alarm the enemy as to produce an abandonment of the siege.

Hanyost gladly embraced the alternative, leaving his brother as a hostage for the faithful execution of his mission; being assured that Nicholas should die if he faltered in the enterprise. Schuyler having procured sundry shots through his garments, that he might show he had run for dear life, departed with his Indian comrade for the enemy's camp. They had arranged between them to approach St. Leger's position from opposite directions, and were not to appear acquainted with each other, if they should meet. This affair was wisely planned, and most skillfully and adroitly executed. The instrument was well chosen. He was well known as a loyalist, and the parties to whom he first addressed himself were no unwillng auditors, nor in an unfavorable mood to be deeply impressed and even awed by his ambiguous language and mysterious manner. The native American Indians, like the followers of Mahomet, were ever inspired with a peculiar respect and even reverence for idiots and lunatics. Fraternal regard strongly prompted Hanyost to apply all his energies and to leave no effort untried to secure the complete success of his mission, and relieve his brother from the fate that was hanging over him. He was completely successful, and having followed the retreating enemy to Wood Creek, he there left them, and returned to Fort Schuyler the same evening, and gave Col. Gansevoort the first intimation of Arnold's approach. It was not until Schuyler's arrival at the fort, that its commandant was able to solve the problem of St. Leger's sudden departure and precipitate flight.

Hanyost returned to the German Flats when his brother was released from confinement, to the great gratification of his mother and relatives, but he was too strongly imbued with sentiments of loyalism, to resist giving a permanent adherence to the interests of the crown, and in the fall of the same year went to Canada and remained there until the close of the war, when he returned to the Mohawk valley, where he died about forty-five years since.

The project of sending Schuyler in advance to announce Gen. Arnold's approach to the besieging forces, has been attributed to that officer. Such an idea however is not characteristic of the man. The forces on the march were not equal to the enemy then before Fort Schuyler, in point of numbers, but they were chiefly composed of continental light troops, enured to service and accustomed to obey, and the patriotic militia of the country had again rallied to the defense of their homes and families, eager for the strife and determined on revenge. Under such circumstances, knowing the strength of the garrison, and being, without doubt, well advised of the position and numbers of the enemy, the American forces all told were a match for their opponents in the neighborhood of the fort, and it was by no means likely St. Leger would again attempt to interrupt the approach of the provincials by offering battle on any other field, and by dividing the strength hazard the safety of his camp in another sortie. Reflections somewhat like these would be presented to the mind of the American commander, who was brave and intemperately rash, and who would delight in scourging the men he had denounced as a "banditti of robbers, murderers and traitors," and therefore would be less likely to suggest a stratagem to avoid a battle than some one possessing a different temperament. The probability is that this project did not originate with Arnold, although on reflection, while impatiently waiting at Fort Dayton for reinforcements and supplies, he acquiesced in the measure, at the same time, perhaps, doubting its success.

Nothing further occurred during the residue of the year 1777, within the present confines of the county, worthy of particular notice. Death had visited almost every dwelling in the upper valley, and mourning and lamentations were heard in every hamlet; but hope cheered the survivors, and the alliance with France, brought to a successful issue by the favorable aspect of American affairs at the close of the year, caused universal rejoicing throughout the whole country.

Unmolested by the enemy in the fall of 1777 and the spring of 1778, the inhabitants had planted their fields, expecting to reap an abundant harvest in due season; but in this they were sorely disappointed. Fort Schuyler, an important post, commanding the western entrance, by water communication, to the Mohawk valley, was thirty miles distant from the principal settlements at the German Flats, and presented no barrier against sudden irruptions of the enemy, who could easily avoid that fortress, and fall upon the inhabitants below, from almost every direction; and during the summer of this year the work of devastation was vigorously prosecuted.

June 25th, 1778.—The following appointments were this day made by the governor and council, to the regiment of local militia in the German Flats and Kingsland districts:

Field officers and Regimental staff.—Peter Bellinger, colonel; Frederick Bellinger, lieutenant-colonel; George Demoth, adjutant; Rudolph Steel, quartermaster.

Michael Ittig, captain; Jacob Baulcom, 1st lieutenant; Frederick Frank, 2d lieutenant; Patrick Campbell, ensign.

Henry Harter, captain; John Demoth, 1st lieutenant; Peter Ja. Weaver, 2d lieutenant; John F. Bellinger, ensign.

Jacob Small, captain; George F. Helmer, 2d lieutenant; Jacob D. Petrie, ensign.

Henry Staring, captain; Theobald Baker, 1st lieutenant; George Weaver, 2d lieutenant.

Soverenus Cassleman, captain; Henry Huber, 1st lieutenant; Jacob G. Klock, 2d lieutenant.

Frederick Getman, captain; Jacob Meyer, 2d lieutenant; John Meyer, ensign.

Henry Eckler, captain; Conrad Orendorff, 1st lieutenant; Timothy Frank, 2d lieutenant; Adam A. Staring, ensign.

The nine companies organized in August, 1775, were reduced to seven in about eighteen months of active war. The most of this loss was sustained at Oriskany. The names of Herkimer, and Shoemaker have entirely disappeared from the rolls, and the Petries have but one representative left.

The Mohawk chief, Brant, with a small party of Indians, attacked a settlement of seven families, called Andrustown, in the present town of Warren, in the month of July, plundered the inhabitants, burned up all the buildings, killed four persons, among whom was an aged man by the name of Bell, and his two sons. One other man perished in the flames of his own house. The rest of the inhabitants were carried away captives, and all the property that could be removed was taken by the Indians.

This achievement was perpetrated for the purposes of the plunder, as Brant was then collecting a large force at Oghkwaga, or Unadilla, for a more important and far more serious expedition, in its effects, which he led in the following month. Brant wanted provisions, and took this method of replenishing his stock. The Indians made a hasty retreat, and were not overtaken, although pursued by a party of Americans from the German Flats. After reaching the scene of desolation, the provincials interred the dead, and with several friendly Indians followed the marauding party as far as the Little lakes, in the south part of Warren, when finding the object of their pursuit beyond their reach, they gave up the chase. There were a few white families at the lakes, called Young's settlement, and the principal man was Young, the patentee, to whom the lands had been granted by the crown in 1752. This man was a tory in feeling, but was not known to have committed any open acts of violence against the country. His nearest neighbor sympathized with him; and when the Americans found these people had been spared by Brant and his party, they plundered and burned their houses, in retaliation for the destruction of Andrustown. John Frank, then one of the committee of safety of Tryon county, from the German Flats district, and long known in this county as Judge Frank, was one of the party who went in pursuit of Brant.

The Palatine settlements at the German Flats were doomed to suffer again under the scourge of Indian warfare, about the last of August or the first of September of this year. At this period there were two stockadoed defenses called forts, midway these settlements east and west. Fort Herkimer, near the south bank of the Mohawk river, containing the stone church and the stone mansion of the Herkimer family, and some other buildings, was surrounded by a ditch; and Fort Dayton, on a somewhat elevated spot of ground in the westerly part of Herkimer village, a few rods from the site of the present court house. Fort Herkimer, so called, was inclosed with a ditch and stockades during the French war in 1756, and Fort Dayton was constructed a year or two previous to the time now under consideration. These defenses, and others of like construction, erected in the Mohawk valley, were intended to be used as places of refuge for the inhabitants, in cases of sudden incursions by the enemy in their plundering and murdering expeditions, and to store public property when necessary. They were a sufficient defense against the tories and Indians, who were never incumbered with arms heavier than the musket and rifle, and, with few exceptions, their armaments were small, consisting of cannon used in firing signal guns to warn the distant inhabitants of some impending danger. The first liberty pole erected in the valley was raised at Fort Herkimer, in the spring of 1775, and was cut down by White, sheriff of Tryon county, who came from Johnstown with a body of militia for that purpose; and it was probably afterwards burned by this common hangman.

There were then about seventy dwelling houses on both sides of the river in the neighborhood of these forts, besides barns, other out-buildings and mills, with a large population for the number of dwellings. The earth had yielded an abundant harvest and the crops had been mostly secured. Brant's long stay at the Unadilla without striking a blow on some one of the exposed points of the frontier, excited a suspicion among the inhabitants that he might be meditating an attack upon them, and a party of four men were sent to watch his movements, who falling in with the enemy three of them were killed, and the fourth, John Helmer, saved himself by flight, and returning to the Flats about sundown, gave notice that Brant with a large force was approaching and would be down on the settlements in a short time. Forts Dayton and Herkimer now became the asylums for the terror-stricken inhabitants, to which men, women and children fled for safety, taking with them their most valuable effects, such as could be moved; but their crops, cattle and buildings were abandoned of course, to the disposal and tender mercies of the enemy. There were many among them in whose recollections the scenes of 1757 and 1758 were vividly fresh, and the apprehension of the ruin that awaited them must have been painfully severe.

Brant, at the head of three hundred tories and one hundred and fifty-two Indians, approached the confines of the settlements just at nightfall, but the weather being unpropitious and the night dark, he made a halt near Shoemaker's, his tory friend, and remained there with his forces until morning, unconscious that his approach had been notified to the inhabitants in time to allow them to escape. The untiring vigilance of the chief set him early afoot, and in the gray of the morning the whole valley was illuminated by an almost simultaneous blaze of houses, barns, stacks and barracks of hay and grain and other combustible materials. A sorrowful sight, to the people in the forts, who saw their houses and other buildings, with the produce of the season's labor, entirely consumed by fire. But this was not all, nor did the destroyer here stay his hand. As soon as it was light enough to discern objects at a distance, the tories and Indians collected all the stock that could be found, and every thing that could be gathered was driven or carried away.

Almon's Remembrancer states that there were 63 dwelling houses, 57 barns, 3 grist-mills and 2 saw-mills burnt, with most of the furniture and grain kept therein; 235 horses, 229 horned-cattle, 269 sheep and 93 oxen taken and carried away. Only two persons lost their lives in this affair. The Indians were compelled to be content with their plunder, such as it was; they got neither scalps nor prisoners this time, nor did they make any attack upon the forts. Soon after the enemy left the valley with their booty, a party of between three and four hundred militia followed in pursuit as far as the Unadilla, but this expedition was fruitless, except in finding and burying the bodies of the three scouts who went out with Helmer to watch the movements of Brant.

Shortly after the events above narrated, William Dygert, who had been taken prisoner by Brant on Fall hill some time in July or August, was recaptured by the Oneida and Tuscarora Indians and restored to his friends. This aggression at the German Flats did not long go unpunished, and a severe retribution soon overtook the Indians by the invasion and destruction of two of their chief towns, Unadilla and Oghwkaga, the particulars of which do not come within the scope of this work.

Mavor, vicar of Hurley, in Berkshire, England, said there was no race of people on earth save the Anglo-Saxon, who to maintain and carry out a principle of civil government, would submit to the ravages, devastations and destruction of property, and bear the consequent destitution of all the necessities of life, inflicted by the British armies during the revolutionary war.

Is not the fate of the Palatines somewhat remarkable? Twice during the latter half of the seventeenth century the houses of their ancestors, on another continent, had been visited by the severest calamities of cruel and exterminating war, when the whole surviving population were driven by a ruthless soldiery into the fields and forests to perish by want or exposure; and when a few thousand of the survivors landed in this country most of them were compelled to endure twelve years of serfdom under a corrupt and peculating colonial government, and finally when seated by the kind hearted and benevolent Burnet at the German Flats, their land of promise, and the *ultima thule* of all their hopes, they were twice doomed in the last half of the eighteenth century to see their fair fields laid waste, their dwellings and crops destroyed, their flocks and herds driven away to slaughter and themselves reduced to destitution and want. And on one of these occasions many of them were slain, but more were dragged into captivity. Surely this last visitation must have been extremely severe; but severe as it was no thought of submission to the crown obtruded itself upon their minds.

Although the lower portions of the Mohawk valley, and the white settlements south and east, were repeatedly visited by the enemy subsequent to the destruction of the German Flats in September, 1778, and the year 1779, the Palatine or German Flats settlements in the upper section of the valley seem to have been exempted from invasion for more than eighteen months, and the whole valley proper was comparatively quiet during the winter of 1780.

On the 3d of April, 1780, a party of about sixty tories and Indians fell upon the settlements in Rheimensynder's bush, a few miles north of the Little Falls, and burnt a grist-mill in that place. A tory by the name of Cassleman was with this party. They came and returned by the way of Jerseyfield. They took John Garter and his son John prisoners at the mill, and captured three men in the road, one of whom was Joseph Newman; at the same time, or on the same day, John Windecker, Henry Shaver, George Adle, Cobus Van Slyke and one Youker or Uker, with several others, were taken at Windecker's father's house, some distance north of the mill. The enemy carried off nineteen prisoners, twelve of whom, collected in one house, surrendered to less than half their number of straggling Indians without making any resistance or an effort to escape. All of these prisoners returned at the close of the war, except John Garter, who died in Canada, and George Adle, who escaped either on the way out or soon after he got to Canada and returned before. John Garter and a man named Espley, another prisoner, preferring colonial freedom, beset as it then was with privations and dangers, to a Canadian prison, agreed to make an effort to escape, and hired an Indian to pilot them through the wilderness; but understanding they intended to blow up the magazine before they left, or making that a pretense for his conduct, he disclosed their intentions to the British officers, when Garter and Espley were punished severely for their temerity. Espley got back, but Garter died in consequence of the severity of the punishment inflicted upon him.

There was a blockhouse in this settlement called Rheimensnyder's Fort, to which the inhabitants resorted at night for safety and protection. When the Indians made their appearance on this occasion many of the inhabitants fled to the woods, or otherwise secreted themselves. The objects of this expedition seem to have been accomplished by burning the mill and the capture of a few prisoners.

After this visit in April, the inhabitants in that part of the county, except two or three tory families in Salisbury, abandoned their farms and retired into the lower valley. Except the retreat of Sir John Johnson through the county, near the close of the year, after the battle at Klock's field, and the arrival of Gen. Van Rensselaer at Fort Herkimer soon after, in pursuit of the Greens and Rangers, whom he was very careful not to overtake, there is no other event worthy of notice. Johson's sable allies having deserted him and taken to their heels, and the gallant knight having left his Greens and Rangers to take care of themselves as they best could, he did not feel that it would be very prudent to mark the progress of his retreat with the usual burnings and slaughter which had hitherto betokened his visits to the valley.

The events of 1781 now claim the reader's attention. The destruction of Fort Schuyler by flood and fire, in the month of May, led to the abandonment of that post and the withdrawal of the garrison to the German Flats. The works had been materially injured by a heavy flow of water produced by long and incessant rains, and on the 13th of May a fire broke out at mid-day, which rendered the place indefensible. The fire was attributed to design and that suspicion was never removed.

While great Britain held her sway over the provinces, controlled the western Indians and desired to command the fur trade, defensive positions at the carrying place from the Mohawk river to Wood creek were no doubt important. Old Fort Stanwix when first built was almost in the heart of the Indian country, and commanded the approaches by water from Canada by the way of Oswego; but during the revolutionary war it was too far advanced into the wilderness to afford any protection to the white settlements below, against the predatory system of warfare carried on by the enemy. That post was easily avoided whenever the enemy came over by the way of Oswego, by passing to the south of it from the Onondaga and Oneida lakes. Most of the expeditions, however, sent against the Mohawk valley, came by the way of the Unadilla, that being the most available point to strike the settlements in that valley, the Schoharie creek, or on the west banks of the Hudson. Several small parties, however, approached the settlements on the Mohawk by the way of Black river.

Mr. Solomon Woodworth, commissioned May 11th, 1780, a lieutenant in Col. John Harper's regiment of New York levies, was afterwards, on the 8th March, 1781, appointed 1st lieutenant in Col. Fisher's regiment of Tryon county militia, "in the place of William Lard taken by or deserted to the enemy." I do not find any record of Mr. Woodworth's appointment as a captain. Acting under one of the above appointments, he, with a company of forty rangers, was stationed at Fort Dayton, for the purpose of scouring and traversing the wilderness country north of the German Flats. Woodworth was a brave man. Once during the war he was taken prisoner, but made his escape, and returned suffering very considerable hardships; at another time he defended a blockhouse north of Johnstown, and single-handed drove away the enemy. Lieut. Woodworth left Fort Dayton with his company to reconnoitre the Royal Grant. Having proceeded a few hours on the march, an Indian was discovered who was immediately fired upon, when the rangers found themselves involved in an inextricable ambuscade, and completely surrounded by an Indian force double their own numbers. The conflict that followed was severe and sanguinary, as might well have been expected from the character of the combatants engaged, and a hand to hand fight left but fifteen of the Americans, who escaped to tell the sad fate of their brethren. Some of this party were taken prisoners, but Woodworth and about half of his men were killed on the spot.

This fatal encounter took place about three miles north of Herkimer village, on the east side of the West Canada creek, in a deep ravine, where now may be seen the mound of earth, under which rest the remains of the gallant Woodworth and his brave companions. The killed, it appears, were all collected and buried in one common grave, unshrouded and uncoffined, with no monument to tell where rest the brave but unfortunate defenders of American liberty.

On the 6th of August, a German settlement called Shell's Bush, three or four miles north of Fort Dayton, was visited by a party of these formidable asserters of the rights of the crown. Donald McDonald, a Scotch refugee from Johnstown, with a party of about sixty Indians and tories, with whom was Empie and Cassleman, two famous traitors, the latter being the same man who was with the party that attacked Rheimensnyder's bush in April, 1780, made their appearance in the Shell settlement in the afternoon of the above day, when most of the inhabitants had retired to Fort Dayton, for protection. Some indications of this hostile movement must have been previously discovered, or the inhabitants would not have sought the protection of the fort. There was, however, one man, John Christian Shell, the husband of a brave and resolute wife, and the father of six sons, who determined to brave out the storm, let come what would. He had a strong blockhouse on his farm, well constructed for purposes of defense against marauding parties of tories and Indians; and he resolved to fight rather than run. The first story of logs had no openings except a doorway or entrance, well protected by a massive door, and loopholes through which the besieged could fire upon their assailants. The floor of the second story projected over the lower part of the building, and had apertures in the projecting floor, affording ample means of annoying any enemy who might approach the building to fire it or break open the door below. Shell had a good supply of arms and ammunition to stand an ordinary siege. When the enemy made their appearance, Shell and his sons were in the field at work, but his two youngest, being twins only eight years old, were so far off he could not save them when he retired to his blockhouse, and they were taken and carried to Canada. Having gained his castle and secured the entrance, Shell and his little garrison were resolute and alert, and kept up a spirited fight from two o'clock until dark. Some of the incidents are worthy of particular notice. Shell's wife was active in loading the pieces fired by her husband and four sons. McDonald several times attempted to set fire to the building, but failed. His men were several times compelled to retreat, in consequence of the galling fire received from the party in the blockhouse. McDonald made an effort to force the door with a crowbar, but was wounded in the leg while so engaged, and none of his party being near enough to rescue him, Shell did not hesitate a moment to unbar the door and drag the wounded tory leader into his fortress. This capture not only secured Shell against being burnt out by the enemy, but afforded an ample supply of ammunition to the little garrison, whose stock was becoming rather short. To save his life, McDonald gave up his cartridges to be used against his followers. A short respite took place between the belligerents, but the enemy returned and made a vigorous effort to take the blockhouse by assault. They came up to the walls and thrust the muzzles of their pieces through the loopholes, when Madam Shell by a blow upon five of them with an axe, rendered them useless; this being followed by several deliberate shots from the little garrison, compelled the assailants to retire to a respectful distance. Just at dark, Shell practised a little stratagem which induced the enemy to suppose that troops were approaching from Fort Dayton, whereupon they fled to the woods, taking with them Shell's two little sons. After providing for the tory commander in the best manner they could, the family started for the fort, which they reached in safety. Some of McDonald's Indians visited him, after the family went away, but finding he could not be removed, they left him to the mercy of the Americans, with a message to Shell that the welfare of his little boys depended on the treatment bestowed on McDonald. The wounded prisoner was taken to the fort the next day, when his leg was amputated. The enemy's loss on the ground was quite severe, eleven killed and six wounded. The little boys, on their return after the war, stated that nine out of twelve wounded which the enemy started with, died before they reached Canada.

In the following year Shell and two of his sons, being at work in the field not far from his block-house, were fired upon by a party of Indians secreted in a wheat field, and he was dangerously wounded. The sons remained with their father until a party from the fort came to their relief. One of the sons was, however, shot dead and the other wounded, before the guard arrived. John Christian Shell did not long survive his wounds, and thus closed the life of a brave and resolute man and a pure and devout Christian. During the short cessation in the attack on the block-house, Shell addressed his Maker in a hymn of deliverance from peril, used by the early German reformers.

The Shellsbush settlement is on what is usually called Gens Purchase, embracing perhaps some portion of the Royal Grant, and it will be observed that the name of Shell, Schel or Shaul does not occur among the patentees of Burnets field, nor is the name found in the list of Palatines remaining in New York, or taken to Livingston Manor, of the first two companies that emigrated. Enough is still known of him to authorize the conclusion that he was a German Lutheran, and he or his ancestors may have come over with the third body of immigrants in 1722, or at a later period. The singularly rude and unharmonious account of Shell's conflict with the tories and Indians, contained in Campbell's Annals of Tryon county, has contributed very much to keep that event fresh in the recollection of the descendants of his German neighbors.

After the defeat of the expedition led by Major Ross, aided by Walter N. Butler, and which fell upon the lower valley on the 24th of October, like an avalanche of lava, burning and destroying every thing in its course, the enemy retreated in a northerly direction through Jersyfield. Col. Willett having ordered the destruction of their batteaux, left at the Oneida lake, arrived at the German Flats by forced marches, in order to intercept Ross's retreat on the west Canada creek, unless he should return to Buck's island on the St. Lawrence river. On the morning of the 29th Willett with four hundred of his best troops with sixty Oneida warriors, provisioned for five days, started in a northerly direction from Fort Dayton along the West Canada creek. The first day's march of the Americans through a snow storm was severe, and at night they camped in a thick forest on the Royal Grant. Here Col. Willett, having ascertained during the night, by means of his scouts, the locality, position and force of the enemy, remained until the next morning when he started well prepared to give battle to the foe, determined to inflict a justly merited and suitable chastisement upon the marauders; but Ross being equally alert, and quite as anxious to avoid the action as his opponent was to bring it on, and being well advised of the proximity of his antagonist, was in full retreat as early as the Americans had started in the pursuit, and it was not until afternoon that Willett came up with a party of the enemy's rear. A smart skirmish ensued, when several of the enemy were killed and taken prisoners, among the latter was a tory, Lieutenant John Rykeman, and the remainder fled. The Americans overtook the main body of Ross's party soon after, when a running fight was kept up between the pursuers and pursued until the latter crossed the creek late in the day. Butler succeeded in rallying his men and made a stand on the west bank, when a brisk action took place between the parties on opposite sides of the creek, during which the enemy had about twenty men killed, and among them was Walter N. Butler. The death of this officer was followed by the immediate and confused flight of his men, and Willett pursued his terror stricken foes until compelled to desist by darkness and the fatigue of his men, who had been on foot all day and more than half the time fighting. The enemy continued the retreat all night and marched thirty miles before they made a halt.

Col. Willett says, "strange as it may appear, it is nevertheless true, that notwithstanding the enemy had been four days in the wilderness, with only half a pound of horse-flesh per man per day, yet in this famished condition they trotted thirty miles before they stopped. Many of them, indeed, fell a sacrifice to such treatment." The British had six hundred and seventy men in this expedition, which closed the active offensive operations of the enemy at the north for the year.

Walter N. Butler's Death.

According to the most authentic tradition we now have of Butler's death, derived from Major Thornton, late of Schenectady, who was a captain under Col. Willett, in the pursuit of Ross and Butler, on their retreat from Johnstown, there seems to be a somewhat different version given to this affair, than that heretofore published. Thornton stated that Ross and Butler, with their party, encamped on Butler's ridge in the town of Norway, on the night before the Americans overtook them, having traversed the forest from

Mayfield the day before. That Col. Willett was fearful the enemy had escaped him in consequence of his having made the detour to Fort Dayton, or that they might have gone a more northern route than the one usually taken, to reach the Black river or Oneida lake. A light autumnal snow had fallen during the night. Thornton was sent out from Willett's encampment as early in the morning as objects were visible, with a few men, and among them was an artilleryman, for the purpose of reconnoitring and finding the enemy's trail, if there was one to be found. The party separated into files of two for the purpose of examination, moving towards the West Canada creek. The artilleryman was with Capt. Thornton, and they had been sometime afoot without discovering any traces of the enemy, when they began to fear they were not on the right course; they continued on, however, until they reached Butler's ridge, when, from their examinations, they were satisfied there had been an encampment the night before, although the snow on the ground rendered the question somewhat doubtful. Having communicated this fact to Col. Willett, Thornton and his companion struck what they supposed was the enemy's trail, and continued their course in pursuit, little expecting to find the enemy near at hand. It was not long, however, before they heard voices, and looking in the direction of this noise they saw a small scouting party, who had probably been on the lookout for Willett, coming up in a direction partly from their rear. Thornton and his comrade avoided this party by hiding in the underbrush. After this scout had passed them long enough to allow an advance with safety, as they believed, they struck the fresh trail and continued the pursuit cautiously, expecting every moment to be overtaken by Willett's advanced guard in force.

The artilleryman was soon killed, by a volley from a thicket in advance; and when hit by the ball he jumped two or three feet into the air. Willett's forces followed the enemy to the creek, the southerly bank being covered with large hemlock trees and a thick undergrowth. A heavy, dense fog hung over the creek, when the American advance got into it for the purpose of crossing, which being suddenly lifted by the wind, exposed them to the enemy on the opposite bank, who gave them so warm and unlooked-for a reception that they retired momentarily up the creek bank, behind the trees and into the bush, having some of the party killed and wounded. The fog again settled upon the creek and the parties fired four or five rounds, each at the other, quite at random, as they could not see across the stream at the time. The enemy's fire slackened, and the Americans then went over and found Butler and five of the enemy dead on the bank of the creek. Thornton stated he was among the first who reached the opposite bank, but an Indian was the first of their party who went to the spot where Butler lay dead, near a tree, and looking at him a moment turned and told Thornton who it was. Thornton examined the lifeless body; the hat, with a gold band around it, was then on the head; he pulled it off, saw the bullet hole in the head, and no other wound or fracture about it. When Thornton started on the expedition he wore a thin pair of summer pantaloons, which were pretty much gone when he reached the creek. The Indian pulled off Butler's pants at Thornton's request, and the latter put them on. Major Thornton was confident no one knew or could tell who it was that killed Butler, he being dead before any of his pursuers found him.

The enemy were pursued by Col. Willett, until hunger and want of provisions compelled him to retrace his steps. On their return to the creek crossing, our people heard the cry of a child near the wayside; some of them went in search of it and found a female infant near a large fallen elm tree, which had been abandoned by its stricken and toil-worn mother to a far different fate from that which awaited it. The child was brought away from its cold and comfortless cradle by some hungered and weary rebel, whose heart may have been sorely riven more than once by the hand of its father. Thornton also stated that Willett's forces had a smart brush with the enemy at Black Creek, in the pursuit out.

After Willett's forces recrossed the Canada creek, they turned off in the direction of Mount's place in Jerseyfield, to bury some of their dead. At this time the party had a British sub-officer, a prisoner, who seems to have been abandoned to the tender mercies of the Indians. This man was a tory and had formerly lived in the valley. Anticipating his fate, he inquired of the American officers whether they intended to allow the Indians to massacre him. No direct answer was given to the inquiry, and the officer disappeared before the troops reached Fort Dayton.

This relation of the manner Butler was killed, corresponds with that given by Col. Willet in his official account of the affair. It is fully corroborated by several traditional statements handed down from persons who were on the spot, and who saw and knew all about it. In every published account I have seen, from that of Marshall, in his Life of Washington, down to our own times, no two of them correspond in the precise statement of facts. Col. Willett could not have had any motive in withholding a full and true relation of the facts attending Butler's death. If he had been wounded and afterwards despatched, when discovered, by one of Willett's men, or an Indian, why should not that fact have been officially stated by the commander of the expedition? He had inquired into the matter; it was a subject too important to be omitted. When, therefore, the Colonel says, "he was shot dead, at once, having no time to implore for mercy," we are called upon to pause a little before we pronounce the statement untrue. But, to use a legal phrase, how stand the impeaching witnesses? One says that Butler, in fleeing from his pursuers, *swam* his horse across the stream, and then turning round to them on the opposite bank, defied them. An Indian discharged his rifle at him and he fell wounded. The Indian then *swam* to the opposite bank, found Butler alive and able to supplicate for mercy, but who answered the supplication by burying his tomahawk in Butler's brains. This relation assumes the improbable facts that Butler was entirely alone and unattended by any of his men, otherwise, if only wounded and capable of speech, having a horse at hand, he could and would have been carried a long distance into the wood, while the Indian, axe in hand, was swimming across the stream. Another says he was sorely wounded while standing behind a tree watching a brisk engagement between the hostile parties, on opposite sides of the creek, and that when he fell, his troops fled in great confusion, leaving him uncared for, whether dead or alive, when they had full time to remove him, and ample means at hand to do it. The Indian then crossed the creek and finding Butler alive, shot him again,, through the eye. An Indian never loses a charge of powder and ball, when his tomahawk, his never-failing and favorite weapon, will answer his purpose. And yet another says the enemy had passed the creek, when Butler stopped, dismounted from his horse, and was in the act of drinking water from a tin cup, in full view from the opposite bank, when he was fired at by two of his enemy and fell. The Indian, a Mohawk, immediately crossed the creek, and finding Butler wounded, only, ended his life with a tomahawk. Now let us consider a moment. Was it not quite remarkable that the commanding officer of an expedition, who had been three days straining every nerve to elude the pursuit of a superior, active and vigilant foe, and whose rear guard had been skirmishing nearly the whole day with his enemy's advance, should loiter in his way, suffer all his men to proceed on their route without him; nay, more, that he should deliberately dismount and drink a tin cup of water, exposed to full view of his pursuing enemy on the left bank of the creek. But opposed to this, is Col. Willett's official declaration, that Butler "was shot dead, at once, having no time to implore for mercy," when this last account makes him present when Butler was scalped; and when he, Willett must have been informed, if it was true, that Butler, in the first instance, had only been wounded and afterwards tomahawked.

I have already given quite as much space to the subject as its importance will justify. Many persons had expressed a desire to know which of the several accounts describing the manner and circumstances of Butler's death was the more probable or true one. That is, whether he was shot dead in the first instance, and nothing was known of his person until the body was afterwards examined, or whether he was first identified across the stream, then fired at, wounded, deserted by his followers, and finally shot in the eye or tomahawked. The scalping part of the tragedy was probably performed in the best style of Indian execution.

I have elaborated Maj. Thornton's statement, and, in the main fact, it seems to accord with the official report. Although the memory of the man has been and is still regarded in our county with deep and unalleviated horror, there are many who would still like to be informed of the truth of history.

The route taken by Maj. Ross and the survivors of this cruel expedition, after leaving the West Canada creek, is spoken of by Stone as in the direction of Oneida lake, where the batteaux had been left when the expedition came from Canada, while other writers assume that Ross proceeded to the Genesee country. It is not probable that he would have attempted the latter route in the destitute condition of his men. He reached Granadier island in about eight days after leaving the creek, in a most pitiable condition, having suffered every thing but death by exposure and want of food.

Thus ended the career of Walter N. Butler, a man of enterprizing boldness, but whose heart was a compound of ferocious hate, insatiable cruelty, and unappeasable revenge.

Even Brant himself denounced him as more unrelenting than the *savages* themselves. It certainly can not excite surprise and wonder that the news of his death should have produced one universal shout of joy along the whole Mohawk valley. The miserable man met a fate he but too well deserved, and retributive justice was not robbed of a proper subject.

The losses of the enemy during this expedition were very severe, and the sufferings of the survivors in traversing eighty miles of wilderness, without food or blankets, in cold and dreary weather, were intense. Willett abandoned the pursuit and returned to Fort Dayton, having lost only one man. The surrender of Cornwallis at Yorktown, and other unpropitious events during the year, had produced an apathetic feeling on the part of the enemy.

In June, 1782, a party of the enemy, tories and Indians as usual, appeared at the Little falls for the sole purpose of destroying a grist-mill at that place, for they do not seem to have achieved any other valorous exploit in that way. The grist mill on the falls of the Mohawk became quite important to the inhabitants of the upper valley, as well as to the garrisons of Forts Herkimer and Dayton, after the destruction of those at German Flats, by Brant, a year and a half before. The enemy came upon the party at the flouring mill at night, and accomplished their designs without much difficulty.* At any rate, only a few shots were fired, and one man, Daniel Pétri, was killed. When the Indians entered the mill, the occupants attempted to escape the best way they could. Two of them, Cox and Skinner,

*The following persons were at the mill when it was burned, and all of them, except the millers and soldiers, had brought corn to the mill, and were waiting for their grists. Peter Wolleaver, Christian Edick, Frederick Getman, Marks Rasbach, John Rasbach, Thomas Shoemaker, Lawrence Hatter, Jacob Petri, Daniel Petri, who was killed, Peter Orendorff; Gershom Skinner, and F. Cox, millers; a sergeant and six men from Capt. McGregor's company of continental troops. Two of the soldiers escaped, and five were taken prisoners.

secreted themselves in the raceway, under the water-wheel, and escaped death and captivity; but two others, Christian Edick and Frederick Getman, jumped into the raceway, above the mill, and there endeavored to conceal themselves, but the burning mill disclosed their hiding place and they were taken prisoners. After burning the mill the enemy retired, taking with them several prisoners!

In Stone's life of Brant, the author states that these mills were erected by Alexander Ellice, Esq., a Scotch merchant, "who had, under the favor of Sir William Johnson, obtained a patent of the wild mountain gorge, through which the Mohawk leaps from the upper into the lower section of the valley." This is not strictly accurate. The lands on the north side of the river, from the upper to the lower end of the falls, are embraced in the patent granted in 1725 to Johan Joost Petri and other Palatines, and the lands on the south side are covered by a patent granted in 1752 to Johan Jost Herchkeemer and another person, known as the Fall-Hill patent. Mr. Ellice, in his lifetime, and his family in England after his death, held the title to two of the four Burnetsfield lots on the north side of the river, and to the whole of Vaughn's patent, granted to Col. John Vaughn and others in 1770, the titles to which were derived through Mr. John Porteous, who was many years a merchant at the Little Falls, and died there. The names of the Burnetsfield patentees are given in another chapter, and it is there shown to whom the lots at the Little Falls were granted.

The upper Mohawk valley was not again visited by any serious calamity during the remainder of the contest. The war had not entirely ceased in other quarters, but there was a general subsiding of hostilities, as if by common consent, and the mother country had sickened of the effort to whip her rebellious children into submission. Towards the close of the year the British commander-in-chief directed that no more Indian expeditions at the north should be sent out, and those already on foot were recalled. The house of commons passed a resolution, soon after the news of the surrender of Cornwallis had reached England, declaring "that the house would consider as enemies to his majesty and the country, all who should advise or attempt the further prosecution of offensive war on the continent of North America." In conformity to the pacific sentiments expressed in the above resolution, if a ministerial change should take place, the American people might reasonably expect an entire change in the policy hitherto pursued towards them. The principal historical events of the war will be closed with this chapter, and the compiler, in common with many others, who like him have heard the oftentimes repeated traditional tale of the suffering infltcted upon the frontier settlements of the valley, must express his deep regret that some one had not written out a particular history of the revolutionary transactions within the county, while most of the surviving actors and eye witnesses were living.

In February, 1783, the forces under the command of Col. Willett, were concentrated at Fort Herkimer, the undeveloped object being to surprise and capture the British fortress at Oswego. The expedition failed in consequence of the small number of troops employed, and the want of a proper armament to besiege the place, attended with the unfortunate occurrence of the Indian guide having, when within a few miles of the fort, lost his way, and conducted this little band into a deep forest covered with snow, instead of directing his course to the place of destination. Colonel Willett returned to Albany in time to hear the gladsome news of peace proclaimed, and to rejoice with his emancipated countrymen in that welcome event.

Here closed the great drama of the revolution, which, for almost six years. had presented to the inhabitants of this frontier, little else than one continued scene of desolation, and blood. The enemy were too keen and indefatigable to leave a single out-laying hamlet unvisited at some period during the war, and probably not one in fifty escaped destruction by fire. In the winter and spring of 1780 the inhabitants whose dwellings were not within the protection of forts and block-houses defended by provincial troops, were compelled to abandon their farms and seek a shelter within the armed defenses, so fierce and exterminating had the Indian warfare become in retaliation of the exploits of the Americans during Sullivan's expedition in 1779.

In 1781 it was supposed that one third of the population of the whole Mohawk valley had gone over to the enemy, and another third had been killed or driven from the country, and that among those who remained were two thousand orphan children and three hundred widows The people of the upper valley suffered severly during the war and from the militia organizations before and after the war it would seem they lost nearly half their men capable of bearing arms during that period. But it is not true that one third of the population of the upper valley abandoned their country and its cause and went over to the enemy, nor is it probable that even one in twenty of them espoused the interests of the crown.

My desire to record in this book an historical fact, which illustrates, in a eminent degree, the spirit and bearing of the leading men of the revolution, induces me to append it to this otherwise long chapter, although it transpired at an early period of the war.

Soon after the confirmation of the treaty of alliance and commerce between the United States and France was received in England in 1778, the ministry acting under the authority of recent acts of parliament, sent out commissioners to America to negotiate respecting the difficulties between the two countries, and fully empowered them:

"To consent to a cessation of hostilities both by sea and land.

"To restore free intercourse, to revive mutual affection, and renew the common benefits of naturalization through the several parts of this empire.

"To extend every freedom to trade that our respective interests can require.

"To agree that no military forces shall be kept up in the different states of North America, without the consent of the general congress or particular assemblies.

"To concur in measures calculated to discharge the debts of America, and to raise the credit and value of the paper circulation.

"To perpetuate our union by a reciprocal deputation of an agent or agents from the different states, who shall have the privilege of a seat and voice in the parliament of Great Britain; or, if sent from Britain, in that case, to have a seat and voice in the assemblies of the different states to which they may be deputed respectively, in order to attend to the several interests of those by whom they are deputed.

"To establish the power of the respective legislatures in each particular state, to settle its revenue, its civil and military establishment, and to exercise a perfect freedom of legislation and internal government, so that the British states, throughout North America, acting with us in peace and war, under one common sovereign, may have the irrevocable enjoyment of every privilege that is short of a total separation of interests, or consistent with that union of force, on which the safety of our common religion and liberty depends."

These terms were not acceptable to congress, nor was that body in the least inclined to negotiate on any terms of conciliation with the mother country in the then aspect of affairs. Having thus far single-handed and alone stood up against all adversities and weathered the storms of war, congress and the people, with the aid of the French alliance, now fancied the haven of peace to be full in view. Mr. Laurens, in reply to certain inquiries put to him on the subject, said the Americans would not enter into the consideration of a treaty of peace, without a direct and open acknowledgment of the independence of the states, or the withdrawal of the British fleets and armies. The terms offered in these propositions look very much like a total abandonment of all the antecedent arrogant pretensions of the crown, and to present the case of a mere nominal connection with and not subjection to the head of the British empire. If the hopes of America were elated by the auspicious events which had happened, the fears of Britain checked her vaulting ambition and drove her to propose an accommodation, which, if offered three years sooner, might have produced a reconciliation.

CHAPTER VI.

Miscellaneous Incidents, from 1783 to the Present Time — Hostile Feelings towards the Indians and Tories after Peace — Old England District — Justices of the Peace Appointed in 1772 — 1784 — Immigration before the War — New England Emigration — Character of the Population — Militia Officers — Allusion to the Shay's War in Massachusetts — Justices Appointed in 1791 — Difficulty about the Stamps — Clerk's Office Burnt in 1804 — War of 1812 — Militia of the County — Bounty Lands — State of the County after the War — Cholera — Jail — Court House — Clerk's Office.

The restoration of peace between the former colonies and the crown did not restore internal tranquility within the borders of the upper valley. The surviving inhabitants awoke, not as from a pleasing dream, whose thought, if so it may be called, had run riot in elysium, but to the sad and woeful reality of slaughtered relatives, ruined habitations, wasted fields, and a devastated country. When they first went abroad from the blockhouses, forts and places of refuge, would they not remember the hand which had inflicted the wrong and been made the instrument of a cruel and tyrannous chastisement? The Indians, those who were known to belong to the hostile clans of the Iroquois, could not safely pass through or sojourn in the country. Not a few of them, who ventured upon the hazardous exploit, forfeited their lives. The men who had been almost abandoned by the country, during the whole war; and particularly during the harrassing campaign of 1780, to their own resources and exertions, felt it to be no wrong to shoot an Indian, when and wherever they met him, in peace or war.

But the most sore trial the survivors were put to, and the greatest cause of irritation they had to suffer, was the return of the tories after the peace, claiming a restoration of their forfeited estates, and compensation for property destroyed and taken for public use during the war. A unanimous feeling of resistance to this claim pervaded the whole valley, and, for several years after the war, he must have been a bold and resolute man, who would visit the country a second time on such a mission. If one of these Mohawk tories got out of the country on his first visit after the peace, without meeting with some disagreeable interviews with the German population, he was a lucky man.

The "old England" district, embracing a small portion of the territory in the south part of this county, and a portion of Otsego and Madison counties, on the Unadilla river, erected by the colonial government, was organized as a part of Montgomery county in 1784, and officers appointed by the court of general sessions. Rudolph Shoemaker and Frederick Bellinger were appointed justices of the peace in Tryon county, May 26th, 1772; and George Henry Bell and Andrew Finck, Jr., were appointed to the same office in Montgomery county, July 8, 1784. These persons then lived within the present limits of this county.

The county had received a considerable accession to its population, between 1725 and 1775, from the country below, from Columbia county, New York and Germany, chiefly of German extraction, with some Low Dutch or Hollanders from the borders of the Hudson. The din of war had scarcely ceased along the valley, ere the sturdy New Englander was seen wending his toilsome way along the valley, with his face set towards the Royal Grant, or the woodland regions of Warren, Columbia, Litchfield and Winfield. The earliest New England settlers found their way into the woods north and south of the river, about the year 1785, and from that time forward to 1800, the emigration from the south-part of this state and the Eastern states was very rapid, and exceeded ten thousand the first fifteen years after it fairly set in. The foreign emigration was nothing during this period. The Celt could not be spared, the loyal Scotch and English would not come, and the wars in Germany were consuming the population of that empire. No event of sufficient importance to attract special attention occurred from 1783 to 1791, except the organization of two towns in 1788, which is noticed in another chapter.

I will notice here the first organization after the war, in 1786, October 2d, made in the regiment of local militia in the German Flats and Kingsland districts, and arranged as follows:

Field and Regimental staff.—Henry Staring, lieut. colonel; Peter Weaver, major, 1st battalion; Patrick Campbell, major, 2d battalion; John Frank, adjutant; Melchert Fols, paymaster; William Petrie, surgeon.

1st company.—Jacob Petry, captain; Dederick Petry, lieutenant; William Father, ensign.

2d company.—John Meyer, captain; William Clapsaddle, lieutenant; Henry Frank, ensign.

3d company.—Adam Staring, captain; Liutwick Campell, lieutenant; Lawrence Herter, ensign.

4th company.—Peter P. Bellinger, captain; Joost Herchimer, lieutenant; Peter Fox, ensign.

5th company.—Michael Meyer, captain; Peter F. Bellinger, lieutenant; George Weatirce, ensign.

6th company, (light infantry).—William Colbreath, captain; Daniel C. White, lieutenant; George J. Weaver, ensign.

These militia arrangements must indicate the numbers and strength of the population capable of bearing arms; and although three years of peace had intervened in which there had been a large influx of population, quite enough to make up two companies, we have three organized companies less at this time than there were in 1775. The names of the officers are copied as found in the council minutes. Ensign William Father, I think, represents William Feeter, and George Weatirce, represents George Weaver.

The recuperative energies of the Teutonic race were not long unseen or unfelt when left free to act, and the fields that were laid waste by war for years, again waved with golden harvests and the accomplished woodman's axe was doing its work in the sturdy forest. O! what a priceless boon to man had grown from the stern calamities of a war whose dirge had just been sung by mourning thousands.

A fact which to some extent illustrates the American character has come to my notice while preparing this work for the press. It is this. A considerable portion of the New England emigration between 1787 and 1793 was from Massachusetts. Many of these people had been implicated in or connected with the disturbances in that state which terminated in what has been called Shay's rebellion. Now the history of that affair is briefly this. During the contest recently ended that state had contributed largely in men, money and credit to the support of the common cause, its commerce had been destroyed and its manufactories languished on the return of peace by the introduction of foreign fabrics. The whole debt of the state, domestic and due to the confederation was about $10,000,000, and in the year 1785 a tax of one and a half millions of dollars was levied on the people and property in the state, equal to about four dollars for every man, woman and child in it. With no money to meet this heavy excessive burden the commercial and agricultural classes became more and more indebted to the state. John Hancock resigned the office of governor, and was succeeded by Mr. Bowdoin by a legislative appointment. Soon after his reelection in 1786, numerous symptoms of discontent were exhibited in different parts of the state, and especially in the western towns, whose population was confined to agricultural pursuits.

In August 1786 a convention of delegates from 50 towns convened at Hatfield, Hampshire county "to consider and provide for the grievances they suffered." In consequence of the disorderly proceeding of the people in different parts of the state; little attention was given to the petition forwarded to the government by the convention. The legislature met in September following, passed some stringent laws against disorderly and riotous meetings of the people, suspended the writ of habeas corpus eight months, and took some measures to relieve the public burthens. The disturbances continued and several of the leaders were arrested and confined in Boston jail. The main object of these people seems to have been to prevent the sittings of the courts of common pleas which they alleged imposed a heavy burden on the public. About 1000 met at Worcester, but committed no other offense than to place guards round the houses where the judges put up, to prevent them from holding the courts. While here, Daniel Shays urged them to proceed to Boston and release by force the prisoners confined in jail there.

The project was not carried out. They obstructed the holding of the courts in some of the western counties in the state. They afterwards made an attempt, in 1787, to take the Springfield arsenal. They were met by Gen. Shepard at the head of 1000 militia, and after having three men killed the rest dispersed.

These rebels, as they were called, then petitioned for a pardon for the offenses committed by them, but it was refused because they stated they had reason to complain of the wrongs and sufferings they endured. They had collected in a considerable body at Petersham in the winter of 1787–8, when they were surprised by General Lincoln, who took 150 prisoners, and the remainder returned home or left the state. This was the last of the famous Shay's rebellion. No lives were lost except on the part of these disaffected people. They do not seem to have aimed at the overthrow of the government, but sought relief from unbearable burthens. They took an unwise course. The remedy did not lay in that direction. John Hancock was again elected governor in the spring of 1788. He was a moderate politician of the federal school. The state was federal when the people arranged themselves into parties. In the western part, the seat of these disturbances, the anti-federalists or republicans contended resolutely for victory at the first election under the federal or national constitution, and in some places had a majority. The head and front of this offending could not have been very grievous. There were no executions for treason. There can be no doubt the government of the state was at that time very exacting and intolerant, and the people had not then learned the true method of self-government.

In resuming the history of the county, after the above digression, it may be proper to state the following persons were appointed justices of the peace; ou the 27th March, 1790, George Henry Bell, John Frank, Henry Dygert, Michael Myers and John Bowman, and on the 17th February, 1791, Henry Staring, Michael Myers, John Frank, Patrick Campbell, William Veeder, William Dygert, Jun., Moses Foot, Benjamin Bowen, Hanyost Schoonmaker, Melchert Folts, Lodowick Campbell, Johannes Finck and Abraham Hardenburgh. These persons are believed to have then lived within the limits of this county.

Soon after President Adams's famous stamp act went into operation, and the agent for vending stamps had been furnished with them to sell, the people in different parts of the county became a good deal excited, and a combination was set on foot to destroy the obnoxious stamps, or prevent their being sold. At the fall musters or trainings, the people marched down from the hills, north and south, and up from the valleys, to Herkimer, "armed and equipped as the law directed," to make war on the stamps, with field piece ready charged. They tore down the agent's sign, demanded of him a promise that he would not sell the paper eagles, and otherwise behaved somewhat noisily, but committed no other act of violence. It was a bloodless affair. A number of the leading men were indicted and taken to Albany under arrest, when Governor Jay met them, and after giving them sound and judicous advice sent them home. One can not help thinking that the worthy governor was somewhat annoyed, during the conference, with the reflection "that he, not long before, had been in arms against his king and the mother country on account of stamps and stamped paper."

In March or April, 1804, the county clerk's office was consumed by fire with all the records and papers it contained. Mr. Joab Griswold had held the office of county clerk from March 19th, 1798, and Mr. Elihu Griswold was appointed in his place April 6th, 1804. The office was burned in the night, and it had been arranged previously that the new incumbent should take possession of the office the day after the fire occurred.

"In the war with Great Britain, declared by the United States on the 18th day of June, 1812," the militia of Herkimer county behaved nobly. They claimed no exemption from service when the governor ordered them to the frontier to protect and defend the state from hostile aggression or foreign invasion. It is no disparagement to the militia of any other county, to say the Herkimer militia met these calls and suffered the privations of the camp with a patriotic devotion and zeal not excelled by any of them.

A detached regiment under Col. C. P. Bellinger, had been ordered to Sacketts Harbor before war was declared, under a six months' draft. Others followed soon after, and in 1813 and 1814, volunteers, detached, and the militia en mass, were on the lake and St. Lawrence frontier nearly the whole time. Companies and regiments succeeding others, whose terms of service had expired. The pay granted by the United States was no compensation to the farmer and mechanic, and substituted service could only be afforded by the wealthy. If the sacrifice was great, each man could well console himself with the reflection that he had done his duty to his country. Governer Tompkins bestowed high praise upon the citizen soldiers of Herkimer county, and it was well deserved.

It is now more than forty years since these events happened, and many farms have been and are being located under the operation of the bounty land laws of 1850 and 1855, by the descendants and relatives of those who performed the military service. Although a land recipient under the former law, I can not admire a policy which is dictated by a present expediency and not by a rule of equal and exact justice. There are thousands who are excluded, whose husbands and fathers performed service as meritorious as any now living; and there are other thousands, long since laid in their graves, to whom this little pittance would have been grateful; whose hunger it would have assuaged, and whose cold and palsied limbs it would have warmed. *But these can not vote now.* They are tenants of the graveyard, under an eternal lease; an immovable fixture, and can not swell the population of the illimitable west.

The restoration of peace with Great Britain in 1815, found our population in a state of universal embarrassment, which they did not recover from fully in ten years. The merchants with large stocks of goods on hand, found themselves undersold by more than one-half on the new importations. A series of cold and unproductive seasons, from 1816 to 1820, had cut off the surplus of agricultural products. Farming lands during the war had been sold at very high prices, and were eagerly sought for at nearly four times the value they bore from 1817 to 1825. The county did not produce exportable commodities sufficient to balance the mercantile imports, and *shinplasters* were the circulating medium. Cheesman's *plasters* were a more sure remedy for the public ailments than his *balsams.* Lands sold during the war at such prices that the purchaser, who paid one-third of the consideration money at the sale, and kept the interest on the balance paid up, could not the first ten years after the peace sell them for a price sufficient to pay the balance of principal due. In other words he could not give them away and get indemnity against his bond. The state expenditures in constructing the Erie canal gave some relief; but the completion and opening of that great work brought the grain-growing regions of the west into direct competition with the then staple agricultural product of the county, wheat. The Mohawk valley had more than seventy-five years enjoyed, without competition from the west, the advantages of the Albany and eastern markets. The county recovered slowly from its depressed and embarrassed condition. It lost, however, very considerable of its German population between 1818 and 1830.

The Asiatic cholera has never prevailed in the county to much extent. On its first appearance in this country in 1832, when fright and apprehension nearly paralyzed the whole community, a few cases occurred in several of the villages, most of them fatal, and along the canal. Since that time, however, the county has been nearly exempt from that dreadful pestilence.

In the years 1833, 1834 and 1835, the legislature authorized the supervisors of the county to contract loans to the amount of $10,300 to erect a new jail and purchase a site for it. An annual tax was also levied to reimburse the principal of these loans by installments and pay the interest. The building is of stone, procured at Little Falls, strong and permanent. The interior arrangements are such as to afford comfort to and insure the safety of offenders. Martin Easterbrooks contracted to complete the mason work, and Edmund Varney, Cornelius T. E. Van Horn, Isaac S. Ford, Jacob F. Christman, Warner Folts, Frederick P. Bellinger and Charles Gray, were the commissioners appointed to superintend the erection of the jail.

On the night of January 25th, 1834, the old court house and jail was destroyed by fire. This was an old two-story structure of wood, and had been standing many years.

The jail on the ground floor had been found unsafe, and besides the public buildings at that time did not reflect much credit upon the county. On the 31st of March, 1834, the legislature authorized the supervisors to borrow from the common school fund, on the credit of the county, four thousand six hundred dollars to build a new court house, and directed a tax of five hundred dollars a year to be levied on the county to refund the loan and pay the interest. Francis E. Spinner, Arphaxed Loomis and Prentice Yeomans were named in the act as commissioners to superintend the erection of the building.

The court house is a handsome structure of brick, standing nearly in the center of the village of Herkimer. The jail is on the opposite side of the street. The rooms on the first floor of the court house are arranged to suit the public convenience, but the interior arrangements of the court room may be easily improved. Owing to some defect or oversight in the construction, the long side walls of the house began to give way and swell out, not long after the house was completed. They were however soon secured by iron rods extending across the building. These rods or bars were inserted in their place when red with heat, and being secured with proper fastenings at the ends on the outside of the walls the contraction of the iron brought them quite into place. The citizens of Little Falls did not fail to make an effort at this time, to change the county seat and bring it to them; but with two-thirds or perhaps three-fourths of the population of the county against them, they "hardly made a ripple."

A new fire proof clerk's office, of brick, was erected in 1847. Mr. Aaron Hall, builder.

CHAPTER VII.

Forfeited Estates — Act of 1779 — Persons Attainted under George III — Treaty of 1783 — Attainder of the Johnsons and Butler justified — Rules of Evidence laid down — British Parliament — Further Provisions of the Act — Royal Grant — Extent of Same — Guy Johnson Tract — Herkimer Estates—Motives of the Johnsons — Sir William Johnson — Events of Revolution still Remembered — Reception of Sir John in Canada — Guy Johnson's Conduct as Indian Agent — Judicial Tribunals always open — The Fifth Article of the Treaty of 1782 — The 9th Article of the Treaty of 1794 — Motives of the Loyalists in Embracing the Cause of the Crown — Congress Fulfilled Treaty Stipulations — Its Messages not Well Received by the States — Present Law of Treason.

At the risk of repeating some of the facts contained in the preceding chapter, and of being considered tedious, I venture to submit some further remarks in reference to the "forfeited estates" of British subjects, confiscated during the war of the revolution. The subject is within the scope of an historical research into the annals of the county, because the title to large tracts of land within its limits has been affected by the action of the legislature of the state. Now, when more liberal sentiments seem not only to be entertained by some governments, but by enlightened individuals, in respect to the mode of conducting war, and of inflicting punishment upon individuals, for acts of hostile aggression in cases where, by the public law, no allegiance was due to the injured state, the opinion has been expressed that the confiscated estates of individuals should have been restored at the peace of 1783. This is a very grave question, and will not meet with an affirmative response from any considerable number of enlightened Americans, even at this day, and they, I am sure, are quite as liberal as any other people in the civilized world. The legislature of this state may have laid down and enforced a rigid rule, and one to which there should have been some exceptions. But the distracted state of the country, and the circumstances of the times, called for the exercise of the most stringent measures of defense and protection. Subjugation, confiscation and the halter was the punishment denounced against what was called an unnatural rebellion. "Life, liberty and the pursuit of happiness," was the prize contended for.

The act of October 22d, 1779, declared "Sir John Johnson, late of the county of Tryon, knight and baronet, Guy Johnson, Daniel Claus and John Butler, now or late of said county, esquires, and John Joost Herkemer, now or late of the said county, yeoman," to be, *ipso facto*, convicted and attainted of voluntarily adhering to the fleets and armies of the king of Great Britain, in the cruel and unjust war then waged by him against this state, and the other United States, with the intent to subvert the government and liberties of this state, and the other United States, and to bring the same into subjection to the crown of Great Britain. Their estates real and personal were declared forfeited to and vested in the people of this state.

When George III, on the 3d day of September, 1783, acknowledged the *thirteen* united states "to be *free, sovereign* and *independent* states; that he treated with them as such; and for himself, his heirs and successors, relinquished all claims to the *government, propriety* and *territorial* rights of the same, and every part thereof," no question could be raised by the British crown, nor by its subjects, in regard to any of the antecedent acts of these *free, sovereign* and independent states.

When we examine the traces of blood, and fire, and desolation that marked the footsteps of the two Johnsons, Claus and Butler, through this state, and especially in the Mohawk valley, from 1775 to the fall of 1779, who can justly say this act of attainder, confiscation, and banishment was wanton, cruel or oppressive towards them? Retributive justice demanded the punishment and it was inflicted.

Other persons were convicted and attainted by the same act, some of them civilians, and all the persons named in the act were perpetually banished from the state, and their return to it was denounced a *felony* punishable with death, without the benefit of clergy. Persons adhering to the public enemy, and guilty of treason against the state, after the 9th day of July, 1776, were subjected to indictment and trial; and it is here worthy of notice, that the legislature were so tender of the rights of those who might be complained of and brought to trial, as to declare that the several matters which, by the laws of England, were held to be evidence and overt acts of high treason, in adhering to the king's enemies, should be the rule in like cases when the parties were charged with high treason against the people of this state, making some other provisions to meet the peculiar circumstances of the times.

After exerting an act of high prerogative, which had been done by the British parliament at various periods in the history of that country, and for causes much less justifiable than those which provoked the attainder we have been considering, all proceedings against other parties chargeable with affairs of this character, against the state, were turned over to the courts, where a conviction could only be had upon an indictment and trial or outlawry.

By the attainder of Sir John Johnson it was supposed the whole of the Royal Grant, so called from the fact that the patent granted to Sir William received the sign manual of the king in person, was forfieted. That tract comprises all that part of the county lying between the East and West Canada creeks, the Mohawk river on the south, and the south line of Jerseyfield on the north, which runs from the village of Devereaux at the northeast corner of the Grant, on the East Canada creek in a northwesterly direction to the West Canada creek, intersecting it north of Prospect in

Oneida county, with the exception of Glen's Purchase, a few lots in Burnetsfield, and some few patents in Manheim. The towns of Norway, Russia, Newport, Fairfield, Salisbury, Manheim, Herkimer and Little Falls, contain portions of this extensive domain. The tract of 2000 acres granted to Guy Johnson in 1765, situated in the present towns of German Flats and Little Falls, was forfeited by his attainder.

The Herkimer estates forfeited lay within the present limits of German Flats and Herkimer, and are believed to embrace portions of the Palatine grants; the only case of attainder or forfeiture within the limits of the patent granted to Johan Joost Petri and others.

Sir John Johnson and the wife of Guy Johnson, were the children of Sir William, by a German woman, legitimated a short time before the baronet's death by the solemnization of marriage with the mother. Johan Joost Herkemer is the only instance of attainder and forfeiture by any of the Palatines or their descendants in the upper Mohawk valley. There may have been others who deserved it, and perhaps there was one, but his case did not come within the letter of the statute.

Those who are familiar with all the revolutionary events of Tryon county, can not but be amazed at the infatuated conduct of the Johnson family through the whole of that eventful period. They must, on the outbreak of the struggle, have concluded that all their princely estates in the country were lost to them, and they would henceforth deal with them and the property of their former neighbors as well as trusty adherents, as belonging to the common enemy, to be consigned to indiscriminate destruction; or they must have resolved to act the part of marauders out of mere wantonness and a spirit of revenge.

Sir William Johnson came to this country at an early day, occupying no higher position than that of land agent. By his zeal, ability, good conduct and attention to business, he acquired large estates, and was promoted to the highest honors ever bestowed by a confiding sovereign upon a colonial subject. Many are the vague surmises in respect to the cause of his death, which took place but a short time before the colonists assumed their defiant attitude to the crown. He was beloved and respected by his neighbors and dependants, and he perhaps foresaw all the miseries in store for a country he could not look upon in any other light than his own. He might have died by his own hand, but facts do not authorize this conclusion. There were, it must be admitted, many powerful considerations which should have induced his family to adhere to the royal cause. They had been bountiful recipients of their sovereign's favor. Honors and wealth had been literally showered upon them, and they felt it would be forfeiting all claim to honorable distinction, should they abandon the mother country in the eventful emergency which had overtaken it. They mistook the temper and feeling of their fellow subjects in the colonies, and did not, probably, comprehend the final result of a separation between the two countries. This family did not embrace the cautious policy of having some one or more of their number nominal adherents to the patriotic cause to protect their possessions, which was adopted by others, and some too of much less distinction and note.

The startling events of the revolution are yet remembered by a few now living witnesses, and a more just estimate of the rights and duties of nations, belligerent and neutral, seem to be more generally entertained at this day than during the last century. This no doubt has occasioned the remark that the *provincial* governments had been too stringent in enforcing a forfeiture against the adherents of the crown, and that when the independence of the states was acknowledged, restitution ought to have been made. It should be remembered that the colonies never encouraged but at all times deprecated the employment of the Indians in the revolutionary war, or in any way making them parties in that contest. They knew their situation; that their own country must be the battle field; and that their own frontier inhabitants would be subjected to a warfare and desolation of the most unmitigated severity, not practiced by civilized nations, and like that with which they too recently had been afflicted, to be then disremembered. When these visitations were renewed with a ten-fold severity by those who had previously deprecated this mode of warfare, and when too, the object seemed to be to kill, burn and plunder, and not to subjugate and hold the conquered territory; it was not the surviving sufferer who could forgive or forget the authors of his calamities or the instruments used in the infliction of them.

To one member of this family, as soon as he was able to reach Canada, a regiment was given, called the Johnson Greens, principally composed of refugees, who made continual marauding expeditions into the Mohawk valley, during the war, and the memory of whose deeds were not forgotten at the close of the last century. The other, at the head of the Indian agency at Montreal, retaining a great influence over the western tribes, including most of the New York Indians, was zealously and efficiently employed in retaining them in the service of the crown, and encouraging and promoting expeditions against the frontier colonists, in which they were to be joined. This service was not performed by a slack hand or an unwilling mind. In this work of mischief and revenge he was but too well supported by that shrewd, active, but stern and resolute Mohawk chief, Joseph Brant, who displayed no more of the savage, in his hostile incursions, than should have been expected, perhaps, when the motives of his prompters were carefully scanned.

There may have been instances in which restitution might have found a willing response in the heart of the country; but that was not the case in respect to this family; where was the point of discrimination? That was the great difficulty. Expatriation and adherence to the common enemy were open acts of avowed hostility, so marked as not to be mistaken. If the party left the country and remained out of it until the close of the war, unless on business of an open, pacific nature, and if he failed to return to it, after being required to do so, these were taken as overt acts of hostility, sufficient to authorize sequestration and forfeiture. There could be but one rule prescribed, which must be broad enough to embrace the whole class of offenders, and while hostilities were being carried on, exceptions could not be applied, and when a state of war no longer existed and the country assumed regular and settled forms of government, it so happened that the individual states retained the whole power of remission, and these were not recognized in diplomatic relations, nor could they separately form treaties with foreign governments, or even enter into negotiations. There was no mode of remission or restitution except by individual application to the states; and here the fundamental rules of government had been settled with so much precision and exactness, as to prohibit the legislative department of the governments from granting restitution of the forfeited estates. The poverty of the states and the excited feelings of the people on the subject of the war, rendered any application for recompense entirely hopeless; and it would have been found very difficult to settle upon any rule for granting relief except that of mere grace and favor, and no refugee of that day could be found bold or craven enough to put his loyalty to that severe test. There were cases in which restitution, remission or recompense could not be asked for with even a remote prospect of success, and which, certainly, could not be granted without violating the plainest principles of justice.

The judicial tribunals of the country have always been open to appeals for legal redress, and the legislative department of the state governments has never interfered, and indeed it could not have done so with any effect, being prohibited by the fundamental law. The title to the lands in one county and part of another, in this state, held under the commissioners of forfeitures, has within twenty years been declared invalid by the courts, on the ground of some informality or irregularity, and not because the law itself was unconstitutional. The constitutions of this state have uniformly recognized the grants made by the king of Great Britain, or persons acting under his authority before the 14th day of October, 1775; the constitution of the United States prohibits the state legislatures from passing laws impairing the obligation of contracts.

By the 5th article of the treaty of 1783, the United States did not agree to recommend to the legislatures of the several states to provide for restitution of confiscated estates to *those who had borne arms against them*, but that treaty did provide that there should be no further confiscations or prosecutions against any one, and that instrument being the supreme law of the land, was of course binding on all subordinate authorities. No claim was set up in behalf of those *who had borne arms*, and this is enough to show that no violations of public faith had been committed in respect to that class of adherents to the interests of the British crown.

The treaty designated a class who should be recommended to the favorable consideration of the states, but as before remarked, the difficulty was this; the legislatures could not, or would not, discriminate between those who actually bore arms, and others who counseled, promoted, set on foot and directed a marauding expedition against their country, and humanity will justify the deed. That treaty, it is true, did secure to "persons of any other description," the right to go into any part of the United States and remain unmolested twelve months, to obtain restitution of their confiscated estates. The congress were bound by that treaty to recommend to the states a revision of all laws regarding the estates of British subjects, to render them consistent with justice and equity, and with that spirit of conciliation which ought to prevail on the return of peace, and also to urge upon the states to restore to those who had borne arms against the colonies their properties and estates, on their refunding to the persons in possession the bona fide price paid on the purchase of the confiscated estates and lands. And it was further agreed that all persons having any interest in confiscated lands by debts, marriage settlements or otherwise, should meet with no lawful impediment in the prosecution of their just rights.

By the 9th article of the treaty of November 19th, 1794, commonly called Jay's treaty, American citizens and British subjects, holding lands in the territory of either party, were secured in the exercise of the rights appertaining to them in the same manner as if they were natives.

What just grounds can there be in view of all the facts involved in the case of these forfeited estates, to charge the state governments, and especially our own, with illiberality and a desire to profit by a contingency brought about by no act of its own seeking. The parties who abandoned their homes and properties, acted from choice and not compulsion, except that of duty and allegiance, which they may have thought was due to the king of Great Britain. They cast their bread upon the waters of strife; it returned not to them again. If the colonists had been crushed in the contest, these people would have returned to a wasted and depopulated country, enriched by the spoils of attainted rebels, and ennobled by a sovereign grateful for the service of preserving the brightest jewel in his crown. This was the fortune that awaited them in case of success, and they knew it. They thought this a prize worth contending for, but they misjudged in respect to the chances of success. They had not yet fully experienced the energies of the men whose motto was "one for all, and all for one," when banded together in the great struggle for life, for home, and for liberty. They did encounter those energies, and were overthrown; they grasped for the prize and lost it, and thereby forfeited all claims for restitution to abandoned houses and estates.

The American congress fulfilled its treaty stipulations to the letter, but its messages met with a cold and silent reception from the several states when they spoke of surrendering up estates to those who had been active participators in what was deemed an unjust and cruel war of aggression. While the attainder act, before mentioned, was in full force in this state, and the commissioners of forfeitures were executing their office, the constitution of 1787 was ratified, which declares that "no attainder of treason shall work corruption of blood or forfeiture, except during the life of the person attainted."

CHAPTER VIII.

Biographical Sketches of the Palatine Families; Bell, Beerman, Bowman, Bellinger, Barse, Casler, Dackstader, Editch, Fulmer, Feller, Fox, Folts, Helmer, Herkimer, Herter, Hoss, Hess, Korsing, Kast, Koons, Kones, Landt, Miller, Mayer, Ohrendorff, Petri, Pouradt, Reelle, Rickert, Shoemaker, Smith, Spies, Spohn, Starring, Teymouth, Veldelent, Welleven, Weaver.

The descendants of the following Palatine families are yet extant in the county: Bowman, Dacksteder, under the name of Dockstader, Felmore, by that of Fulmer, Herter, Lant, now known as Landt, Mayor changed to Moyer, Orendros and Orendorf, now called Ohrendorff, Pears changed to Barse, and Pell to Bell, Reckert and Spoon.

I should not omit to mention the name of Miller, or neglect to say, in this place, that the descendants of Johannes, the patentee, have until the year 1854, retained the ownership of the whole or some portion of the lot granted to their ancestor. But the last proprietor of the name parted with the remnant of a patrimony held in the family more than one hundred and twenty-five years; where sire and grandsire had sported their youthful pastimes, and, when maturer years had cast the burthen on them, where they had toiled and endured in obedience to a high command. Earned by a long and tedious pilgrimage in search of a "haven of rest," and consecrated by the sufferings endured through two long and cruel wars, the title has now passed to a stranger, and the "home-farm" is now divested of all the interesting incidents that have been clustering around its hearth-stones through five generations.

The following families soon became extinct, or removed from the county, and no trace of the names, even, can now be found, if they ever had any real existence:

The Beermans, Fellers, Hoss, Korsings, Pouradts, Spies, and Veldelents. The title to the lots drawn to these names passed into other hands before the revolution, and in some instances can be traced back many years before that event. Owing to the great abuses practiced at one period, under the colonial governors, of granting large or extravagant quantities of lands to individual applicants, in some instances to the extent of fifty thousand acres, where there was no pretence of colonization or settlement, the home government directed that no more than one thousand acres should be patented to one person at any one time, and within a limited period after a grant had been made, and the colonial legislature resumed many, if not all the previous extravagant grants. This restriction was, however, materially, if not completely evaded, when the leading families and influential personages in the colony combined to accomplish by indirection, what the home government prohibited. A number of names would be procured to a petition to the governor and council for a license to purchase the Indian title to as many thousand acres of land as there were names to the petition. The license would, almost as a matter of course, be granted, and the Indian deed being obtained, a patent would be issued. When this was done, the real parties in interest, the affair having been previously arranged and understood, would invite their cograntees to a dinner party, and while the glass circulated freely, and the generous wine had done its office, the stool-pigeon men would execute releases of their interest in the lands patented. In this way many thousand-acre tracts were obtained at the cost of a dinner.

Some of the names which so suddenly disappeared from the upper Mohawk valley are found on the Livingston manor and New York lists. The Zellers may, by a clerical mistake, have been written Fellers. Zoller and Zuller are familiar names among the German population of the county. If any of the original patentees gave a dinner for a hundred-acre lot, in this then sequestered region, the consideration may not have been inadequate, when compared with a metropolitan feast.

Great changes took place in the pronunciation and method of spelling the original German names, when translated or changed to English. This was unavoidable with a people who did not comprehend the two alphabets.

The Bell (or Pell) Family.

Frederick and Anna Mary Pell each took one hundred acres of land on the north side of the river, in the Burnetsfield grant, near Herkimer village. The family were never, I believe, very numerous in the county, and before the revolution seem to have been confined to farming, One of this family, with his son, was killed by Brant and his Indians in the attack upon the settlement on Henderson's patent in July, 1778. The "aged man" may have been Frederick himself. George Henry Bell, who married General Herkimer's sister Catharine, was a man of considerable note in the valley during the revolution. He had been well educated and wrote a neat, compact hand, with much rapidity. Although not among the militia officers appointed in 1775, he commanded a company at the Oriskany battle, was wounded there, and afterwards placed on the invalid pension roll. His disability continued through life. Capt. Bell had two sons in the battle, Joseph and Nicholas; the former was killed and the latter run away during the action, which was always a subject of deep grief and mortification to the father in after life. Nicholas was afterwards killed and scalped by the Indians and tories, about a mile from his father's house, on the road passing over Fall hill. Capt. Bell remained on the battlefield with Gen. Herkimer until the action was over, and took charge of the escort which carried his wounded commander more than thirty miles on a litter. He brought with him from Oriskany a gun which he took in a hand-to-hand fight with a British officer, whom he killed. This trophy was long retained in the family and exhibited as evidence of military prowess. Capt. Bell lived on Fall hill, within the limits of the patent granted to his wife's father. His house, built of stone, was surrounded with wooden pickets during the war, as a protection against the enemy.

He was commissioned a justice of the peace of Tryon county, February 2d, 1778, by the council of appointment, again commissioned in Montgomery county, July 8th, 1784, and reappointed March 27th, 1790. It is said of him that he administered justice with great precision, and sometimes with severity, when he had to deal with those who sympathized with royalty. He had two sons and two daughters. One of the daughters married Henry I. Walrad and the other Peter Waggoner. The late Col. Joost Bell was the son of Nicholas, whose strong attachment for his family is said to be the cause of his leaving his post at Oriskany.

The Bellinger (or Pellinger) Family.

There appear to be five persons of this name, grantees of Burnetsfield patent; two of them being married women. During the first quarter of the present century, the descendants of these families were considerably more numerous in the county than they now are.

The name is found among those Palatines who volunteered under Col. Nicholson, in 1711, for the expedition against Montreal, then held by the French. On their arrival at New York, they seem to have been sent by Governor Hunter to the camps, so called, on Livingston's manor, under the pretense of collecting naval stores; and there is strong reasons for believing they were originally seated on the east side of the Hudson river. The emigration of the Palatines to Schoharie appears to have been from the west side of the Hudson, and consisted of those who had been the most restless and unquiet under the hard treatment inflicted upon them, through the instrumentality of the colonial authorities, and the apparent indisposition to conform to the engagements made to them by Queen Anne, when they started for their new homes. Indeed, most if not all the difficulties encountered by the colonial officers originated with the Palatines settled on the west side of the river.

These observations are drawn out in consequence of a tradition, existing in the county, that this family, or some members of it, came from the Schoharie into the Mohawk valley, which seems not to be supported by the documentary history of the times.

In November, 1722, Gov. Burnet, in a letter to the board of trade and plantations, says, "but as about sixty families desired to be in a distinct tract from the rest, and were of those who had all along been most hearty for the government, I have given them leave to purchase land from the Indians .... on a creek called Canada creek."

From what had then taken place, Gov. Burnet would not have said that the Palatines, who went to Schoharie in spite of the efforts to prevent them, had been very hearty for the government, while he censured those who had participated in that exodus, though not in strong language. The similarity of names found among the Palatines on the east side of the Hudson river, and those contained in the patent, must go far, in connection with Gov. Burnet's declarations, to establish the conclusions now advanced.

This family seems to have held a prominent place in the public regard, at the time of the revolution, and were undeviating and unflinching in their attachment and devotion to the cause of the colonists, in the revolutionary struggle. Col. Peter Bellinger, whose regiment was composed of the militia of the German Flats and Kingsland district, and Lieut. Col. Frederick Bellinger, of the same regiment, participated in the bloody fight at Oriskany; the latter was taken prisoner and carried to Canada. Col. John Bellinger, of this family, was also in that battle, as a private. He removed to, and settled at Utica, about the year 1791.

Most, if not all the lands allotted to the patentees, have been held by their descendants down to the present time, in spite of the diffusibility of our laws in regard to real estates. This has probably been effected by means of wills and testaments, for the statute of distributions, in the period of three or four generations, even where the children of each are few in number, would have divided a hundred-acre lot into very small parcels. One branch of this family placed a high estimate upon military titles, and we find the son succeeding the father in military rank and title, with about as much certainty as to an inheritable estate.

Gen. Christopher P. Bellinger.

In pursuing the plan marked out, of grouping the individuals of the stocks of the Palatine families under one head, from their origin to the present time, great inconvenience has been encountered for want of such accurate data as family records would afford.

Gen. Bellinger was born in the town of German Flats, or within the territory formerly embraced within its boundaries. In the prime of life he was a large farmer, and attained considerable wealth. In 1828, when the town of Little Falls was erected, a part of the eastern portion of German Flats, in which was located Gen. Bellinger's homestead farm, was set off to the new town. His native town contained a very large majority of inhabitants of German extraction, among whom his family connections were quite extensive and influential.

In the early division of political parties, he was a republican of Mr. Jefferson's school, and in this respect sympathized with a very large majority of the German population in his town and in the county; and, in the course of a long and active life, enjoyed a large share of public confidence. He was often elected a supervisor of his town, and to other minor town offices; and, for many years, acted as a justice of the peace. He was diligent, careful and upright in the discharge of all his public duties, and bestowed the most watchful care to the public interests committed to his charge. No stronger illustration of this need be produced than the fact that for many years he had no competitor in his town, for any public favor his fellow citizens had to bestow, or to which they could promote his interests or wishes. He was four times elected member of assembly, in the period of fourteen years, and once returned as elected, by the county clerk, when he was not chosen by a plurality or majority of votes.

At the annual election in the spring of 1809, he succeeded by a majority of five or six votes, and his two colleagues were defeated. Thomas Manly and Rudolph Devendorff, two federalists, were elected over the two republican candidates. It has been said that Gen. Bellinger owed his election at this time to a partial belief entertained by some portion of the federalists that he favored the political views of that party. This was a mistake. He was the next year elected on the same ticket with two other well known republicans.

In 1821 he was again a candidate for the assembly, and having a larger number of votes than either of the two other republican candidates running with him, he obtained the certificate upon an alleged informality in the return of the vote from the town of Danube, when one of his competitors, the lowest on the Clintonian ticket, had obtained a considerable majority. At this time the county clerk alone, canvassed the county vote for members of assembly. The constitution of 1777 was still in force, and the political majority in the assembly would determine the character of the council of appointment, which then wielded an immense political power, having nearly all the civil appointments in the state within its gift.

For a time, after the election, it was doubtful which party had secured the majority of the assembly; it was charged against the clerk, who was a republican, or bucktail as then called, and who held his office at the pleasure of the council of appointment, that he had given the certificate to secure the election of an anti-Clintonian speaker and four anti-Clintonian members of the council. The clerk of course denied the charge, insisting he had no right to look behind the returns, and he must take the certificate of the town canvassers as it stood. And although an Irishman by birth, and could talk high Dutch with the most glib-tongued German in the valley, he said he could not make the word Tood read, mean or spell Todd, and therefore he should give the certificate to the candidate having the highest number of votes, after placing those certified to Stephen Tood among the scattering. The general was however unseated immediately after the organization of the house, and Doct. Stephen Todd of Salisbury, the party who had been chosen, took his seat.

Gen. Bellinger in the party split of 1819 and 1820 acted with the section called in that day bucktails; was an ardent admirer of Daniel D. Tompkins, and in the presidental contest of 1824 adhered to the fortunes of William H. Crawford.

In the fall of 1823, he was again elected to the assembly with John Graves, Esq., of Russia, and Dr. Caleb Budlong, of Frankfort. It devolved on the legislature, which assembled in January, 1824, to choose the electors of president and vice president of the United States, or provide by law for some other mode of appointment. A large majority of members elected in 1823 were republicans or democrats, but very much divided in respect to the candidates for the presidency, and a new element of party strife was presented to the assembly, soon after the election of speaker. The Clintonian party had ceased to exist, and the old federal party had been disbanded. At the election in 1823, a new party, called the people's party, composed of Clintonians, federalists and republicans, hostile to the election of Mr. Crawford, sprung up, and, by the united action and votes of this political combination, a large number of members, hostile to Mr. Crawford, were returned to the assembly. It is not my design to present to the reader anything more of the political history of the state than may be required to give a proper view of the position occupied by the individual whose biography is a subject of consideration.

The speaker, Mr. Goodell, of Jefferson, was friendly to Mr. Crawford. Gen. Bellinger was appointed one of the committee of nine members to which was referred the subject of altering the law prescribing the mode of choosing presidential electors. The minorities had combined to defeat Mr. Crawford; six of this committee, however, were supposed to be his friends, and Gen. Bellinger was one of that number, He assented to the report of the bill, by the select committee, changing the mode of election, and voted for it on the final passage. This bill was defeated in the senate, and in November, 1824, at the adjourned legislative session, he voted for Crawford electors. This was the last time he represented the county in the legislature.

When war was declared by the United States, against Great Britain, in 1812, the General had then attained the rank of colonel in one of the militia regiments of Herkimer county. Congress, anticipating that event, had, in April of that year, authorized the raising of 100,000 men, to be drafted from the militia of the several states; 13,500 of which number was assigned to this state. Col. Bellinger was detached by Gov. Tompkins, to take command of the regiment of militia designed for the defense of the northern frontier, and repaired, with his command, to Sackett's Harbor, in May following. The term of service fixed by congress, for these troops, was three months. The object of the government in thus placing a military force upon the frontier, at this early period, was to watch the movements of any armed force that might be collected in Canada, protect the public property that should be collected at the various points designated as military depots, and enforce a rigid execution of the non intercourse law with Great Britain and her dependencies. A good deal of illicit commerce had been carried on, along the frontier; the laws of the United States had been openly and extensively violated, and the authority of her revenue officers contemned; and, when needed, even an armed force, from the *other side*, would sometimes be at hand, to aid the evasion. A portion of the force, under Col. B.'s immediate command, was stationed at points most suitable to assist the civil officers of the United States in executing the laws of the land.

A distinguished American statesman is reported to have said, when delivering a political harrangue on the sabbath, "there were no Sundays in revolutions." His Britannic majesty's liege subjects, acting upon the principle that a state of war abrogated the omnipotent behests of Jehovah, approached Sackett's Harbor with five armed vessels on the 19th of July, 1812; which day, the calendar tells us, was Sunday, with the view of capturing or destroying several American armed vessels at that place. Col. Bellinger's regiment with the crew of an eighteen gun brig, and a few militia collected on that occasion, constituted the whole American force at the harbor when the formidable expedition made its appearance. Although Col. Bellinger was at that time the commanding officer of the post, the arrangement of the batteries for defense, and the direction of the artillery, was supervised by the senior naval officers on that station. The enemy abandoned the object of the visit, after being somewhat crippled by American shot. Gen. Jacob Brown, in a letter to Governor Tompkins, spoke in terms of high commendation of Col. Bellinger's conduct on this occasion. In other letters to the governor, the general spoke of him as "a brave officer, and a worthy man"; "he is one of the best of men"; "the more I have seen of Col. Bellinger, the more I am pleased with him. He is disposed to do every thing for the best."

During a part of this term of service there seems from the correspondence to have been some misunderstanding between Gen. Brown and Col. Bellinger, in regard to the position of the latter. When the colonel was ordered to the harbor the command of the post was no doubt assigned to him, he being the senior officer in service at that point; and it was not until a brigadier's command was ordered out, and Brown assigned to it, that the latter could rightfully assume any control over him.

At the expiration of three months the regiment was mustered and discharged without being paid. In the subsequent campaign of 1814, Col. Bellinger performed a tour of military service on the frontier with the patriotic and devoted militia of the county. Being placed in defensive positions, he had no opportunity of distinguishing himself, except as a diligent officer, attentive to his duty, exacting its performance from his subordinates, and exercising those acts of kindness to the sick of his regiment, which rendered him beloved and respected by his men. His experience in military affairs was wholly limited to casual militia service, and some years after the war closed he was promoted to the rank of brigadier-general. Warm in his attachments, he was confiding to a fault, and consequently was not wholly exempt from the approaches of the artful and designing, although he possessed a strong and vigorous mind. His education was somewhat limited, being mostly confined to the teachings of the German country schoolmaster. He died at Little Falls about seventeen years ago, without male issue, at an advanced age, leaving four married daughters. He was twice married, and his second wife survived him.

MAJOR FREDERICK BELLINGER,

Being another descendent of the Palatine stock, was a native of the county. He embarked in mercantile pursuits, early in life, which he continued with some interruptions to its close. He won the regard and confidence of his fellow-citizens, which was frequently shown by expressions of popular favor on the part of the people of his native town, Herkimer.

He represented the county in the assembly of this state in 1836, with Stephen Ayres of Fairfield and Thomas Hawks of Columbia.

Major Bellinger possessed many amiable qualities, and was highly esteemed by all who knew him. He died at Mohawk, German Flats, leaving descendants. He was twice married and his last wife survived him.

His family, in common with every other inhabitant of the valley, were visited by the scourge of Indian warfare. During the revolutionary struggle, two brothers, descendants of one of these Palatine families, had occasion during harvest to go into the meadow after a load of hay, and as usual one or both of them went armed. One of the brothers had placed his gun against a stump in the field and commenced pitching hay to the other on the wagon. They had not been long engaged in this before they were fearfully warned of danger at hand by the savage yell and the discharge of muskets. The brother on the wagon after seeing the other shot down and marking the man who did the act, succeeded, by the fleetness of his horses and being partly protected by the hay, in making his escape. The young man shot, was killed while endeavoring to reach his gun, by a well known tory, who had lived on Young's patent, in the south part of the county. He had most likely recently joined the sable allies of the king, and was out on a mission to reduce his rebellious subjects to duty; and true to the instincts of his nature and obedient to the orders of his masters, he could shoot down the peaceful husbandman in the harvest field, or drive the hatchet into the head of the unoffending mother while nursing her infant offspring, and hang the scalp lock of both to his belt with as much zest as the most proficient of his nimble-footed compeers. Many long years had rolled over the head of the surviving brother; he had a family and sons grown to manhood, but time had not obliterated from his memory the recollection of a brother's death or the face and form of the man who had done the foul deed. So late even as when Henry S. Whiting kept the stage house in Herkimer, and a line of passenger stages was running between Utica and Albany, when large wood fires and massive andirons were much in fashion, Mr. Bellinger went into the tavern, to see whether some friend or acquaintance had not just then arrived in the stage, with no thought that he should meet face to face the man who many years before had slain his brother.

But there sat the slayer enjoying himself before a rousing wood fire, which had imparted so much heat to the andirons as to make them red-hot. Mr. Bellinger saw and knew the man at once, and, no doubt, considering him a murderer, seized one of the hot irons by the top, drew it from the fire intending to inflict a blow upon the head of his tory acquaintance, which must have greatly disfigured his scalp-lock if the bystanders had not interfered and prevented him. I very much doubt whether this man ever again traveled through the Mohawk valley, or would venture within reach of Bellinger's curling tongs. He rightfully believed himself protected by the guaranties of the treaty of peace, but Mr. Bellinger did not think so, and when prevented from using the andiron, he sought for and loaded his gun, declaring that he would take the life of his brother's murderer. His son interfered, explained how matters stood between Americans and their late enemies under the treaty of peace, and finally took the gun and put it away.

There may be some who will look upon the outburst of fraternal feeling with great disfavor, and overlook all mitigating circumstances which at the moment seemed to justify Mr. Bellinger in his own mind for any act of retaliation, however severe, or even fatal to the individual who had thus unexpectedly and presumptuously made his appearance upon the field of his former hostile exploits.

Let the scenes of the revolution enacted in the valley be remembered; let it be borne in mind too, that this family with many, if not every other inhabiting the German Flats, had been subjected to the severest calamities of an unnatural and cruel warfare of seven years' continuance, had looked upon harvests and houses destroyed, fields desolated, and cattle and horses shot down as if in sport, or driven away to gorge the appetites of an unrelenting enemy, and last of all, but by no means the least inconsiderable cause of irritation and unappeasable hate, who had mourned some relative slain, either in the field of battle, or by stealth and Indian stratagem; when these things are brought to memory, we can not visit with stern rebuke an act, palliated, if not justified, by so many bold and indisputable mitigating circumstances. The treaty of peace had thrown round this man its broad protective shield, and he was therefore entitled to an immunity which he was in no haste to claim a second time.

The Keslaer and Casler Family.

This was, a few years since, and is now, probably, one of the most numerous of the Palatine families in the town of Little Falls. We can trace the name back to the camps on Livingston's manor, and find it on the lists of volunteers in the Montreal expedition. In respect to this county, so far as I have been able to discover, the name has been derived from the two patentees, Johannes and Nicholas Keslaer. The industrial pursuits of this family have been principally directed to agriculture, and this has been attended with such uniform success, that, in most instances, the sons have inherited the home farms of their fathers, through several generations; and, even at this day, the two lots granted to the first patentees, are still possessed by their lineal descendants. John and Nicholas were brothers, no doubt unmarried, and without families, as each drew a lot of one hundred acres; and no more lands were drawn to that name. Another fact bears out the presumption taken: the third generation from one of the patentees, now living, inherit the property, and the combined ages of the three oldest is more than one hundred and eighty years, and making due allowance for the adolescence of the first and second generation, the period from 1725 to 1855 is more than filled up. In a recent interview had with Richard Casler, a venerable patriarch of one branch of the family, and now eighty-nine years old, I gathered some materials for this notice. He was with

Col. Willett's party when W. N. Butler was killed, on the West Canada creek. Capt. Ellsworth, Lieut. Bloodgood and Ensign Show, were the officers of his company. He knew Gen. Herkimer, and says he was a thick-set, stout man, not quite six feet high. The general's dwelling, at Danube, was built before his recollection. He recollected his grandfather Johannes, the patentee. His father, Jacob, and his uncle, John Casler, who died about the year 1816, at an advanced age, were both in the Oriskany fight. Johan Marks Petri, who was also there, killed an Indian, and told Jacob Casler he might have the Indian's gun, and all he had about him, and be welcome, if he would go and get them, which Jacob took and brought away. A small grist-mill was built on the Casler creek, before the war, which, being stockaded, protected it from being destroyed by the enemy. The Petri and Casler families were connected by marriage. Johan Marks Petri owned lot No. 12, at Little Falls, before the revolution, and built a small grist-mill in the first place on Furnace creek. The mill that was burned by the enemy, a relation of which has been given in another place, was on the river, and supplied by water from it. Jacob Casler, probably a distant relation of my informant, and commonly called Black Jacob, by reason of his having black eyes, a very unusual circumstance among the Germans, at an early day in the settlement of the country, had a severe fight with a bear. The contest was for dear life, and whether black Bruin or black Jacob should live to see another day. Casler had gone out, towards nightfall, in pursuit of cattle strayed into the woods, armed with a common bayonet fixed on a heavy stick several feet long, and when passing up a woody ravine some distance from the clearings, the black tenant of the forest saluted Jacob with a hostile growl, which brought him to a halt. The belligerents did not look at each other with much fraternal feeling. One of them prepared himself for an embrace entirely too bearish to suit his antagonist, and when Master Bruin opened his arms to give the unfriendly hug, Jacob thrust his bayonet into the bear's side as far as he could drive it. This only enraged the wounded beast. It did not disable him entirely, nor cause him to retire from the contest. The bear wrenched the bayonet from his side with his fore paws, and endeavored to disarm his foe; but Casler held fast to his stick and in the scuffle the bayonet became detached from it. Jacob pounded his antagonist on the head and back with his club, and the bear tore Casler's clothes and lacerated his limbs and body with his claws; but Black Jacob knew he must conquer or die, and made up his mind to fight as long as he could strike a blow with his faithful club. The issue of the combat was some time doubtful. Casler bled profusely from his wounds, and was nearly exhausted by his exertions. The bear bled some from his first bayonet wound, and exhibited signs of being confused by the repeated heavy knocks bestowed upon his head, when a happy blow over the eye laid Master Bruin on his back. Casler, no doubt, counted his own life among "the spoils of victory" on this occasion, and would have freely given the bear's hide and bruised carcass to be rid of the ungentle scratches he had received. Jacob long enjoyed the reputation, and justly, of a bold and resolute man.

Frederick Casler, a descendant from one of the patentees, died October 19th, 1849, about seventy years of age, and his father, Jacob Casler, died April 1, 1822, aged sixty-nine years. John Jacob Casler, the grandfather of Frederick, died in January, 1811, aged 88 years. This carries his nativity back to 1723, renders it probable that he may himself have been the patentee, Johannis, and overturns the supposition previously advanced, that the two patentees were brothers. The family tradition respecting the purchase of one of the two patented lots from strangers by the sons of John Jacob, may induce a belief that he was a son of Nicholas, and that the lot having been parted with by the father or his other children, had been brought back into the family by purchase. Jacob and George Kesslair, were, it seems, two of the seventeen patentees of Staley's first and second tracts, granted in 1755, chiefly to the Palatines of the upper valley.

Richard Casler, referred to in this notice, died on the 18th of September, 1855. The newspaper obituary notice states his age at ninety-five years. He told me when I saw him, he was then eighty-nine years old. One of his sons was present and confirmed this statement, by saying that was his reputed age in the family. His health was not firm during the latter part of his life, but he was never known to neglect joining his fellow citizens in celebrating the anniversary of American freedom.

The Editch Family.

This name is also found written and printed Edigh, Edich, Itigh, Ittigh and Ittich. Michael Ittich was one of the volunteers under Nicholson in the expedition against Montreal in 1711. This family were seated for a time on Livingston's manor, and employed, as pretended by the colonial authorities, in making naval stores for the British government. Of the four persons of this name who were patentees, I have no means of ascertaining which was the head of the family, or what relationship they bore to each other. Michael Itigh was one of the patentees of Cornradt Frank's patent, granted in 1765, and Hans Michael Ittig, Jun., and Jacob Ittigh, were patentees of Staley's 1st and 2d tracts, granted in 1755. This name is still extant in the county, although not very numerous. I still recollect a Mr. Edick who figured considerably in our courts some twenty or thirty years ago, especially in ejectment suits brought to settle lines between patents and farm lots, with which he was very familiar on the south side of the river in the Staley and Frank patents.

The Fols (or Folts) Family.

The patentee Jacob took lot three on the south side of the river and a short distance east of Frankfort village, and Melgert, now Melchert, took lots two, high and low land, on the north side.

Their descendants are found in the county in considerable numbers, near the spots where the patentees planted themselves in 1725. The reader will notice that two of the name of Volts were appointed first lieutenants in the fourth battalion of the Tryon county militia in 1775. This was a misspelling of the family name. Melch. Folts's name is found on the roll of volunteers for the expedition against Montreal, in 1711, from Haysbury on Livingston manor.

Warner Folts, who was chosen one of the members of Assembly at the general election in 1824, was a descendant of the patentee Jacob Fols, a farmer and a worthy good man. Ambitious of nothing but to act well his part in this life, and "to make a clean breast of it" with all mankind when he took his final leave of this world. He was a good neighbor and a warm friend. He was elected under circumstances which called forth considerable reprehension, at the time, from former political associates and party friends. Such things, however, are not long remembered. The party which had elected him had also returned a very large majority of members to the house, and when he took his seat and became more intimately acquainted with the political men with whom he was expected to act and associate, he felt embarrassed and unhappy, and finally made up his mind "that come what would" he must go with his old political friends.

Melchert Folts, a son of one of these patentees, was appointed paymaster of the regiment of militia commanded by Col. Henry Starring, in October, 1786; elected the first town clerk of Herkimer, in March, 1789, and held the office several years by reelection. He was also commissioned a justice of the peace soon after the erection of the county.

Born May 5, 1746, and died May 2, 1829; his wife Mary died one month later. The combined ages of the two make one hundred and fifty-seven years and three months. Mr. Folts had received a good common-school education, and was an easy and rapid penman. He kept a journal of the principal revolutionary events in the upper Mohawk valley, but, unfortunately, it has been destroyed or mislaid.

The Fox Family.

This name is not yet extinct in the county, and some of the descendants of the patentee, Christopher, reside near, if not upon, the lot taken up by him in the vicinity of the Stone Church, German Flats. Frederick Fox, a son of the patentee, was a first lieutenant of Capt. George Herkheimer's company, 4th battalion Tryon county militia, as arranged in 1775. Peter Fox was commissioned, in 1786, as ensign in Capt. Peter P. Bellinger's company of militia, in the regiment commanded by Lieut. Col. Henry Starring. I do not place Peter on the list of descendants from the patentee, but it is probable he was.

This family is not now, I believe, very numerous in the county, although several of the name, of German descent, are settled in the southern towns. Christopher Fox was one of the volunteers, in 1711, in the expedition against Canada. He then was at Haysbury, on the manor, and was the Palatine list master of that town.

The Helmer Family.

This name is still pretty numerous in this and the adjoining county of Montgomery, but I do not suppose they all claim to be descendants of the Palatine stock, who first came to the upper Mohawk valley. Of the six patentees, in the grant of 1725, two were married women, whose husbands were alive. Philip and Frederick, two of the patentees, were probably children of the other grantees. Lendert Helmer, one of the original patentees of Burnetsfield, was also the grantee of lots Nos. 13, 21 and 38 in the patent or grant made in 1739, called Glen's purchase. John Adam Helmer, with Capt. Demuth and another man, was sent forward, on the day previous to the Oriskany battle, to Fort Schuyler, by Gen. Herkimer, to apprise Col. Gansevoort of his approach. This duty was executed, although some delays took place in reaching the fort, occasioned no doubt by the extreme caution necessary to be observed to avoid a watchful and numerous enemy. Helmer was also one of the messengers sent by the committee of the Kingsland and German Flats district to Albany, with an account of the disastrous result of the battle. Capt. Frederick Helmer, of Col. Peter Bellinger's regiment of militia, was killed at Oriskany.

John Helmer was the only survivor of four men, sent in August or September, 1778, to watch Brant's movements at the Unadilla, who was then collecting his tory and Indian forces for a descent upon the German Flats, which he, at that time, so successfully accomplished. Helmer's three companions were killed at the Edmeston settlement; but he made his escape, and returned in time to notify the inhabitants of the impending danger, and they saved themselves from slaughter and captivity by fleeing for protection to Forts Herkimer and Dayton. I have no means of deciding whether this was the same man sent to Fort Schuyler, by Gen. Herkimer, but suppose it was.

The historians of the revolutionary period mention a man by the name of Helmer, who was arrested, tried by a court martial, condemned and executed as a spy, at Johnstown, in April, 1779. This man, it seems, belonged to the expedition which came from Canada, in the fall of 1778, for the purpose of recovering Sir John Johnson's iron chest. He became disabled, so that he could not pursue his journey back to Canada, and secreted himself in his father's house until spring, when he was arrested. He had left the county with Sir John, and had attached himself to the baronet's fortunes. This man could not have been one of our family of Helmers, as his father, it appears, was settled at or near Johnstown, and the tide of German emigration, before the revolution, flowed westward.

This family, or these Burnetsfield patentees, the Helmers, were Palatine immigrants, but whether they came over in 1710 or 1722 is not certain. They probably composed a part of the second body of immigrants.

The Erghemar (or Herkimer) Family.

Jurgh, Johan Jost, Madalana and Catharina Erghemar, were each, as appears, patentees named in the Burnetsfield grant. One hundred acres, on the south side of the Mohawk river were allotted to each of them. This name is not found in the list of Palatine immigrants who were sent to Livingston's manor, by Gov. Hunter, or of those who remained in the city of New York. We have no reliable information in regard to Jurgh, or George, Herkimer. There is a tradition among the descendants of this family, that two brothers emigrated from Germany, and after being here some years, they were informed that a considerable estate had fallen to them in fatherland, when they concluded they would return to Germany and look after it; but on going to New York, and seeing only a small portion of the broad expanse of water they would have to cross, their resolution failed, and they returned to their then quiet homes on the Mohawk.

This family early exhibited evidence of wealth and thrift far ahead of any of the other Palatine settlers, in the erection of costly stone edifices, and the possession of many broad acres, purchased after Gov. Burnet's grant. This grant professed to set apart one hundred acres to each man, woman and child of the families who had petitioned to be removed to the upper section of the valley, and it may well be assumed this privilege was claimed and acceded to in every instance.

Was the Catharina named in the patent, and who drew lot No. 5, on or near which the former county poorhouse was erected, the wife of Johan Jost? If Jurgh and Johan

Jost were not brothers, and this idea seems to be very much strengthened by the subsequent ownership and occupancy of the lands granted, unless Jurgh died without issue, and left his estate to his brother, the conclusion seems to be that Johan Jost, subsequently known as Hanyost Herkimer the elder, was the son of Jurgh. If Johan Jost was married in 1725, the date of the patent, he probably had no children to whom lands could be granted according to its terms. The fact is well known that lands were granted to children whose fathers and mothers are named as patentees. Madalana and Catharina are not described as married women, and may have been sisters of Hanyost the elder; if this be the true solution of this matter, they probably died unmarried, or sold their interest in the lands allotted to them, for we find some of the same lands in the possession of Hanyost the elder, in April, 1771. This Hanyost left a grandson, born in October, 1751, who was the issue of his second son, Henry.

This name has undergone many changes. In 1752 it was written Herchkeimer, and the same in 1777, by the family. In 1758, Gov. Delancy wrote it Hareniger. In 1756 we find it written Harkemeis. Then, at other periods, Herchamer, Harchamer, Harkeman and Herkermer. In 1775, the family was, in all its branches, somewhat numerous, influential, and esteemed friendly to the popular cause, and all, except the General, residents of the German Flats district; for we find one of them named as colonel and two others as captains in the fourth battalion of the Tryon county militia by the county committee. The name is then written Herkheimer. This colonel, who was one of the general's brothers, afterwards proved recreant, as well as one of the captains, for we find no account of them afterwards. It is not improbable they belonged to the attainted branch of the family.

The patentee, Jurgh or George Herkimer, did not leave any descendants, unless Johan Jost and one or both of the females named were his children, or they left this part of the country before the revolution. We have no tradition or information of any sort, of any persons of that name, except those who trace their descent from Hanyost Herkimer the elder; nor can we find that any of the other Palatine families claim relationship by marriage with the Herkimer family, behind Hanyost the elder's descendants.

GENERAL NICHOLAS HERKIMER,

Gen. Herkimer's Dwelling.

Was the oldest son of Johan Jost Herkimer the elder, who was sometimes called Hanyost, and died in August, 1775, leaving five sons, Nicholas, Henry, Johan Jost, George and John; and eight daughters, Elizabeth Barbara, Lana, Delia, Catharine, Anna, Gertruyd, Anna Maria and Elizabeth. The father of this numerous family was the Johan Jost Erghemar, one of the patentees of Burnetsfield, and drew lot number 36, and he was also one of the patentees of the Fall Hill tract granted in 1752 to Johan Jost Herchkeimer and Hendrick Herchkeimer.

Although a little out of the order of events, I will here give all the information I have been able to collect in regard to the surviving branches of the General's family. Of the four brothers who remained in the country and attached to the revolutionary cause, Nicholas and John died without issue; George left two sons, John and Joseph, who have been dead a number of years. Joseph left one son only, who until very recently resided at the Little Falls. Henry left five sons, Joseph, Nicholas, Abraham, George and Henry. I have not been able to trace out the descendants of Joseph and Nicholas. Abraham removed to Pennsylvania where his descendants are now to be found. George, the General's nephew, left four sons, Henry G., Timothy and George, who in 1854 lived in Otsego county, near Schuyler's lake, and William who had removed to Chautauque county. The General's nephew, Henry, left Joseph, Henry and Robert H. The first named of these three brothers lived in Springfield, Otsego county, in 1854, and the two latter emigrated to Michigan some years ago. The General's sisters were all married. Elizabeth Barbara, the eldest, married Peter D. Schuyler; she was the mother of Hanyost Schuyler referred to in the former chapter of this work. Lana was three times married; her first husband was Warner Dygert; the second, Nicholas Snell; and the third, John Roorback. Delia was married to Col. Peter Bellinger, Catharine to George Henry Bell, Gertruyd to Rudolph Shoemaker, Anna to Peter Ten Broeck, Anna Maria to the Rev. Abraham Rosecrants, and Elizabeth to Hendrick Frey.

These daughters of the venerable patriarch left numerous descendants, and among them are some of our most respectable citizens. The General was not fortunate in some of his family connections, and he was no doubt to some extent damaged by the adherence of a brother and one or more of the husbands and children of two of his sisters to the interests of the crown, to which may be added the equivocal conduct of his reverend brother-in-law. This was no fault of his, however, so long as he performed his whole duty to his country.

The General was commissioned a lieutenant in Captain William Wormwood's company in the Schenectady battalion of militia, on the 5th of January, 1758, by Lieutenant-Governor James De Lancey. The commission, it will be observed, is directed to Han Nicholas Herchkeimer, gentleman. He must have been, at this time, the senior officer of his name, and commanded at Fort Herkimer in 1758, when the expedition of French and Indians attacked the settlements on the south side of the river. This I advance as an inference drawn from the fact of his then holding a militia commission, and being the only person of the same name who did. He was commissioned a brigadier general of the militia of Tryon county, embodied for the defense of American liberty, and to repel every hostile invasion thereof, by the provincial congress, September 5th, 1776. It should here be noticed that in 1775, he had been appointed or elected colonel of the 1st battalion of militia in his county, when that force was organized by the provincial authorities. At the commencement of the revolution he lived in the Canajoharie district of the county and represented the district in the county committee of safety. His younger brother George was a member from the German Flats and Kingsland district. The General was also a member of the committee from his district and chairman thereof in 1776.

He acted as chairman pro tem. of the Tryon county committee of safety in July and August, 1775, and several letters signed by him are found published in the journals and proceedings of the New York provincial convention of that year. Although twice married he left no children at his death, and his family papers have been scattered, lost and destroyed, so that at this day we are left much in the dark as to his early history. In 1760 he resided in the Canajoharie district, and in May of that year, his father conveyed to him five hundred acres of land, portions of Lindesay and Livingston's and Fall Hill patents. This conveyance also covers a small island in the Mohawk river of about two acres. The consideration expressed in the deed is the love and affection the grantor had for his son.

His family mansion had then been or was subsequently erected on these lands, and the home he occupied while living still remains, but little changed in outward appearance, and some of its interior arrangements and finish are left as when first completed although it has long since been possessed by strangers. The two commissions before referred to are now given to the public, believing they will be interesting to the reader.

By the Honorable
JAMES DE LANCEY, ESQ:
His Majesty's Lieutenant-Governor, and commander in chief in and over the Province of New York, and the Territories depending thereon in America.

To Han Nicholas Herchkeimer, Gentleman, Greeting,

Reposing especial trust and confidence, as well in the care, diligence and circumspection, as in the loyalty, courage and Readiness of You, to do His Majesty good and faithful service; Have nominated, constituted and appointed, and I Do, by Virtue of the Powers and Authorities to me given by His Majesty, hereby nominate, constitute and appoint You, the said Han Nicholas Herchkimer, to be second Lieutenant of the company of Militia in the Schonectady Batalion, whereof William Wormwood, Esq., is Captain.

You are therefore to take the said Company into your Charge and Care, as second Lieut. thereof, and duly to exercise both the Officers and Soldiers of that Company in Arms. And as they are hereby commanded to obey you, as their second Lieutenant, so are you likewise to observe and follow such Orders and Directions, from time to time as you shall receive from Me or any other your Superior Officer, according to the Rules and Discipline of War, in Pursuance of the Trust reposed in you; and for so doing this shall be your Commission.

Given under my Hand and Seal at Arms, in New York, the fifth day of January, in the Thirty First Year of His Majisty's Reign, Annoq: Domini one Thousand seven Hundred and Fifty eight. JAMES DE LANCEY.

By His Honour's Command,

Go. Banyer D. Secry.

Sealed. This is on coarse cap paper stamped fourpenny stamp.

The provincial convention of the state, on the 5th of September, 1776, after organizing the militia of Tryon county into a brigade, separate from that of Albany county, adopted the following preamble and resolution:

"And whereas, Nicholas Herkimer, Esq., is justly entitled to be appointed the brigadier-general of the brigade of militia of Tryon county, as well from his military rank in that county as from his great merit and many exertions in the present glorious struggle for liberty: Therefore,

Resolved, unanimously, That Nicholas Herkimer, Esquire, be appointed brigadier-general of the militia of Tryon county, and that a commission issue to him accordingly for that purpose."

In convention of the Representatives of the State of New York,

To Nicholas Herkimer, Esquire, greeting:

We reposing Especial trust and Confidence in your patriotism, Valour, Conduct and Fidelity, do by these presents constitute and appoint you the said Nicholas Herkimer Brigadier General of the Brigade of Militia of the county of Tryon Embodied for the defence of American Liberty and for repelling Every Hostile Invasion thereof, you are therefore carefully and diligently to discharge the duty of Brigadier General by doing and performing all manner of things, thereunto belonging, and we do strictly charge and Require all officers and privates under your command to be obedient to your orders as Brigadier General: And you are to observe and follow such orders and directions from time to time as you shall receive from the present or any future Congress of the United States of America, or from this or any future Convention of the Representatives, or future executive Authority of this State, or from the Commander in Chief for the time Being of the Army of the United States, or any other your superior officer. According to the rules and Discipline of War, in pursuance of the Trust Reposed in you. Provided such orders and directions of the said Commander in Chief or of such Superior Officer be *grounded* on the authority of the present or any future Congress of the United American States, or the present or any future Convention of the Representatives or other Executive authority of this state, or their Respective committees of Safety; This Commission to Continue in force until Revoked by this or a future convention of this State.

Given at Fishkills the fifth day of September in the year of our Lord one thousand seven hundred and seventy six.

By order, AB'M YATES Jun'r, President.

Attest, John McKesson, Sec'ry.

It is not now known whether the General held any civil office under the crown. As the Johnson family controlled all such appointments in the Mohawk valley, it is not probable he did. He was an early advocate for the rights of the colonists, with the rest of the family, except his brother Hanyost, who was attainted under the act of 1779, and removed to Canada where he died in 1787. The family were wealthy and exerted great influence with the German population in the upper districts of the valley.

From the first organization of the Tryon county committee of safety until he was commissioned a brigadier, Gen. Herkimer appears to have been a prominent member of that committee, and was actively engaged in promoting the patriot cause. His services were known to and appreciated by his fellow citizens in the whole valley, and the voluntary revolutionary associations in the colony. It has been asserted that his education was limited. It is probably true his early instruction was confined to the schools of the country, and was only such as was deemed necessary at that day to fit him for the occupation he was destined to follow. He was a farmer.

In June, 1777, Gen. Herkimer, at the head of about three hundred of the local militia of the county, and one hundred and fifty men of Col. Van Schaick's regiment, repaired to Unadilla and sought an interview with Capt. Joseph Brant, the too celebrated Mohawk chief.

Brant had been a considerable time at Oghkwaga on the Susquehanna, collecting an Indian force, and although he had not then made any hostile attack upon the frontier settlements, he held no equivocal language in respect to his own feelings, and those of his people, in regard to the existing difficulties between the crown and colonies. The Mohawk did not speak with a forked tongue, nor can he be charged with duplicity. Herkimer and Brant had been long acquainted; had been friends and quite near neighbors before the chief left his farm at the upper Mohawk castle, now in Danube, and went to Canada with Guy Johnson, in 1775. The particular object of this visit has never been fully disclosed; nor does it appear to have been made without consultation among the leading and prominent men of the day. Gen. Herkimer's conduct, on this occasion, strongly indicates that he went on a mission of peace. It was known that Brant was surrounded by a very considerable Indian force, numerically larger than the expedition which accompanied the General.

A part of the Mohawks had at German Flats and Albany bound themselves by treaty not to take any part in the contest, and it is by no means a forced inference to conclude that Herkimer's object was to persuade Brant and his followers to adopt the same resolution. It was not inappropriate, even if the General designed nothing but a friendly visit and pacific consultation with his former neighbor, that he should be attended with an imposing force. It was no doubt considered important to make a show of strength to the Indians on that occasion, that they might see if they took up the hatchet against the provincials, what they might have to encounter. It was not until after this conference between Herkimer and Brant that the Indians concluded at a council held at Oswego, to take up the war hatchet in favor of the king; and it was then, and not before, that Brant was acknowledged the war chief of the Six Nations. That place according to the usages of the Iroquois confederacy, belonged to Little Abraham, after the death of his brother Hendrik. Abraham having been a party to the German-Flats and Albany treaty of neutrality, was no doubt displaced or superseded as war chief at the instigation of the British commissioners.

Gen. Herkimer held two consultations with Brant, on two

different days, a limited number of each party being present, unarmed. His object seems to have been to ascertain the feelings and intentions of the Mohawk, and the conferences were animated. Here, as on former occasions, Brant was explicit and decided. He told the General the Indians were in concert with the king, as their fathers had been, and they would not violate their pledge.

Brant desired that the Rev. Mr. Stuart, missionary at Fort Hunter, and the wife of Col. Butler, might be allowed to retire into Canada, which the General agreed to, and presented the Indians with several head of cattle, which they slaughtered immediately. The conference ended, and Herkimer returned home.

If this was intended as a hostile demonstration, rather than a peaceful visit, the force employed was entirely insufficient; and this must have been known to Gen. Schuyler, who then commanded in the northern department. We have referred to this incident in the life of Gen. Herkimer, not on account of its importance, or any very striking or peculiar features it may possess, but to endeavor to rescue the memory of a good and a brave man from a most grave and serious imputation. We have endeavored to show, and we think successfully, that the General's visit to his former neighbor was peaceful in its inception and with the intention of inducing Brant not to take up arms against the Americans; it being well known that he left Canada with a considerable party of Indians, soon after he had had a pretty serious misunderstanding with Guy Johnson. Brant was himself convinced that no hostile demonstration was intended, and if any such views were entertained, they must have been abandoned, for the General declared to Brant's messengers, and to Brant himself, he came on a friendly visit.

Now in the face of all these facts, corroborated by concurrent events, is it probable that Gen. Herkimer ever contemplated a foul and treacherous murder? It is certain Brant never suspected any insidious attempt on his life, or, if he did, he possessed the means of successful defense, which have not been disclosed. The General has a right to throw himself upon his former good character, or his friends have for him; and they may well ask that he be acquitted of a charge, foul and dishonorable, based upon a recollection of events which took place sixty years before they are put upon record.

That Gen. Herkimer should have taken all needful precautions to guard against surprise, and protect his command from any sudden attack by Brant and his followers, is quite natural. This it was his duty to do, even if he was compelled to strike down Brant to accomplish his object; and this would have been quite a different position from that he is made to assume, in the life of Brant, by Col. Stone. In the one case, he is made to stand out the premeditated aggressor; concerting measures to destroy a man he had invited to meet him in a consultation of peace, and who held his safe conduct, which, by all the laws of war, was his shield and protection; and in the other case, he shows a settled resolution not to be circumvented or surprised by an artful, inveterate and resolute foe, without being prepared to strike a blow that must have been instantly fatal to the aggressor.

The latter view of this question entirely accords with the whole tenor of Gen. Herkimer's life to its close, which happened a few weeks subsequent to this event. All hope of inducing the Indians to remain neutral, in the contest between the colonies and mother country, had not then been abandoned by the former, and this was well known to the General; any rash or unguarded act, on his part, would have precipitated an event which all must have deplored, and who would have felt more keenly the severity of Indian retaliation than the General's connexions and neighbors? This expedition was set on foot by Gen. Schuyler, and if, in its inception, it was intended as a hostile demonstration against Brant and his followers, it was most strangely and clumsily conducted. But this could not have been its object, nor the design of its projectors.

The approach of the British army from the north under Gen. Burgoyne, and the concentration of the enemy under St. Leger, at Oswego, Indians, Tories, Canadian and others, produced great consternation in the Mohawk valley, and Gen. Herkimer on the 17th of July, 1777, issued the following spirited and patriotic proclamation:

"Whereas it appears certain that the enemy, of about 2000 strong, *Christians* and *savages*, are arrived at Oswego, with the intention to invade our frontiers, I think it proper and most necessary for the defence of our country, and it shall be ordered by me as soon as the enemy approaches, that every male person, being in health, from 16 to 60 years of age, in this our country, shall, as in duty bound, repair immediately, with arms and accoutrements, to the place to be appointed in my orders; and will then march to oppose the enemy with vigor, as true patriots, for the just defence of their country. And those that are above 60 years, or really unwell, and incapable to march, shall then assemble, also armed, at their respective places, where women and children will be gathered together, in order for defence against the enemy, if attacked, as much as lies in their power. But concerning the disaffected, and who will not directly obey such orders, they shall be taken along with their arms, secured under guard to join the main body. And as such an invasion regards every friend to the country in general, but of this county in particular, to show his zeal and well-affected spirit in actual defence of the same; all the members of the committee, as well as all those who, by former commissions or otherwise, have been exempted from any other military duty, are requested to repair also when called, to such place as shall be appointed, and join to repulse our foes. Not doubting that the Almighty Power, upon our humble prayers and sincere trust in him, will then graciously succor our arms in battle, for our just cause, and victory can not fail on our side."

We have, in another place, briefly noticed the battle at Oriskany, in which Gen. Herkimer commanded the brave

American militia, and were induced to do so from the consideration that many of the inhabitants of the territory now composing this county, were actors in that bloody drama; and not because it came within the scope marked out by the writer when he commenced a work which was intended to be purely local. In the published notices of that event, full justice has not, in the estimation of many, been done to the motives and character of Gen. Herkimer. That he was a good and brave man, can not be questioned, and now, when all the circumstances attending that unfortunate event are calmly considered, no one is disposed to doubt his fixed and unwavering devotion to the patriotic cause; and yet we can not but see that the unfortunate results of that day were owing more to unjust and unmerited aspersions, combined with the characteristics of the men composing the little army, than a want of capacity or inattention to the safety of the troops on the part of the General.

The little army commanded by Herkimer, then hastening by forced marches to the relief of Fort Schuyler, was composed entirely of undisciplined militia, little used and not inclined to submit to the discipline of war, and among them were several members of the county committee of safety, who had theretofore exerted almost unlimited control in all matters relating not only to civil government, but to the movement of troops called out for defense upon the frontiers.

The General was advised that a body of hostile Indians would intercept his approach to the fort, and he sent forward a messenger to Col Ganesvoort advising that officer of his position, and concerted a signal, whereby the arrival of the messenger at the fort was to be announced to the General. As soon as the messenger arrived a spirited sally was to be made by the besieged against the beleaguering army, in order to divert the enemy's attention from Herkimer, who designed a rapid approach, and would have been able to pass the point of expected attack and reach the vicinity of the fort unmolested. Unfortunately the General's messenger did not reach Col. Ganesvoort at the hour expected, and the anticipated signal was not heard in the camp near Oriskany.

General Herkimer's forces were not sufficient to warrant him to risk an action with the enemy single handed. On the morning of the 6th of August, while waiting for the signal of the sortie from the fort, several of the General's officers and some of the committee of safety urged an immediate advance to the relief of the garrison, but the General was reluctant to peril the safety of his little army, composed of his neighbors and friends, and desired to wait the arrival of reinforcements, or until he was notified his express had gained the fort. But the enthusiasm of his followers could not be restrained, nor were his subordinates disposed to treat his opinions with the respect and consideration to which they were justly entitled. This was not all, some of them charged him with cowardice and disaffection to the country; he still adhered to his resolution of delaying a forward movement until it was known whether Col. Ganesvoort had been advised of his approach; and instead of meeting with a proper submission from his subordinate officers, some of them in passionate words charged him to his face with being a tory and a coward. The alternative thus presented to the citizen general was one of great delicacy and immeasurable responsibility. On the one hand it was his duty to march to the relief of the beleaguered fortress and aid in preserving it from falling into the hands of the enemy, but he was yet without any reliable information that his express had reached or could reach Col. Gansevoort in any event, or even that Fort Schuyler itself was not then in possession of St. Leger; on the other, his little army, composed entirely of the militia of the county, fathers, sons and brothers who had recently passed from a state of almost hopeless despondency to the extreme elation and uncontrollable resolution, was no match for the enemy in numbers, and besides if it had been it was alike the imperative duty of the General, by all prudential means, to preserve his men from needless slaughter and captivity, and above all other things not to allow them to become ensnared in an ambuscade from which they could not be extricated. This the General told his insubordinate officers who had so causelessly and cruelly taunted him with cowardice and toryism. He moreover told those who had been the most clamorous for an immediate forward movement, and most liberal in their epithets, that they would be the first to turn and run when the enemy made his appearance. This appears to have been verified to the letter when the action commenced. But what could the General do? To remain in camp only eight miles distant from the fort would lead to further outbreaks of insubordination, and circumstances might happen whereby he would be seriously compromised. He had been informed of the spot where he would be attacked on his march, and he seems to have adopted all the precautions to prevent surprise, that his small force, the nature of the ground and the condition of the country, then a dense wilderness, would allow; although writers differ on this point. It is not intended to repeat in this place any of the events of a battle which filled the valley with mourning.

The troops were ordered to march, and they obeyed with alacrity. After proceeding a short distance Herkimer and the principal part of his men found themselves involved in an inextricable ambuscade, with no alternative but to fight or surrender.

The General's horse was killed under him early in the action, and his leg was at the same time broken by a musket ball; in this situation he directed his saddle to be placed upon a small hillock, where he rested himself, and coolly and firmly issued his orders to his troops. When requested to place himself in a less exposed situation, he answered as a brave and true man would in like circumstances, "I will face the enemy." He found himself surrounded by his neighbors, family relatives and friends, in a position from which they could not be extricated, and where but a few hours before he had told them he did not wish to have them placed; and himself disabled so that he could not walk. While the battle raged the fiercest and the savage yell was loudest, he took his flint, steel and tinder box from his pocket, and lit his pipe, which he smoked with great composure.

The deliberation and coolness exhibited by the commanding officer on this occasion infused into his men a spirit of unconquerable resistance; and it is not unlikely there were some, who in the morning had heard his courage doubted and his prudential motives assailed, if they did not participate in this aggression, that felt keenly the wrong which had been done, and were the more resolved they would not see any further indignity heaped upon him. The General's conduct through the whole of this eventful day was admirable, and greatly contributed to produce order and combined action in his little army.

After the action, General Herkimer was conveyed to his own home, in the present town of Danube, a few miles east of Little Falls, where his leg, which had been fractured below the knee, was amputated. The published statements in regard to this operation do not agree. It was no doubt unskillfully done. The leg, flesh and bone were cut off square, without taking up or tieing the large blood vessels, and he consequently died of an hemorrhage. He was, in his last moments, collected, cheerful and resigned. When he became satisfied that the hours of life with him were numbered, he called for the Bible and read to those around him the thirty-eighth psalm, commencing with the earnest invocation:

"O Lord, rebuke me not in thy wrath; neither chasten me in thy hot displeasure."

Thus closed the life of Gen. Nicholas Herkimer. The name of Herkimer was at an early day bestowed on a tract of country erected into a county which was the place of his birth, as an appropriate memorial to one who had laid down his life in a heroic defense of that country, and the liberty of its citizens.

The General's loss was keenly felt and sincerely deplored

by the people of Tryon county, and the country generally deeply sympathized with his friends in their bereavement.

In October following his death, the continental congress passed a resolution appropriating five hundred dollars for the erection of a monument to his memory, and in communicating the resolution to the governor of this state, the congress said:

"Every mark of distinction shown to the memory of such illustrious men as offer up their lives for the liberty and happiness of this country, reflects real honor on those who pay the grateful tribute; and by holding up to others the prospect of fame and immortality, will animate them to tread in the same path."

Gov. George Clinton, when he sent the resolution and letter to the committee of safety in Tryon county, remarked:

"Enclosed you have a copy of a letter and resolves of congress for erecting a monument to the memory of your late gallant general. While, with you, I lament the causes, I am impressed with a due sense of the great and justly merited honor the continent has, in this instance, paid to the memory of that brave man."

Reader, have you seen that monument, erected by a grateful country, to the memory of a good and brave man, who offered up his life for its liberty and happiness?

Have you seen the proud memento that reflects real honor on those who paid the grateful tribute; and which holds up to others the prospect of fame and immortality?

Descendants of the Palatines; sons of the Pilgrim Fathers; and ye, who have sought an asylum "in the land of the free and the home of the brave," since that monument was *resolved* to be erected, can you point out the spot where it stands, and have you read the inscriptions by which the republic has bestowed a "great and justly merited honor" "to the memory of that brave man?"

In what direction shall the thousands, who daily pass through the valley at a speed which almost annihilates time and space, turn themselves for a momentary glance at the indestructible memorial which proudly attests a nation's honor and gratitude? Or where shall they look for its mouldering ruins, after seventy-seven years' exposure to a severe and destructive climate?

But why ask questions that have been answered more than three-quarters of a century, and when no other response than that already given will ever be obtained? Although the national congress has been remiss in executing its own resolve and redeeming its solemn pledge, our state has perpetuated the name of HERKIMER so long, at least, as the republic shall stand.

Some writers have gone so far as to call in question Gen. Herkimer's prudence, if they do not doubt his capacity as a military commandant, in the disposition and arrangement of his forces in the march to Oriskany, on the morning of the battle. The writer of this sketch feels no disposition to become the partisan, but as these remarks have not been made by military men, so far as his observation has extended, he can not assent to the justice of any such conclusions drawn from the historical facts stated. The material error committed was the forward movement until reinforced, or the signal to be given from the fort was heard. Now let it be borne in mind that Gen. Herkimer was not in command of regular troops, nor the chief of subordinate officers, and his powers as commanding general might be circumscribed by the county committee, a large number of which, it appears, were in attendance. He doubted the expediency and propriety of breaking up his camp, and resisted until overruled by a necessity that knows no law and admits of no restraint whatever. His character as an officer was assailed, and his motives as a man were impugned. The state of things in his camp no doubt impressed him with the strong conviction that one act of insubordination might well be followed by another, which would prove more fatal to those engaged in it, and perhaps to himself and those who remained faithful to him, than any hazard he might incur by a combined movement of his whole force. If only a part of his small army had advanced, it is apparent every man would have been cut off and the remainder, with himself, would have shared the same fate; or, if they had not, he would have been greatly censured for permitting his troops to be attacked in detail.

General Herkimer is in no respect justly chargeable with committing an error by giving the order to march. It seems to be very well authenticated that front, flank and rear guards were thrown out and accompanied the march of the forces. The strength of these covering parties, or the distance they marched from the main body, is not stated.

In passing the marshy ground at the creek, it is very likely the flankers were compelled to fall into the advancing column, in order to cross on the bridge and causeway, and enable them to keep up with the line of march. Here was the spot the enemy chose to occupy in ambush. We might as well blame the commanding officer for taking this road, when there was no other, as to censure him for any disorder in the march consequent upon passing this defile. When seeking grounds to censure the conduct of others, we may overlook points very material to be considered. Surely the men of the revolution, and especially those of the Mohawk valley, were not to be told that the only mode of meeting an Indian attack was in solid column, or in regular formed lines.

It is said the line of march was so irregular, and the attack so sudden, there was no opportunity of forming the men. In what manner would any officer acquainted with Indian warfare arrange his men, except to direct each one to take his cover, and watch the movements of the foe, and as he uncovered to deliver his fire? Why then seek to charge want of capacity for not doing what would have been condemned on all hands as unwise and extremely disastrous? A conflict with the northren Indians, in our dense forests, is almost an individual, hand-to-hand affair, depending more on personal prowess and skill, for success, than combined movements in column or line. This can not be better illustrated than in the words of an eloquent address delivered by the late Governeur Morris, before the New York Historical Society: "Let me recall, gentlemen, to your recollection, that bloody field in which Herkimer fell. There was found the Indian and the white man, born on the banks of the Mohawk, their left hands clenched in each others' hair, the right grasping, in a gripe of death, the knife plunged in each others' bosom; thus they lay frowning."

Some authors have stated that Gen. Herkimer was sixty years old when he died. He was not born until after April, 1725, and it is highly probable, when we take into consideration the facts before stated, his father was not then married. He might have been about fifty years of age at his death, but some collateral members of the family say, he was not over forty-seven or forty-eight when that event happened.

The following letter being pertinent to the subject in hand, on account of the facts stated in it, should have a place in this publication:

German Flats, Committee Chamber,
August 9th, 1777.

Gentlemen: Just arrived Capt. Demuth and John Adam Helmer, the bearer hereof, with an account that they arrived with some difficulty at Fort Schuyler, the 6th of the month, being sent there by order of Gen. Herkimer. Before he set out for the field of battle, he requested some assistance from the fort, in order to make an effort to facilitate our march to the fort. Two hundred and six men were granted. They made a sally, encountered the enemy, killed many, destroyed the tents of the enemy, and came off victorious to the fort. The commander (of the fort) desired them to acquaint us, and his superiors, that he is wanting assistance, and thinks to stand out so long that timely assistance could come to his relief.

Concerning the battle: On our side, all accounts agreed, that a number of the enemy is killed; the flower of our militia, either killed or wounded, except 150, who stood the field and forced the enemy to retreat; the wounded were brought off by those brave men; the dead they left on the field for want of proper support. We will not take upon us to tell of the behavior of the rear. So far we know, they took to flight the first firing. Gen. Herkimer is wounded; Col. Cox seemingly killed, and a great many officers are among the slain. We are surrounded by tories, a party of 100 of whom are now on their march through the woods. We refer you for further information to the bearer. Major Watts of the enemy is killed. Joseph Brant, William Johnson, several known tories and a number of Indians.

Gentlemen, we pray you will send us succor. By the death of most part of our committee members, the field officers, and General being wounded, every thing is out of order; the people entirely dispirited; our county at Esopus unrepresented, that we can not hope to stand it any longer without your aid; we will not mention the shocking aspect our fields do show. Faithful to our country, we remain,

Your sorrowful brethren,

The few members of this committee.

attested PETER J. DYGERT, Chairman.

To the Chairman of the Committee of Albany.

The reader will detect the mistakes in the above letter, although of little consequence now. Neither Brant or Johnson were killed or hurt in the least, except in feeling, although in the subsequent years of the war there were many in the valley who would have much rejoiced had a quietus been placed on Brant at Oriskany.

Gen. Herkimer's will appears to have been used as an exhibit in a suit in chancery, and is now deposited in the office of the clerk of the court of appeals. It bears date February 7th, 1777. He is described in it as a resident of Canajoharie, Tryon county. His first wife, was a sister of Peter S. Tygert, and his second wife, Maria, the daughter of the same person, was well provided for in the will. Some time after the General's death, she married again, and removed to Canada. This Mr. Tygert lived near Gen. Herkimer, and survived the revolutionary war several years. He made eight devises of real estate, comprising nineteen hundred acres of land. There are besides, twenty-seven pecuniary legatees named in it, to whom various sums of money were given and directed to be paid by his residuary legatee. He gave to his younger brother, George, his "home-place," containing five hundred acres of land, and constituted him the residuary legatee. George, who was with his brother at Oriskany, died in 1786, leaving seven children, all of whom were living in 1820.

The executors named in this will, were, Hanyost Shoemaker, John Eisenlord, John Tygert and the testator's wife. The will is signed, Nicholas Herckheimer. It was proved October 4th, 1783, before Christopher P. Yates, surrogate of Tryon county, and George Herkimer admitted the administrator with the will annexed.

John Herkimer

Was the son of George Herkimer before mentioned, the nephew, and not the grandson of the General. On the death of his father he inherited with his brother and sisters the estate devised by his uncle, and he occupied the family mansion until about the year 1814.

In the prime of life he was an active politician and occupied a somewhat prominent place in the public regard. While a resident of Montgomery he represented that county in the assembly of this state, and was one of the judges of the court of common pleas. After the town of Danube in which he lived in 1817 was annexed to Herkimer, he was appointed one of the county judges and held the office some years. He was commissioned a major in the regiment of New York Volunteers, commanded by Col. John Mills, by Governor Daniel D. Tompkins on the 30th day of March, 1813, and served with his regiment at Sackett's Harbor in the late war with Great Britain, and was in the action when Col. Mills was killed.

In the early political divisions of the country he acted

with the republican party, and when the split in that party took place under Governor De Witt Clinton, or in the year 1819, he became one of the leading opponents in the county to the views and pretensions of that gentleman.

At the first general election after the adoption of the new constitution of 1821, his political friends contemplated placing his name before the public as a candidate for the state senate. This nomination would have been equivalent to an election in a district where his party could safely count upon a large and certain majority. The county then being a congressional district, could not be so safely relied upon to return an Anti-Clintonian member unless the heavy adverse vote in the town of Danube, where Major Herkimer lived, could in some way be overcome.

Preferring a seat in the United States house of representatives to one in the senate of this state, he told his leading political associates if he could have the congressional nomination he would see to it that the vote of Danube should not defeat him; and it did not. He was put in nomination and chosen at the general election in November, 1822. The period of President Monroe's last term was drawing to a close, and numerous aspirants were early in the field as candidates for the succession. Messrs. Adams, Crawford, Calhoun and Clay, the three former members of Mr. Monroe's cabinet, and the latter a member of congress and speaker of the U. S. house of representatives, had been attached to the old republican party, and were men of eminent and distinguished talents. The qualifications of these gentlemen were presented to the country and their claims actively canvassed by their respective friends. General Andrew Jackson was also in the field, but his pretensions, at first, seem not to have been favored by all the leading republicans of that day. It had been usual for members of congress to designate the candidate for the presidency, in caucus, and such a meeting was to be held during Judge Herkimer's term. He early declared his preference for Mr. Adams, and as nearly all the members, except those who favored Mr. Crawford, had avowed their intention not to attend the caucus or be bound by its proceedings, it was for a time doubtful what course Judge Herkimer would pursue. It was believed that a very large majority of his republican constituents were in favor of Mr. Crawford, and conforming to their request he attended the caucus, composed of a minority of the republican members, which presented Mr. Crawford's name as a candidate, then voted for Mr. Adams, and declared his intentions to support him in the approaching canvass. We do not design to go into any discussion of political questions, except so far as it may be necessary to give a sensible relation of the incidents that have taken place, which may be proper to notice. The electoral colleges failed to choose a president, but Messrs. Jackson, Adams and Crawford, having the highest number of votes on the list, the election of one of the three devolved on the House of Representatives. Judge Herkimer favored the election of Mr. Adams, in the house. This event took place in February 1825. He died at his residence in the town of Danube, some years ago, aged 73 years, without leaving any male descendants. After leaving congress, he was a number of years engaged in the ardous pursuits of private life, and had become enfeebled by too much exposure in an unhealthful climate. We have not noticed the part Judge Herkimer took in the canvass of 1824-25, with any design of arraigning his conduct before the public, or of imputing any wrong to him. Many distinguished republicans of that day acted with him, and if they misjudged the sentiments and wishes of their constituents, numerous occurrences of that sort have happened before and since.

The Herter Family.

This name is generally pronounced Hatter. We do not find the name among those who took a prominent part in the early stages of the revolution. Henry Herter was appointed first lieutenant in Capt. Frederick Bellinger's company of the Tryon county militia, in 1775. Although the lands allotted to the patentees, Apolone and Lawrence Herter, were on the south side of the river, it was not long before one or both of them, or some of their descendants, moved to the north side of the river. Some of the family were at the Great Flats at the time of the French expedition, in 1757, where one of the Herters, who was a militia officer, was taken prisoner, with his wife and family, and carried into captivity, with the other Palatine prisoners, to Canada, where they were detained about twelve months. Mrs. Herter gave birth to an infant daughter, while crossing the St. Lawrence river, in a birch-bark canoe. Humble as was the birth and state, at that time, of the captive's daughter, she was destined, in after life, to fill a large space in society, at Herkimer and elsewhere. She married Michael Myers, a short biographical sketch of whom can be found in another chapter. Mrs. Catharine Myers survived her husband many years, and it seems but as yesterday that I saw the venerable matron walking along our streets. She died September 4th, 1839, aged eighty-one years and four months. The old people now living say that when young and in the prime of life, Mrs. Myers was a lady of rare personal beauty. She was the grand-daughter of one of the patentees. The male members of this family, of the first and second generation from the patentees, have often been spoken of, as a noble looking set of men, tall, well-formed, and full of health and animation. It has been remarked that the female branches of this family, at one or two degrees farther remove from the original stock, have not lost the family pre-eminence of raising handsome children, both male and female, but particularly the latter. Whether all this has been brought about by intermarriages and crossing the blood, or is an inherent quality of this family, the biographer is not required to determine.

Mrs. Nancy Etheridge, the relict of Joab Griswold, who died September 26th, 1840, aged fifty-seven years, a lady of rare personal attractions and graceful carriage, was a daughter of Mrs. Myers. I must beg the reader to note that I am not a professed connoisseur in such matters, and that, if I repeat "common fame," in this case, I am not uttering a fabulous tale.

This family has lost some of its number by emigration to other states, and to other counties in this state; it is still very numerous, and probably the most numerous of any in the county, who are descendants of the primitive Palatine stock.

Some of the family, Nicholas and Philip, emigrated to Deerfield, Oneida county, after the revolution, and settled there. Nicholas died at Deerfield, in the summer of 1855, at the venerable age of ninety-three years. He was quite familiar, personally, with the principal events of the war in the upper valley, and took much satisfaction, in his advanced years, in handling his cane, and showing how Indians and tories were killed.

The Hess Family.

The descendants of Augustines Hess, the patentee of lot number ten at Little Falls, are yet found in the county in considerable numbers. As there is but one person of that name among the patentees, he was probably a young man and unmarried. From an examination of the church records of the Rev. Mr. Rosecrants from 1763 to the close of the last century, it appears that this family were somewhat numerous at that time in the Mohawk valley.

Augustine Hess, one of the members of the Tryon county committee of safety from the Kingsland and German Flats districts, which first met on the 2d of June, 1775, was a son of the patentee, and a member of the committee some time. From this circumstance he must have held a reputable standing among his neighbors, and been considered a true friend to the country; a fact to which his descendants may refer with pride and satisfaction. I can not ascertain when the family parted with their title to the lot granted to the patentee, but it must have been so long since "that the memory of man runneth not to the contrary."

Augustines Hess, the elder, who was also one of the patentees of Staley's first and second tracts, was killed in July, 1782, by the Indians near Fort Herkimer, on the south side of the river. He was shot dead while on his way to the fort for protection with his family. He was a very aged man, and among the last survivors of the Palatines.

The Kast Family.

Johan Jurgh Kast, and his son Johan Jurgh Kast, Jr., were patentees, and each drew a small lot on the Great Flats, and seventy-acre wood lots on the uplands, in the Burnetsfield tract. In 1724, a small grant of eleven hundred acres was made to this family, or rather to the wife and children of the elder Kast, situated in Schuyler and surrounded by Cosby's manor, on which some of the descendants of the family resided many years. The elder Kast had two sons, Johan Jurgh and Lodowick. I do not find any traces of the latter; he may have died young and unmarried. Johan Jurgh, the younger, had two sons, Conrad and Frederick. Conrad was taken prisoner during the French war in 1757, and was taken to England to be exchanged, and after his return to New York he enlisted in the British army and never returned to the Mohawk valley. Some of the descendants of Frederick are still found in the county. The ancestor of this family probably came over with the second company of immigrants in 1710. At an early period in the history of the settlement of the valley, this family were wealthy and prosperous farmers, having pretty large possessions.

The Petrie Family.

The genealogy of this family can be traced with considerable accuracy to the parent stock. Johan Joost Petrie was one of the Burnetsfield patentees, and lands were allotted to him, his wife Gertruyde, and his son Mark, or Marks. This name is found among the volunteers who went with the expedition against Montreal in 1711, under Col. Nicholson. He arrived in New York with the second company of Palatine immigrants in 1710, accompanied his countrymen to the camps on Livingston's manor, where he remained until he removed to the German Flats. He was tall and well formed; even more than "six feet high and well proportioned." From what I have heard of him, he very much resembled, in stature and appearance, the best of the ancient German race. He and Coenradt Rickert were the leading men of the little colony which first came to the German Flats. He early won the confidence and good will of the colonial government, and it is no doubt owing to this circumstance that he was first named in the license given by Governor Burnet to purchase the Indian title to the lands afterwards granted, and also the first named in the patent. He was selected with others to search out the "promised land." The eighty-six acre lot, then and long afterwards called the Stone Ridge, was allotted to his wife. This lot is described as wood land, "lying in the middle of the great flatts." The present village of Herkimer, or the compact part of it, is mostly on this lot. Surrounded by rich alluvial flat land, subject to inundations, there was no other site for the hamlet unless resort was had to the higher lands northerly of the low lands. I think this allotment was made as a compliment to the wife and her husband. When it became known that safe building lots could only be had on this ridge, dissatisfaction was expressed by the other settlers that they were excluded, and Mr. Petrie divided the large lot into smaller parcels, and gave them to the owners of the adjoining low lands. It has been said that no written conveyances were ever made by him and his wife. I have not made any particular inquiries in regard to this fact. It is not probably one of those cases that would come within an anti-rent, roving commission, with the attorney-general at the head, to hunt up some spot to which the state could assert a paramount title, otherwise the good people at the county seat might be called on to show their papers.

It seems very probable that Mr. Petrie was one of the principal men in the settlement called the German Flats, from the first planting of this little frontier colony, until 1757, or till his death. Up to that time he had been employed by the colonial government, and had accumulated considerable wealth.

When the French and Indians attacked and destroyed the settlements on the north side of the river, 11th November, 1757, the particulars of which are given in a former chapter, all his property, save the land, was taken and destroyed, and he with his family were carried into captivity. He was the individual named in the French account of this affair as "the mayor of the village of the Palatines;" and in speaking of the losses sustained by the inhabitants, the writer states that "the mayor of the village alone has lost 400,000" livres.

The writer here means the livre tournois of France, equal to eighteen and a half cents in value of our currency; quite a large sum this must have been for those times. This was no doubt an exaggeration. All accounts, however, concur in stating that his private losses were very heavy. He had on hand a very large sum in silver, which was taken by the enemy. Whether this money was a part of his private fortune, or had been placed in his hands to purchase government supplies, is not certain, although family tradition speaks of it as private property. Mr. Petrie was detained some time in captivity, and while in Canada was frequently compelled by the Indians to wear a cap with tassels and small bells, and dance for their amusement; a mark of distinction shown him in consideration of the office he held when taken prisoner. He was one of the copatentees with Philip Livingston and John De Peyster of a grant of six thousand acres of land made in 1740, being six lots in a tract called Henderson's or Petrie's purchase, now in the towns of Columbia and Warren.

This patriarch of the Petrie family died before the commencement of the revolutionary war, leaving a large number of descendants, although he had but one child, a son, when he first came to the German Flats. Nearly all the inhabitants of the name in the county were descended from the same stock.

Mrs. Petrie, the wife of Johan Jost, was a lady of education and considerable refinement, far above what was found in the German peasantry of that day. It has always been believed that her father was a man of wealth and distinction in Germany, and that her marriage with Mr. Petrie was not in accordance with the wishes and feelings of her family.

I am somewhat perplexed in having to deal so much with probabilities, but the great lapse of time that has intervened since the happening of the events I have undertaken to write an account of and the present period, and the want of precise, accurate recorded information in respect to those events, compels me to assume as probable facts, what may be, after all, a pure fiction. My intention is not to place on these pages any matter resting wholly on vague tradition, unsupported by cotemporaneous testimony having strong marks of authenticity.

Finding the name of Johan Jost Petrie among those who were for a time seated on Livingston's manor; finding in the Documentary History of the state, that those Palatines who had been temporarily lodged on the east side of the Hudson river had given the existing government but little trouble about a permanent settlement, and that many of them had volunteered under British officers to fight the battles of their adopted country; and finding Gov. Burnet, at a later day, declaring in an official letter he had given about sixty Palatine families "who had been most hearty for the government," permission to settle on a tract by themselves, I feel authorized to say what I have in respect to Mr. Petrie, the patentee, and the Petrie mentioned in the Documentary History, being the same man. But, after all, this seems irreconcilable with the idea that he was a married man in 1711, and if he was not, the lady he did marry must have joined him in this country, where a long contemplated union took place. This corresponds with the family legend of a young lady leaving country, home and parents, defying old ocean's storms, cleaving to the man of her choice in his rude wilderness home. The crown land commissioners bestowed the Stone Ridge lot upon this lady as a token of respect and mark of special consideration.

John Petrie, a son of the patentee, was a member of the Tryon county committee from the German Flats and Kingsland district, which met in June, 1775, to consider the state of affairs between the mother country and the colonies, then rapidly approaching a crisis. In a letter addressed to Guy Johnson, the committee say they had met "to consult the common safety of our rights and liberties, which are infringed in a most enormous manner, by enforcing oppressive and unconstitutional acts of the British parliament, by an armed force in the Massachusetts Bay."

The same gentleman was appointed by the Tryon county committee, on the 16th August, 1779, one of the delegates from the county to a state convention, called to consider proper measures "for appreciating the currency, restraining extortion, regulating prices and other similar purposes."

I have been shown a commission granted by Sir Henry Moore, bart., captain-general and governor-in-chief, &c., &c., issued to Ded'k Marcus Petrie, gentleman, dated October 13th, 1768, in the eighth year of the reign of George III, by which Mr. Petrie was appointed "to be Ensign of a company of Militia Foot in a regiment in Albany county, of which company George Henry Bell Esq. is Captain." Mr. Petrie continued to hold this commission till the country changed rulers, when he was appointed a lieutenant in the Tryon county militia. He was killed in the Oriskany battle, being then attached to Col. Peter Bellinger's regiment. At the time of writing this notice his widow was still living, an aged and venerable matron. It was thus early and effectively that we find the members of this family "doing battle for the right," and one of them laying down his life in defense of the just rights of his country. Surely such deeds ought neither to be blotted out or forgotten.

John M. Petrie, who represented the county in the assembly of this state, in 1808, and 1809, with Westel Willoughby Jr. and Aaron Budlong, was a nephew of Lieut. Petrie, the son of the patentee, Mark Petrie, and consequently the grandson of Johan Joost. John M. occupied the Burnetsfield lot, number 46, some time. It was owned by his father when he died. This son afterwards changed his residence to a farm on Glen's purchase, a few miles north of the Little Falls, where he died, respected, full of years, and his loss regretted, leaving several descendants. Two brothers of the Petrie family, Jost D. and John D., sons of Ded'k Marcus Petrie, are yet in the recollection of the writer. They each possessed a goodly share of sundry broad acres, which were inherited by their children after their deaths. Daniel Petrie, one of this family, was killed in the attack upon and destruction of the mills at Little Falls, in 1782.

John Conrad Petrie, who is described as an orphan, twelve years old in 1710–11, was a brother of Johan Joost, and remained on the manor when the latter came to the German Flats. We find John Conrad still at the camps in November, 1715.

The Reelle Family.

I do not find this name on Livingston's manor, or New York list of Palatine emigrants. Lot number 15 lowland, 30 acres, and 15 woodland, 70 acres, at the German Flats, were granted to Godfrey Reelle, and lot number 10, on the south side of the river, was granted to Godfrey Reele, Jr. This name is not familiar in the county. Christian Reall, settled, near Deerfield Corners, Oneida county, with several other Germans from the upper valley, before the revolution. In the second year of the war, the settlement was destroyed by the enemy, but the inhabitants escaped to a stockade fort, below, in the now town of Schuyler. After the war, Mr. Reall returned to Deerfield, and occupied the farm he had been driven from by the tories and Indians. There is a small stream in Deerfield called Reall's creek, which empties into the Mohawk. Not long after the revolutionary war, some members of the family, or all of the then survivors, removed to the "western country," now Onondaga county, and settled on the Military tract, where several of the descendants now reside. One of this family has recently returned to the county, and is now a resident of Little Falls; but he comes under the name of Reals. Eighty years have passed, and we again see a descendant of this Palatine stock among us. Christian Reall, moved to Onondaga and was there when quite an old man.

THE SHOEMAKERS.

There were two brothers of this name, in the list of patentees; Ludolph, afterwards called Rudolph, and Thomas. They were, both of them, young and unmarried, when they came to the German Flats. Rudolph had several sons, and one of them, Johan Jost, married the daughter of an Englishman, in 1775, by the name of Smith, the fame of whose eccentricities and devotion to the British crown still occupies considerable space in the unwritten history of the valley.

At the commencement of the revolution, Johan Jost had been one of his majesty's justices of the peace in Tryon county. He was not friendly to the cause of the colonists, and it was at his house that Lieutenant Walter N. Butler, Hanyost Schuyler, and a number of white soldiers and Indians were taken prisoners, in the night, by a party of American troops sent from Fort Daytan by Col. Weston.

Butler, soon after the Oriskany battle, had been sent down to the German Flats, on a secret mission, with the appeal of Sir John Johnson, Claus, and the elder Butler, to the inhabitants of the Mohawk valley, inviting them to give in their adhesion to the crown, and send a deputation of their principal people, in order to compel an immediate surrender of Fort Schuyler: promising kind treatment, and protection from Indian vengeance and retaliation for losses at Oriskany, in case of compliance. It was this address which drew from Gen. Arnold the denunciatory proclamation noticed in a former chapter. Some vigilant friend of the country had given notice of this clandestine meeting, and the tory caucus was broken up in the midst of Butler's midnight harangue.

Mr. Shoemaker, although disaffected, was not molested in person or property, and we must therefore conclude he was rather a passive than active adherent of the king. Brant halted near his house in 1778, the night before he with his Indians fell upon and destroyed the property of the inhabitants at the German Flats, but took no scalps or prisoners. With the exception of one member of the Herkimer family, I do not find any other name of note belonging to the Palatine emigrants or their descendants who faltered in their duty to the country and the cause of humanity.

Rudolph I. Shoemaker, born in 1776, who represented this county in the assembly of this state during the session of 1812-13, was the son of Johan Jost, before named. He was a farmer, and lived and died in the present town of German Flats, not far from the present village of Mohawk. He was a man of ardent temperament, and a warm supporter of the war of 1812.

Robert Shoemaker, a younger brother of Rudolph I., was appointed sheriff of the county in 1817, and held that office several years under the old council of appointment. He was often a contestant for popular favor in his native town, German Flats, against General Christopher P. Bellinger, and sometimes came off victorious, but he has often told me his victories were hard won. He was a gentleman of considerable general intelligence, and a prompt, efficient officer. Inheriting a portion of the paternal estates, gathered and enlarged by prudent and frugal hands, he devoted much of his time to agriculture, although he was not unmindful of political preferment when opportunity offered. He represented the county in the assembly in 1822, with Simeon Ford and Stephen Todd. At a late period in life, the spirit of immigration took hold of him and he removed with his family to northern Illinois, where he died many years ago. I have not the means of stating the fact with certainty, but from my knowledge of Mr. Robert Shoemaker, and his apparent age when I first saw him, I conclude he was born during the revolution.

Thomas Shoemaker, the patentee, raised a pretty numerous family, and some of his sons were not backward when danger and duty called the inhabitants of the valley to arms. His son Thomas participated in the Oriskany battle, and afterwards his wife and one of his children, Christopher, and a son of John Shoemaker, then quite young, were taken prisoners and carried to Canada. Mrs. Shoemaker and her child returned from captivity before the close of the war, but the other child did not come back until after. There are now many descendants of this branch of the Shoemaker family in the county as well as some of the other stock.

In looking into the Documentary History of the state, I find the name "Schumacher" among the Palatine immigrants of 1710, from which the present name, Shoemaker, is derived.

The Smith Family.

Two of this family cast their lots on the north side of the Mohawk, on the Great Flats, and two on the south side. The Schmidts were among the emigrants of 1710, and seated for a time at the camps on Livingston's manor. Adam Michael Schmidt was a volunteer, in the expedition against Montreal in 1711. The descendants of the patentees are yet found in the county in considerable numbers, but emigration has diminished them to some extent. Colonel Nicholas Smith, now one of the oldest inhabitants of the city of Utica, if alive, and whose parents were killed by the Indians and tories at Herkimer during the latter part of the revolutionary war, was a descendant of one of the patentees. John Smith was assigned as an ensign to Capt. Eisenlord's company of militia in 1775. In common with the other patentees of Burnetsfield, this family had its share of suffering during the French and revolutionary wars. Some branches of it have held the lands assigned, in regular succession, one hundred and thirty years. Maria, the wife of George Smith, lived to the unusual age of ninety-six years. She died in 1817.

The wife of Joseph Smith was overtaken during the revolution, on the east side of the west Canada creek, by a party of Indians, tomahawked and scalped. The Indians left her, supposing she was dead. She revived after a time, and with much suffering found her way home across the creek. She recovered and lived to a very advanced age.

The Starings.

There were six males, and one married female, of this name, patentees of Burnetsfield. The Starings were formerly pretty numerous in the county, but of late years, they have lost some by emigration. I am not aware that a single lot, granted to the first patentees, is now retained in the hands of their descendants; and it is quite certain, that lot 13, at Little Falls, set apart for Mary Eva, the wife of John Adam Staring, was sold many years previous to the revolutionary war.

I do not find this name enumerated among the Palatine families on the Hudson river, or with those who remained in New York, and it does not seem possible that it could have been derived from any of those contained in the lists of immigrants published. This name appears to have been uniformly written in all the ancient manuscripts, which have come under my observation, as copied from the patent. In this case, as in every other relating to the families who first settled in the upper Mohawk valley, all the parties were near relations, and may not have comprised more than two families.

Hendrick Staring, or as he often wrote his first name, Henri, was a man of some note during the revolutionary war and subsequent to that event.

He was a native of the county, and lived and died within the limits of the present town of Schuyler. He was one of the few fortunate survivors of the Oriskany tragedy, and from that time held a prominent place as a militia officer in the district. He was the son of one of the Palatine families, but I have been unable to ascertain with certainty his father's name. Born after his parents came to the German Flats, his infant years were cradled in the wilderness, and his days of manhood were occupied with the stirring and dangerous events incident to two border wars, unparalleled in severity, and the often repeated destruction of crops and all means of human subsistence. Even the devastations of fatherland, which drove his ancestors to seek repose and protection in a wilderness, beyond the verge of civilization, would not exceed, in all the inflictions heaped upon the devoted heads of the German peasantry of the Palatinate, the cruelties practiced by the combined efforts of French and British loyalism, stimulating Indian ferocity with rum and bribes. These were not the times when parents could venture to send their children to their distant school-house for the purpose of instruction. The population was scattered over a broad extent of wilderness; and few, if any, had the means or the opportunity of instructing their children at home. Col. Staring's education was quite limited, but he possessed a sound and vigorous mind; he was brave, active and zealous in defeating the schemes and counteracting the efforts of the enemy, so far as his limited position would allow. He had, in the course of the war, become a leading man in his neighborhood, and attracted the attention of the royalists, who made several fruitless efforts to capture or destroy him. But the untiring vigilance of the Indian could not always be guarded against; and the Colonel, late in the fall of the year, supposed to be October, 1781, was so unfortunate as to be surrounded and captured near Fort Herkimer, with Abraham Wollever, by a party of Indians. The captors were much elated with their success, and hurried off with their prisoner into the deep recesses of the forest, where it was supposed they intended to inflict upon him a lingering death by torture.

The Colonel understood this to be their intention, and for a time, no doubt, felt some disquiet and a fervent solicitude to get rid of such uncomfortable companions. He had no relish for a stake-burning and as little desire, probably, to have his ears saluted with the music of an Indian pow-wow; and therefore contrived during the night, after he was taken, to make his escape and return to the fort after an absence of two days and two nights. He felt it was no disgrace to turn his back upon an enemy on an emergency of this kind, and thereafter avoided being placed in a like predicament.

He lived near the small stream called Staring's creek, in Schuyler, on which there was a small grist-mill burned by the French and Indians in 1757, and being rebuilt the mill was again destroyed during the revolution. He was a man of thrift and owned many broad acres of land, some of which have been retained by the descendants to a very recent date, if they are not now the owners. The reader who may be curious to see the particulars of the Colonel's capture and escape will do well to consult the Annals and Recollections of Oneida County, published by Judge Jones.

At the treaty of peace in 1783, Colonel Staring was a prominent and influential man and enjoyed the confidence of his countrymen almost without stint. He was a member of the convention from Montgomery county, called in 1788, to consider the present constitution of the United States, which had been submitted to the several states for ratification or rejection. He was an ardent friend of Governor George Clinton, an anti-federalist, and he with a large majority of the convention, when elected, were opposed to the ratification of the constitution.

It has been often asserted that he was absent on the 26th of July, 1788, when the final vote was taken on the resolution to ratify the constitution, having been detained from attendance by the management of one of the prominent advocates of the measure. This can not be true if the members composing the convention and voting on the resolution have been accurately given by Mr. William Jay, who states in his life of John Jay (vol. I, p. 266), there were fifty-seven members in all elected, and this was the number besides the president, Gov. George Clinton, which voted on the resolution, there being a majority of three in favor of it.

Mr. Hammond (vol. I, page 21 of his Political History), thinks Mr. Jay's statement incorrect. He sets down the whole number of members elected to the convention at sixty-seven, consequently there must have been nine absentees on the final vote. Ten states had ratified the constitution when the final vote was taken in the New York convention. The assent of nine only was required to give the constitution effect. The ratification by New Hampshire on the 21st of June, 1788, she being the ninth state, was not known at Poughkeepsie where the convention was in session, until some time in July. The news from Virginia which ratified on the 26th of June, reached the New York convention in all probability before the 26th of July. This changed the whole aspect of the controversy going on in the convention, and must have placed Governor Clinton and the majority in a very embarrassing position. By a rejection New York would have seceded from the confederacy, and being then one of the smaller states her condition in that case must have excited the most intense apprehensions. This was felt and expressed by some of the leading and influential members of the majority, who gave the resolution such form of expression as they hoped would quiet the public and still preserve to the state her place as a member of the union.

Indulging somewhat in speculation, I can not refrain from saying, if Mr. Hammond's account of the whole number elected be right, it is fair to presume that the nine absentees were anti-federalists, unless they were kept away by some other cause than voluntary absence.

There is no doubt the Colonel was a great admirer of good horses, desired to possess those of the best blood and most improved breed, and if he did loiter a little from his place in the convention to indulge his fancy in examining Baron Steuben's stud, his vote could not have defeated the ratifying resolution had he been present. If we may now judge him by all the characteristics of his life he was the last man in the convention to swerve in the least from opinions once formed.

His friend, Governor George Clinton, was reelected in 1789, but his adherents were defeated in every direction, showing that the Governor had a strong hold in the confidence and affections of the people, and could stand up against the influence of a powerful party at home backed by all the influence of the general government, then directed by Alexander Hamilton.

Upon the organization of this county in 1791, Colonel Staring was appointed first judge of the court of common pleas, by Governor Clinton, which office he held many years. By the constitution of 1777, first judges of counties held their places during good behavior and until sixty years old. The selection of laymen for the bench at that early day in the history of the state was not unfrequent, and especially for the courts of common pleas, and even one of the justices of the supreme court organized soon after the adoption of the constitution, was not a lawyer. I allude to John Sloss Hobart, who held the office of United States senator, from this state, from January to May 1798.

Many amusing and curious anecdotes are still remembered and repeated of Judge Staring's mode of administering justice during his judicial career. He was an honest, straightforward man, but he entertained very peculiar notions of his powers and duties as a judge. Some of his decisions while on the bench were considered by the lawyers rather in the light of judicial novelties, than as chiming in exactly with common law precedents. The country was new, however, and the demands of justice comparatively small. He no doubt performed the duties of his station, notwithstanding his limited knowledge of legal principles and restricted elementary education, with quite as much success, and with as much satisfaction to the suitors and the public as many have done who filled like stations, at far later periods in the history of our country.

The story of the *Yankee Pass*, the fame of which had reached the farthest bounds of New England more than forty years ago, and which I heard repeated west of the Mississippi river in 1819, is no doubt familiar to most of the people in the county, and particularly to those of German extraction. I have been frequently told the whole story was fabulous, and got up to amuse our primitive fathers of the valley at the expense of the judge, or by some one envious of his promotion to such honors; for it must be remembered that no longer ago than the close of the last century the county was not exempt from party strife, nor destitute of men who felt themselves competent to fill any office in it within the gift of the people or government. Stripped of all embellishment, the story, as told, has this extent and no other. One Sunday morning the judge saw a man, on horseback, coming along the highway from the west, and presuming that no one would venture openly to violate the laws of the state, unless justified by the exceptions named in the statute, he asked the man to stop, and seeing he was a stranger, inquired of him reasons why he was thus disregarding his duty and the requirements of the law. The stranger, who is reported to have been a New England Yankee, did not excuse his conduct to the judge's satisfaction, and declining to stop over until the next day, the latter exacted the payment of the fine of six

York shillings imposed by the statute, for the infringement of this branch of it.

After paying his fine, the traveler asked the judge to give him a certificate to that effect, urging the necessity of it to protect him against being again called to account by some other magistrate. The judge had no doubt heard of dispensations and indulgences from the lips of his parents. He thought the request reasonable, and told the traveler to write one and he would sign it. This was done, and the stranger proceeded on his journey eastward. Some few months after this occurrence, the judge having occasion to visit the Messrs. Kanes, merchants, at Canajoharie, on matters of business, was requested by them to pay an order of twenty-five dollars which he had several months before drawn on them, as appeared from the date. It is said he was much surprised by this demand made upon his purse, and at first denied having given the order, but finding the signature to be his handwriting, and making particular inquiries in respect to the presentation of the order and the individual who brought it to the store, he came to the conclusion that the paper presented to him for payment was no other than the one he had signed allowing the traveler to continue his journey on Sunday, after paying his fine. It was then called the *Yankee Pass*, from a supposition that no one except a native of New England had the cunning and audacity to practice so keen and grave a joke.

The act to prevent immorality, in force at that time, contained several exceptions, and among them was one allowing any one to travel on Sunday twenty miles to attend public worship, and this fact was quite as likely to be known to the traveler as some others he was no doubt quite familiar with. He must have known Judge Staring and the Kanes, and was well enough acquainted in the Mohawk valley, and with the standing and business occupation of its inhabitants, to know that the judge's order on the Messrs. Kanes would be honored at sight, or he would not have attempted the cheat; and, besides, it was necessary for him, to prevent detection, to make the order payable as far distant as practicable from the judge's residence.

I do not make these suggestions from any disposition whatever, to shift the paternity of this joke from the Yankee traveler, if he was one, on to the shoulders of any other person, not claiming nativity in the far famed land of Yankeedom.

From whatever nation this individual may have claimed descent, foreign to the Mohawk Germans, he had been long enough a denizen to become quite naturalized, and familiar not only with the names of the principal inhabitants of the valley, but with the pecuniary standing of some of them. He knew that Judge Staring had dealings with the Kanes, and hence believed the order would be paid when presented, or we must award him the palm of being the most accomplished *guesser* that ever emigrated from the land of wooden nutmegs and bass-wood hams.

I have indulged somewhat in these speculations on the assumption that the story was founded in fact, and to give place to a new version as to the origin of this affair, which excuses the Yankee from being the projector, although it leaves him under the serious imputation of being what the law terms a *particeps criminis.*

The new version is this: One of the judge's sons had become enamored with a fair, blue eyed daughter of one of his father's neighbors, and had resolved, with her consent of course, to make her his *frau*, but found himself rather *short*, as the phrase now is, of the means to carry out the object of his desires in a manner befitting his standing and position as son of the first judge of the common pleas, who was a wealthy farmer, and a gentleman of standing and influence in the county. There may have been some Guelf and Ghibelline feud existing between the heads of the two families, that prevented the early accomplishment of the young man's wishes. At any rate, whatever may have been the cause therefor, the judge, it seems, kept the purse strings tied rather too tight on this occasion, and the son was thrown on his own resources to devise the *ways* of obtaining the needful to celebrate his intended marriage. The young man opened his mind to an Anglo-Saxon friend, relying upon his inventive genius to aid him in carrying out a suggested plan of relief. The son knew his father's credit was good for any amount he would give his name for, and that he had an open account with the Kanes; he knew his father's scrupulous regard for the maintenance of the laws to the very letter, and what he would do in case he found a man traveling on Sunday. The plan was matured and the thing was done. The judge's genuine signature was obtained to the celebrated Yankee Pass, the fame of which is known over this broad land. Necessity was in this case the mother of a successful invention, which has been unfairly attributed to the genius, or cunning contrivance of an individual who was supposed to belong to a peculiar American stock.

This relation was obtained from a source which I know is respectable, and I was assured that the origin of the story and the pass was based on the statements now given. Aside from the facts showing, as I think pretty strongly, that the intention of getting the judge's name to a paper of this kind was not prompted at the moment, and that the party who got it in the manner described, was quite familiar with all the peculiarities of the man he was dealing with, although he may have been wholly unknown to the judge; there is an additional fact worthy of some consideration in balancing probabilities.

The Messrs. Kanes were reported upright, fair dealers as merchants, but were as fond of jokes as they were anxious to sell goods at a large profit to their German customers, and it is not likely, even if they knew the fact in respect to the origin of the order and the purposes to which its avails were to be applied, they would divulge any secrets of that sort, while they would by no means aid a stranger to cheat an old and valued friend and customer.

Judge Staring lived to an advanced age, died in the town

of Schuyler, leaving male and female descendants. He married a daughter of Johan Jurgh Kast, and obtained by purchase and inheritance the title to about six hundred acres of the Kast patent which he left to his children.

I should have noticed in the proper place that one of Judge Staring's children, a little girl about ten years old, was carried off by the Indians during the war. She had gone to one of the judge's relatives near Fort Herkimer, where she could be taken for security, in case of an attack upon the settlements. The woman in whose charge the child was left permitted her to go into the field near the house, where she was seized in a stealthy manner and borne into captivity. The judge was not very forbearing towards his relation for this careless act, as he no doubt fully anticipated the little girl's fate in case her name and parentage should be found out; she was however recovered after the war closed.

The Temouth Family.

The name is written Demot and Dimouth in the Palatine records. Those who were not used to the German method of spelling and pronunciation often wrote the name Damewood. I have found the name printed Damoth and Demuth. John Jost parted with the lot granted him at Little Falls before the revolution, and probably before 1757, as no traces of the family can now be found near that place. The Demuths were in the vicinity of Herkimer during the revolutionary war. One of them moved to Deerfield, Oneida county, before the commencement of hostilities, but that settlement being broken up by the enemy he escaped with his family and returned to the German Flats for greater security. Captain Demuth was with John Adam Helmer in the difficult and dangerous service of carrying a message from General Herkimer to Colonel Ganesvoort during the siege at Fort Schuyler. He also was sent by the committee of safety to Albany with an account of the transaction at

Oriskany and Fort Schuyler in company with Helmer. As Demuth was an officer at this time and Helmer was not, it appears to me undue prominence has been given to the latter by Colonel Stone in the matter of carrying the message to Fort Schuyler, in which Capt. Demuth's name is not mentioned at all, but Helmer is shown to be the principal man.

General Herkimer would not have been guilty of so indelicate an act towards an officer as to make a private his prominent agent in carrying an important dispatch to the commanding officer of the beleagured fort, nor could an officer consent to execute a military service under such circumstances. I make this correction not to disparage Helmer in any way, but in justice to the memory of a man equally devoted with him to the cause of humanity and the just rights of his country. The records of our government sufficiently testify that Capt. Demuth's services were duly appreciated by a grateful people.

Some of the Demuth family emigrated to Onondaga after the close of war with the Realls, where their descendants now reside. There are but very few people of this name, if any, now living in the county. There was a George Damewood who lived at one period during the revolution on the north side of the Mohawk river between Little Falls and West Canada creek.

Since writing out the above I have been informed that two small boys of this family were carried into captivity by the Indians during the war. They were taken at the river bank near Fort Herkimer. At the restoration of peace one of them returned to his family and remained with them, but the other having been adopted into the family of an Onondaga chief, had become so much attached to Indian customs and habits that he could not be induced to quit his savage roaming life. When grown up to manhood he would often visit his relatives who lived not far from the Onondaga reservation and remain with them over night, but he would not on any occasion sleep upon a bed. A blanket and the floor yielded all the sleeping luxuries he required or would indulge in, and it was not often he could be induced to prolong his visit longer than one night. He spoke the English, German and Indian very well, and was often very useful in promoting a friendly intercourse between the whites and Indians.

The Welleven Family, or Wolleavers.

This name is found written Wolleben and Wohleben in the statement of the heads of Palatine families on the west side of the Hudson river in 1710.

Nicholas W., the patentee in Burnetsfield, who was also one of the patentees in Staley's 1st and 2d tracts, died in 1773, leaving six sons, Henry, Peter, Richard, John, Abraham and Jacob; and six daughters, Catharine the wife of Frederick Shoemaker, Mary Sophia the wife of Peter Flagg, Elizabeth who married with Frederick Schute, Lany who married with Frederick Bellinger, and Hannah the wife of John Emgie or Empie. Empie was a tory and went to Canada with his family. Richard, John, Peter and Abraham were in the Oriskany battle; the two former were killed and the two latter returned, Peter slightly wounded. Nicholas Wollever, from whom I had this account of the family, stated he was the son of Peter, and was born August 1st, 1769, and is now nearly 85 years old; says his father was born March 9th, 1732, and died November 17th, 1829, having attained the age of 97 years and 8 months; that his father Peter was taken prisoner during the French war in 1757, and was sent to England for exchange. He was also in the mill at Little Falls when it was attacked and burned by a party of the enemy, which my informant assured me was in June, 1782, and made his escape.

Peter Wollever lived on the farm in Manheim, since known as the Christy place, which he hired of Joseph Brant, the Mohawk chief; and Brant sent word to him, in 1777, that he would come and tomahawk him, if he did not leave the farm immediately. Peter then moved to Fort Herkimer with his family, in the fall of 1777, after the Oriskany battle; where he remained until the close of the war. My informant stated, his father once borrowed money of Gen. Herkimer, to pay the rent to Brant. He had three sons, who attained the age of manhood, Nicholas, John and Henry. His daughters were, Elizabeth, wife of Frederick Shoemaker; Catharine, the wife of Garret Van Slyke, whose father John Van Slyke, was killed on Fink's Flats, during the war; Susan, the wife of Jacob Edick; Hannah, who married a Mr. Furman; Mary, now living, who married a Mr. White and Eva, the wife of Stanton Fox.

Abraham Wollever, one of the patentee's sons, was taken prisoner, in October, 1781, with Henry Staring near Fort Herkimer; soon after he was taken, he was knocked down, tomahawked, scalped by his captors and left; the enemy with their other prisoner, Staring, pursuing their course towards Oneida. Abraham survived this horrid treatment, was out two nights, his feet having been very much frozen, and near sunset of the third day after his capture, he was brought to the fort. He lived a number of years after this event, to recount the story of his sufferings. He was discovered by a party from the fort, who had gone out after horses, which had strayed away. When first seen, he was trying to mount one of the horses, and being covered with blood was taken for an Indian, and would have been killed by his friends, if he had not clung so close to the horse, that they could not shoot him without killing the animal. Jacob Wollever, the youngest son of the patentee, shot the tory or Indian who killed old Mr. Hess. This family have a tradition that their ancestor came into this county directly from Schoharie. This tradition is supported by the fact, that the name is found among those Palatines who were seated on the west side of the Hudson, from whence the first German settlers of Schoharie came. This name is now nearly extinct in the county.

The Wever (or Weaver) Family.

This name is written on the Livingston manor lists, Weber and Webber. Jacob and Nicholas were volunteers in the Montreal expedition, repeatedly mentioned in other parts of this chapter. Peter Ja. Weaver, was an ensign in 1775, in the 4th battalion of the Tryon county militia. Some of the family settled in Deerfield, Oneida county, in 1773, and after the war, other members of the family, from Herkimer, fixed themselves at that place. George I. Weaver was taken prisoner during the war, and was detained in captivity about two years, and some part of the time he suffered very much by the inhuman treatment of his captors. Four hundred acres of land were assigned to this family, two hundred on the north, and two hundred on the south side of the river. A portion of these lands is still possessed by the descendants of the patentees.

Jacob G. Weaver, whether of the same family or not, I am unable to state, was cotemporary with John Jacob Astor, and at an early period of our history, was engaged in the fur trade, by which he accumulated a large estate, which he left to be inherited by three daughters. He was shrewd and active in the prime of life. He died at Herkimer, Nov. 28th, 1820, aged 79 years.

CHAPTER IX.

County when Erected — Statute Boundaries in 1791 — Counties Erected from Herkimer — Winfield — Salisbury — Manheim — Danube — First Counties in the State — Montgomery — List of Patents to Lands in the County — Colonial and Crown Grants Confirmed — Attainder Act of 1779 — Forfeited Estates to be Sold — Bills of Credit — Commissioners of Forfeitures — Lots in Royal Grant Sold — Indian Children — Lots in Jerseyfield Sold — in Glen's Purchase — Bayard's Patent — Guy Johnson Tract — Johan Joost Herkimer — Area of the County — Actual Boundaries — Rivers, Streams, and Lakes — Face of the Country — its Soil, Produce, Minerals, Manufactures, Roads, Canals, and Turnpikes — Newspaper Press of the County — Colleges and Academies — Religious Aspects — Medical Society — Poor-House Establishment — Agricultural Society.

The county was erected on the 16th of February, 1791, from the county of Montgomery, formerly Tryon, and embraced all that portion of the state lying west of its eastern boundaries, except the counties of Otsego and Tioga, which were erected at the same time, and extending to the eastern boundaries of Ontario county, erected January 27th, 1789, and covered, according to the statute designation, all the territory bounded north by Lake Ontario, the River St. Lawrence, and the north bounds of the state; easterly by the counties of Clinton, Washington, and Saratoga, as they then were; southerly by the counties of Montgomery, Otsego, and Tioga. These boundaries were not accurate, even at that time; the true boundaries of the county, as it now is, will be stated hereafter. Onondaga county was set off from Herkimer in 1794; Oneida in 1798; Chenango, from Herkimer and Tioga, in 1798; Cayuga, from Onondaga, in 1799; Cortland, from the same, in 1808; St. Lawrence, from Oneida, in 1802; Jefferson and Lewis, from the same, in 1805; Madison, from Chenango, in 1806; Seneca, from Cayuga, in 1804; Oswego, from parts of Oneida and Onondaga, in 1816; Tompkins, from Seneca and Cayuga, in 1817; and Wayne, from Seneca and Ontario, in 1823. There were only fourteen counties in the state when Herkimer was set-off; and the three then created, Otsego, Tioga and Herkimer, made the number seventeen. There are now eleven whole counties, and parts of two others, embraced in the territory first set off, as Herkimer.

In 1816, parts of the towns of Richfield and Plainfield, in the county of Otsego, were with a portion of Litchfield, in Herkimer county, erected into a new town, by the name of Winfield, and attached to Herkimer county.

In 1817, the towns of Salisbury and Manheim, and all that part of Minden, Montgomery county, now comprised in Danube and Stark, were annexed to the county of Herkimer.

The first counties created, by law, in this state, then a colony, were Albany, New York, Dutchess, Kings, Orange Queens, Richmond, Suffolk, Ulster and Westchester, November 1st, 1683. Albany took its present name in 1664. Montgomery was created, by law, as a county, March 12, 1772, by the name of Tryon, which was altered April 2d, 1784 for reasons well understood by readers of our revolutionary history.

The present county comprises within its limits the following tracts, and parts of tracts of lands granted by the crown, before the revolution, and by the state, since the treaty of 1783.

This mark (*) denotes that the patents are partly situated in Herkimer, and partly in adjoining counties.

Names of Patents or Tracts.	Date.	No. of acres.	Names of Original Patentees.
Adgate's Tract,*	1798	43,907	Mathew Adgate,
Bayard's Patent,*	1771	50,000	William Bayard, Alexander Ellis, and fifty-three others,
Brown's (John) Tract,*	1792	......	A part of 1,920,000 acres granted to Alexander Macomb,
Burnetsfield Patent,	1725	9,400	Johan Joost Petri, and ninety-three others,
Colden's (C.) Patent,	1738	3,000	Cadwallader Colden the younger, and Coenradt Ryghtmeyer,
Cosby's Manor,*	1734	22,000	Joseph Worrell, William Cosby, and nine others,
Colden's (A.) Patent,	1761	4,000	Alexander Colden, and three others,
Frank (Conrad) & Co's Patent,	1765	5,000	Coenradt Frank, and five others,
Fall-Hill Patent,	1752	2,324	Johan Joost and Hendrik Herchkeimer,
Glen's Purchase,	1739	25,076	
Hommedieu's (L) Patent,	1786	4,000	Ezra L'Hommedieu and Nathaniel Platt,
Henderson's Patent,*	1739	6,000	James Henderson, and two others,
Hasenclever's Patent,	1769	18,000	Peter Hasenclever, and seventeen others,
Johnson's (Guy) Patent,	1765	2,000	Guy Johnson. Forfeited by attainder of G. J.
Jerseyfield Patent,*	1770	94,000	Henry Glen, Alexander Ellis, and ninety-two others,
Kass's Patent,	1724	1,100	Johan Jurgh Kass, and his children,
Lindsay's Patent,	1730	3,000	John Lindsay and Philip Livingston,
Livingston's Patent,*	1762	20,000	Philip Livingston, and nineteen others,
Lispenard's Patent,*	1770	9,200	Leonard Lispenard and thirteen others,
Lansing's Patent,*	1753	6,000	Jacob and Abraham Lansing, and Jacob Glen,
McComb's Purchase,*	1792	......	Alexander Macomb,
McNeil's Patent,	1761	4,000	John McNeil, and three others,
Matchin's Patent,*	1786	1,600	Thomas Matchin,
Nobleborough Tract,*	1787	40,960	Arthur Noble,
Moose River Tract,*	....	......	Owned by the state, except 13,080 granted in 1847 to Anson Blake,
Petrie's Purchase,	1740	6,000	John Jost Petrie, and two others,
Royal Grant,	....	......	Sir William Johnson,
Remsenburgh Patent,*	1787	48,000	Henry Remsen, and three others,
Snell and Timmerman's Patent,	1755	3,600	Jacob Timberman, and Johan Joost Schnell,
Staley's 1st and 2d Tract,	1755	34,000	Rudolph Staley, Johan Jost Herchkeimer, Jr., Nicholas Herchkeimer, and fifteen others,
Schuyler's Patent,	1755	43,000	Abraham Lynsen, and twenty-one others,
Totten and Crossfield Patent,*			
Vrooman's Patent,*	1790	9,760	Isaac Vrooman,
do	1786	4,000	do
do	1790	433	do

Names of Patents or Tracts.	Date.	No. of acres.	Names of Original Patentees.
Van Driesen, Peter, ...	1737	1,000	Petrus Van Driessen,
Van Driesen, John, ...	1786	428	Johan Van Driessen,
Van Horn's Patent,*	1731	8,000	Abraham Van Horne, and three others,
Vaughn's Patent, ...	1770	8,000	John Vaughn and seven others,
Watson's James Tract,*	1792	......	A part of Macomb's purchase,
Winne's Patent, ...	1741	2,000	Peter Winne,
Walton's Patent, ...	1768	12,000	William Walton, Jr., and eleven others,
Young's Patent,*	1752	14,000	Theobald Young, and ten others.

The Indian title to Glen's purchase, was extinguished in 1734. The whole tract was subdivided into thirty-nine large lots, of unequal quantities. In 1738 *five* of these lots were granted to Patrick McClaughry and Andrew McDowell, and *eight* to James DeLancey, John Lindsay, and Abraham Glen. In 1739 *three* were granted to Lendert Helmer, *two* to Jacob Glen, *three* to Archibald Kennedy, *three* to John Schuyler, Jr., *three* to Arent Brant, and *three* to Philip Schuyler. In 1761 *three* were granted to Samuel Auchmuty, *three* to William Mitchell, and *three* to William Ogilvie.

The patent for the royal grant was never recorded in this state. The grant was made by the king in council, and not by the colonial authorities, consequently the date and number of acres can not be given from any entries in the Secretary's office at Albany.

The Guy Johnson tract was conveyed by Jeremiah Van Rensselaer, Jacob G. Klock, and Henry Oathoudt, commissioners of forfeitures of the western district of New York, to Benjamin Tallmadge, major in the army of the United States, June 7th, 1784, and by Tallmadge to Caleb Brewster, July 9th, 1794.

The above abstract shows that the title to most of the lands in the county, with the exception of those in the extreme northern part, were granted by the crown before the commencement of the revolutionary struggle, and those grants were recognized as valid by the constitution of 1777. But although declared valid by the fundamental law of the state, this declaration was in effect nothing more than an inhibition upon the legislative power of the state to resume these grants at pleasure. The state was left free to protect itself against the treasonable acts or hostile aggressions of any of the parties holding under these grants. This power was exercised by the legislature and carried into effect to some extent in this county, and this makes it expedient to give that subject a little examination.

The attainder act of 1779 embraced fifty-nine persons, three of whom were married females, and they were also declared convicted and attainted with their husbands of offenses against the act. It had been the practice under the colonial government to include females in the grants by the crown, even when the patents were issued to parties for lands not intended for immediate settlement. At this day a proceeding of this kind against a married lady would seem harsh, discourteous and ungallant. The particular reasons, if any existed, which induced the legislature to adopt a measure so stringent, is not disclosed in the act, and there were none probably which marked them as special objects for confiscation and banishment, except the fact that they were seized in their own rights of large landed estates within the colony, and their husbands had been prominent and influential partisans in the cause of the crown, and continued their active and devoted adhesion to the king to the date of the act. It was expedient to disarm such persons of all the powers of mischief which wealth and appliances would bestow, as well as to punish past and future aggressions against the state; and besides, this was but a slight departure from the British maxim that an attaint of blood cut off the inheritance.

The legislature passed an act on the 12th of May, 1784, directing the speedy sale of confiscated and forfeited estates, requiring the proceeds to be applied to the sinking and discharging the public securities, created for the purpose of carrying on the war. This was the first step taken to dispose of these estates and the functions of the commissioners ceased in 1788. The act of 1784, designated the kind of money and certificates or bills of credit issued by the state, which might be received in payment for lands sold; and one class of bills were receivable at the rate of one dollar in silver for every one hundred aud twenty nominal dollars of such bills; others at the rate of one dollar in silver for every forty of the nominal dollars specified in the certificates, and a certain class of warrants payable in wheat were receiveable at the rate of one silver dollar for every bushel of wheat expressed therein.

Most of these certificates and bills had not been issued, at the date of the act, over four years, and the commissioners of forfeitures were directed not to receive in the aggregate over five millions of dollars in these bills and certificates for lands sold by them under the act. A large nominal sum of public debt was by this process extinguished with a small amount of actual cash, or its equivalent. This was a heavy depreciation of public securities, and was severely felt by the people, who were compelled to take them from the government. The purchasers of the public domain, however, were in no respect losers by the operation. Having purchased these securities at the current specie market price, or at the sum fixed by the continental scale of depreciation, they exchanged them in most instances for some of the best lands in the state, at a price per acre a little more than nominal, and thus accumulated large fortunes, which have been or soon will be wasted by their posterity. These purchasers hazarded nothing; the state warranted the title against all claims, and assumed to pay the debts of any person owning the forfeited estate which existed prior to 9th of July, 1776, and were due to an inhabitant of this state on that day, who had not been attainted or convicted of adhering to the public enemy during the war.

The commissioners of forfeitures of the western district of the state, sold and deeded between September, 1784 and September, 1788, ninety-three lots in the 1st allotment of the royal grant; ninety-one in the second allotment; one hundred and thirty in the 3d allotment; and one hundred and thirty-seven in the fourth allotment.

This proceeding on the part of the state was founded on the attainder of Sir John Johnson, by the act of 1779.

The map made by Lawrence Vrooman, in 1797, shows that Sir William gave by his will to six of his natural children by Molly Brant or Brandt, fifteen thousand acres of this grant, as follows: To Margaret, 2000 acres; George, 3000;

Mary, 2000; Susan, 3000; Ann, 3000; Brandt, 1000; and to William, 1000 acres. The portion of this tract thus devised adjoins the East Canada creek, and is in the present towns of Manheim and Salisbury.

The lots as numbered on the map are, 166 in the 1st allotment; 102 in the second; 136 in the third; and 143 in the fourth. These are the highest numbers, but in several instances intervening numbers below are not found.

A specific half of eighteen lots in Jerseyfield patent, was also sold and deeded by the commissioners of forfeitures, within the periods above mentioned. The original patentees of this large tract were mostly of the Dutch extraction, not German, and residents in Albany, Schenectady and the lower Mohawk valley. None of these names appear in the attainder act of 1779. Some party known to be obnoxious to the penalties of the act, must have been proceeded against by indictment for treason against the state, and the lands declared forfeited on inquisition found. The whole of five lots and a specified half of four others in Livingston's patent was also sold and conveyed by the commissioners. Peter Du Bois, who was attainted by the act of October 22d, 1779, was one of the patentees of this grant, and the sales probably covered his interest, or what remained of it, in the whole patent.

One lot, No. 52, Bayard's patent, was also sold by the commissioners, under the attainder of some of the patentees.

A part of Glen's purchase seems to have been owned by some one obnoxious to the law attainder. James De Lancey was one of the three joint patentees of several lots in this purchase. He was attainted by the act of 1779. Six small lots in that tract were sold and deeded for £1095, New York currency, on the 27th August, 1788, to replenish an exhausted treasury. James Caldwell purchased five of the lots and Michael Myers one of them. Johan Jurgh Kast's little patent of eleven hundred acres in Schuyler, contributed five hundred dollars to pay war expenses. One lot in that patent seems to have been sold to make compensation for treason

127.

400
0 A

114.
0 A
300

107.
290
Ac

94.
220

lusan

00 A

against the state. Surely none of the descendants of that sturdy old Palatine could have been recreant to his country and a traitor to humanity.

Two of the Bayards, grantees in the patent of that name, were attainted by the act of 1779, and if they had not then disposed of their interest, the commissioners of forfeitures no doubt gave their attention to a subject of so much importance, and a portion of that patent is held under a title from them.

Diligent search and examination has been made in the proper quarter to find some evidence of grants under the authority of the state, of the John Joost Herkermer's property, but without success.

Some part of the Herkimer property came into the hands of Alexander Ellice, soon after the revolution. The precise time has not been ascertained by the writer, nor has he been able to lay his hand upon any papers showing the title to have come from the state. This, however, must be so, for Mr. Ellice, being a British subject, would not have been allowed to hold forfeited lands except by a grant from the state.

In respect to that part of the royal grant, devised by Sir William to his Indian children, the sale by the commissioners could not be sustained, and consequently was abandoned in regard to some of them, who had not committed any overt act of treason or offense against the statute. One of these children, however, did bear arms against the colonies, and may have been proceeded against under the attainder act, by indictment. The present titles of a portion of the grant are therefore derived from Sir William's will, through his Indian children, but all the remainder, which passed to Sir John Johnson, as heir at law, is held under the state by virtue of his attainder.

The county covers an area of 1370 square miles, or 887,000 acres, and is bounded on the north by the county of St Lawrence, on the east by the counties of Hamilton, Fulton and Montgomery, on the south by the county of Otsego, and on the west by the counties of Oneida and Lewis. It lies in the central part of the state, between 42 degrees and 50 minutes, and 44 degrees and 5 minutes north latitude, and 1 degree and 43 minutes, and 2 degrees and 14 minutes east longitude from the city of Washington; and is 75 miles long from north to south, and about 26 miles in width from east to west.

Rivers, Streams and Lakes.

The Mohawk river runs through the southerly part of the county from the west, on an easterly course, and is the most considerable stream of water in it. The East Canada creek, or kill, as formerly called, takes its rise in Hamilton county and discharges itself into the Mohawk river from the north, and forms the eastern boundary line from the river to the northeast corner of the royal grant.

The sources of the West Canada creek, or kill, called by the Indians Tueghtaghrarow, are traced to the northerly part of the county, and into the westerly part of Hamilton, running a southwesterly course to the southwest corner of Matchin's patent, and thence southerly and easterly to the northwest corner of Walton's patent, it forms the boundary line between Herkimer and Oneida counties. It empties into the Mohawk river from the north, near the village of Herkimer.

The Moose, Black and Beaver rivers, which flow into Lake Ontario, have their sources in the north part of the county, fed by numerous lakes and ponds of pure water, none of which, however, are of any commercial note, but are now often visited by the *amateur* angler and hunter, as they formerly were by the veteran aboriginal of the forest, and sad is the fate of him who is not proof against the assaults of the mosquito and midge. The bite of these insects is very annoying and poisonous to many of the whites. There are two small lakes or bodies of water in the south part of the town of Warren, called the Little Lakes, but there are no others of note on the south side of the Mohawk.

The Nowadaga creek, in the town of Danube, which flows north into the Mohawk river; the Otsquaga creek, that drains the town of Stark, and the head waters of the Unadilla and Susquehanna rivers take their rise in the towns of Columbia, Warren, Litchfield and Winfield, and flow south, are the only streams which are worthy of note on the south side of the Mohawk. On the north side, besides those already noticed, are several tributaries of the Mohawk and East and West Canada creeks, affording eligible sites and water power for mills and manufactories, improved to a limited extent.

Face of the Country.

The surface is much diversified, and it may properly be called "a hill country," but it is not mountainous, as it has been sometimes asserted. The Adirondack range of elevated lands enters the county on the northeast from Hamilton and extends to the Mohawk at Little Falls, where it is broken through by the river; thence the same range extends southwesterly in the southern part of the county, forming a dividing ridge for the waters running south and those that flow into the Mohawk river. The settlements now extend about thirty miles north of the Mohawk and the most elevated points of land on the north and south sides of the river, are productive of grass, Indian corn, and coarse grains. These remarks apply particularly to the settled parts of the county. The ranges of upland are quite elevated, in some places being eight hundred feet above the waters of the river. The Ostrander hill, south of Newville in the town of Danube, the hill east of Fairfield academy, and an elevated plat in Russia, observable in a clear day, on the road from Little Falls to Middleville, fourteen miles distant in a northerly direction up the valley of the West Canada creek, are prominent points of this description, and still these elevations are not precipitous or inapproachable.

The northern part of the county, remaining in forests, is elevated, but not more broken than the southern portions under cultivation, and along the valleys of the Mohawk and the East and West Canada creeks.

SOIL.

This is somewhat various, depending upon localities. Sandy and argillaceous loams, based on limestone, sandstone and primitive granite gneiss, clay and calcareous loam, calcareous and sandy loam, calcareous loam, sandy and clay loam, are the general characteristics of the uplands. Rich alluvial flats are found in the Mohawk valley, and quite as productive in grains of various descriptions, as any of the best lands in the state. The alluvial flats of the smaller streams are also rich and productive. The soil north of the royal grant is light and sandy, producing fair summer crops, and is pretty well adapted to grazing.

PRODUCTIONS.

Before the war of 1812, and as recent as 1820, the principal productions of this county were wheat, corn, rye, barley, peas, beans, oats, hay and potatoes; wheat and barley forming the chief articles of export to the Albany market; of corn, oats, peas and rye, there was some surplus, and also of fat cattle and hogs. The Mohawk valley and the Schoharie were once the granaries of the Albany and New York markets, even when "York flour" had attained some celebrity in New England, and was preferred there to the southern article. The opening of the Erie canal in 1825, brought a rival into market, against which it was useless to contend—Western New York and the country on the south shores of Lake Erie, where the harvests were gathered nearly two weeks earlier than in Oneida, Herkimer and Montgomery, and the crops in bulk would be in market before the grain growers in those counties had begun their wheat harvests. If there was no difference in the quality of the article produced, the difference in the price of land in western New York, Pennsylvania and Ohio, and that along the Mohawk valley and in the county, and the disparity in the quantity of the yield per annum, made grain-growing an onerous and unprofitable business to the Herkimer county farmer.

During the period of ten years, from 1820 to 1830, agriculture was at a low ebb in the county. Year after year the insect destroyed all the fields of wheat, and year after year the toil-wearied farmer found himself without the means of paying even his small debts, much less to grapple with bonds, mortgages and interest, given to secure the purchase money of his lands.

In 1820, if all the personal or movable property in the county had been sold at a fair appraisal, it would not have produced sufficient means to pay the domestic debt of the county, and probably not more than half of it. But the recuperative energies of the American can not be borne down even by formidable obstacles, nor can "his hopeful and go-ahead resolution" be "crushed out." As early as 1825, some few of our farmers began to think seriously of "changing their mode of husbandry." They abandoned grain growing and turned their attention to grazing, and now the dairy house, and not the granary, is the great point of attraction. Butter, cheese and fat cattle now constitute the staple of the agricultural exports from the county. At one period, Herkimer county cheese stood the first in the market, and it has not lost any of its qualities, but other localities have no doubt improved their productions, still the supply hardly keeps pace with the demand, so that prices do not recede but advance moderately. The business has been quite remunerative for years past to those who bought lands as prices ranged about ten years since. Formerly, the most considerable portion of cheese made was taken to market in the fall of the year; the shipments by canal commencing in September and continuing until the close of navigation, or until all the early made cheese was sent off, and that made late was kept over the winter and sent forward in the spring. But since the rail roads have carried freight, the article is now sent to market as soon as it becomes sufficiently cured to bear transportation in boxes. The raising of broom-corn and the cultivation of the hop has lately attracted attention, and are now being produced to some extent, and on some soils it will no doubt be found quite as profitable as raising grain or devoting the lands to grazing. The soil of the royal grant is said to possess, in an extraordinary degree, the quality of yielding sweet fall pasturage even until covered with snow.

Sawed lumber from the North woods is yet produced in moderate quantities and forms an article of export; and since the construction of plank roads in that direction this business has somewhat increased, and will continue to afford employment for the hardy pioneer lumberman for some years to come.

At no period within forty years have the agricultural interests of the county been as prosperous and healthful as at present, and the domestic or home indebtedness so small; and with the balance of trade largely in its favor, the future prospects of its people are most cheering and hopeful. In the article of breadstuffs, and particularly flour, the consumption greatly exceeds the production, and very considerable quantities of western flour and wheat are annually brought into the county for home use. Wheat is not raised in any quantity; the home supply of corn, oats, rye, buckwheat, potatoes and apples is equal to the consumption; and apples are sometimes exported when the crops are good and the eastern supply short.

Minerals.

Iron ore is found in large quantities in the north part of the county, and formerly in what is called Brown's tract, there were works for smelting the ore, but these have been long since abandoned. This ore is said to have been discovered in the town of Salisbury, but the quantity is not sufficient to afford any encouragement to capitalists to work it, or the quality of it is not as good as that found in other localities at much greater distance from the market, as no efforts have as yet been made to open and work the mine since its discovery. Gypsum has been obtained in small quantities in the town of Stark. Some specimens of lead ore have been found in the county, but neither lead or gypsum has yet been found in sufficient quantities to attract attention. The rock crystal, or false diamonds, were formerly found at Little Falls and at Middleville, nine miles north, on the West Canada creek, in large abundance, and more beautiful than in any other portion of the United States. They were of different sizes, and most of them beautifully clear and transparent, and exceedingly multiform in shape. Those found at Little Falls were taken from the sandstone; and those at Middleville were obtained in cavern or grotto, apparently formed by the crystallization of some mineral waters. Some specimens were found larger than a walnut, with water in the centre, and others with dark spots entirely inclosed or surrounded with clear crystal. The writer was several years ago told by a gentleman, that he took a number of these crystals, obtained at Little Falls, to London, England, and the lapidary informed him that one of them was a *real* and not a *false* diamond; and that he saw the stone submitted to the test of fire. No positive indications of coal have yet been found, and there probably will not be, as the geological formations are not characteristic of that fossil. At present the wealth of the county consists principally in its agricultural products; but we might speculate a moment, in these days of improvement and progress, and fancy the navigation of the Moose river, improved as high up as the iron region of the county, by which the products of the ore beds will be brought to market on the Black river canal.

Manufactures.

These, although not numerous, or employing large amounts of capital, when compared with some other counties in the state, or some other localities in the United States, are respectable, taken altogether, and contribute an important item to the sum of our integral prosperity and wealth.

The manufacture of leather has heretofore been successfully carried on, and several large tanneries have been erected in different parts of the county. Several extensive paper mills are in operation in the county. An extensive building is now being erected at Little Falls, by Mr. George W. Beardsley, to be used in manufacturing paper of various descriptions and qualities, from wood.

Roads, Canals, Turnpikes.

Before and during the revolutionary war, the Mohawk river was navigated by batteaux of light draught and easy transport over the carrying place at the lesser falls. At this time the main traveled road between the East and West Canada creeks, was on the south side of the river. As early as April, 1790, the legislature appropriated "one hundred pounds for the purpose of erecting a bridge across the East Canada creek, not exceeding three miles from the mouth thereof, upon the road from the Mohawk river to the royal grant."

On the 6th of April, 1793, the legislature appointed commissioners, and directed them to erect "a bridge over the East Canada creek, nearly opposite Canajoharie castle, on the public road leading from Tribes Hill to the Little Falls; the building and erecting a bridge over the West Canada creek, on the public road or highway leading from the Little Falls aforesaid, to Fort Stanwix."

The Western Inland Lock Navigation Company, was incorporated March 30th, 1792. The object of this company was to open and improve the navigation of the Mohawk river, and other streams, from the Hudson to the Seneca lake and Lake Ontario, to "encourage agriculture, promote commerce and facilitate intercourse between the citizens" of the state, as put forth in the preamble to the act. The improvements made by the company, in this county, consisted in opening a short canal in the river flats, and the construction of a lock, to avoid a rapid in the river, near old Fort Herkimer, in the town of German Flats; and the construction of the canal and locks, at Little Falls. This work was completed in 1795. The locks were first made of wood, were rebuilt of stone in 1804, and in good condition in 1825, when the Erie canal was opened. On the completion of these works, the river was navigated in a good stage of water, by the large Durham boats, between Schenectady and Lake Ontario. There was a light and commodious passenger boat on the river, in the year 1817. The trip from Utica to Schenectady was rapid and agreeable, but the return was so slow and tedious, that passengers did not incline to embrace it. The entire cost of this company's improvements was about $450,000.

The state owned $92,000 of the stock, and individuals, $140,000. The state wishing to use the waters of the Mohawk and Oswego rivers, and occupy some portion of the company's canal, for the purpose of the Erie canal, and being unable to agree with the company, on the sum to be paid, took the franchises and property of the corporation by appraisal, paying to the individual stockholders, for their interest, $91,616; the interest of the state, at the same rate of allowance, being $60,204·80. This company, it appears, sunk of capital in twenty-two years after their works at the Little Falls were completed, $298,180·20.

The next improvement in roads, which materially affected the interests of the people of the county, was the construction of the Mohawk turnpike. The charter of the Turnpike and Bridge company, was granted April 4, 1800. The road from

Schenectady to Utica, on the north side of the river, was built in an expeditious and unsubstantial manner, of the material found along the line. Although the opening of the Erie Canal, in 1825, materially affected the income of the company, by diverting transportation from the road, it was an immense thoroughfare for travel, until August, 1835, when the corporate franchises of the company and the road itself were transferred to the Utica and Schenectady rail road company, for $62,500, and the successors of the company, now own and control the turnpike, from the west bounds of the town of Herkimer, to its termination on the west bank of the river, at Schenectady. I need not say, perhaps, for the information of any inhabitant of the county, that the Erie canal traverses its territory, from west to east, on the south side of the Mohawk river, passing through the villages of Frankfort, Ilion, Mohawk and the town of Danube; nor that the New York central rail road traverses the county from east to west, on the north side of the river, passing through the town of Manheim, the villages of Little Falls and Herkimer, and part of the town of Schuyler, crossing the Mohawk, near the west bounds of the county; having five passenger and freight stations along the line in the county.

One of the most, if not the most, successful enterprises of modern times, was the the Utica and Schenectady rail road company, chartered in 1833, and now forming a part of the New York central rail road. The original capital was $2,000,000. The road was constructed, equipped for running and opened on the 1st of August, 1836, for a sum somewhat less than capital. It was a pioneer road, and the art of *chisseling* had not then been brought to its modern perfection.

On the first organization of the company, in 1833, after the distribution of the stock, Erastus Corning, John Townsend, Lewis Benedict, James Porter, of Albany; Alonzo C. Paige, of Schenectady; Tobias A. Stoutenbergh, of Montgomery; Nathaniel S. Benton, of Herkimer; Nicholas

Devereaux, Henry Seymour, Alfred Munson, Utica; James Hooker, Poughkeepsie; John Mason and Churchill C. Cambreleng, of New York, were chosen directors; James Porter was appointed secretary; Gideon Hawley, treasurer; Wm. C. Young, chief engineer; and Gideon Davidson, commissioner. The charter required that one director, at least, should be a resident of the county through which the line of the road passed. Messrs. Corning, Townsend, Paige, Devereaux, Benton and Hooker, of the first board chosen, remained in the direction twenty years, and until the consolidation took place, May 17th, 1853. Mr. Young was appointed engineer and general superintendent after the road was finished, and held that highly responsible place until 1851, when he resigned, went on to the Hudson river road, and was succeeded by Mr. Chauncey Vibbard, who had been several years an efficient aid to Mr. Young. Mr. Vibbard is now the general superintendent of the New York central company. It is not too much, nor out of place here, to say, that Mr. Young was a most valuable and efficient officer. There were but few men in this country at that time, who could have taken the charge and active superintendence of an entirely new enterprise, organized and arranged the running of the trains, selected competent and suitable agents to aid him, with better or more complete success than he did. He lived on the road for years, until order and exactitude pervaded the whole line, and at every station, and in every department of service. But it may be said, he did not and could not do all this work alone and single handed. This is true; he had active, able and vigilant assistants on the line, as local superintendents; and Maj. Zenas C. Priest, who entered the service of the company before the road was opened for traffic, and has remained on it ever since, was among the most reliable and efficient of Mr. Young's assistants.

At the time of consolidation, the stock capital of the company was $4,500,000, on which the shareholders received fifty per cent premium in six per cent bonds of the consolidated company, equal at par to $2,475,000, and how much of the two and a half millions of increase to the original two millions was made up by extra dividends in the old company, and how much of surplus has been and will be paid by the trustees to the stockholders of the company, I need not name, to make good the assertion, that the Utica and Schenectady company has turned out the most successful of modern railway enterprises.

The Utica and Schenectady rail road is now enrolled among the things that were, and history teaches by the examples inscribed on its pages. Twenty years the directors of that company served the shareholders without *compensation or reward*, and not only repaid them their whole capital, with interest, but gave them a *little* surplus, and left the original stock unimpaired in the new company. If this success does not show that there was ability, application and integrity in the direction and management of the concerns of the company, it will be extremely difficult to produce an example of this sort that will. I am not aware of a single year, and I marked the progress of affairs with considerable attention, when the annual expenses of the road exceeded thirty-three per cent of the gross earnings. Those expenses seldom reached that sum during the whole seventeen years the road was operated. Why, then, do we now see those expenses reaching to and even exceeding fifty per cent of the gross earnings of rail road companies? I place these facts on the record, and those who have time, and are so disposed, may discuss causes and their effects.

The shareholders of these companies have a remedial power in their own hands, and can apply it once in each year, if they choose to do it. They can know, if they will, whether the laws of the state have been strictly observed by the directors and agents of the company; and they should know, too, whether the principal agents of the corporations have been interested in contracts with the company; or have used the information or knowledge which could only come to them confidentially, for the purpose of dealing in the stock of the companies to which they belong, and speculate on a rise or fall in the market. When men seek places in rail road directions, to control and participate in the contracts for supplies, and when the chief agents of these companies are allowed to be contractors, the stockholders directly, and the general public indirectly, suffer materially.

I will dismiss the subject of rail roads, and go back in order of time a half century or more. March 26, 1803, an act was passed, authorizing certain great roads in this state to be opened and improved, and for that purpose $41,500 was directed to be raised by lottery.

The State road, so called, from Johnstown to the Black river country, passing through parts of Manheim and Salisbury and the towns of Norway and Russia in this county, was laid out and surveyed, and probably opened by commissioners appointed by the governor, pursuant to the authority conferred by the above act. This road was used a good deal in the early part of the present century, when the eastern emigration was flowing towards the present counties of Lewis and Jefferson, the western portion of St. Lawrence and the northern parts of Oneida and Herkimer.

The Fall Hill turnpike and bridge company, incorporated in 1804, was authorized to build a toll-bridge over the Mohawk at Little Falls, and construct a road from the house of Ira Crane in Minden, Montgomery county, to the Mohawk river, thence along said river to Henry A. Vrooman's, in German Flats, and thence to Samuel Abbott's house and Kassler's mills. The object of this improvement was to avoid the difficulties of the road over Fall hill, which was pretty steep and rugged. The bridge was erected and used many years, and until the charter was abandoned. The road was not made.

In the year 1806, commissioners were appointed to lay out and straighten the road on the south side of the Mohawk river, from Schenectady to Utica, where they should judge the same expedient. This road was directed to be opened three rods wide, and the towns through which it passed were required to work it. In all the cases which I have noticed, if any portion of these roads, surveyed by the directions of the legislature, was laid out through improved lands, compensation was made to the owners, and after the roads were surveyed and opened by the state, the towns through which they passed were required to repair and maintain them. This requirement could only be observed where there was sufficient population.

An opinion prevailed at an early day, that the northern travel would leave the Mohawk valley at East Creek or Little Falls, and turn towards the Black river country, but the project of opening and improving a road from Little Falls in that direction was never carried into effect. The people of Johnstown, Utica, Whitestown and Rome, were too much alive to their own interests to allow such a project to get the start of them. The route from Johnstown through the northern parts of Montgomery and Herkimer, crossing the East Canada creek at Brackett's bridge, and the West Canada creek at Boon's bridge, near Prospect, in Oneida county, was much the shortest, and the best adapted to emigrant travel.

The Great western turnpike passes through the southeast corner of the town of Warren, at the Little lakes, a distance of two or three miles. This road does not touch the Mohawk valley. The Minden and Utica turnpike company was incorporated in 1809. The designated line of this road in the county passed through the present towns of Stark, Warren, Columbia, Litchfield, the southwest corner of Frankfort into Oneida county. Some part of this turnpike was completed, and one or more gates were erected to collect tolls, but it has long since been abandoned, the charter having been declared forfeited for a misuser, and the people are not obstructed by the toll-bar.

Col. Jeremiah Drake projected a rail road, to connect with the Utica and Schenectady line, near A. A. Fink's, two miles east of Little Falls, and running northerly a distance of about fifteen miles in this county, to the northeast corner of the Royal grant. He procured an act of incorporation in 1834, had the line of road surveyed and located, and estimates of cost of construction and traffic made up. Col. Drake was sanguine the road would yield a good return upon the investment, but failing to convince capitalists of this fact, he was compelled to abandon the project. The line of the road as surveyed, passed through Manheim Center, Wintonville, Salisbury Center to Devereaux. This line would not have yielded an income quite as prolific as the Utica and Schenectady, but that company and the New York central line would have found it a most valuable auxiliary in furnishing fuel from the North woods.

The plank road mania of 1847–8, in its epidemic progress through the state, visited the county, and roads of this description were constructed in various directions.

The first, in point of time, was the road from the village of Mohawk, through Herkimer and Middleville to Newport, up the valley of the West Canada creek.

The Little Falls and Middleville, connecting the two places named by plank.

The Manheim and Salisbury, connecting Little Falls with Salisbury Four Corners. This line has been extended to Graysville, a village on the Black creek in the north part of Norway.

The Little Falls and Salisbury, connecting the former place with Devereaux at the northeast corner of the Royal grant. The route of this road is nearly on the line of Col. Drake's proposed rail road. The plank road from Utica, passing through Frankfort, Litchfield and West Windfield to Unadilla.

The Mohawk and Ilion, connecting the two places named by plank.

The Frankfort and Utica, extending from Frankfort village to the west line of the county, along the Erie canal.

Ilion and Cedarville, extending from the former village south to Cedarville.

The plank road from Fort Plain, in Montgomery county,

to Cooperstown, passes through Starkville and Van Hornesville, in the town of Stark.

The North Gage and Russia plank road, connects Russia, in this county, with North Gage, in Oneida county.

The Utica, Deerfield and Schuyler plank road.

Although not in the order of time, I may here remark that a charter was granted in 1836, to construct a rail road from Herkimer to Trenton, Oneida county, along the valley of the West Canada creek; but no further effort was ever made to carry into effect the objects of the law. Like many other projects of this kind, its promoters found it difficult to obtain the capital to build the road, although the route was quite feasible and unobstructed by deep cuts and heavy embankments.

The Newspaper Press of the County.

Strange as it may seem to the reader, the history of the newspaper press of the county, although covering only about half a century, has come to rest in tradition, and while itself the recorder of events that have moved a world in arms, and shook crumbling empires into dust, it has failed in this county to place its own existence and career beyond a surmise and a probability; or, the frail memory of man when he makes the effort to speak of dates and limit periods without a written or printed record before him. Tradition is much more uncertain among a civilized people who claim to record events as they transpire, than with the aboriginal natives of this continent, who perpetuate their legends and important national events by reciting them in a full assembly of the tribes, where the young, the old and the middle aged of both sexes are seated around the great council fire to hear repeated and impress upon the memory, the history of their tribe, the exploits in war of their great chiefs and distinguished braves, to describe the limits of their hunting grounds, and to recount the moons and the seasons since the happening of some great event.

In the beginning of the present century, and probably about the year 1802, Mr. Benjamin Cory published the first newspaper in the county, called the *Telescope*, designed to uphold the interests of the federal party. In January, 1805, David Holt a (name long familiar to the people of the county) and J. B. Robins purchased Mr. Cory's interest in the paper and issued another instead of it, called the *Farmer's Monitor*.

The *Monitor* was continued until the summer of 1807, when it was discontinued for want of patronage; Mr. Cory having established another federal paper, which, as the lawyers and merchants of the village were mostly of that party, engrossed nearly all the advertising patronage.

The *Herkimer Pelican* established by Cory, was probably continued until the year 1810. The *Pelican* supported Governor Lewis, and the *Monitor*, it is said, was attached to the George Clinton branch of the republican party.

The fourth paper was established in January, 1810, by J. H. & H. Prentiss, called the *Herkimer American;* it was published several years by them and William L. Stone, afterwards of the *New York Commercral Advertiser*, when Edward P. Seymour purchased the establishment and conducted the paper to "its life's end" in 1831. Mr. Seymour always kept his paper to the true party lines while he controlled it, but he would not refuse to print tickets for the republicans when they had no press in the county.

The *Bunker Hill* made its appearance some time in the year 1810, established by Mr. G. G. Phinney? The political tendencies of this paper were pretty high-toned. The motto, "Live free or die! Death is not the greatest of evils," (*Gen. Stark*), showed its conductor was ready for the fight. Mr. Phinney brought out the *Honest American* about the year 1812. The editorial courtesy of those times was quite pungent, taking the following article as a specimen:

"A Mean Blackguard.—Captain *Consequence*, or in other words, *Charley* Holt, has been pleased, if he ever was pleased, to *daub* in his paper the following ridiculous paragraph against the editor of the *Honest American:*

"'A Dishonest American.—The foolish rascal in Herkimer, who to the disgrace of the name of an editor, is the lickspittle of the *Public Advertiser*, can not expect further newspaper notice, but will be silenced without disturbing our readers by so pitiful a subject.'

"Capt. *Charley* talks of 'silencing us,' but the captain is informed that he nor all the *men* he could raise while a captain in Hudson, will be able to silence us. Capt. *Charley* says we can not expect further 'newspaper notice.' God grant we may not receive any further notice from so mean a scoundrel. This '*pitiful* subject' wishes not to 'disturb' his 'readers.' It is well known, that as far as Capt. Charley's influence extends, he has done more to disturb the republican party than any other editor in the state. An *eternal* good-bye to you, Capt. *Charley*, unless you intend to take other notice of us than that of 'newspaper.'"

This language smacks some of an indictment or prosecution for a libel. These two papers, the *Bunker Hill* and *Honest American* were both discontinued before 1821, and in September of that year, Edward M. Griffin established the *People's Friend*, a democratic paper, at Little Falls, which was published by him until about the year 1832, when several of the leading democrats of the county, to prevent the sale of the establishment and discontinuance of the paper, bought out the concern. Messrs. C. S. Benton & Co., continued the publication of the paper under the title of *Mohawk Courier*, until the proprietors sold out their interest to Josiah A. Noonan. Mr. Noonan transferred his interest in the paper to Horatio N. Johnson who after publishing it some time, sold it to Elias G. Palmer, and again purchased it of Mr. Palmer, and now conducts the paper.

The *Herkimer Herald* made its appearance at Herkimer in 1828, under the direction of Mr. John Carpenter, and advocated the election of General Jackson.

Next in order of time came the *Republican Farmer's Free Press*, in 1830, an anti-masonic paper, established by an association, printed by David Holt and edited by B. B.

Hotchkin. Its life was short. Then came the *Herkimer County Journal* in December, 1837, a whig paper. It was owned by a company, commenced at Herkimer, under the editorial charge of J. C. Underwood, and printed by E. P. Seymour. In about one year Mr. O. A. Bowe took charge of the paper and published it about six years. It was at different times edited by R. U. Sherman, G. W. Smith and A. H. Prescott. Mr. Orlando Squires took charge of the paper in 1849, and removed the establishment to Little Falls, where the paper is now published under the direction of Mr. Daniel Ayer, and has nearly reached the close of the 17th volume.

The *Republican Farmer's Free Press* was transferred to Little Falls, its name changed to the *Herkimer County Whig*, and published by Larned W. Smith, who also issued from the same press the *Inquirer*, a deistical affair. This was not a very long lived concern. It commenced its career in 1834, and closed I believe in about two years.

Mr. E. M. Griffin established *The Enterprise* at Little Falls in 1839, and continued its publication about two years, and then started the *Mohawk Mirror*, a quarto sheet which he published or pretended to publish twice a month. This paper died out in 1844.

Next in order of time came the *Frankfort Democrat*, established at Frankfort in the fall of 1842, by J. M. Lyon, now of the *Utica Gazette*. It was afterwards removed to Herkimer village, and the name changed to *Herkimer County Democrat*. Until 1853 this paper was the organ of the Hunker section of the democratic party, and enjoyed a pretty good patronage. Mr. Robert Earl, who succeeded Mr. Lyon in the proprietorship of the paper, sold out his interest, and the paper has since sustained the other section of that party.

When Mr. Bowe quit the *Journal*, in 1844, he established at Little Falls an abolition journal, called the *Herkimer Freeman*, which he published about six years, using the type and press of the *Enterprise*. Failing to accomplish all he designed and all that his industry and application to his business deserved, Mr. Bowe in April, 1850, started the *Mohawk Times* at the village of Mohawk. Hope again with him "on trembling pinions soared," and the advocacy of "free soil" with a spice of "news and miscellany," was to conduct his bark to a haven of rest. Mr. Bowe soon abandoned this, his last enterprise in the state, in a short time, and established a press somewhere among the green hills of Vermont.

The *Mohawk Valley Sentinel* was established by L. W. Peters and G. W. Gould, at Mohawk in the winter of 1855. It has been conducted by Mr. Peters several months, Mr. Gould having left the concern. Its motto, "Put none but Americans on guard" (*Washington*), very clearly denotes the political bias of the paper.

The *Ilion Independent*, the last to be now chronicled in history, was brought out in February, 1855, at the village of Ilion by Mr. George W. Bungay. It seems to be devoted to temperance and advocates the prohibitory liquor law. Its motto, "Liberty, Equality and Fraternity" show an enlarged and comprehensive benevolence.

Out of the seventeen or eighteen newspapers established in the county during the past fifty-four years, only three of them, the *Courier*, *Journal* and *Democrat* have stood the test of time. The *Sentinel* and *Independent* have not yet passed the ordeal. Fourteen have enjoyed a brief existence, have performed their mission and are now forgotten. The *Herkimer American* attained the respectable age of twenty-one years. The *Courier* and *People's Friend* conjoined have seen thirty-four years. The *Herkimer County Journal* has thrown its banner to the breeze eighteen successive years and rallied its friends to many political defeats in the county; and the *Herkimer County Democrat*, although thirteen years an active campaigner can not claim always to have recorded victories of its friends.

The reader will notice as an act of justice to J. Munsell of Albany, that I am much indebted to his interesting work, *The Typographical Miscellany*, for the important matter contained in this article.

Colleges and Academies.

Fairfield Medical College.

The College of Physicians and Surgeons of the western district of New York, located at Fairfield, Herkimer county, had its origin in the medical school established by the trustees of Fairfield academy, in 1809. This school had acquired some reputation while attached to the academy. It was even such in the second year of its existence, as to induce the legislature of the state to endow it with $5,000, and when it received the rank of college, they generously added to its funds the further sum of $10,000.

The charter of the college bears date June 12, 1812, to which is appended the seal of the university of the state, and signed by DANIEL D. TOMPKINS, Chancellor of the University of the State of New York.

H. BLOODGOOD, Secretary.

In the charter the following persons are named as constituting the first board of trustees, viz.: Westel Willoughby, Jun., Jonathan Sherwood, Luther Giteau, Solomon Wolcot, Isaac Sears, Abijah Tombling, Amos Hale, Simeon Ford, Clark Smith, Joseph White, Alexander G. Fonda, Oliver C. Comstock, John Miller, Isaac Sargeant, Reuben Hart, Amasa Trowbridge, Francis A. Bloodgood, William D. Ford, James Kennedy, Oliver Ellis, Andrew A. Bartow, William Smith, John Stearns and James Hale; they and their successors were to have perpetual succession.

At a meeting of the board of trustees, held Dec. 1, 1812, the following individuals were appointed officers of the college, viz.:

Lyman Spalding, professor of anatomy and surgery.

Westel Willoughby, Jun., professor of obstetrics.

James Hadley, professor of chemistry.

John Stearns, professor of the theory and practice of physic.

The class of 1812-13, as appears by the records, consisted of eighteen medical students. During the session of 1813-14, it numbered twenty-four.

At a meeting of the board, March 23, 1815, T. Romeyn Beck was recommended to the honorable regents to fill the office of professor of the institutes of medicine.

Jan. 30, 1816, the degree of doctor of medicine was conferred on two individuals, viz.: Horatio Orvis and Sylvester Miller. Dr. Beck gave his first course on medical jurisprudence. Number of students, 28 ; 4 graduates.

At a meeting of the board, May 20, 1817, Doct. Joseph White, of Cherry Valley, was appointed president and professor of anatomy and surgery in the college, in place of Dr. Spalding ; at the same meeting, it was resolved, that President White have leave to substitute his son, Delos White, M. D., to deliver lectures on anatomy in his stead.

Jan. 20, 1818, the class consisted of 41 students, of whom 7 were considered worthy of the degree of doctor of medicine.

Jan. 19, 1819, a resolution was passed by the board of trustees, dismissing any student who should be concerned directly or indirectly in digging up any dead human body, for the purpose of dissection in the college.

Jan. 20, 1820, the legislature were petitioned for a law for giving the dead bodies of unclaimed convicts of the state prison, at Auburn, to the college, for the purposes of dissection.

Jan. 23, 1821, Dr. Delos White resigned his professorship of anatomy, in consequence of the difficulty of procuring subjects for dissection. The same year, it was resolved to extend the course of lectures from twelve to sixteen weeks.

Jan. 22, 1822, James McNaughton, M. D., made professor of anatomy and physiology. 62 students ; 14 graduates.

For several years subsequent to this period, the affairs of the college continued to prosper, and the number of students to increase. At the close of the session ending in January, 1827, Joseph White, M. D., in consequence of age and infirmities, resigned his professorship, and was succeeded in the chair of surgery by John Delamater, M. D. Number of students in attendance this session, 144; graduates, 25. In consequence of the increase of students, an additional college edifice was erected, containing thirty-two lodging rooms, and the lecture rooms of the old college edifice were enlarged and rendered more commodious.

1828, number of students, 171; graduates, 33.

1832. This year the number of students had increased to 205; graduates, 39.

1834. The largest class ever assembled at the college was during the session ending in January, 1834, when the number reached 217, of whom 55 received the degree of doctor of medicine. The following year the number was 198.

The organization of the medical department of Geneva college, and subsequently the incorporation of a medical college in the city of Albany, together with other causes, had the effect to diminish the number of students in attendance at the Fairfield college from the year 1834, until the final suspension of lectures in the latter institution, by the faculty; yet the numbers continued to be respectable, and probably would have been until the present time, had the proper efforts been continued to sustain it. During the year 1836, the regents confirmed the following alterations, by which the professorships stood as follows:

Westel Willoughby, M. D., emeritus professor of midwifery.

James Hadley, M. D., professor of chemistry and pharmacy.

T. Romeyn Beck, M. D., professor of materia medica and medical jurisprudence.

James McNaughton, M. D., professor of anatomy and physiology.

John Delamater, M. D., professor of practice of physic, and diseases of women and children.

Reuben D. Mussey, M. D., professor of surgery and midwifery.

Subsequently, Frank H. Hamilton, M. D., succeeded Prof. Mussey in the chair of surgery, and with this exception, the faculty remained as above during the operation of the institution. The last course of lectures was given during the winter of 1839-40. The number of students in attendance was 105, of whom 26 received the degree of doctor of medicine. Since the cessation of medical lectures, the college buildings have undergone material modifications, and have been thoroughly repaired, for enlarging the accommodations of Fairfield academy, for which purpose they are at present appropriated. Lyman Spaulding, M. D., was the first president of the college, and was succeeded in office by Joseph White, M. D., in 1817, who resigned in 1827. The venerable Prof. Willoughby succeeded Dr. White, and held the office until his decease.

Fairfield Academy.

This institution was incorporated March 13th, 1803, by the regents of the university of this state, and has been in successful operation ever since. The first board of trustees consisted of Moses Mather, Thomas Manley, Nathan Smith, Samuel Giles, Westel Willoughby Jr., William Griswold, Alvah Southworth, Cyrus M. Johnson, John Meyer, Jonathan Hallet, Abijah Mann, Mathias B. Tallmadge, Samuel Wright, William Smith, Benjamin Bowen, Charles Ward, Clark Smith, Thomas Bennett, Moses Wheeler, Francis A. Bloodgood, Aaron Hackley, John Snell, John Herkimer and Henry Coffin, and the school was opened under the supervision of the Rev. Caleb Alexander, as the principal, and under his care and management of about ten years, the institution became extremely popular, and was esteemed the best academic school in the country. It enjoyed a wide field of patronage and usefulness, the first twelve or fifteen years of its existence, it being the only school of the kind in central or western New York in which thorough academic instruction could be obtained.

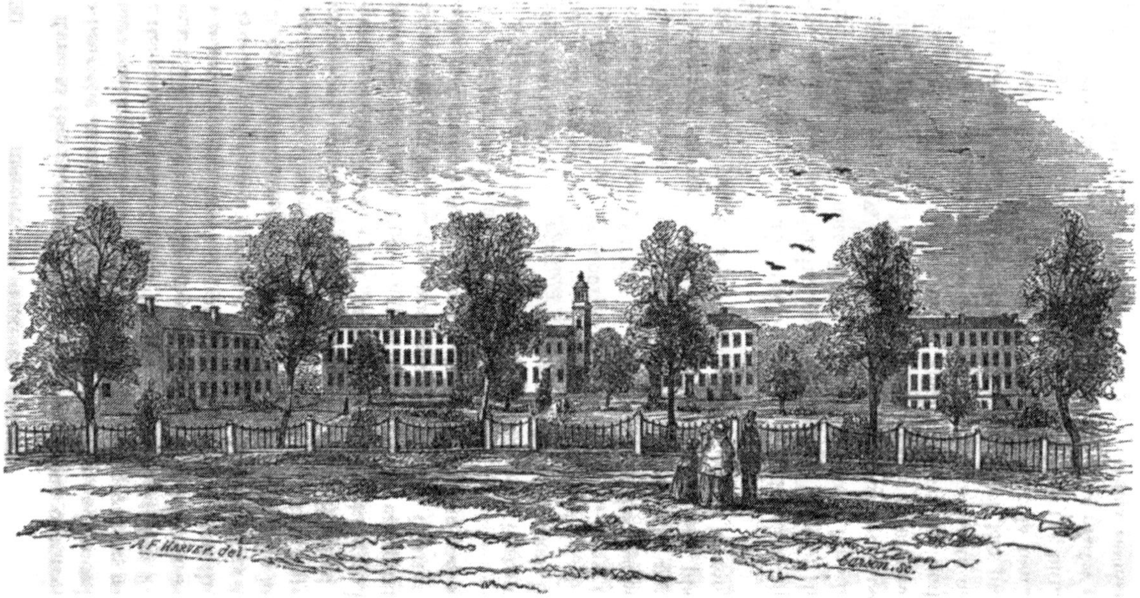

FAIRFIELD ACADEMY.

Even at this late day it is not an unfrequent occurrence to hear the members of the legal profession, advanced in years and living in the central, western and northern parts of the state, speak of their having been educated at Fairfield. The same remarks may no doubt be made with truth by many engaged in other pursuits, or have devoted themselves to medicine or divinity. Fairfield Academy has sent out many worthy and excellent men, and some who have distinguished themselves in public life and in the learned professions, and it may well have done this. She had the young and aspiring talent of the country flocking to her halls, and she maintained sound, thorough and enlightened instructors. The trustees and patrons of this institution have just grounds to felicitate themselves on the past success of the school.

At former periods the aid of the state has been bestowed, with sparing munificence, and it may be with as much liberality as justice to other institutions and the ability of the state would allow. It is however gratifying to know that this institution, the oldest in the county, and the first established in a now wide-spread, populous and wealthy region of country, enjoys a permanent endowment which places the successful progress of the school beyond a contingency.

No people ever committed a graver mistake than those who make up their minds that almost any body or thing will do for a school teacher. Those who look for cheap instructors, without inquiry as to qualifications, err exceedingly. The youthful mind is quite as capable of erroneous as rightful impressions when engaged in learning, and all experience teaches us how difficult it is to eradicate error and impress truth in its place in the mind of the pupil; hence the importance of placing in our schools teachers capable, accomplished and experienced. "Set the blind to lead the blind," and what will be the end? The reader will, I hope, bear with me a moment longer. It has seemed to me, we regarded less than we should the permanent endowment of our academic schools. I mean such an endowment as would give a permanent annual income sufficient to carry the institution through all temporary adversities that may overtake it in the progress of years. This enables the trustees to retain an efficient corps of teachers and maintain the usual grade of instruction, and when prosperity returns no changes will be required to meet that fortunate exigency. There are no people within the pale of civilization who practice expediency so much as the Americans in accomplishing proper objects and achieving just results. This may be the mighty lever that has brought the country to its present elevated position; but are the foundations sufficiently strong and adamantine to sustain us in that position? The truths of science can only be reached by keeping on the right tract and within its orbit; and who can lead and direct the neophite save the accomplished master, the experienced teacher and guide?

Caleb Alexander was a native of Northfield, Massachusetts, who graduated at Yale College, and having been admitted to the ministry, settled as pastor over the church at Mendon. He came into Western New York as a missionary in 1801, and I am enabled through the kindness of one of his descendants to consult his journal, from which I have made some extracts:

"August 10, 1801. Having received my commission from the Rev. Nathaniel Emmons, D. D., President of the Massachusetts Missionary Society, having obtained the consent of my church and congregation and committed myself and family to the direction and disposal of God, I began my missionary tour to the people in the western parts of the state of New York."

He visited various localities on the North river, in Saratoga, Schenectady, Albany, Schoharie, Otsego, Madison, Oneida, Cayuga, Onondaga, Ontario and Herkimer counties, and finally reached Norway, in this county, November 10,

1801, and remained until 23d, visiting and preaching at Fairfield, Norway and Salisbury. At this period Mr. Alexander says, that Fairfield contained 2065, Salisbury, 1694 souls, and the whole county, 14,503.

While at Fairfield and Norway, on this occasion, he made arrangements for opening a school at the former place. A frame building was erected, and in May, 1802, he returned from Massachusetts with his family, and commenced in good earnest to lay the foundation of an institution which gave birth to the Academy. During the whole period of his engagement at the head of the Fairfield Academy, he preached alternately at Fairfield, Norway, Salisbury and at other places in the northern part of the county.

He left Fairfield in 1812, and took charge of the academy at Onondaga Hollow, where he remained engaged in teaching and preaching, giving a portion of his attention to farming, until he was called home to give an account of his stewardship, at the venerable age of 73 years.

Mr. Alexander was the author of several educational works, and among them were his Latin and English Grammars, which were of high repute in their day, although he sold the copy right of the "Grammatical Elements, or a Comprehensive Theory of English Grammar," &c., to Isaiah Thomas and Ebenezer T. Andrews, of Boston, in 1793, for $133·33. His education was as thorough and complete as could well be obtained in this country at the time he graduated, and he evinced no lack of energy and application in subjecting his acquirements to the severe test of writing out an elementary treatise on the English language.

The present trustees of this institution are Charles Willard, Sidenis Teal, David W. Cole, Jarius Mather, William B. Porter, Roswell D. Brown, George Pierce, James Seaman, Thomas A. Rice, Richard R. Smith, Henry Tillinghast, Lorenzo Carryl, Jeremiah Cory, Varnum S. Kenyon, Ezra Graves, William Lamberson, Parley Arnold, Horace Ford, Jeremiah Smith, Alden S. Gage, William Mather, George

W. Philips, Asa Chatfield and John Green. Jeremiah Smith, president of the board of trustees, Jarius Mather, secretary.

The Academy at Little Falls in the county of Herkimer,

was incorporated by the regents of the university of this state, October 17, 1844.

The trustees named in the charter were, Nathaniel S. Benton, Arphaxed Loomis, Frederick Lansing, George H. Feeter, William C. Craine, David Petrie, Henry Heath, Martin W. Priest, Harry Burrell, Richard N. Casler, Albert G. Story, Zenas C. Priest, Thomas Burch, Nathan Brown, Soloman Petrie, Stephen W. Brown, Henry Eysaman and William Ingham.

The whole value of academic property, consisting of lots, buildings, furniture, library and apparatus, as appears from the first annual report of the trustees made December 8th, 1845, was $14,849·38.

Merritt G. McKoon, Esq. A. M., opened the school, as principal teacher, and the same has been continued to the present time, under the direction of different instructors.

The citizens of the town and surrounding country exhibited a generous liberality in donating funds towards the erection of the splendid stone edifice occupied as the academic building.

The present trustees of this institution are, Nathaniel S. Benton, Arphaxed Loomis, Harry Burrell, Martin W. Priest, Albert G. Story, Thomas Burch, Zenas C. Priest, John Beardslee, Seth M. Richmond, James Feeter, William J. Skinner, William Ingham and Philo Reed.

The academy at Herkimer was incorporated in 1838 or 1839, and was subject to the visitation of the regents of the university. It flourished a few years and was finally abandoned for want of patronage.

This school, as is well known, was located in one of our most pleasant villages, containing a population, able of itself to form the nucleus of a very liberal support, but owing to some serious difficulty, originating with some of the faculty, the school unfortunately failed to command the public confidence.

West Winfield Academy.

Incorporated by the regents of the university, February 14th, 1851.

The trustees named in the charter are, William Stuart, Alonzo Wood, James M. Rose, Walter Palmer, Joseph Harding, Joel Wadsworth, Rufus Wheeler, Zenas Eldred, J. L. Moore, David R. Carrier, Ira Walker, Samuel Smith, H. D. Kellogg, Orange Holmes, Newton Wilcox, William McLoughlin, Levi S. Knight, Alvah Barker, Hiram Brown, L. G. Holmes, T. W. Morgan and N. M. Morgan.

The present value of the academic buildings, library and apparatus, at the date of the application, was stated at $3,200. The location of this institution in an elevated and healthful district of country, easy of access, and being surrounded by a vigorous and wealthy population, must make it an inviting spot for youth to pursue academic studies, and it should not fail, as it seems to me it need not, to become highly useful and influential in disseminating classical instruction over a wide and extended territory. The academy, thus far, gives promise of much usefulness.

Religious Aspects of the County.

I shall not add one word to what has been said in the introductory chapter, in reference to the small show now made in this important and interesting branch of our local history. If the extracts from the two missionary journals, here presented to the reader, contain truthful views of our condition, more than fifty years since, we must know our situation in this respect has changed, and we doubt not for the better. Reliable data to show these facts are beyond my reach. There is, or has been, an organized Bible society in the county. Unfortunately, its records and proceedings can not be obtained, to exhibit its operations and prospects.

The state census of 1855, affords materials for the following brief table of statistics respecting the religious aspects of the county. The United States census tables of 1850, give as the whole number of churches in the county, 54. The Methodists have only 8, and the Presbyterian only 2 in those tables. I notice this because I have learned not to confide implicitly in statistical evidence of this character. Differences like these can not easily be reconciled or accounted for:

	Churches.	Members.		Churches.	Members.
Baptists,	12	713	Methodist Episcopal,	28	1430
Catholics,	2	744	Presbyterian,	10	345
Congregational,	1	72	Protestant Methodist,	2	50
Dutch Reformed,	6	498	Universalist,	7	141
Episcopal,	3	74	Union Churches,	9	275
Free Will Baptists,	3	152	Whitfield Calvinists,	1	5
Lutheran,	4	94			

Presenting an aggregate of 88 churches and 4,593 church members, or persons attached to the several churches, and conforming to the rituals in discipline, government and doctrine. This, then, I apprehend, does not embrace among the Protestant congregations, at any rate, the whole number of persons attending religious services in those congregations. The above number is only one in four of the adult population of the county, and one in eight and four-tenths of the whole number of inhabitants. A beggarly account of empty pews, when we assume, as we should, that the capacity of the churches is equal to seating the whole population of the county.

The Rev. Caleb Alexander having performed a missionary tour to the western parts of this state in 1801, by the directions of the Massachusetts missionary society, I have transcribed such portions from the original journal as are of local interest:

NOVEMBER, 1801. — *Tuesday*, 10.—Rode east 11 miles, to Norway, dined at Lieut. Smith's, in the morning delivered a sermon on Rom., vii, 7, 8, "The carnal mind is enmity against

God, for it is not subject to the law of God, neither indeed can be. So then, they that are in the flesh can not please God." After lecture a conference was formed in which we had much free conversation on religious subjects. Here is a Presbyterian Church of about 27 members, of whom some appear to be pious. At their request I agreed to visit them, next Friday preach a lecture and attend a church conference on the subject of their difficulties. Lodged at Lieut. Smith's.

Wednesday, 11, rainy and snowy, rode 6 miles south, to Mr. Nathan Smiths, in Fairfield; very muddy, chilled with the storm and much fatigued.

Thursday, 12, rainy and snowy, pain in my limbs, kept house all day visited by Capt. Griswold. By him I learned that religion is in a low state in this town. There is a Congregational Church, but no officers, and no meeting on the Sabbath. Proposed to call the church together and converse with them. The storm and badness of traveling rendered it unadvisable to attempt to collect the church.

Friday, 13, returned to Norway, dined at Deacon Brownson's, preached a lecture at a Mr. Cook's; text, Prov., xxix, 1: "He that being often reproved hardeneth his neck shall suddenly be destroyed, and that without remedy." After lecture attended a conference with the church on the subject of difficulties, and agreed to meet them again next Monday morning at nine o'clock. Lodged at Mr. Cook's.

Saturday, 14, breakfasted at another Mr. Cook's, returned to Fairfield and wrote journal.

Lord's Day, 15, delivered two sermons in the school house near Mr. Nathan Smith's. A. M. text 2 Tim., iv, 7, 8: "I have fought a good fight, I have finished my course, I have kept the faith, henceforth there is laid up for me a crown of righteousness, which the Lord the righteous judge shall give me at that day." P. M. text Acts iv, 11, 12: "This is the stone which was set at nought by you builders which is become the head of the corner, neither is there salvation in any other. For there is none other name under Heaven given among men whereby we must be saved." A full assembly and attention. The people contributed $2·33 cents for the use of the M. M. Society.

At Steuben the people contributed $6·96 cents for the use of the M. M. Society.

Monday, 16, rode early to Norway, met with the church at Mr. Newland's and attended all day to the settling of difficulties of long standing. It appeared that in many instances they had been irregular in their proceedings, which served to be the principal cause of the contentions and animosities existing among them. These were all canvassed and reduced to a happy train of accommodation. Adjourned to meet on Saturday morning, at which time I agreed to preach a lecture and to administer the sacrament of the Lord's Suppor on the next Sabbath so be that all difficulties should be settled.

Lodged at Mr. Lewis Hinman's, and spent the evening in preparing papers to be laid before the church on Saturday.

Tuesday, 17, breakfasted at Mr. George Cook's, dined at Mr. Moses Mather's, returned to Fairfield. There has been some attention to religion in Norway, several have attained a hope and give evidence of true piety. The church consists of 37 members, incorporated three years since by the Rev. Mr. Marsh in union with the associate churches of Morris County Presbytery. Mr. Marsh preached here two years and is now settled in Ballstown. In Norway are two Baptist churches, one on the open communion and the other on the close communion plan. The open communionists are Armenians in sentiments.

Wednesday, 18, visited. In Fairfield is a Congregational church of 24 members, some attention to religion. This town contains 2065 souls, no minister; some Baptists and some never attached themselves to any denomination. The royal grant is a tract of land 20 miles square of excellent soil, situate north of the Mohawk, and between the two Canada creeks and contains Salisbury, Fairfield and Norway in which are 3606 souls and no minister. The county of Herkimer contains 14,503 and no minister, excepting illiterate Baptist preachers, who are exerting every possible means to gain converts to their denomination.

Thursday, 19, rode east 4 miles to Salisbury, in Montgomery county, called upon Aaron Hackley, Esq., and preached a lecture on Titus, iii, 5, 6: "Not by works of righteousness, which we have, but according to his mercy he saved us by the washing of regeneration and renewing of the Holy Ghost, which he shed on us abundantly through Jesus Christ our saviour." A decent congregation in the school house. There is a Presbyterian Church of 36 members, belonging to the Northern Associate Presbytery of Morris County Presbytery. A Baptist Church has lately been established here. There has been in this place last summer much attention to religion, and almost every convert has joined the Baptist communion through the vigorous exertions of the Baptist teachers itinerating. Salisbury contains 1694 souls, a Presbyterian meeting house.

Friday, 20, cold; extremely bad riding, delivered a lecture P. M. in the school house, on Rom., i, 16: "I am not ashamed of the Gospel of Christ." The people contributed $1·12 cents for the use of the M. M. Society. Returned to Fairfield and called on Mr. Nathan Smith.

Saturday, 21, rode early in the morning to Norway, very cold and rough riding. Convened with the church at Mr. Ruland's, and attended to the difficulties and controversies existing among them. After much conversation, explanations and mutual confessions it was unanimously agreed that they would all make a public confession to-morrow in the presence of the congregation, and renew their covenant with God and one another. During the whole of the transaction they all appeared to manifest a tender, charitable and forgiving spirit, and it appeared that their divisions arose more from mistake of judgment than error of heart. Went to Mr. George Cook's for lodgings.

Lord's Day, 22, cold, snowy and very bad traveling, the church and congregation convened about half-after eleven. Delivered a sermon, text John xv, 5: "He that abideth in me and I in him, the same bringeth forth much fruit." A full and attentive assembly. An inflammation in my throat and nose rendered speaking very difficult. Read the confession of the church for their past misconduct, read their covenant to which they all gave consent, administered the sacrament and took tea at Lieut. Smith's. The congregation contributed $2·44 cents for the use of the M. M. Society. Returned to Mr. Nathan Smith's.

Monday, 23, set out from Fairfield on my journey homewards. Cold weather. Rode south 7 miles to the Little Falls, with a view of taking a boat to fall down the river to Schenectady. Found the Mohawk covered with ice, then rode up the river 7 miles to German Flats to take the stage. Finding that the stage is not to run till to-morrow I crossed the Mohawk to Herkimer Court House, 2 miles. Around the Little Falls the country is hilly and very rocky near the river. On the northern bank are seven locks and a canal for the conveyance of boats. Here is a village of 40 houses, several merchant stores, mechanical shops and a new meeting house of hexagonal construction. The people are principally English, and they seldom have preaching. The place abounds in vice, especially profanity. Since my arrival on the river, I have heard more cursing and swearing, horrid oaths and imprecations, than in ten years past. They fell chiefly from the lips of boatmen. In some taverns were English and Dutch farmers drinking and swearing, and the English appeared to be the most abandoned. They regard not the presence of a clergyman, for the dominie drinks and swears as much as the common people. At the German Flats I observed au old Dutch stone chapel. There is a Dutch clergyman who preaches to the people every second Sabbath.

On the flats in the town of Herkimer is a handsome flourishing village. Nine years since there were only two Dutch buildings in the place. There is now a handsome street, a meeting house, a court house, a gaol, about 30 elegant dwelling houses, a printing office, merchant stores and several mechanical shops. No minister. Religion appears to have no footing here.

Between Fairfield and the Little Falls is a Dutch settlement, called Manheim; rich farms, a meeting house, and a minister. Meinden, another Dutch settlement, lies south of the Little Falls; no minister. Hasenclevers hills, north of Herkimer courthouse, about 8 miles, and 7 west of Fairfield. No preaching. Schuyler Short Lots lie N. W. of Herkimer; many English, a Baptist church and some Congregationalists.

In the whole county of Herkimer, there is neither a Presbyterian nor Congregationalist minister. The people seem, in general, to be growing up in ignorance and wickedness. A resident missionary might do much good in this county.

Tuesday, 24. Took the stage at Herkimer, and passed through the German Flats, Minden to Canajoharie, 26 miles. In Minden is a Dutch Reformed church, and one at Canajoharie, which are supplied by Dutch clergymen.

The Rev. John Taylor, of Massachusetts, performed a missionary tour through the Mohawk and Black river country, in 1802, and believing the subject would not be uninteresting, I have transcribed such portions of his journal and remarks as relate to this county. He commenced his journey July 20th, 1802, and on his way out he reached the Mohawk valley on the 26th of the month, and his journal proceeds:

"*Manheim*, the last town in Montgomery county—extent 6 by 6—vacant, not a large congregation.

"*Salisbury*, north of Manheim—extent about 6 by 8 miles; contains not far from 1700 souls. One Presbyterian chh, vacant. The people, it is said, are tolerably well united and wish to settle a minister.

"Rode this day 36 miles. Weather extremely hot and dry. The people in the towns thro' which I have passed, are something sickly with the dysentery and influenza.

"*Herkimer*, Little Falls. The Albany stage arrived at the public house which I now am at, one o'clock last night."

The journal then gives an account of the loss from the stage and recovery of some boxes of books. "This parish," Little

Falls, contains six or seven hundred inhabitants. They have a new meeting house, but do not improve it.

"Before I go to Utica, I have concluded to visit Fairfield and Norway. About 3 o'clock I left the river, traveled 8 miles, and called on some of the principal men in Fairfield, and found things respecting religion very discouraging. I offered to tarry and preach the next day, but it was thought y[t] no people would attend. I find that people are universally in the midst of their harvests, and it is extremely difficult for them to attend lectures. At night I arrived at Norway, 6 miles north of Fairfield.

"*Norway*, bounded east by Salisbury, west on Canada creek, south on Fairfield. A young gent. by the name of Johnson, has preached in this town several sabbaths, and the people have hired him for 3 or 4 sabbaths to come. But it is in this town, as in all those parts. There is a mixture of Baptists, of Methodists, Universalists and Deists. In the various parts of the town, there is preaching by sectarians of almost all kinds, every sabbath.

"There is one Methodist church, numerous; two Baptist churches, and part of a third; no meeting houses...... The people almost universally inclined to hear preaching, of their various sects. I have concluded to visit this place and several other towns in this quarter, near the close of my mission, should I be able to make it convenient.

"29th July. I this morning left Norway for Utica, and arrived at Utica about 5 o'clock, having traveled 23 miles. I passed through a corner of Schuyler, and found the people to be generally Baptists; from there I passed into Deerfield, upon the Mohawk. There is a considerable congregation of Presbyterians. In Deerfield the people are Baptists, and are vacant."

I will observe in passing, that Norway at this time comprised most of the present town of Newport, and all the town of Russia, and the country north.

On his return from the north part of Oneida county, in September, Mr. Taylor continues:

"24th. Rode to the royal grant, 6 miles; found that in this part of the town of Norway the people are all Baptists, and that they had not appointed a lecture. I accordingly passed on ten miles to another part of the town, called Pottersbush. Here I found a church of 30 persons, and was received with gladness.

25th. Too much fatigued to preach.

26th, Sunday. Preached to about 200 persons—very attentive. Administered the Lord's Supper. After meeting endeavored to settle a difficulty in the church, but could not effect it. Rode 1½ miles to visit a dying person, and baptise a child. This town is almost ruined by the methodists and baptists, [I suppose he means so far as regards his own denomination] and the difficulty in the congregational chh has had a very bad influence. The chh is proceeding upon ye advice of Mr. Alexander" [the Rev. Caleb Alexander, then having charge of Fairfield Academy], "which I think is very wrong. 2 of the best members of this chh are become baptists in sentiment, and they came forward and stated their difficulty between their consciences and their covenant—and no one in ye chh supposes that they are not conscientious in the matter—and yet Mr. Alexander advised the chh not to dismiss y^{m}, but to proceed to excommunion, and brought the chh to a vote that there was no possible way by which any member could be separated from the covenant only by excommunication. This is what is stated to me by ye most judicious members of the chh, and I think this will be ye ruin of ye congregational interest in this town.

27th. Rode ten miles to *Salisbury* [county of Montgomery], having previously appointed a lecture this day. Preached to about 150 persons—appearances good. Had a conference in the evening—as many present as in the afternoon. This people, like most others in these parts, is very much divided, and the methodists prevailing."

The voluntary system of supporting religious institutions, which prevails in this county, is the only one which can be recognized, or would be tolerated, by a population made up of almost every nation, kindred, tongue and language in the civilized world. The inconveniences of this system are hardly seen and scarcely felt at this day, and we can only hope they may be less, far less, than the evils and inconveniences that have heretofore grown out of systems established by law and supported by governments.

COUNTY MEDICAL SOCIETY.

This venerable society was organized on the 5th day of August, 1806, at a general meeting of the physicians of the county, held at the Court House, pursuant to an act of the legislature of the state, regulating the practice of physic and surgery, passed April 4th, 1806.

Dr. George Rogers was chosen chairman, and Dr. Westel Willoughby, Jr., secretary, for the day. On canvassing the votes for officers of the society, Dr. Westel Willoughby, Jr., was elected president; George Rogers, vice-president; Andrew Farrell, secretary; and Amos Haile, treasurer.

Drs. Amos Haile, Andrew Farrell, Jonathan Sherwood, Rufus Crain and Isaac Sears, were chosen censors.

The names of the physicians present at this meeting were, Westel Willoughby, Jr., George Rogers, Andrew Farrell, Amos Haile, Abijah Tombling, David Perry, Jonathan Sherwood, John Eastman and Samuel Redfield.

The first Tuesday in January in each year, was assigned as the anniversary of the society. At the annual meeting, held at the court house in January, 1807, the society resolved, that to entitle a physician to become a member of the society, he must either produce a diploma from some medical society in the United States, agreeable to the late law of this state, or a voucher that he is a reputable physician.

Westel Willoughby, Jr., M. D., was appointed a delegate from the society to meet the delegates from the other counties in the state, on the first Tuesday in February, 1807, to form a state medical society.

Drs. Benjamin Hazen, Nathan Harwood, James Hadley, Isaac Sears, Jacob Abrams and William Traver, were admitted members of the society. A committee was appointed to form a code of by-laws, who reported the same at an adjourned meeting, on the 5th of May, following, which were adopted, and ordered to be printed. Dr. Willoughby was requested to deliver a dissertation before the society, at the adjourned meeting in May, 1807. In 1808, at the quarterly meeting in May, a seal was ordered to be procured for the use of the corporation; and at the anniversary meeting in January, 1809, the meetings of the society were reduced from four to two annually, and a fine of one dollar imposed for nonattendance.

Having thus briefly noticed the establishment of this highly interesting and beneficial institution, I shall continue my historical abstract to the present time, noticing as I pass, any marked or interesting incidents. Dr. Willoughby was continued president of the society, until January, 1816, when Rufus Crain was elected, who held one year, and was succeeded by James Hadley, who also held the office one year, and was succeeded by Westel Willoughby, M. D., in 1818. This year the society passed an order, that the county censors of any incorporated medical society should not proceed to examine a student for a license to practice physic and surgery, unless he produce a certificate of having attended at least one session at one of the medical colleges in the United States or in Europe, after the first day of January, 1818.

Dr. Willoughby held the office of president of the society until January, 1837, when he delivered a farewell address, for which, and for his constant and unwearied exertions for the interest and welfare of the society, a vote of thanks was tendered to him. The society also, by resolution, requested a copy of the address, and also a copy of a communication that day made by him, to be deposited in the archives of the society. In 1818, a vote was taken to apply the funds of the society to increase the library of the medical college at

Fairfield, on condition that its members could have the benefit of the library during the recess of the lectures at the college. In January, 1819, a resolve was passed, that every medical practitioner in the county who was not then a member, be notified by the secretary to attend at the next regular meeting of the society, and connect himself therewith, pursuant to the act passed in 1818.

In January, 1823, an order was passed to apply the funds of the society, in the hands of the treasurer, to the benefit of the College library, in accordance with a previous resolution. The funds afterwards received were also appropriated to the same object. In 1825, the society asked the trustees of the college to pass a resolution, that all the books purchased by its funds should be delivered to the society, when the college should be located in some other place than Fairfield. In 1828, the society adopted resolutions of condolence with the families of Drs. Bryan, Willard and Todd, who died the preceding year, and requested biographical sketches of their lives to be deposited in the archives of the society. The society had not met with a more severe loss in one year. These gentlemen were of high professional repute, and of great personal worth. The society in 1830, had its attention called to evils of intemperance, and resolved unanimously to discountenance the use of ardent spirits; and the annual meetings were changed to the first Tuesday in June, in each year.

In 1831, measures were taken to procure a medical topographical survey of the county, in accordance with a circular from the state medical society. I have not noticed that the several committees, appointed under the resolution, to procure the survey, ever made any reports. Dr. Calvin W. Smith was designated as the candidate to the state medical society, for the honorary degree of doctor of medicine.

The society this year, 1832, took measures to petition the legislature, to restore that part of the revised statutes, regulating the practice of physic and surgery, repealed by the act of 1830; and appointed a committee to circulate memorials for that object.

In 1837, the society adopted a regulation requiring the physician employed at the county poor house to make an annual report of his cases of practice; that the library committee should make an investigation into the state of the society's library, count the number of books on hand, and compare the treasurer's reports, and the augmentation of the library for the preceding five years. Also, that each member of the society be requested to keep a record of all the deaths which might occur in his practice, the age of the patient, the diseases of which they died, and how far said deaths were caused by intemperate habits of life, and report thereon to the society. This was a very important regulation, easily carried into effect by the members of the profession, and if strictly attended to, would afford useful and important information. We must abandon all hope, for the present, at least, of obtaining accurate information by the agency of state regulations, in respect to the statistics of births, marriages and deaths. The medical profession could well supply the number of births and deaths, and without much trouble and no expense. Annual abstracts of these would present actual results within a small portion, and would entitle that profession to the gratitude of the country. We must now resort to tables compiled in foreign countries, upon a far distant continent, if we desire to ascertain the probable duration of human life, or calculate the value of an annuity. These are the best data we have. They approximate to the truth, or they are supposed to do so, or they would not be used. We should, however, long since have laid the foundation for results, applicable to our own climate, population and condition of society, which would no doubt have been more accurate and satisfactory.

Doct. Harvey W. Doolittle was chosen president of the society in June, 1837, was succeeded by Dr. Calvin W. Smith for one year in June, 1838, and was again chosen in

1839, and held the office by annual election until June, 1842.

In January, 1839, the society adopted the following:

"Whereas, by the dispensation of Divine Providence, since our last meeting, this society has been deprived of one of its most valuable members, and community one of its brightest ornaments, in the death of Doct. John Holmes:

Resolved, That the members of this society will wear the usual badge of mourning for thirty days, as a testimony of their high respect for their deceased friend; and that the secretary be a committee to present the condolence of this society to the relations of the deceased."

At the semi-annual meeting in January, 1840, the society adopted a like resolution on the announcement of the death of Dr. Calvin W. Smith, and appointed a committee to write a biographical sketch of the lives of Drs. Smith and Holmes.

The professors of the Medical college at Fairfield, having resigned, and the trustees of that institution having failed to procure the appointment of others to continue the lectures, the society, in 1843, took effectual measures to reclaim, secure and preserve the society library, which had been deposited in the college under the care of the trustees and professors of that institution, as before noticed.

In June, 1842, Doct. Lester Green was elected president of the society, and a resolution was adopted, pledging the influence of the members to forward any feasible plan for resuscitating the Medical college at Fairfield, and tendering the use of the society's library to the trustees of the college when the professorships should be filled and the lectures resumed.

At the annual meeting in 1843, Doct. Green was reelected president. The whole number of volumes on the catalogue of the society's library was 590, of which 473 were brought from Fairfield, 54 were charged to members and 63 were lost or missing. The society adopted a set of by-laws, regulating the safe keeping and use of the library. Doct. Alfred E. Varney was chosen president at the annual meeting in 1844, and the delegate to the state society was requested to lay before that body the opinion entertained by this society, "that it was the duty of the medical faculty generally, to memorialize the legislature of this state to procure the passage of a law to prohibit the sale or use of any secret compound as a medicine," and to ask the state society to adopt measures to lay this subject before the legislature at the next session. These proceedings were rescinded at a subsequent meeting. Some doubts having been entertained, growing out of the legislation of the state in respect to medical societies, in regard to the legal existence of the society, a resolution was adopted in January, 1845, to continue the association as an organized body, and the unanimous opinion of the society to that effect, was declared.

The republican principle of rotation in office, even without emolument, seems to have obtained some footing in the society, and Dr. Abram Snyder was chosen president in June, 1845. A resolution was passed to raise a committee to present the condolence of the society to the family of Doct. Westel Willoughby, deceased, and request a biography of his life, and also that the society would wear the usual badge of mourning.

At the annual meeting in 1846. Doct. Caleb Budlong was elected president; Dr. Walter Booth in 1848, and Dr. Abram Snyder again in 1849. Drs. J. R. Brown, Wheeler, Griffith and Snyder delegates to the National medical association. Drs. Brown and Wheeler were appointed a committee to prepare and present to the society a biographical sketch of the life of Dr. Lester Green. The transactions of the society at its annual meeting in June, 1847, do not appear to have been recorded, nor is the death of Dr. Lester Green noticed except as above mentioned.

Dr. Harvey W. Doolittle was elected president of the society in 1850 and 1851. Drs. Booth, Brown, A. F. Doolittle and D. Belknap were appointed delegates to the National medical association in 1850. In June, 1852, Dr. A. Green was chosen president, and Drs. A. F. Doolittle, C. A. Griffith, A. Hawn and W. Booth, appointed delegates to the National medical association. The proceedings of the society this year were important and interesting, but they are such that I shall not venture to publish them so long as the society hold them under the injunction of secresy.

The society, at its annual meeting in June, 1853, elected Dr. Walter Booth president, and appointed Drs. Budlong, Griffith, Hawn and Parkhurst delegates to the National medical association.

The proceedings of the semi-annual meeting of the society in January, 1852, are deeply, nay more, solemnly interesting. Although crowded for space, I shall let those who know the *man* better than I did, pronounce his eulogy on these pages. Dr. C. A. Griffith presented the following resolutions, which were unanimously adopted:

"Whereas, It has pleased the Allwise Disposer of events to remove from this life our late friend and brother, Harvey W. Doolittle, one of the oldest, most eminent and highly respected physicians of this county, and who was for many years president of this society; Be it therefore,

Resolved, That we deeply deplore the loss sustained by his bereaved family, by the medical society, of which he was long an active member, and by the public at large, in the death of that excellent man and physician, Dr. *Harvey W. Doolittle*, whose professional attainments, not less than his own personal qualities, contributed to render him a most useful and estimable member of the community:

That we know and cherish his qualities as a man and a citizen; that we admire his sound judgment, his scientific knowledge and philanthropic spirit, which gave him a desirable eminence in his profession:

That we loved and lament him as a friend, and we doubt not his translation to a higher and happier sphere, where the pains and cares of this transient life give place to unbroken rest and unspeakable felicity.

Resolved, That as a mark of respect for the talents and

virtues of our departed brother, the members of this society will wear crape on the left arm for the space of thirty days.

Resolved, That a copy of these resolutions be sent by the secretary to the family of the deceased, and that copies be also furnished to the editors of the several newspapers in the county, with a request to publish the same."

A committee was appointed to prepare a biographical sketch of Dr. Doolittle's life.

Dr. W. H. Parkhurst was chosen president of the society in 1854, and Drs. Doolittle, Booth, Parkhurst and Griffiths, delegates to the National medical association. At the annual meeting in June, 1855, the following officers were chosen: Drs. Abm. Hawn, president; I. E. Casey, vice-president; C. A. Griffith, secretary; A. Green, treasurer; A. F. Doolittle, W. H. H. Parkhurst, F. B. Ethridge, A. Miller and S. Smith, censors; delegates to the national medical association, Drs. J. R. Brown, A. Hawn, I. E. Casey, and C. A. Griffith. The president of the society, Dr. Parkhurst, read the annual address. Biographical sketches of the lives of Drs. Doolittle, Snyder, Belknap and Sherwood were presented and deposited in the archives of the society. My abstracts must close for want of material. I do not find any record of the proceedings of the semi-annual meeting in January, 1855, in the manuscript document from which the preceding notes were compiled. I would have been pleased to have given a more extended and particular account of the doings of a body of professional gentlemen, in which the community at large have so great an interest, and upon whose professional progress so much depends to sooth and alleviate "the ills that flesh is heir to," but my chapter is fast growing to a volume.

It must suffice to say, that this society held its regular meetings for nearly fifty years, elected all its officers, secretary, treasurer, delegates to the State medical society and censors, on whom it enjoined the most rigid and careful attention in examining students for admission to practice.

That fines were imposed for nonattendance at the stated meetings, but their collection was not at all times rigidly enforced. The initiation fees appear to have been punctually paid, and from a small beginning the society had collected a very respectable medical library. Members were annually designated to deliver discourses on subjects relating to the practice of medicine, and members were invited to report special and unusual cases coming under their observation and care. The archives of the society must be replete with important and interesting information.

The common remark, "that Americans are careless of human life," is most strikingly illustrated in our treatment of this profession. We are quite as likely to deliver a valued friend or dear relative, laboring under some critical or latent disease, into the hands of some "quack doctor," who knows no more about the anatomy or organism of the human system, than a Malay does of ethics, as we are to search out the best-read and most experienced medical practitioner.

The county has sustained, if it did not produce them, several men of eminence and distinguished ability in this profession. But the avaricious grasp of the "almighty dollar" may strike down science and the arts and accomplishments, or invite them to new fields of enterprise and exertion in the westward track of emigration, and leave us nothing but a dull stultified mass of imbecility. There is no reason, within human cognizance, why the country, and such a country as ours, should not uphold and maintain men of eminence in all the professions and pursuits of life. No man with us holds the tenure of his existence and his labor on a lease from another. None are so poor but he can cast in his mite to the erection of the splendid monument of American progress; there are thousands who lack the will. Progressive ignorance is a broad and steep declivity which must quickly land us on a platform of anarchy or under a throne of absolutism.

The Poor House Establishment.

This county was among the first in the state to come under the provisions of the act of November 27th, 1824. The board of supervisors met at Herkimer, May 5th, 1825, and appointed Abijah Beckwith of Columbia, Robert Shoemaker of German Flats, and William Griswold of Fairfield, a committee to examine into the subject of establishing a poor house in the county and to report at a subsequent meeting of the board. This committee reported on the last Monday of May, 1825, when the supervisors resolved to purchase the property in German Flats, near the line of the canal formerly owned by Mr. Gillespie, for the sum of two thousand dollars, to be appropriated to the purposes of a county poor house; appointed Samuel Etheredge and Gideon Johnson to negotiate the purchase, and Rudolph J. Shoemaker, Alfred Putnam, Lauren Ford, John B. Dygert and Caleb Budlong superintendents. The supervisors also directed their clerk, as soon as the proper officers had taken possession of the house, to cause public notice of the fact to be published in the *Herkimer American* and *People's Friend*.

On the 16th November, 1827, the supervisors resolved by a vote of 10 to 6 to abolish the distinction between town and county poor in accordance with the provisions of an act of the legislature then recently passed. Up to this time each town had supported its own poor at the county establishment, that is, such persons as had according to existing laws become settled in the respective towns, were, when supported at the public expense, known as town paupers. The new system had not worked to the public satisfaction, either through defects in the management or want of proper accommodation as to buildings and grounds. On the 16th of December, 1827, the supervisors resolved to ask the legislature for authority to sell at their discretion the "present county poor house establishment, and purchase a more suitable piece of land and erect buildings thereon for the future reception and accommodation of the paupers of the county." A law was passed to this effect, but no immediate action seems to have been taken under it. In November, 1829, the supervisors authorized the county superintendents of the poor to provide for support out of the county house, idiot and lunatic paupers. In 1837, the question of disposing of the poor house was again agitated, although at the annual meeting that year the superintendents were authorized to purchase a part of the Steel farm for the use of the county, which was subsequently effected. In 1839 and 1840, the question of a sale and change of location was discussed by the supervisors, and there appears to have been a settled opinion that something should be done, but what it should be, was very difficult to settle upon. The legislature again passed laws on the application of the board of supervisors, allowing a sale and change of location. In 1842 the superintendents were authorized by the board of supervisors to sell the "present poor house and the small piece of land contiguous thereto for five hundred dollars," a pretty clear indication that the house was not considered of much value and was deemed entirely inadequate to the purposes it had been devoted. It was agreed on all hands that the time contemplated by the resolution of 1828 had fully arrived, but the difficulty about the new location and the plan of a new house were not very easily settled. The legislature in 1844 vested in the board of supervisors full power to sell out the old establishment, purchase a new site and erect suitable buildings thereon.

An active and exciting controversy of nearly three years' duration was kept up in the county before a majority of the supervisors made a final disposition of the subject. That body was almost equally divided on the question of the new location. The centralists were very urgent to keep it on the south side of the river, or near the centre of the county, while the supervisors of the northern and eastern towns were very zealous to have the poor house establishment removed from the Erie canal. While the contest existed, the towns placed their best and most influential men in the board of supervisors, when Greek met Greek in the tug of war. After the board had appointed commissioners to select a new site, the friends of the river location carried a resolution at a subsequent meeting of the board, to rebuild on the old site, and after repealing all former resolutions of the board relating to this subject, adjourned. Before any further action was taken in reference to carrying this project into effect, this resolution was repealed, and the matter was again entirely afloat, and continued undetermined some time.

At a meeting of the board, on the 17th March, 1846, the supervisors, by a vote of 11 to 7, sanctioned the contract for the new buildings, made by the commissioners previously appointed, and directed the superintendents of the poor to deliver and assign to the said commissioners all moneys and securities belonging to the county poor house establishment. The board had, at a meeting held on the 15th January, 1846, fixed upon a new site, by a vote of 10 to 9. The commissioners who superintended the erection of the new establishment were, George W. Alton, George Burch and Cornelius T. E. Van Horne.

The new Poor House is located in the town of Herkimer, on the west side of the West Canada creek, on the road from Herkimer to Newport, and about two miles south of Middleville, and far enough from the canal and rail road thoroughfares to discommode roaming mendicants, which I conclude was the leading object of the advocates of the change. The establishment is large and commodious, and well adapted to the benevolent purposes for which it was erected. The supervisors of this county now perform all the duties in respect to pauper relief that formerly devolved upon the overseers of the poor by law.

County Agricultural Society.

A society to promote the improvement of this important branch of our industrial pursuits, was organized under the act of April 7th, 1819. The objects of the society met the approval of the non-agricultural portion of the people of the county to a considerable extent, and some exertions were made to induce the farming community to attend the annual fairs and exhibitions, but the coercive tax authorized by the act to sustain these county institutions was not looked upon with favor in that quarter, and after one or two efforts to make a respectable show, the affair was abandoned.

A reorganization of the society was had in the county, under the act of May 6th, 1841, and the annual exhibitions which have taken place have been highly creditable to the agricultural, manufacturing and mechanical interests of the county. It could not be expected that the extent and variety of show would be as large as in the more populous and wealthy counties. The proceedings of this society are found published with the annual transactions of the State society, and I will not recapitulate them. I notice with regret, the fact, that of late years the society has been sustained mainly by the population in the southern and western parts of the county, while the northern and eastern sections do not seem to have participated in these annual social meetings and industrial exhibitions, with the zeal and alacrity which might well be expected from an intelligent, wealthy and progressive population.

I must close this notice of the society with giving the last annual meeting of its executive officers.

At the annual meeting of the officers of the Herkimer county agricultural society, held pursuant to adjournment, at the Remington House, in Ilion, on the 2d day of January, 1856, the following members were present, viz.: Messrs. McKee, Morgan, Bonfoy, Smith, Jones, J. B. Smith, D. Bonfoy, Hawks and Wilcox.

Resolved, That Wm. Stewart, Esq., be appointed chairman, *pro tem.*, and Hon. Jonathan Jones, secretary.

The following gentlemen were elected officers for the current year:

President—Geo. B. Judd, Frankfort.

Vice President—Duane Richardson, Schuyler.

Secretary—Wm. Dygert, Frankfort.

Treasurer—J. A. Rasbach, Ilion.

Resolved, That an executive committee of nine persons be appointed, whereupon the following gentlemen were chosen: Daniel Mason, Frankfort; James Folts, Frankfort; Geo. W. Joslin, Frankfort; Ezra Graves, Herkimer; Samuel H. Kinney, Litchfield; Wm. P. Pryme, Schuyler; J. D. Ingersoll, Ilion; Lemuel F. Hawks, Columbia; Amos Gilbert.

Resolved, That a corresponding secretary be appointed, from each town in the county.

The following gentlemen were then chosen: Conrad Oxner, Columbia; Ralph Simms, Danube; L. B. Arnold, Fairfield; Amos Mann, Frankfort; E. W. Patridge, German Flats; Samuel Earl, Herkimer; Jeremiah Kinney, Jr., Litchfield; Josiah Davis, Little Falls; John Markell, Manheim; Seth Fenner, Newport; Benjamin Hurd, Norway; Wm. Coppernoll, Ohio; Stephen Pryme, Russia; Lorenzo Carryl, Salisbury; Amos Bridenbecker, Schuyler; Daniel Hawn, Stark; Chas. Delong, Warren; Gardiner Hinckley, Wilmurt; E. W. Willcox, Winfield.

Resolved, That the secretary furnish each of the corresponding secretaries with a printed subscription to solicit persons to become members of the society.

Resolved, That the vice president act as chairman of the executive committee.

Resolved, That the several examining committees be direted to report in writing, the result of their examinations, before the delivery of the address.

Resolved, That the executive committee meet at the house of D. M. Golden, in Frankfort, on the first day of February next, at 10 o'clock A. M.

Resolved, That the secretary furnish the several papers of the county, with the proceedings of this meeting.

Resolved, That the next annual meeting be held at the Remington House, in Ilion, on the first Tuesday of January, 1856. Adjourned.

CHAPTER X.

1783 TO 1855.

Political Parties — Origin of, in this State — George Clinton — Leader of the Anti-federalists — Montgomery County Anti-federal in 1788 — Herkimer County, Federal from 1791, to 1800 — Judge Sanger — State of Parties change in 1801 — Jay's Treaty — Alexander Hamilton — Germans Anti-federalists — Mathias B. Tallmadge — Object of his settling at Herkimer — Success and Defeats of the Republican Party for 19 Years — Restrictive Measures of the U. S. Counsel of Appointment — Robert Williams — Removals from Office — Contest in 1810 — Henry Hopkins — Clintonians and Bucktails — Meeting of the latter in 1819 — Secretary superseded — Success of Federalists in 1819 — The Reason of it — Policy of the Leaders — Federalists succeed in 1820 and 1821 — Clinton elected Governor, in 1820 — State Convention of 1821 — Popular Vote in the County, for and against — Prospects of Parties — Simeon Ford, Richard Van Horne, Sanders Lansing, Sherman Wooster — Democratic Success — New Constitution adopted — Success of Democrats, from 1822 to 1847 — Political Excitement in 1824 — People's Party — Electoral Law — Michael Hoffman — Democratic Assembly Ticket defeated — Presidential Election — Martin Van Buren — William H. Crawford — Aspect of the Election — Democratic Success in 1825 — Silas Wright — Prospective Troubles continue among Democrats — Call of a Convention to amend the Constitution of 1821 — Position of the Democratic Party in the County — Convention Law originated in this County — Vote for Convention — Vote for Delegates — Vote for and against Constitution — Democratic Party defeated in 1847 — Henry P. Alexander elected to Congress in 1848 — Review of the Chapter — Vote amending the Financial Article — Senate Document No. 70 — 1831, Characteristics of Population.

Distinct political party divisions and distinctions do not seem to have assumed any very definite shape, the first twelve years after the adoption of the Federal constitution. Until the formation of that instrument in 1787, and its submission to the states for ratification, there was no general subject on which the people of the states could well divide and array themselves in national party lines. New York was opposed, under the leadership of Gov. George Clinton, to *the formation of a new government*, or any material change in the articles of confederation, and this was emphatically declared in the resolution of the legislature at the time the three delegates, Messrs. Lansing, Yates and Hamilton were appointed to attend the national convention. When the constitution which emanated from that body came before the people of the country for consideration, and while under advisement, New York was the great battlefield; and in none of the states was the opposition to its ratification more decided, animated and emphatic than in this. A strong anti-federal feeling predominated among the inhabitants of the whole state, and notwithstanding the conditional ratification by the state in 1788, Gov. Clinton was able to sustain himself until 1795 against all the power and patronage of the general government, wielded by Gen. Hamilton and other distinguished adherents of President Washington's administration.

This fact shows most clearly that the ratification before mentioned was compelled by the necessities of the case, and was not a voluntary acquiescence. The people of the Mohawk valley placed as high an estimate upon the character and services of the commander in chief of the American armies as any other; they held the name of Washington in deep reverence and profound respect, but they had fought the battles of their country, and conquered for it independence and peace under the banner of New York. Theirs had been a seven years' campaign without retirement to winter quarters, and they felt little inclination to surrender to others any portion of the boon so dearly purchased. On the question of ratifying the federal constitution, Montgomery county was decidedly anti-federal.

From the organization of Herkimer county, in 1791, to 1800, federal members were chosen to the assembly, except the two years the county was represented by Judge Sanger, and the year before Oneida county was set off from Herkimer.

I assume that Judge Sanger was an anti-federalist in

1793-4, when he represented the county, because he was elected to the senate in 1800 by the republicans, and afterwards acted with the federalists. The members of the assembly elected in 1797, seem to have been taken from both parties; or rather, one anti-federalist was that year elected. The great influx of population from New England between 1790 and 1800 had changed the political aspect of the county, and especially in that part of the territory set off as Oneida, in 1798.

The political contest which preceded the election of Mr. Jefferson in 1801, had arrayed the voting population of the county into two political parties, which in that day were known as federalists and republicans; and it is a fact not unworthy of notice in this place, that while the eastern population seated within the territory of Oneida county, almost unanimously acted with the federal party, the immigration to Herkimer seems to have been more equally balanced, although a considerable majority of that population which settled in this county adhered to their New England proclivities.

The federalists, at that early day, possessed another great advantage over their opponents which was not unimproved. The establishment of county seats at Herkimer and Whitestown opened a new field for the legal profession, and it was not long left unoccupied by gentlemen of great weight of character, standing and talents, as their subsequent political and professional career abundantly shows. The mercantile interest was also strongly attached to that party, and the men at that time engaged in commercial pursuits, controlled much of the money capital of the country. The establishment of trade upon a permanent and favorable basis with England was by this class of our population deemed most essentially important. The commercial treaty negotiated by Mr. Jay with great Britain in 1794, had been assailed and denounced, by the planting or agricultural interests with persevering zeal and ardor; while other portions of the population not particularly identified with those interests, evinced their disapproval of the treaty and the negotiator by mobs and riotous burnings in effigy, unmistakable evidence of a misdirected popular feeling Such was the state of party feeling, its bearings and influences upon society, that a republican lawyer or a republican merchant was seldom to be found in the country villages or at the county seats in this part of the state, where it would be now difficult to point out one of either class who does not profess the true democratic creed of some sort.

The survivors of the revolution were slow to see the necessity of a strong government; the very name was distasteful and odious. They had gone through one war "to crush out" what they believed a monstrous evil, kingly rule, and they had yet to feel the necessity and be satisfied of the propriety of having any connection or intercourse with kings or kingly governments; and besides, the leading federalists were strongly suspected of sympathizing with Great Britain, then engaged in active hostilities to put down republican France. Alexander Hamilton, although nurtured in the revolution, was known to be favorable to strong and high toned governments; I say known, because his project of a constitution read to the convention at Philaphia in 1787, was spread far and wide over this broad land. He was *the* leader of the federal party in this state and exerted no small influence with that party in other states. And although he was a great man, holding rank with the most solid and brilliant of his compeers of the revolution, it must be confessed he was not an adroit and skillful manager of a political party.

I do not believe, and never have, that the masses belonging to the federal party, when it maintained a political existence, ever gave their full adhesion to the extreme notions of some of their leaders; nor do I suppose every man professing to belong to the republican party is bound to adopt and defend the unwise or pernicious notions of some of his so called political friends, but, after all, the character of the leader is impressed upon his party, which must stand or fall according to the estimate placed by the popular judgment upon the principles and measures enunciated.

At the period under consideration, the opening of the nineteenth century, the whole framework of our government was but little more than an untried experiment, so far as respected its actual workings. We had gathered some strength as a nation, and the hopes of the old stepdame for an opportunity of resubjugation had become very much darkened. But it is not my purpose to write a treatise on governments, or the history of political parties outside the confines of the county, any farther than may be needful to explain results as we have found them.

The German population of the county was strongly imbued with the anti-federal feelings, when the federal constitution was ratified. After political parties assumed the names of federalists and republicans, a very considerable majority of that population was found acting with the latter; it was not brought out, however, to act effectively, until the April election in 1800. An able and efficient body of men, lawyers, merchants and others, had settled at Herkimer, whose influence, in conjunction with others in the county, decided the political character of the members.

Before the period here mentioned, Mathias B. Tallmadge, a republican lawyer, and connected by marriage with the family of Governor George Clinton, settled at Herkimer. I can not give the actual time Mr. Tallmadge came into the county, but I find he was elected a delegate to the convention of 1801, from this county, with Evans Wharry and George Rosecrants. He was afterwards elected to the senate of this state, in April 1802. Mr. Tallmadge was, no doubt, sent into the county as a political leader, and by this movement Governor Clinton extended his family influence to an important point in the state, then fast filling up with population from the older southern and eastern counties, and from the other states, particularly New England. It is not improbable that Evans Wharry, a native of Orange county, well known to, and a fast friend of Governor Clinton, was mainly instrumental in bringing Mr. Tallmadge into the county.

Mr. Tallmadge's contemporaries do not speak of him in terms of extravagant praise. He was not equal in point of talents and energy of character to any of his leading opponents. But the soil was congenial to his touch, and the harvest ripened to his hand; and such was the veneration and respect for the name of George Clinton in the Mohawk valley, and so deep seated was the anti-federal feeling in the county, strengthened and embittered by some of the acts of the federal government under the administration of John Adams, and particularly the stamp act, that it only remained to select the candidates, print and circulate the ballots, and the election from that moment became a "fixed fact," so far as this county was concerned. Mr. Tallmadge was appointed United States judge for the district of New York in 1805, and soon after removed from the county.

During the period of nineteen years, from 1800 to 1818, inclusive, republican members were elected to the assembly, with one solitary exception, and then that party only sustained a partial defeat in the county. At the spring election, in 1809, Thomas Manly and Rudolph Devendorff, federalists, and Christopher P. Bellinger, republican, were chosen members, the latter by some five or six votes. The federal party that year, for the first time since 1799, achieved a political triumph. This event has been charged to the restrictive measures of the general government, under Mr. Jefferson, which weighed heavily upon the navigating and grain-growing interests of the country.

Wheat had fallen from twenty-four shillings a bushel, before the embargo, to six shillings after that measure was enforced, and products found no foreign market. Daniel D. Tompkins was then governor, and the freehold vote in the state upon the choice of senators showed a little over seven hundred republican majority. Under the constitution of

1777, the political majority in the assembly controlled the choice of the council of appointment, composed of one senator from each senate district. It so happened, there was not, at this time, a single federal senator from two of the districts, and the majority in the assembly were forced to choose two members of the council who had been elected as republican. This was a gloomy prospect for those who were hopefully looking to the enjoyment of the "spoils of victory." While the republicans were reposing in security, supposing every thing would be safe with the casting vote of their favorite governor, the dominant party were actively engaged in looking up some disaffected republican senator, who could be brought over to their views. The constitution of the state had given the civil list appointments into the hands of the federalists, and all they lacked was instruments by which to exercise their power. They however found the man they wanted, in the person of Mr. Robert Williams, of the Middle district, who had been a Burrite, Lewisite, Clintonian, and was elected to the senate by the republicans. He, it appears, was one of the trading politicians of that day, who set themselves up to the highest bidder; and he met the fate in after life that all such men deserve — the scorn and contempt of his former friends, and the studied neglect of those he had recently served. The federal council, after its organization, went to work with a zeal that met a warm response from its friends in every quarter of the state; but was far from being very agreeable to their opponents. This council appears to have done a pretty large and extensive business in the way of removals and appointments to office.

The party in power were no doubt induced to this course in view of the election of governor, about to take place, in the spring of 1810. The federalists had contested the election the previous year on the merits of the measures pursued by the national administration, and had succeeded. Those questions, though of grave importance, still remained to pass the ordeal of the popular judgment at the ballot box, but were not the only elements that entered into the contest, which became unusually excited and animated. The federalists were in office, and the reelection of Governor Tompkins would postpone to an indefinite period all hope to the federal party of a permanent restoration to power in the state and union; and the republicans were smarting under their recent defeat and consequent loss of office, by the treachery, as they alleged, of one who should have been a friend.

Mr. Hammond says, that "contrary to the expectation of both parties, the republicans were not only successful, but their success was complete. They achieved an entire and complete overthrow of their opponents. Tompkins was reelected by about ten thousand majority. The republican candidates for the senate succeeded in all the four districts, and in the assembly the republicans had a majority of almost two to one."

It does not come within the objects of this publication to discuss the causes which produced the above result, or to speculate upon motives that may or may not have actuated political men or parties. At the election in April, 1810, the republican party in the county regained its ascendency, and the members of the new council of appointment were careful to revise and correct, in 1811, all the mistakes of their immediate predecessors.

A word of explanation should here be given in reference to the spirited, uniform success of the republican party in the county during the period of nineteen years. I have stated one exception. On a further examination, I find another. At the spring election, in 1815, Henry Hopkins, a gentleman who had uniformly acted with the federal party, was elected to the assembly with John McCombs and William D. Ford. One of the republican candidates first put in nomination died a few days before the election, and Mr. Hopkins was chosen by a majority of nineteen votes over George Paddock, who was taken up and supported by the republicans.

Many of the leading republicans in the county were, between 1816 and 1820, known as Clintonians; they sustained the measures of Governor De Witt Clinton, and selected candidates to the assembly friendly to that gentleman, who were of course chosen. I believe the members elected in the county, the three years previous to 1820, did not act with the bucktail opposition (so called) against the governor. Disaffection in the republican ranks manifested itself pretty decidedly throughout the state, towards the close of the governor's first term, and a meeting was called at the Court House in Herkimer, in the spring of 1819, to organize and nominate an assembly ticket. The meeting, although not very numerous, was composed of a considerable number of active republicans, and attracted some attention. John Herkimer, then one of the county judges, and afterwards member of congress, was appointed chairman. Michael Hoffman, Esq., submitted a series of resolutions, setting forth the grounds of complaint against the governor, and among them was one condemning, in pretty strong terms, the action of the council of appointment in removing Martin Van Buren, and appointing Thomas J. Oakley, a leading and distinguished federalist, to the office of attorney general. The resolutions were adopted and published, with my name appended as secretary. For this act of *insubordination*, the secretary was complimented with a supersedeas as a justice of the peace at the following July session of the council of appointment. The same meeting nominated candidates for members of assembly in opposition to the ticket already in the field friendly to Governor Clinton.

This division among the republicans brought out the federalists, who, on the eve of the election, nominated a full assembly ticket, which was chosen by a handsome majority, although the anti-Clintonian or bucktail republicans abandoned their ticket, and generally voted for the Clintonian candidates.

The result of the election showed a clear federal majority in the county at that time, and this was probably the fact;

not arising out of any material change in the political sentiments of the population within the territorial limits of the county before 1817, but from the annexation, in that year, of the three eastern towns from Montgomery county, Salisbury, Manheim and Danube.

The federal party in the county, like that of the republican in Oneida, although twenty years in a minority, was neither dead nor asleep. Its wakeful and recuperative faculties were extremely facile. Whenever at a gubernatorial or senatorial election, it became expedient to poll a full freehold vote, their strong and tried men were put upon the local tickets, and the elections were canvassed with a zeal and animation that betokened a confident assurance of success. The annexed towns had usually given a pretty strong and reliable aggregate federal majority, when attached to Montgomery county. Of the candidates presented by the federalists in 1819, one was selected from Manheim, a gentleman of influence and weight of character, with a view, no doubt, of impressing our new neighbors with the notion that their interests were to be carefully looked after, and their prominent men not neglected. Candidates were taken by that party from each of the remaining towns at the two succeeding elections. In adopting and pursuing this policy, the federal party, under the circumstances, evinced a good deal of political skill. I well remember speaking with a Clintonian republican, Robert Shoemaker, on the subject, who remarked, it would do very well unless it provoked jealousy in other parts of the county.

At the succeeding spring elections, in 1820 and 1821, the federalists achieved two more victories in the county, and then rested upon their honors more than a quarter of a century. It had, I believe, become a fixed common law principle with the political parties in the county, when it was entitled to three members of assembly, to select one of German and two of English descent, as candidates. This rule may not have been observed in every instance during thirty-six years, and if not, the exception was extremely rare.

The contest for governor in 1820, between the bucktail and Clintonian parties was, no doubt, one of the most severely contested of any that had taken place in the state for many years. The freehold vote in the county was 1226 for Clinton, and 947 for Tompkins. Mr. Clinton's majority in the state was only fourteen hundred and fifty-seven, and although he escaped defeat, his opponents held the political power of the state by having a working majority in each legislative branch. The federalists as a party supported Mr. Clinton, notwithstanding some fifty *high-minded* gentlemen, of great personal worth, talents and wealth, renounced their connection with that party, declared it dissolved, in a published manifesto, and avowed their intention of supporting Mr. Tompkins. A portion of the old republican party adhered to Mr. Clinton, and a perfect reunion of the dissevered fragments did not take place until General Jackson's election in 1828, and in the meantime most of the *high-minded* gentlemen had gone over to the Adams party. This brief view of the aspect of affairs outside of the county, seems necessary to enable us to appreciate more justly the true state of things at home. There were several provisions in the constitution of 1777, framed and adopted while the country was in a state of war, and when it was believed too many guards could not be thrown around the exercise of the powers of self-government, such as the veto power, vested in a council of revision, composed of the chancellor and justices of the supreme court, who held their offices during good behavior; the power of appointing all the civil and military officers in the state vested in the governor for the time being, and four senators, and the restriction upon the elective franchise, confining the choice of governor and senators to those citizens who owned a freehold of the value of two hundred and fifty dollars, which attracted public attention, and became the subject of discussion among politicians and in the public press. This subject, if properly managed, could be used as an effective instrument to produce a political crisis, and the opportunity was not neglected by Mr. Clinton's opponents. It is not my purpose to inquire after the reasons, or to discuss the motives which induced that gentleman and his leading friends to oppose the call of a convention to revise the constitution of 1777. Whatever may be the exact truth in respect to this matter, the people were told, and they believed, that he and his friends were in fact hostile to the measure, and with this impression strongly fixed in the public mind, the convention was called, and the result in the choice of delegates was precisely what every intelligent politician in the state expected.

The majority of the popular vote in the state for the convention, was seventy-four thousand four hundred and forty-five. In this county the aggregate vote for it was 1598; against, 1627. The election of delegates took place on the third Tuesday of June, 1821. The republicans, or democrats as they were now called, had been defeated the previous April, and the Clintonians controlled the only newspaper in the county.

Although the current of public opinion in the state was setting strongly in favor of the democratic party, the condition of affairs in the county did not afford much prospect of success in the election of delegates to the convention. Mr. Simeon Ford, a gentleman whose private character was without reproach, of highly respectable talents, and who had long been a leading member at the bar in the county, had been elected a member of the assembly in 1820, and reelected in 1821. His capacity for business and industrious habits, rather than brilliant displays of oratory, rendered him an efficient member of the house, and one of the prominent Clintonian leaders. He was a politician of the old federal school, and had been long a resident of the county. It was considered very important by Governor Clinton and his friends to secure Mr. Ford's election as a delegate to the approaching convention. In view of the great interests at stake, no man in the county was better qualified by experience and ability to grapple with the accumulating difficulties of the times, and which eventually precipitated his party, for a time, into a hopeless minority.

I think the Clintonian and democratic conventions met at Herkimer, on the same day, to select candidates to be supported at the election for choosing delegates; and if this was not the fact, the Clintonians had made their nominations. It was known to the democrats that Mr. Richard Van Horne, of Danube, was a candidate on the ticket with Mr. Ford, before they made out their ticket. The democrats were neither hopeful nor sanguine, and their convention was not very numerously attended, but we had come resolved to make up a ticket, win or lose. During our deliberations it was stated in the convention that Mr. Van Horne was in favor of the extension of the elective franchise, and a modification of the veto, and appointing powers, and had given verbal assurances to that effect. It was somewhat difficult to make out a ticket, not on account of the pressure of claims by the friends of candidates, but for the want of the right sort of men, and none were envious of the distinguished honor of being defeated. We finally nominated a ticket, consisting of Sherman Wooster, Sanders Lansing and Richard Van Horne.

It was urged in the convention, that by placing Mr. Van Horne on the democratic ticket, we should render his influence in the town of Danube less hurtful to Messrs. Wooster and Lansing, than it would be if he was left off. To the surprise of some, and contrary to the sober expectations of many, Messrs. Lansing and Wooster were chosen delegates by a majority of four hundred and thirty six. It was generally believed the Clintonians were opposed to the extension of the elective franchise, and this damaged their ticket with the non freeholders, to some extent. But considerable apathy prevailed among Mr. Clinton's friends at the polls of election which I attended. I always attributed this to dissatisfaction, in a certain influential quarter, in respect to Mr. Ford's third nomination, although the avowed reasons for non interference in the election, was, that the individual approved of the call and objects of the convention. There is no doubt, I think, that the minds of many people in the county, became settled and fixed in favor of the measure, after it was generally known that the call of the convention had been sanctioned by such an immense majority of the voters in the state.

After finishing their labors at Albany, the convention adjourned, submitting the new constitution to be approved or rejected by a vote of the electors. At a special election, held in the month of February, 1822, the constitution was ratified by a vote of 75,422 for it, to 41,497 against it; showing a majority of 33,925, in the state.

Without riots, bloodshed or the least disturbance in the machinery of government, this civil revolution was accomplished, and the large approving vote was followed by the most salutary effects. I do not wish to be understood in this remark, to refer to mere party politics. It showed to the civilized world, that Americans were capable of self-government; that old and well established principle of the fundamental law of the social compact, could be abrogated when found inconvenient or unsuited to our condition, with the same order and peaceable decorum which usually attend our annual elections. The vote in this county, on adopting the new constitution, was, 1583 in favor, and 1254 against it.

The first election in the county, under the new constitution, in November 1822, resulted favorably to the democratic party, and from that time, to 1847, I am confident no candidate, other than an avowed democrat, was elected to any office by the people. I shall notice the exceptions in due order of time, when the regular county-convention nominations were set aside or disregarded. I should notice the fact in this place, that a democratic paper was established in the county, by Mr. Edward M. Griffing, in 1821. It was called *The People's Friend*, and published at Little Falls.

The presidential controversy in 1824, produced the ephemeral nondescript called the *People's Party*. It lived one year, and no longer. Its leaders were in favor of almost every body, or any body for president, except William H. Crawford. Some of my readers, if I should have any, may think I do not treat this subject with the impartial pen of an historian. I wish to call things by their right names, and tell the plain unvarnished truth.

At the November election in 1823, Christopher P. Bellinger, John Graves and Caleb Budlong were chosen members of assembly, and were not unfriendly to Mr. Crawford. The electors of president and vice-president were then appointed by the legislature, and it was supposed, and such was no doubt the fact, that a majority of the legislature chosen that year, were, when elected, favorable to Mr. Crawford, assuming he would be the regular nominee of a democratic congressional caucus, and it hence became necessary in order to defeat Mr. Crawford in this state, to change the mode of appointing electors, and with that view early in the session of 1824, a bill was introduced into the assembly directing the appointment of electors to be made by the people through the ballot box by general ticket, at the annual election preceding the expiration of the official term of the presidency. I do not use the cant phrase of the day "*restore* the election to the people." The people never had exercised that power directly, and therefore it could not be *restored* to them. The bill passed the assembly, but was indefinitely postponed in the senate, which was virtually a rejection. At former periods in the history of the states, the federalists and republicans when in the minority in the legislatures, on which would devolve the appointment of electors, made efforts to change the law and refer the subject to the people directly, but the majorities in both instances considered it a sort of clap-trap affair and retained the power in their own hands. The rejection of the electoral law placed the democratic party in a very unenviable predicament. The democrats had now placed their necks under the axe which they used to decapitate the Clintonians three years before. The current of popular opinion set against them with a force perfectly resistless. Party drill, regular nomination, and personal appeals did not avail any thing. The democratic county convention met as usual and nominated candidates for assembly, and concurred in the several state and senatorial district nominations. The same convention nominated Michael Hoffman to be supported as a candidate for congress. This was Mr. Hoffman's first appearance on the political arena in the county as a candidate for an elective office.

A meeting not very numerous, I believe, subsequently convened at Herkimer, and nominated John Herkimer member of congress for reelection, and Samuel Dexter, Jr., Warner Folts and Jacob Wire for the assembly. These gentlemen had all of them acted with the democratic party during the last four years. This was a *Peoplish* movement, and it was understood at the time that the Clintonians proper or federalists did not appear openly in the affair, although they must have secretly encouraged it from the support given by them to the ticket at the election. There had not been during the summer and fall any organization of a people's party or any indication showing disaffection in the democratic ranks in the county. A large majority of the party in the county was supposed to be friendly to Mr. Crawford against all the other candidates, and when the convention met to make nominations, there was a fair prospect of an old-fashioned field fight between the veteran parties. Mr. Herkimer was an Adams man, and Mr. Hoffman an avowed Crawfordite.

The Clintonians generally supported what was called the people's ticket, and after the election, during which a good deal of bitter feeling was exhibited, the canvass showed that Mr. Clinton had 134 majority over Col. Young; Hoffman over Herkimer 244; the average of people's assembly ticket over the democratic was only 49. The democratic assembly candidates received the entire support of the party in good faith, yet all of them left it within a few years and attached themselves to other political organizations, and Messrs. Dexter and Folts were on the best of terms with the democratic members of the house during the whole session. This political tornado was not confined to Herkimer county alone, it swept over the whole state, and Mr. Clinton, who only two years before had been so reduced in popularity in consequence of his course on the convention question, that his friends dared not to venture his being a candidate for governor against Mr. Yates, was now elected by 16,906 votes over Col. Young.

But the eleemnts of dissolution existed in this people's party at its very formation. The only bond that brought them to act in concert, was the defeat of William H. Crawford; that once accomplished, and the union became a rope of sand. Mr. Clinton, whose position made him the strongest man in this state, among the coalesced minorities, did not favor the pretensions of Mr. Adams by any avowed or overt act of adhesion or preference. He expressed an opinion, before the question was actually decided, that Gen. Jackson would be chosen by the house of representatives; founded on the belief that the house would choose the candidate highest on the list and having the greatest number of votes, and thus conform its action to the declared will of the largest popular vote. These facts with others that might be here repeated clearly show, that Mr. Clinton did not sympathize with the Adams and Clay sections of the people's party which combined at the November session in 1824, to secure a majority of the electoral vote in this state for their respective favorites.

Much surprise has been expressed, that Mr. Van Buren and his friends did not at once consent to change the mode of appointing electors, appeal to the popular vote of the state, and some of his warm friends and the advocates of Mr. Crawford's election censured him and them for not doing so. Mr. Van Buren possessed a clear and comprehensive political sagacity; this his greatest and most bitter opponents allowed and feared. The disturbing and disquieting controversy growing out of the Missouri compromise, had not been forgotten. The south had enjoyed eight presidential terms, and the north one, since the adoption of the constitution. The sectional preferences and prejudices of the north were against the candidate preferred by Mr. Van Buren, and many of his influential friends in this state; and there was but little prospect of controlling or changing the direction of those prejudices and preferences, except through the agency of a regular caucus nomination, made by the republican members of congress, and even that might fail in the absence of any great national question on which an appeal could be made to the patriotic feelings of the people. A regular nomination could not be obtained for Mr. Crawford, and the era of good feeling doctrine promulgated under Mr. Munroe's administration had soothed the political asperities which had existed between the old republican and federal parties, not a little sharpened by the events of the war of 1812. A democratic electoral ticket pledged to support Mr. Crawford, would probably have obtained a plurality of the votes given in the state, if backed by a regular congressional nomination, and the friends of all the other candidates had presented, and in good faith supported, separate tickets; but if the minorities should combine, as they did in the legislature, and divide the candidates for the electoral college, assigning a given number to each of their favorites, and go down to the election with but one ticket, there would not have been much question as to the result. The democratic ticket might have succeeded, if there had been no issue on the electoral law; and that issue would not have been raised, if there had been only two candidates in the field for the presidency.

That there would be a democratic majority elected, on whom would devolve the appointment of the electoral college, and that such majority would act in accordance with the wishes of Mr. Van Buren and his friends, if the caucus system was strictly adhered to, was quite as certain in July, 1823, as it was at the meeting of the legislature, in 1824. That there would be no choice by the college in

December, 1824, was pretty well settled in the minds of politicians before the New York election in November, 1823, so that the whole object aimed at by the friends of the several candidates was, to place their respective favorites in a position to be chosen by the house of representatives. That was the issue in this state, and this indicated too clearly to be mistaken what course Mr. Crawford's opponents would take in case a plurality or majority electoral law should be passed. Even the loss of the election did not place the power of choosing democratic electors out of the reach or beyond the control of the democratic party; if there had been no dishonorable violation of the most solemn voluntary pledges, Mr. Crawford might have as easily obtained the whole thirty-six electors as four.

At the November election in 1825, the democrats regained the ascendency in the county by a majority of about six hundred, and the Clintonians lost the election in the state. This result again placed the political power of the state substantially in the hands of the democratic party. From this time to 1847, the democrats invariably elected their regularly nominated members of assembly, and with one exception, in 1846, their county officers. The candidates of the party never failed of an election by the people during the above period, with the exception noted, although in that time, the state had been several times lost and won to the democratic party, and the country had seen the election of two whigs to the presidency, General Harrison, in 1840, and General Taylor, in 1848.

The rejection of Mr. Van Buren by the Baltimore convention in 1844, the disaffection manifested by a section of the democratic party in this state against Governor Bouck, who was elected in 1842, and the disagreement among leading democrats in regard to the canal policy of the state, had combined to produce a feeling of estrangement in the democratic ranks, which was distinctly exhibited at the annual election in 1846. Governor Wright was then a candidate for reelection. My intercourse with Governor Wright, political and social, had been, for twenty-two years, intimate and cordial. I had contributed my feeble exertions to his elevation to the senate of the United States, and never regretted having done so. After the development of the difficulties in the democratic party in the state, and they had sufficiently shown themselves prior to the election in 1844, to satisfy any considerate man, that a disruption was at hand, which must soon overwhelm any man occupying the executive chair, I objected to and advised against his acceptance of the office of governor, and thereby vacate his seat in the senate of the United States. Mr. Wright had other friends who viewed this subject in the same light, and who were governed by the same disinterested motives that I was, and they did not hesitate to express their opinions on the subject. I do believe he did not cheerfully consent to leave Washington, and that he had strong forebodings of the fate that awaited him in the event of his coming in direct contact with the bitter family feuds at home. I need not speak of Gov. Wright's character and standing as a public man or private citizen; other and abler pens than mine, have already inscribed a just memorial of them on the page of history. He was a strong, able and popular man. What I have said and shall say in regard to Mr. Wright, may not seem to be exactly in place in the local history of a county which did not claim him as a resident, but I have an object in alluding to him in this place in consequence of his name being connected with our local affairs. His nomination for reelection was apparently acquiesced in by the party, and nothing appeared to disturb the smooth surface except the little anti-rent ripple which originated in Albany, Columbia and Rensselaer counties, and had now began to attract some attention; but there was a secret under-current operating strongly against his success. So confident were his active friends of achieving an easy victory in the state, that in several instances they did not observe due precaution in selecting candidates who could secure the general support of their party friends. Such was the case in respect to the nominee for sheriff in this county, and the nominee for congress in the district, composed of Herkimer and Montgomery counties. The former was nominated in the county convention by a small majority of a strongly contested vote, and the latter in the district convention by the casting vote of a member, whose object was to present the man who could be the most easily defeated at the polls. Sections of the democratic party in both counties organized opposition to these nominations, presented other candidates, and with the aid of the whigs defeated the regular nominees of the party. Mr. Wright must have been a good deal damaged in this county by this contest among his friends. I say friends, because the successful candidates and their supporters claimed to be his friends. His majority in the county was nine hundred and ninety-four, several hundred less than in 1844.

Previous to 1846, considerable discussion had taken place in the state, respecting its financial condition, and the expediency of imposing restrictions upon the power of the legislature to borrow money, and contract a state debt. The judicial department of the government had been found inadequate, not from the inefficiency of the judicial functionaries, but from want of numbers, to dispatch the business brought before it, and the delays of litigation were nearly equivalent to a denial of justice.

At the legislative session in 1844, the two houses passed the resolutions of which the following are the titles:

1. "Resolution proposing certain amendments to the constitution, in relation to state debt and liability."

2. "Resolution proposing an amendment to the constitution in relation to the court of chancery."

3. "Resolution proposing an amendment to the constitution, in relation to the supreme court."

The amendments embraced in these resolutions came up for consideration at the session in 1845, and were agreed to by two thirds of all the members elected to the senate, but failed of receiving the requisite majority in the assembly. Although there was a democratic majority in the house, as well as in the senate, a marked diversity of opinion existed among the members of the majority, in respect to the constitutional amendments then under consideration, and the project of calling a convention to revise the constitution of 1821, which had been introduced into the assembly. While one section of the democratic members strongly favored the financial amendments, the other section did not yield them a hearty assent, or its cordial support, although willing to place them before the people for their adoption or rejection. The position of these two sections was reversed on the judicial amendments. The whigs, as a party, generally favored the judicial amendments, but were strongly opposed to the financial. That party however were not inclined to go in favor of any measures, or any policy, which would defeat the calling of another convention, to new-model the constitution. To use their own language, "they went for a new deal," with the hope of securing some of the prominent offices of the state from which they had been excluded for nearly twenty years. I shall not attempt to discuss the various questions presented, and views entertained for and against the call of another convention. On one side it was urged that the legislature could not constitutionally pass any law, authorizing the call of a convention, inasmuch as the existing constitution prescribed a mode in which amendments to, or alterations of that instrument could be made entirely different from that then under consideration. On the other side, it was insisted, that the whole subject was at the disposal of the electors, and if on submitting the question to the people, a majority should decide in favor of a convention, that one might, and should be convened. It is quite certain that the convention of 1821 did not suppose that instrument would be altered or changed, except in the manner pointed out in it; and it is equally certain, that the convention of 1846 must have considered the act initiating its existence might be justly characterized as revolutionary: otherwise, direct authority would not have been conferred upon the legislature, to provide for taking the sense of the electors in respect to calling future conventions. The financial convulsion of 1837, and the commercial embarrassments of 1840 and 1841, consequent upon the great inflation of prices in 1839, followed by an unexampled depression in the state stocks, attributed mainly to the recent rapid increase of the state debt, had contributed to infuse into the public mind a strong and settled conviction, that to avoid interminable taxation and embarrassments, the legislative power over the finances and credit of the state, must be strictly defined and limited to a very narrow circle.

The democratic party of this county had taken ground at an early day in favor of an amendment to the constitution, to the effect that every law passed by the legislature proposing to create a debt by the issue of state stock, or impose a tax for certain purposes, in order to become effectual, must be submitted to, and sanctioned by a direct vote of a majority of the electors of the state, at an annual election. This proposition, subsequently modified and amended, and known as the People's Resolution, was adopted by a convention held in this county, in the year 1837. Its paternity was afterwards attributed to a distinguished politician of the county, through a mistake as to its origin. The rough draft of the resolution was shown to me in my office, by my then law partner, in his own handwriting, and I am confident that he alone was the author of it. The substance of that resolution now composes a part of the seventh article of the present constitution of the state. When first brought out, the project attracted but little attention outside of the county, but it became one of the standing resolutions of the county conventions for several years, and was finally adopted as a cardinal point in the democratic creed, first in the county, and then in the state.

The passage of the law calling the convention originated, I am fully convinced, with the politicians of this county;

and, although I do not mean to say their object was confined to the adoption of the financial restrictions, and it probably was not, still that measure incited their unceasing vigilance and most active exertions. The act calling the convention was approved by Governor Wright, and became in form a law. The vote in this county on the question of convention or no convention, was, 4,346 in favor, and 86 against it. At the election of delegates, Michael Hoffman had 1,470, and Arphaxad Loomis 1,468 votes, about two-thirds of the democratic strength in the county. There was no organized opposition, and the scattering vote was small. When this constitution was submitted to the people for adoption, less unanimity seemed to prevail in the minds of the electors. The vote for it was 3,382, against it 1,029, and on the question of admitting our colored population to an equal suffrage with the white, without property qualification, the yeas were 1,442, and the nays 3,156, showing 187 more votes on the equal suffrage question, than the aggregate for and against the constitution. The aggregate of the whole vote for governor in 1844, was a little over 7,295, and in 1846, 5,633. This shows that nearly 3,000 of the electors of the county did not participate, either in the call of the convention, or the adoption of the constitution.

The changes proposed in the fundamental law by the convention of 1846 were much more extensive than those made by the convention of 1821. It was thus that a great revolution in the institutions of a state was brought about, founded, when the movement commenced, on the single complaint against improvident acts of legislation in respect to the finances and credit of the state.

The above figures show that one-half of the electors of the county did not approve of the constitution by an affirmative vote. The convention had incorporated a provision into the constitution restricting the power of the legislature to pass laws of a certain character, except by a majority of all the members elected to each branch, three-fifths of all the members being present, in which case the absence of a member operates as a negative upon the law, which, in many instances, may be only temporary and affecting the rights of only a few people ; but in fixing the fundamental law of the state, it only required the majority of the voices of those who might choose to speak to control the destinies of millions. It is not my object to write a political treatise, and I therefore forbear further remark. I have aimed to give a true statement of the events of this period, and believe I have done it.

At the succeeding annual election, in 1847, the county performed a complete political somerset. James Feeter, in the first district, and Lawrence L. Merry, in the second, whigs, were elected to the assembly by considerable majorities, and Thomas Burch, whig, was chosen senator in the senate district. The defeated candidates were two radical democrats and one hunker. This was preparatory to the canvass for the presidency in 1848. Hitherto, for a period of about forty years, the people of the county had not been represented in the congress of the United States, by a man who was not known and recognized as a republican or democrat, but Henry P. Alexander, a highly respectable whig, was this year elected to congress from the district composed of Herkimer and Montgomery, and was not very badly beaten when again a candidate in 1850.

I hardly need say, in this connection, that the whig party has not obtained any ascendency in the county since 1847, except in the election of Mr. Alexander.

It is now, 1855, sixty-four years since this county was erected, and it may not be uninteresting to some to take a brief view of the state of political parties in it during that period. It is in no respect of any moment, except to show the current of public feeling at home in regard to the political questions which have agitated the country since the foundation of the national government and the formation of political parties, consequent upon the diversity of opinions not only in respect to the federal constitution of 1787, but also in regard to what was esteemed the true principles and proper form of government to be adopted by the American states, as well as the fair and just interpretation of that instrument. The subject of American politics and American political parties, derives all its interest and importance from the fact that the state and national governments are administered conformably to the popular will, enunciated in the form prescribed by written fundamental rules. Since the county was organized, the representatives in the popular branch of the legislature, the assembly, have been elected wholly, or in part, by the anti-federal, republican and democratic parties fifty-four years. I use these names to designate the same political party in succession at different periods of time. I should add here a word of explanation; the above period embraces every year when the candidate elected was nominated by the political party above designated. Of the twelve state senators elected from the county at different times, two were federalists, nine were republicans and one was a whig. There have been three state conventions to modify, alter and change the state constitution, and republican delegates were chosen to each, except Richard Van Horne, in 1821. Six republican electors of president and vice-president have been selected in the county, and one whig. In respect to the members of congress sent from the county, I have had some difficulty in ascertaining the whole number. From the best information within my reach, there were twelve in all; and of these, one was a federalist, nine were republicans or democrats, one was an independent, chosen in opposition to the regularly nominated candidate, although he claimed to be a republican, and one was a whig.

There are but few counties in the state, if any, in which the population has shown such steady and uniform adherence to the republican or democratic party, and where the political men of that party have been so frequently elected to office by the people. And I am proud as a citizen of the county, to record the fact, that hitherto there has not been a single instance, save one, of corruption and malconduct charged against our public men, and those who have "gone to that bourne from whence no traveler returns," now "rest from the labors of life's toilsome pilgrimage," leaving behind them fame and characters untainted and untarnished.

The financial article of the constitution of 1846 has been recently modified so as to allow the legislature to contract a debt to a limited amount to complete the state canals. A majority of the electors in the county who voted on this modification, were in favor of the amendment. The vote was a small one, and affords no evidence of a change of opinion in the county favorable to an unlimited grant of power to the legislature over the credit and finances of the state. This review closes with the year 1854, and will not be resumed by the author of this work.

NOTE.—The reader, I doubt not, will excuse a brief allusion to a subject which has, on more than one occasion, attracted public attention.

The governor, in his annual message to the legislature in 1831, had directed attention to the accumulating surplus revenue of the United States, under the operation of the tariff laws, and the senate of this state raised a select committee consisting of Mr. Benton, Mr. Mather and Mr. Deits, to whom that part of the message was committed. The members of the committee gave the subject their early and earnest attention, made up their minds to present a report to the senate, and designated Mr. Benton to prepare it. In the mean time, as Mr. Hammond states, the assembly, on the 10th of March, passed a concurrent resolution, without a division, declaring that the surplus revenue ought to be annually distributed among the several states, without alluding to the constitutional incompetency of congress to act on the subject. I transcribe what Mr. Hammond says in vol. II, of the Political History of New York, page 353. "It [the resolution] was sent to the senate, but was by that body referred to a select committee, of which Mr. Benton was chairman, who, on the 4th of April, made a long and able report, in which they discussed the constitutional question in relation to the powers of congress to make the proposed division without decidedly expressing their views on the question." [Senate Documents of 1831, No. 79.] Mr. Hammond seems to infer that because the committee withheld a decided expression of opinion as to the constitutional power of congress to make the distribution under the power then vested, that the committee entertained doubts on that subject. This conclusion does great injustice to two of that committee, Messrs. Benton and Deits, at any rate. The whole argument of the report on this point, which Mr. Hammond says was an able one, went to show that congress had no more power to create a surplus for the purpose of distribution, than it would have to build a church, school house or an academy within the territorial limits of one of the states. The committee could not fail to see that they were discussing a subject submitted to their consideration by the executive department of the government, and which had been acted upon by a coordinate branch of the legislature, without any allusion to the constitutional question; and they felt unwilling to meet the difficulties which seemed to them insurmountable, other than by presenting the argument against the exertion of the power by congress in the best possible light and in the most forcible manner they could, and leave the subject without any other expression of opinion. Had the committee entertained any other views, or no decided views at all on the subject under consideration, would they have elaborated an argument in support of principles they repudiated or about which they felt indifferent? There is no subject of constitutional power or legislation, over which the people of this country should be more watchful or guarded than the "money power," wherever it may be exerted, whether by the state or United States.

CHAPTER XI.

1791 TO 1855.

William Orendorff, Aaron R. Clark, John Bowman, Samuel Bennett, Samuel Perry, Nathaniel Foster, John Allen.

The catalogue of crime of the higher grades is quite brief. It is believed there was no trial or conviction from 1791 to 1798, when Oneida county was set off. I have gleaned from criminal records of the county only six trials which resulted in convictions and acquittals.

On the 31st of May, 1809, William Orendorff was tried and convicted upon an indictment for a rape, and sentenced to the state prison during his natural life.

On the 5th of June, 1811, Aaron R. Clark was tried and convicted before Mr. Justice Van Ness of the supreme court upon an indictment for manslaughter, and sentenced to the state prison for three years and three months.

On the 15th of September, 1812, John Bowman, who had been previously indicted for murder, was arraigned before Justice Van Ness of the supreme court, D. V. W. Golden, Walter Fish and George Rosecrants county judges, and J. Ingham, assistant justice, and plead not guilty. The following are the names of the jurors empanneled to try the case: Augustus Carpenter, Lucius Wetherby, Benjamin Benjamin, Jr., Jabez D. Wolf, Oliver Miner, James Alexander, Daniel I. Petry, Jost I. Petry, Ezra Mallory, Gibson J. Stranahan, Joseph Pooler and Sheldon Harvey. There were nine witnesses sworn on the part of the prosecution, and examined. Not any witnesses were called and sworn on the part of the prisoner.

The entry of the verdict and sentence pronounced by the court is recorded in these words: "The jury found the prisoner *guilty*, and he was sentenced to be hanged by the neck until he was dead, on the fourth day of December next, between the hours of 11 o'clock A. M. and 1 o'clock P. M."

John Bowman was a lad not over ten years of age when he was tried and convicted for this crime. He was ably defended by Daniel Cady, Esq., now one of the justices of the supreme court of the fourth district. Bowman had killed one of his playmates, a small girl younger than himself, and the point insisted upon by Mr. Cady in the defense, was, that he was too young to possess a mind and judgment capable of understanding and appreciating the nature of the offense he had or was about to commit. The jury thought otherwise, and brought in a verdict of guilty. The judgment of the court was not executed. The sentence was commuted by a law passed November 10, 1812, to imprisonment for life in the state prison.

Samuel Bennett was convicted upon an indictment for manslaughter, on the 12th of December, 1822, before Mr. Justice Platt of the supreme court, and judges Holt and Herkimer of the common pleas, and sentenced to confinement in the state prison at Auburn for ten years. Simeon Ford, Esq., the district attorney, conducted the prosecution, and Messrs. Hoffman and Maculey defended the prisoner. In this case the counsel for both parties exerted all their powers for conviction and acquittal, and a Herkimer audience have seldom witnessed more able forensic efforts than were displayed on this occasion.

At the September term of the oyer and terminer in this county in 1826, Samuel Perry was arraigned on an indictment for murdering his wife. The court consisted of Nathan Williams, circuit judge of the fifth circuit, and Hiram Nolton, Sanders Lansing and John Mahon, county judges. The jurors sworn were Jeremiah B. Cooper, William Williams, Henry F. Orendorff, Elnathan Harvey, Peter House, Henry Dockey, Milton Philleo, Joseph Griswold, Eli Fortune, John

Eysaman, James Van Valkenburgh and Suffrenus Snell. The whole panel having been exhausted by peremptory challenges and challenges for cause, the two last named jurors, Van Valkenburgh and Snell were summoned to sit as tales. George H. Feeter, district attorney, assisted by Abijah Mann, Jr., and David Bucklin, Esqs., conducted the prosecution, and Lauren Ford, Michael Hoffman and Oran G. Otis, Esqrs., defended the prisoner. Twenty-three witnesses were called by the prosecution and examined, and two only on the part of the defense. The trial commenced on the 14th day of September, and on the 16th the jury pronounced the prisoner *guilty* by their verdict. The prisoner's counsel tendered several exceptions to the ruling of the court during the progress of the trial, and the judgment upon the verdict was respited to allow the supreme court of the state to examine and give judgment upon those exceptions. The social position of the prisoner, the alleged or supposed causes which prompted the commission of the offense, and the estimable character always borne by the unfortunate victim murdered, conspired to excite in our community a deep and intense feeling. The court room in which the trial was conducted, although not as large as some in our cities and most populous counties, was quite spacious. Long before the court convened to open the trial, this room was filled almost to suffocation with an anxious and deeply excited audience; the avenues to the room were so densely thronged with people seeking admission that ingress and egress by the officers of the court was at times very difficult. I felt a strong desire to hear this trial, as I had never been present at the traverse of an indictment for murder, but my human endurance could not stand it. I once, during the trial, under the auspices of the district attorney, got into the court room, and after remaining a short time made my escape from it, and was compelled to remain an outsider. Many others were excluded from hearing the trial, and for the like reasons.

The respite of the judgment rendered it necessary for the

prisoner to be present, when the supreme court should make a decision on the exceptions taken on his behalf, in order that the sentence of that court might be pronounced, in case the exceptions were overruled, and with the view of removing the prisoner to Albany, the sheriff of the county, John Dygert, Esq., had brought his conveyance to the jail, when a short delay occurred in starting, to permit the prisoner to execute a testamentary disposition of his property. While the will was being prepared, the sheriff's officers visited the cell where the prisoner was confined, and found him dead, or so nearly dead that he survived but a short time. He had cut his throat with a razor. This act was performed with a strong and unflinching hand, and sure instrument. The jugular artery was severed, by a long deep gash, which ended life almost as soon as made.

When the grim messenger of death bore the tidings of this man's fate to the chancery of Heaven, think ye, did the recording angel, as he registered it, drop a tear of regret upon the record, and blot it out for ever? This suicide was committed in the month of October, following the conviction, and between the two periods, Perry had devised plans of escape from prison, and flight to Canada. He had considerable pecuniary means, and was therefore enabled to subsidize fit instruments for his purpose; but all his plans were defeated by the vigilance of the public officers, and the care taken for his security.

The next capital offense appearing on our criminal records, is the case of Nathaniel Foster, indicted for the murder of Peter Waters, a St. Regis Indian. This trial was opened on the 16th and closed on the 17th of September, 1834, at the Court House in Herkimer, before the Hon. Hiram Denio, circuit judge of the fifth circuit; John B. Dygert, Abijah Osborn, Jonas Cleland and Richard Herendeen, county judges; and a jury consisting of the following persons: John Davis, John Harder, Henry Ostrander, James F. Fox, William Bouck, Peter Rickert, William Shoemaker, James Shoemaker, Lester Green, Nicholas A. Staring, Earl Trumbull and Peter Bell. James B. Hunt, the district attorney, assisted by Simeon Ford, Esq., conducted the prosecution, and Joshua A. Spencer, Aaron Hackley, George H. Feeter, Lauren Ford and E. P. Hurelbut, Esqs., appeared for the prisoner. The record shows there were five witnesses called and examined on the part of the prosecution, and five by the prisoner's counsel. The jury rendered a verdict of ***not guilty***, after a consultation of about two hours. That Foster deliberately shot the Indian, at a time, too, when he was in no immediate danger of assault from or by the Indian, and that this act was premeditated, there can not be much doubt, if there is any reliance to be placed on human testimony. Foster and the Indian had for some months lived near neighbors on Brown's tract, so called, in the north part of the county. Both were hunters of the wild game of the northern forests, and were probably envious of each other's success, if they had no substantial causes of complaint to produce hostile feelings between them. Foster was an old man, upwards of sixty winters had bleached his locks, and the Indian was in the prime of life, stout, athletic, and like all his people indulged in the use of "fire-water," when he could get it, and was easily irritated and passionate. On the morning of the day the Indian was killed, he and Foster had a scuffle, and the latter was slightly wounded by the Indian. Some bystanders interposed and parted them, or Foster would probably have been more seriously hurt. Shortly after this, the Indian and several whites started off in a boat and bark canoes on a hunting excursion on the Seven lakes, and Foster followed or preceded them five miles by land, to a point in one of the lakes, where he shot the Indian, who was then alone in his canoe, but there was another bark canoe near by, containing two white men.

On the trial, the prisoner's counsel proposed to ask one of the witnesses on the stand if he had ever heard this Indian threaten to kill Foster, insisting the evidence was competent and tended to prove that Foster was in "imminent danger" of being killed himself by the Indian; submitting the sufficiency of the proof to the consideration of the jury. Objections to the admissibility of this testimony being made, the presiding judge of course sustained the objection, and ruled that such evidence was not competent; one of the county judges concurred with Judge Denio, but the other three judges holding the evidence was admissible, the circuit judge was overruled by a majority of the common pleas bench. This was a novel decision in our criminal courts, and will not, probably, be often followed in trials for murder. The majority of the court must have held, that when an American Indian threatens to take life, the danger becomes imminent, from the inflexible pertinacity he has always evinced in carrying such threats into execution. *Id certum est quod certum potest*, is a sound legal maxim, but it will not do to apply it to the future actions of an Indian, any more than to an Anglo-Saxon. It is very difficult to say what effect such evidence had upon the minds of the jurors, or might have had in a case where the killing of an Indian was not involved. It is not very material to discuss this point to any great extent, when the reasons for the acquittal are so well known as they were when the verdict was given, and even at this day. Three-fourths of the jury were of German descent, whose memories still lingered on the traditional scenes of woe and desolation inflicted upon the families of their ancestors, by the Indian races, who never claimed the protection of the laws of civilization, or submitted to the municipal regulations of the whites. I do not intend to impute any moral wrong to the twelve men who held Foster's conviction or acquittal at their disposal, much less will I seek to impeach their judgment or motives; but truth and candor compels me to express the belief that, if, under the same circumstances, a white man had been killed by Foster, instead of the Indian, he would have been found guilty. Foster was not a bad man, although a hunter and an inhabitant of the forest nearly all his days; he was not inclined to provoke quarrels with any one. The Indians visited the wilderness between the settled parts of St. Lawrence and Herkimer and Hamilton counties, and claimed the whole country as hunting grounds, although their title had been long extinguished. This seemed to produce an unfriendly feeling between the hunters of the two races, which proved fatal to some of them, but the red men were the greatest sufferers.

The next case in the criminal annals of the county, was that of John Allen, who was arraigned on an indictment for murder, before Philo Gridley, justice of the supreme court, of the fifth district, Ezra Graves, county judge, David Humphreyville and Morgan S. Churchill, justices of the sessions, on the 5th of September, 1849. George B. Judd, district attorney, conducted the prosecution, and Messrs. V. Owen and R. Earl, the defense. Thirty-nine witnesses were called and examined by the prosecution. The jury empanneled to make "true deliverance" found the prisoner *not guilty*, under the *direction* of the court. This is the substance of the entry in the proceedings of the court, and those familiar with the expressions used, will conclude that the prosecution failed to make out a case of probable cause of guilt, against the prisoner. The murder was charged in the indictment, to have been committed in the town of Schuyler, in the winter of 1848–9. The lifeless body of a man was found, bearing strong marks of violence having been inflicted upon it, and sufficient to produce death. It was identified to be that of a foot pedler, traveling about the country, with goods of some value. It was also believed he had a small amount of money with him. The circumstances connected with this sad affair, produced a strong impression on the public mind, that the man had been murdered, in order to obtain possession of his goods and money, or that he was killed in defending himself against a violent robbery. The popular excitement in our community ran to a pretty high pitch, and a just indignation at the commission of so foul a deed, was loudly expressed. The officers of justice were soon on the alert, and the district attorney ably and resolutely performed his duty, and if he failed to convict the man indicted and arraigned, that failure can not justly be charged to a want of industry or energy, on the part of the prosecution.

This ends my catalogue of capital offenses against life, for a period of nearly sixty-four years, since the erection of the county. In all that time there have been two convictions for murder, but no public execution by the hangman. May the good Providence of God, and a just regard of our population to their duty and obedience to the laws, continue to avert from us all cause for such an exhibition of punishment.

We can not and do not claim to be exempt from the commission of crime in the lower grade of offenses, but the calendar has not been large, nor have the instances been grave or serious. The petty larceny fraternity have not yet quite left us, or abandoned their business, and there have been those who indulged in acts of felonious appropriation upon a larger scale, so as to come under the definition of *grand* larceny.

Bands of counterfeiters and persons engaged in passing counterfeit paper money, and spurious coin, have heretofore infested the county, the rigor with which these law-breakers were prosecuted, and the vigilance of the public officers in detecting and ferreting out these depredators upon the public, has long since cleared the county of this class of offenders. I do not mean to say we have not had instances of offenses of this sort committed in the county within twenty years, but the cases have been rare within that time compared with the period between 1820 and 1830.

Upon a careful review of the statistics of crime committed in this county the present century, and comparing them with other counties in the state, and other communities, we find much to encourage a hope that the future in our progress will present more gratifying results than the past, and that the moral sentiment of the population of the county in this respect, as in every other duty of life, may be found the highest and best of any in the state.

CHAPTER XII.

Biographical Sketches of Stephen Ayres, Alexander H. Buell, Robert Burch, Stephen W. Brown, Benjamin Bowen, Dan Chapman, Atwater Cook, William H. Cook, Rufus Crain, Henry Ellison, John Frank, Simeon Ford, David V. W. Golden, Gaylord Griswold, Joab Griswold, Elihu Griswold, John Graves, David Holt, Michael Hoffman, Stephen Hallett, Philo M. Hackley, Henry Hopkins, Sanders Lansing, John Mahon, Thomas Manly, Jacob Markell, John Mills, Michael Myers, William Petry, George Rosecrants, Nathan Smith, Ephraim Snow, Henry Tillinghast, Stephen Todd, Abijah Tombling, Edmund Varney, Richard Van Horne, Evans Wharry, George Widrig, Westel Willoughby, Chauncey Woodruff, Sherman Wooster, Samuel Wright.

The writer has indulged in some personal gratification in collecting and writing out the biographical sketches presented to the reader's attention in this chapter. That gratification would have been greatly increased, if the means of doing more ample justice to the subject had been within his reach, and he could have included every name found in the official list printed in the appendix. He was familiarly acquainted with very many of the individuals of whom he has written, and take them as a class, or individually, with one exception, for purity of character, elevated and patriotic purpose in action through life, they should not have a second place on the scroll of fame. Their sphere of action was limited, but they bore the same relation to the people of the county, that others filling higher and more elevated positions held in respect to the communities they represented. There have been and always will be, I suppose, grades of excellence in official men; some may have no excellence at all, but this can not be said of those whose biographies are found in the succeeding pages of this chapter.

STEPHEN AYRES

Was a native of Massachusetts, and born at Braintree, February 16th, 1770. He came into this state with his father, Jabez Ayres, in the year 1792, who settled in the town of Salisbury, where he made his clearing, raised his family, and went to his final rest, leaving the subject of this notice to inherit a good farm and a large share of his energy of character. Mr. Stephen Ayres purchased a lot of land in the then town of Norway, now Fairfield, in the fall of 1792, which he brought under cultivation and on which he lived until his death. He was a practical surveyor, an occupation he occasionally pursued until age incapacitated him from service in the field. In the course of a long and active life he had traced many of the lines of lots on the patents on the north side of the river, and could designate the boundaries of lots, and describe and locate the corner trees from memory, many years after he had quit the active pursuits of his profession, and indeed many years after he had made his survey. His son, Hiram Ayres, was called on, not many years before his father's death, to trace the lines of a lot at a distant point on the Royal grant, from the family residence, and when told the number and location of the lot, Mr. Ayres described to his son with particular exactness, the corner of the lot where the survey commenced, and lest these landmarks might have been removed or destroyed, he also described a peculiar witness tree, and its course and distance from the true corner, when surveyed about twenty years before and not since visited by him.

In 1836, Mr. Ayres represented this county in the Asembly, with Frederick Bellinger and Thomas Hawkes. He was not ambitious of political preferment, although he deservedly enjoyed the confidence and esteem of his fellow citizens. In stature he was full six feet, and "well proportioned." He was of that class and school of men who reasoned well and endeavored to act wisely. He chose to be governed by the results of his own reflections, and the

Engraved by J C Buttre from a Photograph

Alex. H. Buel

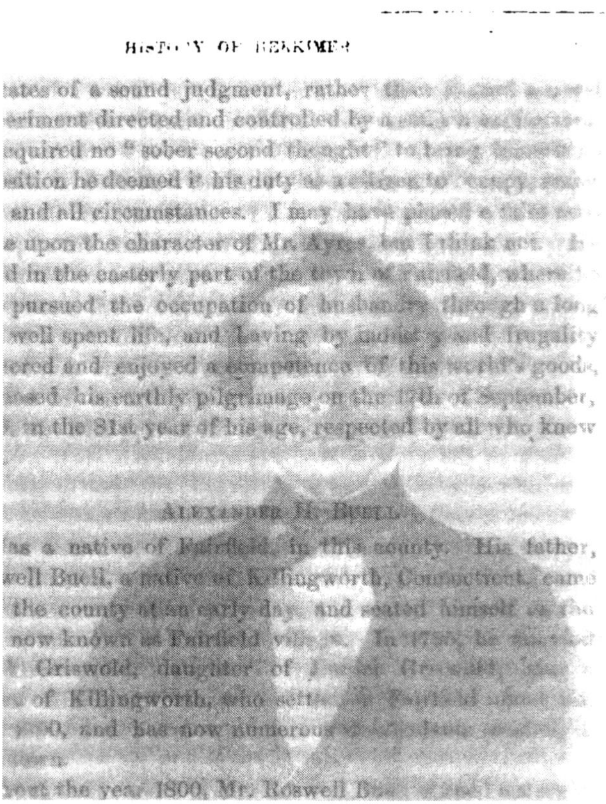

dictates of a sound judgment, rather than hazard a novel experiment directed and controlled by a sudden excitement. It required no "sober second thought" to bring himself to a position he deemed it his duty as a citizen to occupy, under any and all circumstances. I may have placed a false estimate upon the character of Mr. Ayres, but I think not. He lived in the easterly part of the town of Fairfield, where he also pursued the occupation of husbandry through a long and well spent life, and having by industry and frugality gathered and enjoyed a competence of this world's goods, he closed his earthly pilgrimage on the 17th of September, 1850, in the 81st year of his age, respected by all who knew him.

ALEXANDER H. BUELL

Was a native of Fairfield, in this county. His father, Roswell Buell, a native of Killingworth, Connecticut, came into the county at an early day, and seated himself on the spot now known as Fairfield village. In 1795, he married Sarah Griswold, daughter of Daniel Griswold, also a native of Killingworth, who settled in Fairfield about the year 1790, and has now numerous descendants residing in that town.

About the year 1800, Mr. Roswell Buell opened a store in Fairfield, and was some time engaged in the mercantile business. He was distinguished for his enterprise and benevolence. He donated an acre of land to the trustees of Fairfield academy, in 1802, on which the first academic edifice was erected. In the midst of an active and useful life, he fell a victim to the epidemic which prevailed in the winter of 1812-13, aged 40 years. His affairs were somewhat involved by this sudden event, and after the settlement of his estate was effected, only a small patrimony remained to the surviving members of his family. His widow still lives, and at the close of 1855, has attained the venerable age of 86 years.

Alexander Hamilton Buell, the subject of this notice, was

born July 14th, 1801. The loss so early in life of the counsel and sustaining aid of a father, when both were so much needed, was no doubt viewed by young Buell as a severe calamity. He soon seemed to appreciate the circumstances which surrounded him, and was fully impressed with the idea that he must be the artificer of his own fame and fortune; that success could only be looked for through his own exertions. The position in which he was placed had great influence in moulding his character and developing those traits which led to his subsequent success in life as a merchant. His opportunities for an accomplished academic education were somewhat limited by his engagements as a clerk in the store of Mr. Stephen Hallett, then one of the principal business men at Fairfield. His time at school was however well employed, and he sought to make up by diligence and studious application during his leisure hours, what he lost while engaged in the store of his employer.

A marked feature of young Buell's character is developed in the following facts: During the first three years of his employment with Mr. Hallett, and he commenced at the age of 14, he was diligent and attentive as a clerk in the store, supporting himself by his own exertions, and at the same time superintending the affairs of his widowed mother with all the efficiency of a man of mature years, and with a kindness and solicitude that carried with it a sweet and soothing solace. Nor was this all; his sisters, orphaned like himself, were not unfrequent recipients of presents from the surplus of his earnings. He had become so accomplished in business, several years before he reached his majority, that he was repeatedly sent by his employer to the city of New York to purchase goods to replenish his store.

Mr. Buell, at the age of 21, became a partner in business with his former employer, and at Mr. Hallett's death, assumed the sole proprietorship of the business at Fairfield. He subsequently, in connection with different individuals, extended his mercantile business into the neighboring towns and villages in the county; afterwards, giving scope to a clear and comprehensive mind, and the exertion of an excellent business talent, his commercial operations were extended to counties in this state remote from his native home; and he did not finally stop until he reached the distant shores of the Pacific ocean; even California was not neglected by the accomplished and successful Fairfield merchant. I am not aware that Mr. Buell ever thought of removing to New York, where fortunes are so rapidly made and marred in commercial pursuits. He was several times gratified and honored by the confidence of his townsmen, in electing him to local offices of trust and confidence. He was a member of the assembly from this county in 1845. This, I believe was his first appearance at Albany as a legislator. He was placed at the head of the important committee on banks and insurance companies, in a house in no respect destitute of men of talents. Although it is not usual to select the chairmen of the leading committees from new members, the appointment in this instance was judicious, and the compliment well deserved. In this new and untried position, Mr. Buell sustained himself in every respect to the satisfaction of the house and his friends. An ardent politician of the Herkimer school, and I use this term because our neighbors in other counties charge us with being "of the strictest sect," it was his duty and his pleasure to square his official conduct to suit the feelings and opinions of his constituents.

Mr. Buell was chosen member of the 32d congress from the 17th congressional district, composed of Herkimer and Montgomery counties, at the November election, 1850. His competitor was a personal friend, and then the member from the district, Henry P. Alexander. The canvass was briskly conducted and adroitly managed by the contestants and their friends. The district was one in which there could not be much doubt when the whole vote was polled and party lines strictly drawn as "in olden time." He was married to Miss Harriet E. Gruman, of Clinton, Oneida county, November 9, 1840. Before taking his seat in the congress, to which he had been elected, Mr. Buell closed his connection with most of the mercantile establishments in which he had been interested, over which he could not well exercise a personal supervision. He won and enjoyed the confidence and regard, not only of the business community, but of his political friends and associates. By his industry, application and unwearied exertions, he accumulated a fortune, enough to satisfy the reasonable desires of an ambitious man a little removed from the commercial and financial emporiums of our state, where few men are counted rich who are rated under a million of dollars, where comparisons serve only to stimulate to hazardous experiments, and even wild and imaginary speculations. He must, of course, have been punctual in all his pecuniary engagements, and prompt in all his other business relations. His surviving townsmen have cause to remember him for his public spirit, and the worthy recipients of charity never solicited his aid in vain.

Mr. Buell died at Washington city on the 31st January, 1853, after a brief and painful illness, in the 52d year of his age. The house of representatives passed the usual resolution of condolence; and while a monument in the congressional burying ground commemorates his official connection with that eminent body of American statesmen and his death, his mortal remains, distinguished by a suitable memorial, have found a final resting place in the grounds of Trinity church, Fairfield, by the side of which repose the remains of a father, brother and an infant daughter. His wife, two sons and a daughter, survived him.

Robert Burch

Was born in Killingsly, Connecticut, December 3d, 1761, emigrated from Berkshire county, Massachusetts, into this state, seated himself in the present town of Schuyler in 1799, and died on the farm he had opened and reduced from a wilderness state, on the 26th of June, 1830, in the 69th year of his age.

Devoted to agricultural pursuits, Mr. Burch bore the even tenor of his way through life unobtrusively, and left several sons, who are among our prominent and active business men.

He was one of the members of the assembly from this county at the sessions of 1811 and 1812, at a period when national and state politics very much engrossed public attention. He possessed a quick apprehension and a sound and discriminating judgment. He was diligent and attentive to his public duties, and was careful in those times of high party strife to be prepared to vote promptly when the question was propounded by the speaker. I have heard an anecdote repeated of him to this effect. His seat in the house was near that of Mr. Brayton, a member from Oneida, with whom he was on terms of friendly, social intercourse, although they differed on political subjects. Mr. Burch was always in his seat and prompt to respond in a pretty audible tone of voice when the roll was called on a division. Mr. Brayton may have been, and probably was, classed among the leading men of his party. Now for the anecdote. On one occasion, after a pretty stormy debate and close vote on a division, Mr. Brayton accosted his political adversary and said to him, "Burch, how does it happen that you are always so prompt and ready to vote, your party friends following your lead to a man, and you seem to give yourself but little trouble in regard to matters before the house?" Mr. Burch coolly remarked, "I'll tell you, sir, how it is; your name being called next before mine, I am careful to notice how you answer, and, always on questions of this sort, vote against you, and feel assured I am quite right." The question may have been prompted by some momentary feeling of irritation under defeat; the answer shows that the respondent was fully satisfied he had done his duty.

A few years after Mr. Burch settled in Schuyler, some of his former neighbors "at the east" sent him some branches of a dwarf evergreen, too frequently found in the soil of New England, not only to remind him of his former home, but as they said, "to keep him from being homesick." A pretty good antidote that for any such ailment in one then reposing in the luxuriant valley of the Mohawk.

Stephen W. Brown

Was a native of Williamstown, Mass. He was several years engaged in mercantile business, in the town of Salisbury, in this county, which resulted favorably. He removed to Little Falls in the year 1830, with a view to a more extended field of business operations, and to give a wider scope to a mind fertile in expedients. He was liberal and public spirited, if not to a fault, so far as regarded his pecuniary resources, it may well be said, he indulged his generous feeling to the extremest limit of prudence. He was active, ardent and almost incessantly engaged in business. Always among the first, and with the foremost, in any local business enterprise that required associated capital, and combined personal exertion, to carry it forward to a successful result; or in founding and rearing some public institution, permanently beneficial to the locality where it was to be established. After his removal to Little Falls, he was several years engaged in trade at that place, which he finally relinquished, and devoted his whole time and attention to the affairs of a manufacturing establishment, which had been brought into existence mainly through his personal exertions. He closed his mercantile business in 1843.

He was chosen sheriff of the county at the November election, 1837, and held the office one term. He was a popular officer; kind and agreeable in manners, and cheerful in disposition, he had many friends, and very few, if any, enemies. With an almost inexhaustible flow of kindly good feelings, and hopeful in the extreme, anticipated results were sometimes counted as accomplished, when in fact actual realization was not within the measure of a fair probability. His character, as a man, was irreproachable, or if not so, the tongue of blame has not blazoned his faults to the world. He was a reformer in almost every thing relating to politics and civil government, and exerted his influence, effectually at times, to correct some of the flagrant abuses of the bad men of the legal profession, which were oppressive. I say bad men, for I know that only a few of that honorable class, would descend so low as to commit the faults which, through his agency, were immediately and successfully remedied by legislative interference. He was suddenly and violently attacked, when absent from home on business, with a fatal malady, from which he did not recover. He survived but a few days, after his return to his family at Little Falls.

The monument erected to his memory, by those who knew him well, and appreciated his worth, bears this incription:

STEPHEN W. BROWN
Died May 30th, 1846,
Aged, 49 years.
This stone is erected by his
neighbours to evince their
high estimation of his character.

Benjamin Bowen

Was a native of Rhode Island. He came from Newport, in that state, to Fairfield, in 1787, where he purchased a farm and settled. He remained at Fairfield until 1792, when he removed to Newport, and commenced the erection of mills at that place, and laid the foundation of the prosperity of that pleasant and thrifty village. He was a man of great activity and enterprise. He was a member of the legislature in 1798, elected on the same ticket with Gaylord Griswold, Henry McNeil, Nathan Smith, Mathew Brown, Jr., Lodowick Campbell and Isaac Foot. This was the only time that I find he was chosen a member of either branch of the legislature. He was appointed one of the judges of the county courts October 30th, 1800, and held the office nearly five years, and probably as long as his political friends had the bestowment of patronage. He died at a somewhat advanced age, leaving no male descendants in this county. His only son emigrated to Alabama with his family in 1819, and died there. I believe Judge Bowen also died in Alabama, but I am not certain of this fact. Thus the name of one of the earliest and most enterprising pioneers of the northern part of the county has become extinct, but a memorial of his active and zealous efforts to make the "desert blossom as the rose" still remains.

Dan Chapman

Was a native of the state of Connecticut. He came into the county at an early period after its erection, and settled on the Stone ridge, Herkimer village, where he engaged in mercantile pursuits, but the ledger balances showing a deficit, he abandoned the weights and measures of merchandising, and betook himself to those of the legal profession. He must have been admitted to the bar previous to May, 1804; his name does not appear on the roll of attorneys commencing at that date. He was appointed surrogate of the county March 23d, 1803, superseded in 1807 by an adverse council of appointment, reappointed in 1808, and held the office until November, 1816. He seems to have escaped some of the political vicissitudes of the times during his last period, that appear to have been visited upon the sheriff and county clerk. The federal party held the appointing power of the state in 1810 and 1813, and if political conformity preserved to him the seals of probate and administration, Mr. Chapman must have been exceedingly adroit and flexible. He quit the profession about the year 1820, and removed to Oneida county. He again returned to this county, and after remaining here a short time removed to Montgomery county, where he died a few years since at a very advanced age. He was a subaltern officer in the revolutionary army, and enjoyed the gratuity of his country in his old age, which softened and assuaged the "ills that life is heir to." He was not successful in accumulating wealth, although his life was morally and religiously irreproachable.

Atwater Cook

Was born in the town of Salisbury, in this county, December 17, 1795, of parents in moderate circumstances in life, who were of English or Anglo-Saxon extraction. His father lived to attain a pretty advanced old age.

Like most young men of that day, Mr. Cook's education was limited to the course of instruction taught in the country schools of that time, but he was endowed with a strong and vigorous mind, a sound and discriminating judgment, and much practical good sense. He experienced some of the vicissitudes of life and the "charms of its varieties" were not unknown to him at the commencement of his career of manhood. He resolved, by just and laudable efforts, to overcome all obstacles to the attainment of a reasonable competence and the enjoyment of the confidence and good will of his fellow citizens. He early turned his attention to the dairy, and was among the first of our farmers who abandoned grain-growing and resorted to grazing. His exclusive attention was not given to agriculture. At different periods of his life he was engaged in mechanical and mercantile pursuits.

Mr. Cook was many years one of the justices of the peace of his town; the duties of the office he discharged with ability and satisfaction to the people. He also held other town offices of confidence and trust, and exerted, when he chose, no inconsiderable influence among his fellow citizens. When in the prime of life, he bestowed considerable attention, by reading and study, to the cultivation of a sound and vigorous understanding. At the general election in

1830, he was chosen one of the members of assembly for the county. Nicholas Lawyer, of Danube, and Olmsted Hough, of Schuyler, were his colleagues. Mr. Cook was an attentive and industrious member of the house during the session of 1831, and was active and efficient in his exertions to promote the interests of his constituents in regard to local legislation, and especially in removing the alien dead weight which had many years pressed so heavily upon the village of Little Falls.

Although not trained to public debating, he spoke several times during the session on important subjects before the house, and was listened to with great attention. He was much respected, and his familiar acquaintance with the internal local affairs of towns and counties, made him a useful member. In 1839, Mr. Cook and Benjamin Carver, represented the county in the assembly. This time his party was in a political minority in the house.

It may truly be said of Mr. Cook, he possessed a mind of considerable conservative tendencies, still he was a man of progress. He lived in a progressive age, and belonged to a progressive race, and he failed not to meet the exigencies of the day and the hour when action was called for. He was among the first in the town of Salisbury to initiate the temperance movement, and he continued, through life, to give the cause his warmest advocacy and most hearty support. He was equally active, prompt and devoted to every movement which would tend to ameliorate the condition of his race, or promote the welfare and best interests of the community where he lived.

Mr. Cook's health was quite infirm during the latter years of his life, and he suffered much and acutely, from severe sickness; neverthelesss, his death was sudden, and unexpected to his friends at a distance. He died at his family residence, in Salisbury, February 14th, 1853. He was then the oldest male inhabitant, born in the town. By industry, strict application to business, and a watchful providence of his yearly gains, he had accumulated a competence of wealth, for all human purposes, which he left to be enjoyed by his family.

WILLIAM H. COOK

Was a native of this state, and came into Norway, in the fall of 1792, from Dutchess county. He settled a short distance westerly of Norway village, where he devoted himself to farming and merchandising, pretty extensively, and if I have not been misinformed, made some effort at the milling business, which did not in the end amount to much, in the way of increasing his we lth. He was appointed sheriff of the county, March 17th, 1802, and was annually thereafter appointed, until 1806; when he was left out of commission but was again appointed sheriff, in 1807, and held the office one year longer. This ended his official career in this county, and it might have been well for him if he had never tasted office.

Mr. Cook was in the battle of Tippecanoe, fought on the night of the 6th of November, 1811, between a small American force, under Gen. Harrison, and a numerous body of north-western Indians. He died at Vincennes, Indiana. Jabez Fox, a native of Connecticut, came into this county about the year 1810, married a daughter of Mr. Cook. He was admitted as an attorney, at the Herkimer county common pleas, in January, 1813. Mr. Fox pursued his profession a few years at Herkimer, and then removed to Little Falls, in 1818, or about that period. He was elected county clerk, under the then new constitution, at the general election, in 1822, to hold for the term of three years, from the 1st day of January following. He died at Herkimer, in January 1825, at the age of 35 years.

DOCTOR RUFUS CRAIN

Was a native of Western, Worcester county, Massachusetts, and the second son in a family of ten children. His father, Isaac Crain, was born in Coventry, Connecticut, and his mother, whose maiden name was Putnam, and a near relation of Gen. Israel Putnam, was also a native of Western. His early education was entirely sufficient to enable him to study and practice the medical profession with much success. He studied under the direction of Dr. Ross, of Colerain, Mass., who is spoken of as an eminent and successful practitioner, and after completing his course, formed a connection in business with his late tutor, which terminated when he came to this state in 1790.

His first object was to fix himself at Cooperstown, Otsego county, but passing through Warren on the route to his place of destination, being pleased with the country and the inhabitants, and finding many of them from New England, he changed his determination and seated himself in Warren, which at that time was destitute of a physician. Here he devoted himself to his profession with the characteristic zeal and assiduity of a young New Englander, and in a few years found himself enjoying the rich fruition of an extended and lucrative business. His position in a country town containing as good lands as any in the county, enabled him to engage in agricultural pursuits, which he prosecuted with success in connection with his professional business, which received his chief attention, to nearly the close of his life. Doctor Crain came into the state early in life and formed a connection by marriage with an influential family of the town in which he died. He was one of the early patrons of the Medical college at Fairfield, and devoted himself earnestly and efficiently to its success. He, like hundreds of others who left the then over populated and not very prolific soil of New England, near the close of the last century, had determined to try his fortune in Western New York, as then called, and he came, as he once told me when we were riding together from Herkimer to Little Falls, resolved on success. "Yes, sir," said he, in reply to a remark of mine, "a young man with a good profession and a fair share of talents, need not fail, he can not fail in a new country, if he is prudent, industrious and attentive to business. He can, if he wills to do it, establish a reputation and accumulate a competence." With a mind so constituted, success in life could only have been prevented by a series of disastrous events, beyond the control of the individual whose fate is affected by them, and against which human foresight could erect no guards.

Although uniform and decided in his political principles, Doctor Crain did not usually take an active part in the contests which agitated the country, and especially his adopted state, during many years of his life, in reference to public measures. He preferred to devote himself to the more peaceful and congenial pursuits of his profession, and these were not often affected by the success or defeat of his party friends.

In the course of a long and useful life, Doctor Crain was often called upon by the confidence and partiality of his townsmen to perform the duties of various local offices in his town. He was appointed one of the judges of the court of common pleas of the county on the 24th of February, 1817, and superseded in March, 1820, for political causes. He was again reappointed in March, 1821, February, 1823, and April, 1828, and held the office until 1833, when he was left out of the commission at his own request. The doctor was enough of a politician to be struck down whenever his opponents could reach him.

In the presidential contest in 1828, between President Adams and General Jackson, Doctor Crain was the democratic candidate for elector in this congressional district, and was chosen to that office. The presidential electors were then chosen by districts. When I say he was the *democratic* candidate, I suppose the fact that he favored Jackson's election is sufficiently indicated. If it is not, then I will say he was one of the twenty electors of this state who voted for the general in December, 1828. The selection of Dr. Crain to perform the great and important trust of declaring the will of a constituency in the choice of the highest elective office in the world, was alike due to his social position and political standing. De Tocqueville thinks we have adopted a most happy expedient in our mode of electing a chief magistrate, combining, as it does, the "respect due to the popular voice with the utmost celerity of execution, and those precautions which the peace of the country demands." The last part of the sentence might have been omitted, for the American people have not yet seen the time when they would go seriously to work cutting each other's throats for the sake of any candidate for the presidency, and probably never will.

Doctor Crain possessed a large fund of anecdote, and was very social and hospitable. He died in the town of Warren, September 18th, 1846, having arrived at the mature age of three score years and over, leaving a handsome estate to the inheritance of two descendants, a son and a daughter.

Henry Ellison

Was, I believe, a native of one of the New England states. He came to this county, and settled in the town of Herkimer, at an early period of its history, on the West Canada creek, several miles north of Herkimer village, where he was many years successfully engaged in farming and tanning. He was a sagacious, intelligent man, although, like most of his compeers in age and occupation, his early school education was limited. A sound judgment, industry and frugality, make ample amends for the absence of mental adornments, in the industrial pursuits of life, where the latter can have but little application.

Mr. Ellison was chosen an elector of president and vice president, in 1836, and gave his vote in the state college of electors for Martin Van Buren, as the successor of Gen. Jackson. To him a most grateful office, the remembrance of which he long cherished. This selection was due to his character, as a man, and his political standing with his party. He was a strict economist, in public affairs, as well as in his domestic relations. He accumulated an ample estate, which he left to his posterity. Mr. Ellison died about six years ago, at his residence in Herkimer, at a pretty advanced age.

JOHN FRANK

Was the son of Conrad Frank, a palatine emigrant, and one of the patentees of the grant commonly called Staley's 3d tract. John was appointed a justice of the peace for Montgomery county, March 27th, 1790, and afterwards commissioned as one of the justices of Herkimer county, February 17th, 1791, and appointed one of the judges of the county courts, March 27th, 1794, and held that office until 1799 or 1800. From my recollection of him, he was small in stature, and when young, must have been a remarkably energetic man. He was in the prime of life and vigor of manhood, during the dark and calamitous period of the revolution, and one of the committee of safety, in the German Flats and Kingsland districts. The name is spelled Frink, by Campbell and Stone, when giving a list of the members of the committee, from different districts of Tryon county.

When the news of the destruction of Andrustown, by Brant and his dusky servitors, on the 18th of July, 1778, reached Fort Herkimer, Judge Frank was among the foremost and most zealous of the resolute patriots, who volunteered to repel and punish the marauders. Brant, having the advantage in time, was too wary and nimble-footed for his pursuers. He had accomplished his objects, and had no wish to encounter, in a hand-to-hand fight, an exasperated and resolute foe, although not his equal in numbers.

Brant's escape being fully ascertained when his pursuers reached the Little lakes, their mortification and disappointment was distinctly manifested in plundering and burning the habitations of Young and Collyer, two decided tories who had given "aid and comfort" to the enemy, on his way to Andrustown, and who had not been molested or injured by Brant and his followers. This application of the *lex talionis* would be considered rather severe at this day, when not provoked by some active participation in aggression, on the part of the sufferers. But let it be remembered, that the tory inhabitants of the country, although they might, from policy, refrain from being seen with arms in their hands, making war upon their liberty-loving neighbors, were at all times active and diligent in conveying intelligence to their hurt; and ever ready to supply the king's adherents with provisions, and shelter them from pursuit, when required or needful, and whose humanity was never known to give a sympathetic tear of sorrow or regret, at the manifold and unspeakable sufferings inflicted upon their nearest neighbors, and former fellow subjects; and we can not, and should not condemn them for any acts of retaliatory severity, short of taking life. I crave indulgence, for justifying by argument, what some may from tenderness set down in the catalogue of wrongs.

There is not, in my judgment, any grounds for supposing Judge Frank disapproved of the conduct of his companions, in their dealings with Young and Collyer. What had he seen within a few hours? A small, secluded hamlet of seven families, remote from the track of war, invaded for the mere object of plunder, everything valuable that could be removed carried away, five of the inhabitants killed, the remainder driven into captivity, and every house and other building in the settlement, reduced to ashes by the invader's torch.

Judge Frank closed a long and eventful life, in the town of German Flats, about 15 years ago. When the infirmities of age had bowed his venerable head, so that he could no longer stand or walk erect, he retained to the last, and in a remarkable manner, the full possession of a sound, vigorous and intelligent mind. His residence was near the south bank of the Mohawk river, nearly opposite to Herkimer village, and a few rods west of the site of old Fort Herkimer. He had seen the infant German settlements, on the north side of the river, twice destroyed. Once, by the French and Indians, in 1757, and again, by the Indians and tories, in 1778; he had also seen the settlements on the south side of the river, devastated by the French and Indians, in 1758, and again by Brant and his followers, in 1778. He lived to see his country again involved in the war of 1812; the patriotic alacrity of his countrymen, as they marched to the frontiers for her defense, and he saw that struggle closed by an honorable peace. And, he lived to see what cheered the ardor of his noble heart, and soothed the anxieties of his declining years, his country free, prosperous and happy.

Simeon Ford.

In 1816, when I came into the county, this gentleman was a prominent and leading member of the bar, a position he had held several years. He came into the county previous to 1797, and after his admission to the bar, was associated in the profession with Mr. Gaylord Griswold, until the death of the latter. Being the junior member of the firm his partner, as was then the fashion, stood first on the list, as the recipient of political favors and promotion. Mr. Ford was appointed district attorney of the county, early in the year 1819, and held the office until May, 1823, the duties of which he performed with ability, and most untiring fidelity. He was a sound, well read, criminal lawyer, and a good advocate, and in saying this, I must not be understood as intimating he was not in other respects eminent in his profession. He always conducted his prosecutions as if he believed, and felt, the prisoner was guilty, and it was his duty to convict. The rogues often stood appalled, when the grand-jury came into court with true bills against them. Mr. Ford again held the office of district attorney a short time in 1836. He had, previous to 1820, been several times a candidate for popular suffrage, more with a view, as I suppose, of gratifying his political friends, than with a confident expectation of success. Not because the candidate was unpopular with his party, or was in any respect unfit for the place. The reader familiar with the history of Herkimer county politics, in former times, can well understand, why Mr. Ford should be defeated in a popular election, at the times referred to.

No man in the county had stronger hold upon the feelings of party friends, or stood higher in their estimation, than Mr Ford, and they were ever ready to place him as a candidate before the people, when a chance of success should occur. At the annual elections, in the spring of 1820 and 1821, he was chosen member of assembly. His legislative career was limited to the two sessions of 1821 and 1822, during which, if he was not the party leader, he was an influential and prominent member of the house. He was attentive, watchful and industrious, and Governor Clinton could not have had a more ardent and devoted supporter of his policy, than Mr. Ford was. Old associations, and long tried attachments, clustered around him, and he could not bear to see them dissipated, without making an effort to prevent it. He had always been the advocate of the canal policy, enunciated by Mr. Clinton, which was strongly assailed by many of the governor's opponents. He was, moreover, deeply imbued with a conservative feeling, in regard to the existing judiciary. It was these views and opinions, commendable in any man, which brought Mr. Ford into the position, a false one, as respected the public feeling, of attempting to stem or turn aside a popular torrent, which eventually swept him and his friends from power for a time. If we claim to justify our own conduct, in public affairs, on the basis of an honest conviction, that what we advocate is right, we must allow the same immunity to an opponent. What the majority may say, in respect to the merits of the question debated, is quite an other matter. Thus much has been said, because many worthy citizens of the county believe Mr. Ford was entirely conscientious in the course he pursued, and they could not but admire his courage and devotion.

Mr. Ford became pecuniarily embarrassed by the purchase of some lands in the Hassenclever patent. Perhaps, other real estate purchases, near Herkimer, were connected with it. At any rate, if he had held the lands in the patent, a few years longer, the result would have been quite different. Instead of suffering a loss, he would have realized a handsome profit by the rise in prices.

In the year 1825, he was appointed by Governor Clinton to an office at the salt springs, Syracuse. He remained there several years. He resigned his post at Syracuse, and removed to Rochester, where he remained five years and then he returned to Herkimer, and resumed his profession in 1832, with all the ardor and buoyancy of a vigorous young man. But his professional business had been broken up, and his former clients had been compelled, in his absence, to seek professional aid and advice in other quarters and among his successors. He remained, however, at Herkimer until about the year 1836, when he removed to Cleveland, Ohio, where he pursued his profession successfully several years, giving much of his attention to the office of prosecuting attorney, which he received when he went to Cleveland, and held at the time of his death, which took place in the year 1839, at the age of 62 years. He was a native of Berkshire, Massachusetts, and removed from Berkshire county into this state. He was high-minded, honorable and generous, almost to a fault. His office was the chief resort of students in the legal profession in this part of the state for nearly twenty years. Few men in the legal profession have been more highly respected in the circle of their acquaintance than Mr. Ford, and few have better deserved it.

David V. W. Golden

Was a native of Beekmantown, Dutchess county. In 1792 he removed to Niskayuna, in this state, where he was several years engaged in the mercantile business. In 1798 he came into this county, and established himself in the present town of Columbia, where he carried on his mercantile business until his death, which took place on the 11th of February, 1814, aged 41 years. Mr. Golden opened the first store in the town, and is reputed to have been quite successful in business.

He was appointed one of the judges of the county courts in March, 1810, and commissioned first judge of the county, March 21st, 1811, and held the office until his death. The records of the courts show that Judge Golden was attentive to the duties of his office. He was a man of considerable note in the county, and was regarded for his honorable conduct and fair dealing.

Gaylord Griswold

Was a native of Windsor, in the state of Connecticut. He settled in the county soon after it was erected, if not before. He is said to have been a man of rare endowments and great energy of character. Thomas R. Gold came into the then western country about the same time, and Mr. Griswold and Mr. Gold made an arrangement that one of them would stop at Herkimer, and the other at Whitestown; the courts in the county then being held alternately at these two places. Mr. Gold, it seems, took the most expanded field of operations, though he was not Mr. Griswold's superior in legal talents. The reader may recollect, that in the chapter devoted to that object, reference has been made to the supposed political feeling of the population of the county at its first organization. Mr. Griswold was one of the strong and vigorous men who aided largely in holding the popular vote subservient to the views of his own party. We find him, in 1797 and 1798, a member of the assembly from the county, having for colleagues men, some of whom afterwards acted with the political party which he opposed. Party lines may not then have been so strictly drawn as they were two or three years afterwards.

We next find Mr. Griswold elected a representative in congress, about the year 1802, from the 15th congressional district, composed of the counties of Herkimer, Oneida and St. Lawrence. It appears, from the recorded events of the times, that Mr. Griswold lived and was in public life at a period when one of those political ebullitions, which not unfrequently visit our state, was about making its appearance, in a contest between Aaron Burr and Morgan Lewis, as candidates for governor. Mr. Hammond, in his Political History, states that "Gaylord Griswold, then a member of congress from Herkimer county, wrote a letter, which was published, in which he urged his friends to support Mr. Burr, as the only means of breaking down the democratic party, and charged the opposition of Gen. Hamilton to *personal resentment against Burr.*"

We must not inflict an injury on the memory of Mr. Griswold, by allowing it to be supposed that this was other than a private letter, written to a political friend, and that its publication was a breach of confidence. However well disposed he may have been to embrace the ordinary or extraordinary means often resorted to by political partisans to break down their opponents, he could not have willingly sought an opportunity of openly charging Gen. Hamilton with being governed by private hatred in his opposition to Col. Burr. Small men will often be guilty of mean and dirty acts, but Mr. Griswold was not of that clan. He was ardent, it is true, high-minded and generous, and knew too well what belonged to his position and character to commit such an act of indiscretion.

Since writing the above, a friend has put into my hands a handbill containing the letter referred to by Mr. Hammond. The letter was written at Washington, in February, 1804, and was not made public until April 23d, 1807, three years after the contest between Lewis and Burr, and when the latter was being proceeded against for treason and high misdemeanor, in attempting, as was charged, to subvert the government and setting on foot a hostile expedition against a power with whom we were at peace. This letter does not show that Mr. Griswold upheld Col. Burr's conduct which led to his arrest as an offender against the laws of the United States, nor does Mr. Griswold charge the opposition of Gen.

Hamilton "to personal resentment against Burr." The letter contains this expression, in reference to Hamilton, and nothing more: "It is a matter of surprise among our federal friends here, how Hamilton can take so important a part. Report says, Hamilton made a long speech in favor of Lansing, and against Burr. I *fear* his personal resentment to Burr, and not policy, governs his conduct." The object of the publication at the time was not to inflict a personal injury upon Mr. Griswold, but to damage the leading federalists in the public estimation. Having placed Mr. Griswold *rectes in curia*, on this point, I leave the subject. He was connected by marriage with the Hooker family, in Connecticut, several of whom emigrated into the state, and were largely engaged in mercantile business. He died at Herkimer March 1st, 1809, aged 41 years, 2 months, and 11 days, leaving a handsome estate, and a family to enjoy it.

JOAB GRISWOLD

Was born at Goshen, Connecticut, June 29th, 1769, and died at Herkimer, August 20th, 1814, aged 45 years. He came into the county at an early peiod after its erection, and settled at Herkimer. Joab, Elihu and Gaylord Griswold, although natives of the same state, emigrating about the same period, and seating themselves in the same locality in another state, did not claim any relationship or affinity. The subject of this brief notice was also one of the active and influential men who exerted themselves so successfully and efficiently in upholding the federal party in the county the first ten years of its organization.

He was rewarded for his devotion and services with the office of county clerk, conferred upon him by his political friends, on the 19th March, 1798, which he held six years, when he was visited by the adverse turn in political affairs. The office building in which the county records and papers were kept, was burned down with all the contents, the night before he was to deliver possession to his successor. This was a singular and probably unavoidable occurrence. Mr Griswold was a lawyer by profession, engaged in agricultural pursuits while he lived at Herkimer, and these constituted his chief engagements, aside from his official employment. He left a family; some of them were residents of Herkimer village until recently, if they are not at this time.

ELIHU GRISWOLD

Was a native of Windsor, Connecticut, and he also came into the county and settled at Herkimer at an early period. He was educated in the medical profession, and was therefore called Dr. Griswold, by way of distinction, although he did not pursue his profession after he settled in Herkimer. When he first came into the county, and for some years afterwards, he, like Gaylord and Joab, was attached to the federal party; but as man is not bound always to adhere to one side in politics, even though he may have been nurtured in a particular school, and at this present writing, floods of people seem to be looking out for new political homes, the doctor placed himself in antagonism to his former political friends, about the year 1801, and made gallant fight with his republican compeers to bring about a political revolution in the county.

Mr. Griswold was appointed county clerk, April 6th, 1804, by Governor Morgan Lewis, or rather by the council of appointment, about the time Governor Lewis was elected. He held the office six years, when he was superseded in 1810; was again reappointed in 1811, and continued to hold it until his death in 1812, when he was succeeded by his son-in-law, Aaron Hackley, Jr., Esq. He was born August 17th, 1756, and died at Herkimer, January 12th, 1812, aged 55 years. He was educated and accomplished; a man of considerable energy of character, courteous, generous and social. It is worthy of notice that all three of these Griswolds died in the prime of life and vigor of manhood. Among Doctor Griswold's descendants were several daughters, all of whom were respectably connected by marriage to prominent and influential citizens of the county. I depart a little from my rule to say one of them married a Mr. Townsend, a merchant in the village of Herkimer, who meeting with reverses in business, made up his mind to seek a home in the far west, and lay the foundation anew of a fortune for his family, by devoting himself to farming.

About the year 1817, Mr. Townsend, with his resolute and devoted wife and several small children, left a home where ease, refinement and elegance had surrounded them, bade a sorrowing adieu to relatives and friends, and started on their journey to the interior of Illinois, over land to Olean point in this state, thence down the Alleghany and Ohio rivers in a flat boat, and from Shawneetown, or some point on the banks of the father of waters, to their haven of hope and rest amid the broad, smiling prairies of the embryo state. An intimate friend of the writer, who visited the family in the spring of 1820, said he found them seated about thirty miles northeast of Edwardsville, on a beautiful prairie, containing several hundred acres, not far from a considerable stream of water, near which is usually found an adequate supply of woodland. Mr. Townsend had erected his log dwelling, farm buildings and yards to secure his farm stock during night, from such pestilent poachers as bears, foxes and prairie wolves, and sometimes two-legged animals called thieves. The visiter, after a brisk ride of forty miles over broad prairie fields, redolent with the wild flowers of spring, encountering often herds of deer, with nostrils distended and antlers erect, not unfrequently followed in full chase by a brown, cowardly prairie wolf, whose voracious gaze was fixed upon a fawn; then the sharp rattle of the usually dull snake, giving timely notice of its dangerous proximity, ever and anon enlivened by the brisk flight of the prairie hen, and the awkward but rapid stride of the wild turkey, arrived near nightfall at Mr. Townsend's place, just as he, with his farm aiders, had returned from the field of labor and were housing the cattle and stock. Although his acquaintance with Mrs. Townsend before she left the state had been slight, he approached the door of the cabin and met a lady on whose countenance he had never seen a more happy and gladsome expression. "O! Mr. S.," said she, extending her hand to him, "I can not express how much satisfaction I feel in meeting one from Herkimer, the dear, dear home of my youth, where still live many cherished relations and friends, and where too is found the revered resting place of an honored and loved father and mother." But turning to her husband and laying her hand upon his arm, she said in a subdued and firm tone, "I am happy with you and my children, and happy in *this* house. I have resolved to be contented and am."

My friend was fed and lodged as sumptuously as could be hoped for or expected by one who had become fully acquainted with the ways of a frontier life and new beginners. The short evening soon passed away in social chat, in which many questions were asked of friends and acquaintances, and many responses given. Just before retiring, Mrs. T. said to her visiter, "we sometimes have nightly doings here which the eastern people, generally, are not accustomed to, and you will not, I hope, be frightened at any unusual noises. Our log walls are a perfect protection. Indeed, the music of our midnight serenaders will not, I dare say, convince you that 'all discord is harmony not rightly understood.'" In the course of the night my friend said he was awoke by sounds more resembling what he would imagine to be the dismal and frantic yell of infernals, than living animals. "Do you hear the music," asked Mrs. T. of her guest, "and what do you think of it?" "Think of it?" he replied, "you must be more than a Roman matron, if you bear these tormenting wolf yells." The concert was soon ended by the crack of a rifle, and the prowling serenaders fled from the habitation of man. After overhauling his defensive weapons, and breaking his fast, my friend left this family, happy in the enjoyment of the present and hopeful of the future, and turned his face towards St. Louis.

John Graves

Was a native of Dutchess county in this state and removed into the town of Russia in 1795, where he selected and purchased by contract a lot in the "wild woods" which he designed to convert into a farm, and make it his abiding place and home. At the age of 19 years he had paid the contract price for the land, when calling for his deed the seller could not make him a title, and he was compelled to find the true owner and again bargain and pay for the lot, which he did. This was a hard and discouraging beginning in life to be encountered by one so young and in a new and wilderness county, but he no doubt believed it better for him to combat the adversities which had overtaken him, where he then was, than to try any new locality or other expedient. The sequel of life with him proved he acted wisely and prudently.

He was elected member of assembly in this county in 1812, on a ticket with Rudolph I. Shoemaker and Hosea Nelson. His majority, although he had the largest vote of any candidate on his ticket, was only 40; and the average majority of the successful candidates was fifty-three. This was at the eve of the eventful period of the war with Great Britain when political party lines were stringently drawn. Mr. Graves supported the war policy of the then national government. He was again chosen member of assembly at the November election in 1823, with Christopher P. Bellinger and Caleb Budlong, and was consequently a member of the house during the stormy session in the winter of 1824, and at the extra session in the following November. The subjects which engrossed public attention at this time are noticed in another portion of this work. He favored the claims of William H. Crawford to the presidency and acted throughout with the republican party of this state in the fruitless effort of securing his election.

Having been chosen sheriff of the county, he entered upon the duties of the office on the 1st day of January, 1829, which he discharged with great fidelity and satisfaction to the public. At the end of his official term he retired from public life to the enjoyments of a domestic home, surrounded by competence and the society of friends who knew and appreciated his worth. He died at Gravesville in the town of Russia on the 16th of February, 1855, aged 76 years, leaving a widow and two sons, one of whom is the Hon. Ezra Graves of Herkimer.

The obituary notice of his death disclosed the fact that he died of consumption after a protracted and painful sickness. Mr. Graves was among the first of the hardy and resolute pioneers who penetrated the wilderness to the northwesterly portion of the Royal grant, where for sixty years he marked the times and seasons as they came and went, and noticed the exit of his compeers as they passed life's threshold to their long rest and silent home. But few remain of those, who, before the year 1800, emigrated into the county for the purpose of settlement, and the sod of the valley shall soon mark the place where that few must rest.

David Holt.

I can give only an outline of the official character of Mr. Holt, for although nearly half a century a resident of the county, where he raised a pretty numerous family in our midst, he is now gone, and they have emigrated to that great field of eastern enterprise, the far west. He was a practical printer, came into the county in 1805, from the city of Hudson, and commenced the publication of a republican newspaper, which he continued a few years and then was compelled to abandon it for want of patronage. He was a short time engaged in editing a republican paper at Herkimer, not far from the year 1811. He held the office of post master at Herkimer many years, and collector of the internal revenue under the general government. He also acted as a justice of the peace, an office conferred by the state government, and was esteemed an excellent magistrate.

He was appointed one of the judges of the county court on the 24th of February, 1817, and first judge of the county in February, 1821, and held the latter office until March, 1825. He adhered to the fortunes of Governor De Witt Clinton, as he had, I believe, to those of George Clinton, and was stricken down in the political revulsions which overtook the former. This was a dark period in Judge Holt's life, but like a true man and one resolved to do his whole duty, he resumed his mechanical trade, and again managed *bank* and handled *quoins* although he was poor.

Judge Holt was engaged for a brief period in printing the *Republican Farmer's Free Press* at Herkimer; he then removed to Little Falls, and printed the *Mohawk Courier* while that paper was published by C. S. Benton & Co. He may have remained a short time in the office after Mr. Noonan bought the establishment, but I think he did not. He then removed to Albany where he was engaged in type setting more than ten years, and from thence he went to Wisconsin where some of his sons had settled. Now he no longer " moves the *lever* that moves the world."

> " Alike to him is time or tide,
> December's snow or July's pride;
> Alike to him is tide or time,
> Moonless midnight or matin prime."

He met the reverses of life with resignation and fortitude. He many years, as the reader must conclude, from a perusal of this brief notice, enjoyed a large share of the public confidence, worthily bestowed, and exerted an influence in political affairs not yet forgotten.

Michael Hoffman.

In attempting a brief sketch of the life and public career of Mr. Hoffman, I feel some embarrassment at the outset. Our personal and political relations for many long, long years had ripened into a deep seated and almost fraternal regard, but in the evening of his, and I might say of my own days, it was our fortune to differ on some questions of domestic policy, that in no respect to my knowledge disturbed in the least our personal relations, and that circumstances can in no respect induce me to do the least intentional wrong to his character or fame. I know I am touching a delicate subject to speak of myself in this connection, and only do it to enter a broad and unqualified disclaimer at the threshold to meet all ungenerous cavilings and unkind surmises in regard to the motives and objects that induced me to perform a labor which should have been undertaken by abler hands.

Mr. Hoffman was born on the 11th of Oct., 1787, at Half Moon, Saratoga co., in this state. His father was a native of Germany, and his mother though born in this country was of Protestant Irish descent. Her parents emigrated directly from the Green isle, and by this means the pure blood of the Teuton and the Celt mingled in his veins. He commenced the study of medicine in 1807, and obtained the diploma of M. D. in 1810. For some cause, and what I am unable to state, he abandoned the pursuit of this profession, commenced the study of law in 1811, and was admitted as an attorney in 1813. This must have been the date of his admission in the supreme court, or at the common pleas of some other county than Herkimer. His name is found on the rolls in this county entered December 14th, 1815. My acquaintance with him commenced soon after the month of March, 1816; he was then in an office with Aaron Hackley, Esq., at Herkimer, and probably as a partner. It was about this time, and also afterwards, that papers came to the office in which I was a student at law endorsed "Hackley &

Hoffman, Attys.," Mr. Hackley had established himself at Herkimer in 1807, and at the time I now speak of was county clerk. As Mr. Hackley was chosen member of assembly in the spring of 1817, and left the clerk's office at the commencement of that year, the partnership I speak of may not have commenced until that period.

By his assiduous attention to his profession, the force of a strong native talent, very much improved and cultivated in after years, aided by the desire of his partner to promote his welfare, Mr. Hoffman had reached the front rank in his profession in the county when about thirty years old. He had lost four years in his medical pursuits.

He was an earnest and zealous advocate, and conducted the trial of his causes, from the opening to the close, with unabated ardor and confidence, and although beaten by the ruling of the court, or the finding of the jury, he would never admit he was conquered. He seldom failed to bring forward all the points of fact and law applicable to his case, and to present the strongest in such a form as to attract the attention of the court and jury. He was prone to adhere to the technicalities and precision of legal precedents, and in urging them he might waive points that involved, to some extent, the substantial merits of the case. At any rate, he seldom, if ever, failed to do full justice to his cause and his client to the extent of his duty as counsel.

Mr. Hoffman's constitution was neither robust nor firm, and the labor of a long and intricate trial at the circuit would sometimes nearly exhaust him; but he always bore up under these infirmities with an almost unconquerable resolution. He was afflicted many years with an internal chronic affection, which eventually proved fatal.

I am not aware that Mr. Hoffman had participated, to any great extent, in the political contests of the day previous to 1819; in the spring of that year, he attended a political meeting held at the Court House in Herkimer, and offered a series of resolutions disapproving the course of Governor De Witt Clinton, and urged their adoption by the meeting in an able and eloquent appeal. The resolutions were adopted, and the disruption of the republican party in the county into Clintonians and bucktails took place at that time. After the nomination of a federal assembly ticket, the disjointed sections attempted to coalesce, but were defeated at the election.

About this time, Mr. Hoffman removed to Waterloo, Seneca county, which had recently been established as a county seat, and opened an office in connection with Mr. Bartow, a young gentleman who had studied with him, and who, I believe, was a relative; but owing to the impaired state of his health, and some severe domestic afflictions, he returned again to Herkimer, and resumed the practice of his profession, after an absence of a few years. He was appointed district attorney of the county, by the county court, at the May term, 1823, and held the office until the December term, 1825. He was again reappointed in March, 1836, and resigned the following September.

I have elsewhere noticed Mr. Hoffman's election to congress in 1824. This was his first appearance before the people of the county as a candidate for popular favor. He sustained himself nobly through an excited and stormy canvass, and was vigorously and efficiently supported by as resolute and active body of friends as ever, in this or any other state, was brought out to support a candidate. He was known to be a man of the first grade as to talents. His character was beyond and above reproach of any sort; he was moreover a sound democratic republican. If he at any after period of his life thought differently on the subject of national politics, it matters not; he was then a firm national democrat. He came out of the contest a victor, beating his competitor by only 246 votes, while every other democratic candidate running on the same ticket, or voted for at that election in the county, were beaten by majorities ranging from 43 to 138. There were then sixteen towns in the county; he obtained small majorities in ten of them, and his opponent in six. The peculiar circumstances which attended this election, and the marked public favor with which Mr. Hoffman's name was received, could not and did not fail to place him in the front rank of the democratic party in the county, and among the prominent men of the state, which position he maintained seemingly without any effort, while he lived. He was again chosen member of congress in 1826, 1828 and 1830. In 1828, he was elected without opposition. His course during eight years' service in the house of representatives was marked by an able and assiduous attention to his public duties, and the places assigned to him on the different committees of that body showed the distinguished appreciation in which he was held by the presiding officers of the house and his colleagues from this state. I do not propose to notice the particulars of his congressional career. This may be the proper place for an extended review of that subject, but my limits will not allow it. It must suffice to say, he favored the election of General Jackson to the presidency in 1828, and his antecedent political action was directed to that object. He was a decided advocate for free trade, and opposed to protective tariffs; against the reincorporation of the United States bank, and sustained the Maysville veto message of the president. Although a state rights republican in the strictest sense of that term, when applied to a northern politician, he strenuously upheld President Jackson's administration, even to an approval of the celebrated nullification message, sent to congress in January, 1833, calling on the two houses to pass the necessary laws to enable the government to collect the national revenue in the state of South Carolina.

While in congress, he occupied prominent places on important standing committees of the house of representatives, and during his last term he was chairman of the committee on naval affairs, a position which brought him into confidential communication with the executive departments of the government. It has been usual in the practice of our government, and especially when the speaker of the house accorded in political sentiment with the president, to consult the heads of the executive departments in respect to the constitution of the five executive or strictly departmental committees. This course enables the government at all times to designate the individual member with whom, as the organ of the house, it would be thrown into confidential communication on delicate and important national questions, when the public interests require that the intentions and objects of the government shall not be promulgated to the world, and that the popular representative branch of the government shall sustain the executive department.

Mr. Hoffman was very averse to being placed at the head of the committee on naval affairs. The subject was spoken of at the time, but his friends were not able to find out any satisfactory reasons for his objections. The administration at this time possessed his unlimited confidence, and the president, General Jackson, could not fail to consider Mr. Hoffman an able and efficient supporter upon the floor of the house. His objections must have been purely personal, as he finally consented to accept the post.

The political struggle was very active, acrimonious and bitter during the whole eight years of General Jackson's administration, but I am not aware that Mr. Hoffman, in public debate, indulged in personal allusions to his political opponents, or denounced the individual conduct of his antagonists. He assailed the policy and measures of the opposition with so much zeal as to provoke the ire of George Poindexter, a senator from the state of Mississippi, who called on Mr. Hoffman for an explanation or retraction of words spoken or written by him. This being declined, Poindexter challenged him to single combat with mortal weapons. There were two reasons, and pretty strong ones, why he could not fight, even if he had been the aggressor; the laws of his state were extremely severe against duelling, and a deep seated religious conviction forbade his making an effort to take the life of a fellow being by single combat, or to expose his own by being shot at, without an attempt to cripple his opponent. His personal friends at Washington insisted, however, that Poindexter was not justified by the code of honor in calling him out, and that he might decline the challenge without violating the duello. The whole matter was referred to southern gentlemen, who, without any hesitation, decided that under the circumstances of the case, Mr. Hoffman could with honor decline to meet the challenger. There were not ten electors in his district at this time who did not approve of his conduct, as well in regard to this duel, as his course in other respects, as their representative, which was emphatically declared at a county convention of his political friends not long after the affair happened; yet when an election for member next came round, he did not command voices sufficient for a renomination, and his name was not presented as a candidate, nor did he, by any means known to me, seek a renomination. The known hostility of the president to a renewal of the United States bank charter, Mr. Van Buren's rejection, as minister to Great Britain, by the senate, and the pretty evident indications of General Jackson's preferences in respect to his successor, had produced an almost unexampled excitement at Washington, and in the public mind throughout the country, on the subject of politics, and the aggressive action of intemperate partisans appeared to find no restraint in the courtesies of civilized life. In giving Mr. Hoffman's statement of this affair, which the reader will find below, I am not aware that I violate any confidence or do any act disrespectful to his memory. It is a brief and terse summary of the transaction, and placed him on high, honorable grounds.

"WASHINGTON CITY, Feb'y 26, 1832.

"Dear Sir: The public papers advise you of the manner in which I have been hunted and abused. Illness, which still confines me, has prevented my early expose to you of this matter.

"My first letter was a full and satisfactory answer: 1st, that

I had not procured the *publication.* 2d, that the *conclusions* of the editors, sometimes called in the correspondence, *imputations,* were not made on any *request* or *suggestion* of mine. 3d, a brief *statement* of what Clement had said to me. 4th, that I had spoken of these in conversation with my colleagues, who had informed me that he had made similar *statements* to them; and 5thly, that for the *truth* of his *statements* I had at *no* time vouched.

"Davis' note objects that the 2d paragraph of that letter was *irrelevant* and *exceptionable.* I know that what is *relevant* can not be *exceptionable* or *offensive.* In my first note on the 4th point, I had not been as explicit as I might be. To obviate his objection to irrelevancy, and to render that part of my former note too explicit for cavil, I stated that it was *relevant,* and added in express terms, as I had before said in substance, that I had repeated these statements made by Clement to me, in casual conversations. After this no objection is made on the ground of *irrelevance.*

"Indeed, it had been *made* and *waived* in Davis' first note, because in that note, after making that objection, he expressly narrowed down the controversy to the single point of agency in procuring publication. Asking an answer to this *alone* was a waiver of all other matters either of exception or inquiry.

"The concluding paragraph of my second note, repeats by express reference the denial in my first. I contend then, that by this reply, P. was *concluded* in his only inquiry and *excluded* from all other inquiry whatever.

"But it is right that you should understand all this miserable quibbling. The printed card, as well as the violent and intemperate "call" on me and others, was a design to muzzle the press, cut out the tongue and prevent the utterance of what Clement had stated. Meantime he was almost daily employed in making denials in the Telegraph on the subject, not only of the truth of what he had stated, but also that he had made any such statements. After these denials, however clearly it may be proved that he made these statements, he can not, I think, be successfully employed as a witness to prove that his statements to us were true.

"In this view of the subject you will duly appreciate the reason why the second paragraph of my first letter was deemed exceptionable; why it was not published in the Telegraph, and why I was challenged because I would not make my answers in *substance* and *form* as my "inquisitors" in their holy office thought proper to order.

"My concluding note sums up the matter as it *then* stood. But these *honorable* men, after they were told the correspondence must close, push in a reply. To understand, answer and refute its sophistry and falsehood, it is only necessary to underscore the words "statements," which always mean the relations of Clement, and "*imputations*" which throughout the correspondence, and in the very nature of things here, means the "*conclusions*" of the editors from those *statements*.

"Davis had required me to say that 'you do not vouch or believe the truth of the *imputations* cast on Governor Poindexter,' &c. I declined this as unnecessary. He did not ask me *either* in relation to the *statements*. I did not decline doing *either* as to the *statements*.

"But in his supplemental letter he argues while he states that I was required to vouch *or* believe as to the *imputations*, and refused to do either, it left it to be inferred that I *believed* the *statements* of Clement, and for that *single* cause I was challenged. But I had in my very first note said I had at *no* time vouched for the truth of his *statements*.

"So much for the sophistry of that supplement on its face.

"Suppose I had said I believed every word that Clement stated to me; ought I to be *shot* for yielding a belief to a man whom Mr. P. had introduced to the senate as the *witness of truth* against Mr. Van Buren? According to Clement's letter the senator had sought him out, and in his character of senator asked in a letter for the precious information; and this man, who admits he raised the corpse of Hicks, reluctantly yields to the solicitations of the senator and makes the disclosures. Yet the senator reads that letter, and I was to be shot for merely hearing the same witness speak.

"I am sick and too fatigued to write more, and must lie down. Yours, MICHAEL HOFFMAN.

N. S. BENTON.

Mr. Hoffman was very urgent that Mr. Sandford should be reelected to the senate of the United States, in 1831, and wrote several letters to the members of the legislature on the subject; but a strong belief that he was interested in the United States bank, coupled with a desire to bring out a man who would be *available* as a candidate for governor, induced the republican members to select with great unanimity another individual. Another fact had strong influence upon the democratic members of the legislature, to induce them to bestow the office upon William L. Marcy. He was known to be the confidential friend of Martin Van Buren, and the war waged against that gentleman by the combined opposition, gigantic in intellect and power, did not fail to draw around him at that time, the deep sympathies of the friends of Andrew Jackson, in this state as well as elsewhere, and they were therefore prepared to throw around him as strong a bulwark as could be erected.

On Mr. Hoffman's retirement from congress, he was appointed one of the canal commissioners of this state, in the year 1835; he held the office but a short time. He suffered a heavy pecuniary loss by having been a surety for a young man, a distant family connection, I believe, and he surrendered all, or nearly all, his property in arranging the unhappy affair, and procuring a final discharge from his liability. This occurrence reduced him from comparative ease and comfort in pecuniary matters, to the necessity of again resorting to the labors of his profession, which continued to engross his attention until the year 1836, when he was appointed by the president and senate, register of the land-office, for the Saganaw district, in Michigan, where he remained until after the general financial explosion, in 1837. I have to say, that Mr. Hoffman was appointed first judge of the county, in June, 1830, and held the office until April, 1833; and that he again held the office of district attorney of the county, a short time, in 1836.

He represented the county in the assembly, with Arphaxad Loomis, in 1841 and 1842, and with Peter H. Warren, in 1844. His party was in a minority in the house, in 1841, but, it had regained the ascendency in both branches, in 1842, when democratic state officers were elected, and a series of financial measures were initiated and carried through the legislature, for the avowed purpose of reviving the credit of the state, which had suffered pretty severely from causes not necessary here to discuss, and concerning which the two political parties of the day did not agree. A direct tax was levied to aid the funds, appropriated for the Erie canal enlargement, and the construction of the lateral canals. Mr. Hoffman was at the head of the committee of ways and means, and labored assiduously to perfect and carry through his favorite measures. He was willing to levy a tax, to resuscitate the credit of the state, and keep its faith unimpaired with its creditors, in regard to existing obligations and indebtedness, but he was not disposed to go one step beyond that. The financial officer of the state, A. C. Flagg, then recently elected comptroller, favored this policy. The consequence was, that the further progress of the public works on the canals was suspended, for the time being, and the state stocks, and the state credit, soon regained their former healthful position. These measures were approved by William H. Seward, then governor of the state, an ardent and enthusiastic advocate for the speedy completion of the canals. It was repeatedly stated during the discussion of these measures, that the people would not willingly be taxed to support or aid the construction of the canals, or even to bring the finance and credit of the state into a healthful condition. Mr. Hoffman and his friends, it seems, did not misjudge the public feeling on this subject. Governor Seward convened an extra session of the legislature, in the summer of 1842, to provide the means for carrying on the public works, but the majority was intractable, and adjourned without doing anything, but to take the per diem and mileage allowed by law.

The session of 1844 was not prolific of any great or interesting questions of legislation, and although a majority of the democrats elected to the assembly was friendly to what was called the "canal policy," and elected a speaker who was known to differ from Mr. Hoffman in regard to the "stop and pay law," there are few, if any, instances in the history of the legislation of this state, when a single member exerted such powerful influence as did Mr. Hoffman during this session. He did not trouble himself to advocate many of the measures brought before the house, but he took unwearied pains to oppose and defeat every project he considered unsound, impolitic or mischievous, and he seldom failed.

The election of Mr. Polk, in 1844, brought into the executive chair of the United States an individual with whom Mr. Hoffman had served in congress; and this intimacy, it is said, was the reason why the president nominated Mr. Hoffman to the senate as naval officer in the city of New York, against the remonstrances of a member of his cabinet from this state. During the progress of the controversy on the tariff question, and with South Carolina, he felt, and often expressed, a deep anxiety in regard to the issue of events and the fate of the country. His mind not unfrequently forboded an appeal to force, which he deprecated in the strongest terms, and urged the adoption of conciliatory measures so far as these could be tendered, by a modification of the tariff, in order that confidence might be fully restored between the antagonistic sections of the country. Happily his fears and sombre anticipations were not realized, nor could they well be under the wise and energetic administration of Andrew Jackson. The man who, by one sentence from his pen, could compel the ruler of thirty-four millions of people, and one of the first continental powers of Europe to fulfill the obligations of a solemn treaty, whose conditions had been violated, was not to be "frightened from his propriety" by any threats of domestic treason. His advice to his countrymen to "ask for nothing but what was right, and submit to nothing which was wrong," and his known patriotic devotion to the best interests of his country, had seated him too firmly in the hearts and affections of the American people, to be disturbed by the denunciations or threats of sectional politicians. But it is not my purpose to eulogize General Jackson in this place, or speak of him outside of the nullification controversy.

Mr. Hoffman's appointment to the lucrative post assigned him by the partiality of the president, and in my judgment it was not undeserved under the circumstances of its bestowal, placed him in a condition where, by the application of the prudential regulations which had governed him through life, he soon retrieved his fortunes, and he was enabled to leave his family, on his demise, possessed of an ample competence. His former connections with the financial policy of the state, as settled by the legislation of 1842, no doubt produced his election in Herkimer county, in 1846, to revise the constitution of 1821, although he was then a resident of the city of New York. The convention met at the Capitol, in the city of Albany, on the 1st day of June, 1846, and it is probably needless for me to state, that Mr. Hoffman participated largely in the initiatory proceedings of that body, or that his course in the convention in any respect disappointed the public expectation, founded upon the antecedents of his public career.

Although every portion of the fundamental law, when under revision, presents questions of the most grave consideration, there are no doubt some points of more engrossing importance than others. Mr. Hoffman was named chairman of the committee to which was referred that part of the constitution relating to

"3. Canals, internal improvements, public revenue and property; public debt, and the powers and duties of the legislature in reference thereto; and the restrictions, if any, proper to be imposed upon the action of the legislature in making donations from the public funds; and in making loans of the moneys or credit of the state."

Broad and comprehensive inquiries, imposing great labor to analyze and digest, and much power in debate to illustrate and defend the details of a constitutional article involving such varied and deeply interesting subjects. Mr. Hoffman, from this committee, reported two articles, each comprising several sections, on the 30th July, 1846. They were the outlines of the existing 7th or financial article of the present constitution. The debate was opened by him on the 11th of September, by an able and elaborate argument, showing the condition of the finances and debt of the state, its inability, except from taxation, to meet any increased liabilities, and urged upon the convention the necessity and expediency of placing some restraint upon legislative discretion over the subject, which, he insisted, was not to be depended on. He occupied the whole of one day in elaborating his views on this occasion. I can not even attempt a synopsis of his argument. The debate which followed was highly interesting, and exhibited much talent in the members who participated therein, and was finally closed on the 7th of October, when, having been considerably modified while under discussion, the two originally reported articles were incorporated into one, and was adopted by a vote of 77 to 9. Some of the most important modifications to the original reports were moved by Mr. Loomis, but whether with Mr. Hoffman's assent, I do not know. If he felt it incumbent on him to carry through this favorite proposition, he did not confine his whole attention to this one subject. He participated largely in the doings of the convention generally, and evinced great ability, research and experience. He voted for the restricted right of suffrage imposed by the constitution upon the colored population; and voted for the separate submission of the articles conferring free suffrage on this class of citizens. There was no incongruity in these votes.

Mr. Hoffman's legislative career closed with the adjournment of the convention. It had been an unusually long and varied one, twelve of the twenty-one years since his first election to congress; and it may with truth be said, he occupied, during this period, a distinguished and prominent position on the political stage. He was nearly twenty years the recipient of official favors of some kind, and enjoyed the popular confidence of the citizens of this county in a somewhat remarkable degree. His health, which had been rather infirm some time previous to 1847, gave way more rapidly under the accumulated difficulties of deep seated chronic disease, about that period, and he closed his earthly pilgrimage at Brooklyn, Kings county, on the 27th day of September, 1848, aged 61 years.

He held the post of naval officer when he died, and his remains were brought to Herkimer for interment. He was a man of generous impulses, strong personal attachments and unwavering political principles. In private life, his character was wholly blameless; as a public man his reputation was unsullied by any acts of peculation upon the public, or any efforts to further the prospects or promote the interests of his political friends or his party, by a prostitution of patronage, or the partial appropriation or application of the public treasure to promote similar objects. While in congress, he represented a district which called for no appropriation for local objects, and that was the condition of his county when he was in the legislature. I do not mean to say he was more pure than any other man living in his day; but he was not assailable on points that some men have been.

Stephen Hallett

Was a native of the town of Salisbury in this county, and was born there in the year 1787. He was the son of Major

Jonathan Hallett, an officer of the revolutionary army. What business he was engaged in antecedent to the year 1820, I am not informed of; he that year removed to Fairfield village, where he engaged in merchandise and also carried on the same business in the town of Norway. Mr. Hallett was appointed by the council of appointment, sheriff of the county in 1821. The designation of the candidate was made by a county convention, and the recommendation of that body was approved by the council. He was reappointed in the winter of 1822, and at the November election of that year was chosen sheriff of the county under the provision of the constitution of 1821. His term of office expired on the 1st of January, 1826. He was a prompt and efficient public officer, and possessed a pretty full share of the "irrepressible energies" of a Herkimer politician of the dominant party. He was intelligent, public spirited and humane. He died at Fairfield, November 19th, 1827, aged 40 years, leaving a family to mingle tears for their bereavment, with the regrets of friends and neighbors for their loss.

If he had faults I know not of them,
And if I did, why should I note them?

PHILO M. HACKLEY

Was born at Wallingford, New Haven county, Connecticut, in October, 1776, and died at Allegan in the state of Michigan, the 24th of October, 1849, aged 73 years. Aaron Hackley, his father, removed into this state with his family and settled in the town of Salisbury, in 1795. Within a few years of this event, Philo M., the son, removed to the village of Herkimer, and established himself in the mercantile business, which he pursued with varied success, nearly twenty years. He had been well educated, was gentlemanly in his deportment, and a high-minded and honorable man. He was a federalist in politics, and not ashamed to avow it on all proper occasions; was one of that talented and influential body of men, who early established themselves at the county seat, who during several years exerted a potent political influence in the county. He was well informed on most subjects, and active and zealous in promoting the success of his party. His political friends were not unmindful of this, but sought out several occasions to show their grateful attachment to a true and worthy adherent of a cause which they no doubt believed was worthy of their best efforts to sustain. He was appointed surrogate of the county in 1807, but a political revolution displaced him the following year. He was appointed sheriff in 1810, another change in the appointing power transferred the office to a political opponent.

The succeeding ten years found him enjoying the comforts of private life, although a period of very considerable political excitement, and during which the country had passed through a foreign war, and its institutions had been subjected to the severest tests. At the spring election in 1819, he was chosen member of the assembly on a ticket with James Orton and Jacob Markell. The election of three old fashioned, although highly respected federalists, was an unusual occurrence in the county. The causes which produced this change in the ascendency of parties in the county at the above and two succeeding elections, are explained in another chapter. He did not after this hold any prominent office. He lived several years at Little Falls, and removed from thence with his family to Auburn, in this state, about the year 1839, where he remained five years and then went to Michigan. He met the vicissitudes of life with the characteristic resignation of a Christian. He left several children at his death, who had settled in different parts of the country, none of whom, however, were residents of this county. The American people, and especially the descendants of the old Puritan stock, are, I believe, the greatest antigregarians of any in the world.

Henry Hopkins

Emigrated into the county at an early day and settled in the village of Herkimer, where he engaged in merchandizing, and carried it on for some time. He received the appointment of sheriff of the county in 1813, and had the good fortune to hold the office two years against John Mahon, the perpetual successor of federal sheriffs in those days. He was intelligent, gentlemanly, kind and social, and personally very prepossessing in appearance. Full six feet high and very "well proportioned." He was quite popular as a public officer, and being highly regarded by his fellow citizens of all classes, he did not fail to attract the special attention of his political associates.

He was put in nomination for the assembly in the spring of 1815 by his party, with Thomas Manley and Mathew Myers, and was elected. One of the republican candidates, George Paddock, died only five or six days previous to the election, and there was not time in those days of bad roads and tardy movements to assemble the county convention and present another candidate previous to the election, and the voting went on as usual. Mr. Hopkins led his ticket by a few votes, and beat his dead competitor by 19 majority. The canvass shows that 1368 votes were cast for Hopkins and 1349 for Paddock. The election was a very close one, and each party appears to have placed their most prominent and popular men before the people. The average majority of the two highest on the republican ticket was only 22½ over their two highest opponents. I notice a fact which presents the remarkable uniformity of the freehold vote of that day. There were two senators to be chosen in the western district that year, and the federal and republican parties each presented two candidates. There were then eleven towns in the county, and each federal nominee received an equal number of votes in every town except two, and so it was with the republican candidates. The losses and gains among the candidates running on the same ticket were in Herkimer and Schuyler, and those losses and gains between the candidates running on opposing tickets were equal. The difference being only four in about nine hundred cast by each party. A greater uniformity prevailed in 1809, when there were six candidates, three supported by each party, and a variation of only two votes between the highest and lowest of each set. Mr. Hopkins was a candidate for reelection the next year, 1816, but failed of an election by 133 votes, although the highest on his ticket. He died at Herkimer in November, 1827. I have not found any memorial of his final resting place, except in the fond recollection of those who knew him, nor am I aware that he left any descendants.

Sanders Lansing

Was born at Albany June 17th, 1766. He was the youngest of four brothers: John, formerly chief justice of the supreme court, chancellor, and delegate to the convention of 1787, which formed the constitution of the United States; Abraham G. and Garret G., late of Oriskany. He had one sister, Mrs. Barent Bleecker of Albany. On the 10th of December, 1789, he married Catharine, the eldest daughter of Abraham Ten Eyck of that city. He was educated to the legal profession, and was appointed register in chancery on the promotion of his brother to the chancellorship. He was of the ancient Dutch lineage, who came from Holland in the glorious days of Petrus Minuit, Wouter Van Twiller, Willem Keift or Petrus Stuyvesant, representatives of their high mightinesses, the states general. It matters not, however, when they came or where they were from, their descendants were here on the day of our nation's birth, and claimed the right to be numbered among her children.

Mr. Lansing removed into the county with his family, in 1820, and settled at Little Falls, where he was several years engaged in closing up some extensive land agencies, in which the collateral branches of his family were interested. He was chosen delegate to the convention, in 1821, with Sherman Wooster and Richard Van Horne, called to revise the constitution of 1777, although quite a stranger to the great mass of the electors. The name was no doubt familiar to a considerable portion of the population, but he was known individually to only a few of them. His course in the convention was marked by that cool deliberation, and sound judgment, which great experience and a practical knowledge of the working of our system would very naturally lead him to adopt. He was not a visionary theorist; nor was he opposed to a change in the fundamental rules of government, when that change was required to conform them to present exigencies, and advance the best interests of the state. He did not often engage in protracted forensic debate; and this was probably owing to his withdrawal from practice in the courts, soon after he came to the bar. A majority of his constituents in the county approved of his official acts, and he lived many years after this event, to mark the upward and onward progress of his native state, endeared to him by grateful recollections of the past, and hopeful prospects for the future.

Mr. Lansing was appointed one of the judges of the county courts, in March, 1821; reappointed, in 1823, by the governor and senate under the new constitution, and held the office until 1828. I can venture to say, that he never neglected attendance at court a single term, during this whole period, unless prevented by sickness. His rule was, that no man ought to accept a public office and neglect to perform its duties, whatever they might be.

Judge Lansing also held the office of master in chancery, and commissioner to perform certain duties of a justice of the supreme court at chambers. The latter appointment was conferred after he left the common pleas bench. He was a gentleman of great purity of character, and held in strict observance those rules of conduct that divine revelation enjoins, as he believed, on all who would secure a happy future. He left only two sons. My attention was always attracted to the uniform exactness, and methodical precision, in which he transacted all his business, whenever I made professional calls upon him. This I attributed to early training. Some would say this was a national characteristic. Well, if this be so, the peculiarity is the child of education, and is called "national," when applied to the people of Holland, because they uniformly observe the thorough rules of instruction, and an exact method of training as far as they go. I can not regard Dutchmen, native or a descendant, as the only people of all the Caucasian races who are constitutionally or by nature endowed with the particular mental faculty of attaining method and exactness in the transactions of life.

Mr. Lansing resided in the town of Manheim, several years preceding his death, and died there, September 19th, 1850, aged 84 years, 3 months, and 2 days; his beloved and respected consort died on the 23d; a grandson, on the 20th, and a granddaughter on the 24th of the same month. Within the period of a week, four members of a family were placed in the silent grave. This occurrence was somewhat remarkable, in regard to the rapid succession in which the events happened, as there was not at the time any epidemic diseases that touched three of the cases.

John Mahon

Was born in Ireland, and came to this country when quite young. After remaining here a few years he went back to Ireland and again returned to this country. He crossed the Atlantic three times before he was sixteen years old. He lived several years with "blind John Smith," who carried on merchandising in a small way at or near Utica. He was in this county some years before 1800, and acquired all his education after he left Ireland. His first wife was a daughter of Judge John Frank, of German Flats, in which town he resided, some years acting as constable and deputy sheriff. Being connected by marriage with a German family, he acquired and spoke the provincial dialect with all the fluency of a native German of the Mohawk. He was a man of much energy of character and great native talent. I knew him well more than thirty years, and in all that time never heard him speak in any other terms than of strong dislike and execration of the government and institutions of his native country. My curiosity was sometimes so strongly excited as almost to tempt me to inquire of him the particulars of his parentage, but he was not a man to gratify other people's curiosity only when it suited himself. I always imagined his ancestors had suffered some deep wrong, or what he believed to be so, from the British government in Ireland.

He said he was indented out to service for a limited time to pay the expenses of his first passage. I am not aware that this practice continued after the revolution. He was appointed sheriff of the county in 1808, and held the office two years. He was again appointed in 1811, and held the place till 1813; and in 1815 he was again reappointed and held two years more. He seems to have come into office and gone out on every political change in the council of appointment. He was an active and efficient public officer, and a very ardent politician, as the reader will probably conclude by this time. He never asked any favors from his political antagonists, and was very careful not to be too liberal in granting them. From 1817 to 1821, he was engaged to some extent in private pursuits, and upon the restoration of the republican party to political power in the state, in the latter year, he was appointed clerk of the county, and held the office until January, 1823. In 1819, he was actively engaged in organizing an opposition in this county against Governor De Witt Clinton. He was the prime mover and leading spirit in that movement, and did not fail to extend his exertions to the close of the election in 1820, when Clinton and Tompkins were rival candidates for the gubernatorial chair.

On his exit from the clerk's office he was appointed one of the county judges in February, 1823, and held that office until 1833. This was the close of his active political career. Judge Mahon died at Herkimer in October, 1851, aged 78 years. He left one descendant, a son, Patrick Mahon. I am not aware he had any attachments for the predominant religious faith of his native country. I do not think he had any; and it is this circumstance which seems to throw obscurity over his origin and early life. This is one of many cases often presenting themselves to our view, which exhibits in bold relief some of the striking peculiarities of American institutions. An alien orphan, destitute alike of money and education, immigrates to our country, and by application and industry acquires both. But this is not all. He does not loiter at the foot of the official ladder. He secures the confidence and good will of the people whom he can rightfully call his fellow citizens, and enjoys for nearly forty years high and important official trusts, and only leaves them when about to go to a last and final resting place. Judge Mahon possessed some very marked peculiarities. I never heard that the vigor of his intellect had been in the least impaired from the time he quit public life to his death. But this is no place for questions not relating to public life and character. The grave throws a mantle over our foibles, and let that be the end.

Thomas Manley

Was a native of Dorset, Bennington county, Vermont. He came into the present town of Norway, in the spring of 1789, opened a small clearing, and erected his log cabin, and brought his family into the town the next year, 1790. It will probably be noticed, that Norway was first organized in 1792, but its territory has been subsequently very much circumscribed. Mr. Manley being among the first settlers on the northern part of the Royal grant, and a man of energy and force of character, was a prominent man in his town. He held the office of supervisor fifteen years, and was twice commissioned by Governor John Jay superintendent of highways in the county of Herkimer. These commissions respectively bear date April 4th, 1798, and March 8th, 1800. One of his sons, Dr. Manley, of Richfield, Otsego county, told me his father, the first year he came on to the grant, put up a bark hut as a sleeping place for himself and his hired man, and a store room for such few things as they had, requiring protection from the weather. They used a blanket to cover the entrance of their primitive lodge. The needful cooking was done at the fire outside. As they were then quite destitute of such substantials, in the way of food, as beef, pork, mutton and lamb, the forest was resorted to, to supply deficiencies, and the white rabbit being numerous, were taken whenever occasion required. Not having the fear of cholera before their eyes, and being intent in felling the forest and opening their clearing for a small crop, they did not stop to enquire into the origin and causes of diseases, but threw their culinary offal down near the door of the hut, where a considerable quantity of rabbit bones had of course been accumulating. Mr. Manley and his companion were one night disturbed by an unusual noise outside, but near their hut: listening a moment, they concluded, from the cracking of the rabbit bones, that some strong mouthed native of the forest was making a night meal of them. Manly took his gun, and moving the blanket door gently aside, fired in the direction of the heap of rabbit bones; a terrific growl was the only response, except the echo of the discharge in the surrounding dense forest. The night was dark, and having struck up a light with steel and flint, and recharging their gun, they cautiously examined the ground about the hut, but found nothing except some traces of blood. The animal, although wounded, was not disabled from making its escape. Early the next morning, Mr. Manley and his companion took the blood trail into the forest, and in about an hour found a good sized bear, weary and faint from the effects of his late night feast, and the unkind treatment he had received. The bear was killed, in the hope that the meat would give the captors a savory change in animal food. But it was poor, and the meat was coarse, dark and tough.

Mr. Manley was an agriculturist, and was highly respected in his town and in the county. He was elected a member of the assembly in this state in 1799, on the ticket with John Mills and John Myer; again in 1809, with Rudolph Devendorff and Christopher P. Bellinger; and again in 1820, with Simeon Ford and Daniel Van Horne. He was uniform and adhered with unwavering tenacity to his political principles and party in this county more than sixty years. It is no slight evidence of the good feelings of his friends, or of his standing in the county, that his name was often presented by them as a candidate for member of assembly, as well when there was a fair prospect of success, as when this chance was quite doubtful. He died in Norway, where he lived 63 years, on the 21st of January, 1852, aged 88 years and six months. He was born in August, 1763. In closing this notice, I need hardly add, that such a man as Mr. Manley must have been highly esteemed while living, and died regretted by all who knew him.

Jacob Markell

Was born in the county of Schenectady, on the 8th of May, 1770, about two miles west of the city. His parents were Germans, or of German descent. He received his English common school education, while quite young, at Schenectady. This name is found in the list of Palatine immigrants, who came over in 1710, but his ancestors were not among the Burnetsfield patentees. Judge Markell's father came to Stone Arabia, in the present town of Palatine, Montgomery county, at an early period, but whether before or at the close of the revolution, I have not been able to ascertain. Young Markell's health was not robust, and he was placed in Maley's store, in Albany, where he served out a clerkship. He married, when twenty years old, at Palatine, and removed to Manheim, and commenced farming, which he carried on during the remainder of his life, until he became too infirm, in consequence of age, to attend to the laborious duties of that occupation. When he first came to Manheim, he opened a small country store, and manufactured pot-ashes, a business that yielded a good return while the country was new, and timber plenty. He was an acting justice of the peace, almost time out of mind, and held the office of supervisor in the town of Manheim *twenty-seven* years. When that town remained attached to Montgomery county, he held the office of judge of the court of common pleas, and was elected to congress for one term, during Mr. Madison's administration, and in the war of 1812. He was elected one of the members of assembly from Herkimer county, in 1819, on the same ticket with James Orton and Philo M. Hackley, and closed a long and well spent life at the residence of his son, John Markell, Esq., in Manheim, with whom he had lived the two preceding years, on the 26th of November, 1852, aged 82 years, 6 months and 18 days, after a very brief illness. His wife survived only seventeen days. She was about five months younger than her husband. They had lived together after marrriage about sixty-two years, and raised a family of children. She was as well, apparently, as she had been for many years previous, when her husband died, but immediately after his funeral she sank under her afflictions, and yielded her life to the messenger that never calls but once.

Judge Markell was very methodical in all his business affairs, and with other qualities possessed a shrewd and intelligent mind, which, from long practice, had become considerably imbued with legal principles, and especially those in reference to domestic relations. Hence, when his faculties were unimpaired, he wrote most of the wills made in his town, was usually called upon to adjust, settle and arrange important and difficult questions or matters of business between neighbors, was often entrusted with the administration of estates, and the guardianship of infants. In view of the facts already stated, I need hardly say, he possessed, in an eminent degree, the confidence and good will of his townsmen.

In the prime of life, he was capable of exerting a political influence, which was usually felt by his opponents.

John Mills

Was born in the town of Chatham, Columbia county, New York. He came into the town of Columbia about the year 1790, and was by occupation a farmer. In stature he was just what one would wish, being, "six feet high, and well proportioned," and in all respects a fine looking man. He was truly one of nature's noblemen; his conversational powers were good, was fond of company, pleasant and agreeable in his manners; few men possessed the art of pleasing to so great an extent. He seldom said a foolish thing, and never did a mean act. He had the faculty of accommodating himself to the company he was in, and of going with his whole mind into the subjects which were the topics of conversation; and whether light and frivolous, or sound, substantial and grave, it made no difference to him, he was at home in either, and whatever he said was listened to with attention. His countenance and manner, in fact, the whole man, changed to suit the company, the subject matter and the occasion. He could look pleasant or serious and grave, or frown with great severity. He was honest and fair in his dealings, and was deservedly popular. Had many friends, and few, if any, enemies. He was a kind hearted, good neighbor, never had lawsuits or difficulty himself, and did much, by example and otherwise, to preserve friendship and good morals in society. He was several times supervisor of the town, and usually held some town office, although the political majority was against him. He was elected to the assembly of this state, in 1799, and was frequently a candidate and lost his election, not for want of fitness or popularity, but because he belonged to, and acted with, the federal party, which was in the minority.

He died in 1836, at the age of 76, having always resided on the farm on which he first located, and helped clear with his own hands.

A highly respectable correspondent says :

"I lived within three-fourths of a mile of Capt. Mills some thirty years, and was in almost all sorts of company with him. I knew him well. His education was limited. I think him the best specimen of a man I ever knew. I was also acquainted with his father ; he was a real Yankee. His mother was low Dutch."

Michael Myers

Was born at Auville, New Jersey, February 1st, 1753. Although of German descent, he was not from the original Palatine stock of the upper Mohawk valley. The name is not found in the list of Palatine immigrants who came to the colony in 1709 and 1710. His ancestors may have been among those who composed the third emigration in 1722. With a view of giving as much of the early history of the prominent public men who labored in organizing the county, as well as to aid in establishing the liberties of the country, as might be any way interesting, I have endeavored to reach that object in respect to the subject of this notice, and have failed. Mr. Myers was with the American forces at the battle of Johnstown in 1781, where he was severely wounded in the leg, and from the effects of which he never recovered. He was then about twenty-eight years old. The American forces in this action were composed of levies and militia; it may therefore be presumed that he had come into Tryon county before or during the war. Upon the organization of the county courts, he appears to have been appointed one of the judges and a justice of the peace, February 17th, 1791. He was several times reappointed, but was left out of the civil commission in 1805.

He was elected the first member of assembly after the erection of the county and reelected the following year, and was in attendance at the winter sessions of 1792 and 1793. Judge Myers had been a resident of that part of Tryon or Montgomery county now embraced in Herkimer, several years before 1790. He was elected to the senate in the spring of 1795, took his seat at the following session and served his full term of four years. After this he does not seem to have occupied any prominent official station. His successor in the senate from this county was John Meyer, who was several years one of the county judges, and in 1800 appointed the first judge. He served but one year of his senatorial term, and left the county about the year 1802. John and Michael were not relatives. The former retained the German usage in writing the family name; I think the latter did not.

Judge Michael Myers was many years a prominent and influential politician in this county, but he attached himself to that political party which found but few adherents among the Germans in this quarter, when the people ranged themselves as federalists and republicans. He was appointed by President John Adams, commissioner of stamps for this county, but stamped paper, bearing the impress of the American eagle even, fared no better in the upper Mohawk valley in 1797–8, than that showing the lion and the unicorn and a jeweled crown, encircled with England's loved motto, "HONI SOIT QUI MAL Y PENSE," did among the Bostonians, in 1765. "Dunder and Blixum," muttered the German in his provincial dialect, "what for gant I gif mine node any more to bay for der horse or der gow I puy, mitout I bay dwenty-fife zents for der baper mit der stamb." "Why, neighbor Hanyost," responded the Yankee follower of Shays, "I guess all them tarnel Britishers have kum back to Filladelfa agin, and ar ony putin on the tax to show who's who;

darn the old tories, I won't stand it, that's sartin." The stamps came to a bad market, and the commissioner's periodical returns showed a good supply on hand of those first sent.

Judge Myers possessed a good share of energy, and his position gave him opportunities of laying the foundation of one of the most splendid fortunes in the state, and it was believed by many of his townsmen that he had accumulated great wealth in the purchase and sale of wild lands, at an early period after the close of the war. Although at his death his fortune was ample, it was by no means so extended as it might have been, if he had retained the interest in the lands purchased in his name, connected with others. He seems to have had a good many transactions with the late John I. Morgan, in those speculations, and when we compare the reputed wealth of these two gentlemen at their respective demises, it will not be supposed the judge's actual share in these original purchases, retained by him, was nearly as large or beneficial as the public records seem to indicate. He may not have been as confident in respect to prospective value of real estate as his partners were, and alienated at the prices paid, three shillings and three pence per acre, with a small advance. This must have been a moderate price for lands in the 20 townships, even in 1791. Lands in the Royal grant were sold in 1785, at $2·50 per acre.

Judge Myers died at Herkimer, February 17, 1814, aged 61 years and 16 days. He left numerous descendants, sons and daughters, those who yet survive have sought homes in other parts of our broad country. I believe there is not at this time a single male descendant of this stock now in the county, but there are several in different parts of this state, and in other states of the union.

Peter M. Myers who was appointed county clerk in 1810, was a son of Judge Myers. He held the office one year, under this appointment, when by a political revolution in the counsel of appointment he was removed, and again by another change in politics in 1813, he was reappointed and held the office two years. Mr. Myers has been dead many years. He left descendants, several of whom remain in this state.

Doctor William Petry.

I now introduce to the reader a native of Germany, who did good service for the country during the revolution in the capacity of physician and surgeon, as well as in other respects. He was born near Oppenheim, December 7th, 1733, came to this country in 1763, and married Salome Wolf, the daughter of Mr. John Wolf of Cosby's manor, December 22, 1766. Dr. Petry was a Bavarian, no connection of the Petrie family from the Palatinate, and before he came to America, he served as a surgeon in the Prussian army. Having obtained a professional diploma in Germany, he of course must have previously received a classical and professional education. He was interested in a store or employed in selling goods before the revolution, at the present village of Herkimer; the out-break of the war put a stop to that business for a time, although he seems to have reengaged in it in 1784. He did not feel a very strong sympathy for the royal cause, for we find him on the 2d of June, 1775, attending a meeting of Tryon county committee of safety as a member from the German Flats and Kingsland district. He continued a member of that committee several years and probably until the state government was organized. I also perceive he acted as a justice of the peace during the war. He was employed as a surgeon at Fort Dayton in 1776 and 1779. He was General Herkimer's medical adviser, and did not concur in the treatment of the young French surgeon who amputated the General's leg below the knee several days after it was shattered. I also notice an account for medicine and attendance, by direction of the commissioners of Indian affairs, on some Indian children, and on " Scanando's daughter when beaten with a stone by an Indian." As a memorial of the past I transcribe the following:

"At a council of appointment held at Poughkeepsie, April 27, 1781: Present:—His Excellency Governor Clinton, President. The Honorable Abraham Ten Broeck, Stephen Ward, Arthur Parks, Esqrs., Members.

"*Resolved*, That William Petry be Surgeon of the Regiment raised for the immediate defence of this state, whereof Marinus Willet, Esquire, is Lieutenant Colonel Commandant. State of New York, ss:

"The aforegoing is truly extracted from the minutes of the council of appointment. Robert Harper, Clerk."

In April, 1782, Doctor Petry was appointed by the council of appointment surgeon of the regiment of state levies commanded by Colonel Willett. He was present at the Oriskany battle and wounded in the leg, from which he suffered a good deal of inconvenience. He dressed General Herkimer's wound on the battle field. It is understood that at this time there was not as much cordiality between the general and the doctor as had previously existed. As the latter was then one of the county committee of safety, he may with the other members of the committee have disapproved of the general's policy in regard to an immediate march to the relief of Fort Stanwix. It is reported of the doctor that he was not strictly a noncombatant at Oriskany, that after the first assault by the enemy he was very active in encouraging the militia, and forming them so as to present a combined resistance to the enemy. His former experience in the Prussian service enabled him to afford essential aid on that occasion. He was with his regiment under Col. Willett in October 1781, when that brave and active officer pursued Ross and Butler's party on their retreat across the country to reach their boats at the Oneida lake, and when the latter was killed after crossing the West Canada creek. He also accompanied his regiment under Willett in February, 1783, on the expedition to capture by surprise the

British fortress at Oswego, which failed of success, not however by any fault of the American commander.

Doct. Petry was actively engaged in his profession, nearly the whole length of the Mohawk valley, during the revolution, and before and after, he being the principal physician and surgeon in the county, until nearly the close of his life. He always went armed during the war, in going the round of his visits. He was somewhat brusk in manners, and firm in his resolves. Many anecdotes are told of him, some of them quite amusing and characteristic of the man. Not being within call at the moment when an operation was required upon one of the men of his regiment, several of the young American surgeons were called in, and while they were consulting what to do, he returned, and coming into the room where the disabled man and the doctors were, asked the Yankee surgeons to retire a few minutes, as he wished to confer with the wounded man. While they were absent he amputated and dressed the limb, and then sent for them to return, and remarked that they might now consult as long as they pleased. After the peace he again engaged in mercantile business at Herkimer, which he continued till near the close of life. He died at that place, August 6th, 1806, aged nearly 73 years. He left several sons and daughters, and of the latter is the mother of the Messrs. Earls. His memory has been, and still is, highly cherished by the old German inhabitants of the county, who knew him. His descendants still retain the paternal estate, for which they entertain a high regard.

When the doctor had made up his mind, on almost any subject, all further debate with him was not of much use. His family residence was a little distance from the Court house, and the compact part of the village, where he often resorted to hear aud talk over the news of the day, with his neighbors and old revolutionary compeers, who were never at fault for fruitful themes of discussion, when modern affairs did not present them. He had become very deeply interested in regard to the stamp act, passed under Mr. Adams's administration, and stoutly denied the justice and propriety of compelling the American people to buy stamped paper for their ordinary business, as they had just got through with a long war to get rid of it. He became very much excited on the subject, when, one day, he was in the village where the stamps had been long and warmly discussed, and arguments, pro and con, wholly exhausted, the old gentleman returned home greatly vexed and annoyed, the din of stamps, and stamp acts ringing in his ears, when the peculiar voice of a flock of guinea hens, on his premises, arrested his attention; the innocent cry of the poor hens sounded to him very like stamp act, and he could not endure it. He ordered his boys to kill them at once, for he would not, he said, have any d—d stamps about him. The innocent hens were beheaded for the treasonable cry of stamps. I can not better close this brief notice of the doctor, than by giving in this place a copy of his diploma, translated from the German.

We, ordained by Grace an Electoral-Palatine MEDICAL ASSEMBLY; appointed Privy Counsellor, and First private Physician, DIRECTOR and ASSESSORS, Court Physicians and City Physicians, &c.,

Do hereby testify and make known that the proprietor of this, named WILLIAM PETRY, born in *Neustein*, in the *Electoral-Palatine* Bailiwick of OPPENHEIM, came to us with a dutiful petition to be examined in the art of *surgery*, according to the graceful *Electoral Royal Medical Order*. Therefore, after producing his authentic indentures, showing that he had regularly studied surgery for three years with *John George Heuser*, the City Surgeon of the Electoral Palatine Bailiwick of OPPENHEIM; then studied with *Schimdt*, the City Surgeon here in Manheim, one year and a half, and attended the *Anatomical School* in *Berlin;* after that served one year in the Royal Prussian Hospital, in Dresden and Torgau, also served as company surgeon during four years in the Estimable *Schenckendorf's Infantry Regiment*, and in like manner served two years among the *English Grenadiers;* and that during all the time he practiced the surgical and anatomical art. We had no hesitation to comply with WILLIAM PETRY'S petition to give him the customary examination. In which examination, as to all questions about wounds in general, *contusions*, *tumors*, *fractures*, *luxations*, anatomical and surgical operations, he having answered to our perfect satisfaction; and in our presence, also to our satisfaction, attended to several practical cases in surgery. We all agree that he is a skillful and well instructed surgeon, which we hereby attest to him by virtue of our usual seal and with our own hands. Manheim, 8th Febr., 1763.

Consilium Medicum Electorale Palatinum

[L. S.] P. J. WALCK, JC. SCHROTT, Medico.
FRANCISCO HELM, Actuarius.
M. PRIA.

GEORGE ROSECRANTS

Was the son of the Rev. Abraham Rosecrants, who for many years presided over the German congregations in the Mohawk valley. George was born on the 15th of March, 1764, on Fall hill, in the present town of Little Falls. His mother was a sister of Gen. Nicholas Herkimer. He died December 21st, 1838, at the place of his birth, aged 74 years, 9 months and 6 days. He had four brothers, Henry, Abraham, Joseph and Nicholas, and three sisters. He left one son, Abraham G., now living, and five daughters. Although of German descent, he did not belong to the original Palatine stock, and therefore the sketch of his life and family belongs to a different chapter of biographies.

Mr. Rosecrants was called pretty early into public life. At the age of thirty-five, he was elected to the state convention with Evans Wharry and Matthias B. Tallmadge, from this county, which was called in 1801, to act upon certain propositions in respect to the power of the members of the council of appointment, and limiting the number of members of assembly. In 1805 he was appointed one of the judges of the court of common pleas, which office he held until March, 1821. In 1812, he was appointed by the legislature one of the electors of president and vice-president of the United States, and voted with the other electors of this state for De Witt Clinton, in preference to James Madison. He was one of the members of assembly from the county, in 1817 and 1818, and was chosen a state senator at the spring election in 1818, and held that office the full term of four years. This closed his official career. He was a member of the council of appointment in 1819, and warmly attached to Governor De Witt Clinton while that distinguished statesman occupied a prominent position in the councils of the state.

It must be evident to any one familiar with the history of political parties in the county, that Judge Rosecrants was of the old republican school of politicians. In voting for Mr. Clinton, in 1812, for president, if he erred at all, he erred in common with a majority of his political friends in the legislature, who had nominated Mr. Clinton in opposition to Mr. Madison.

Judge Rosecrants possessed good sound sense, and a discriminating judgment. He was industrious, diligent and attentive to his public duties, and highly esteemed for his many amiable qualities as a private citizen. He was a warm admirer of General Andrew Jackson, and much elated at the general's election to the presidency. When not engaged in public life, Judge Rosecrants devoted himself to agricultural pursuits on one of the most delightful farms in the county, situated on Fall hill.

Nathan Smith

Was a native of Massachusetts, came into this county in 1790, and opened a country retail store, in company with Naham Daniels, a few miles from the present village of Fairfield, on the farm recently occupied by Robert Alexander, and now by his descendants. They, at the same time, carried on the manufacture of pot-ashes. Mr. Daniels removed to Newport two or three years afterwards. Mr. Smith then removed to Fairfield village, where he continued the mercantile business for some time in connection with his brothers William and Samuel. He was many years a prominent politician in this county, and his first appearance in the legislative halls of the state appears to have been in 1798, associated with Gaylord Griswold and five others. This was the year that Oneida was erected. I state the fact that one at least of Mr. Smith's colleagues, Mr. Griswold, was, in after life, a leading and influential politician of the federal school, and more than fifteen years after his first election, Mr. Smith was associated with the republican party. He was again chosen member of assembly, and was in his place at the sessions of 1801 and 1802. These successive elections, at a period when the political opinions of candidates were drawn out and freely expressed, lead to the conclusion I have formed in regard to his early political attachments.

He was appointed a judge of the county courts and justice of the peace, in March, 1805, but it does not appear he was again commissioned in 1808 and 1811, and no other person seems to have been appointed at either of those periods to fill his place on the common pleas bench. Judge Smith was chosen a senator from the western district at the election in 1805, and held the office two full terms by a reelection in 1809. In February, 1808, he was chosen by the assembly one of the council of appointment. This great political machine had the previous year been in active operation under the direction of Gov. Lewis, who had been elevated to the executive chair by the combined votes of the federal and a section of the republican parties; but a large portion of the latter were very much opposed to the governor, and were arranging themselves in formidable masses to defeat his reelection. The governor and his council of 1808, sought to strengthen themselves by the removal from office of every unfriendly republican; but as usual on such occasions the official patronage was principally bestowed upon Lewisite republicans, or quids, as then called. The federalists, although they had supported Lewis's election, were not permitted to taste the "loaves and fishes" of office, and one of those not uncommon occurrences in New York politics had happened, in which the whole patronage and emoluments of place were bestowed upon a section of the republican party, and that section in this instance was the least numerous and influential of the two in the several counties of the state. The rivalries and jealousies of the potent and wealthy families existing in this colony at the out-break of the revolution, and who embraced the popular cause, was often exhibited at the elections, and for nearly forty years after the peace of 1783, this great political star chamber, the council of appointment, rewarded the faithful and punished the insubordinates with unerring precision. Woe to the official who failed to support the regular nominations of the party; from that moment he was a doomed man. The election of Mr. Tompkins to the executive chair, and the return of more than two to one members of assembly friendly to the new governor, with a majority in the senate, gave note of preparation for one of those periodical removals and appointments which often visited the state before and since the time now being considered.

The council of which Judge Smith was a member proceeded in the work of "crushing out insubordination" with a zeal and dispatch that in a very few months produced a change of individuals in nearly all the civil offices in the state.

The application for the charter of the Bank of America with a capital of $6,000,000, was made at the session of 1812, and Judge Smith was still a member of the senate. This application was generally opposed by the republican members and favored by the federalists. Governor Tompkins was by no means friendly, and on the 27th of March, prorogued the legislature until the 21st of May following, assigning as a reason for this act that the applicants had used or attempted to use corrupt means to procure the charter. The bill had passed the assembly by a vote of fifty-eight to thirty-nine, and was sent to the senate, when on a motion to reject, the vote was thirteen to fifteen and failed. The prorogation took place soon after and caused great excitement and some violence and outrage. This was a strong executive measure, but if, as was then and still is believed, a bill was about to be forced through the legislature by corrupt appliances, any legal and constitutional measure might be adopted to defeat it. The governor was sustained by the public judgment and this showed pretty conclusively the popular belief in the charges of corruption.

When the legislature met, on the 21st of May, the senate immediately proceeded to consider the bill to incorporate the stockholders of the Bank of America. As may be well supposed under the circumstances, the opposition to its passage was long and ably conducted, but the bill finally passed the senate by a vote of seventeen to thirteen, Judge Smith voting for it. The early history of the bank legislation of this state, exhibits scenes of the most revolting character, highly discreditable to the state. The public mind was not only satisfied, but had a surfeit of such matters, and for many years after chartering the Bank of America, but few applications for laws of this sort were presented to the legislature. The last attempt to procure bank charters by bribery of members was made in 1825. The effort was exposed and severely punished, as all such acts should be, if the purity of legislation is to be preserved. This remarkable fact is shown in the history of the passage of the Bank of America charter. The vote in favor of the bill was considerably increased in the assembly, after the exposure of the corrupt conduct of the agents of applicants; and why the senate should have entertained the bill at all, after these acts were known, must surpass the comprehension of modern legislators. During the bank legislation of 1829, 1830 and 1831, very serious doubts were entertained in relation to reincorporating any of these tainted charters. One of them was rejected in the senate, and on winding up its concerns exhibited a beggarly account of insolvent assets.

I have alluded to this subject in this place only because Judge Smith was an actor in chartering the Bank of America, and that was an event of his public life, in which he participated. It is due to his character and fame that I should say in this connection, I am not aware that he was in any respect damaged by the vote he gave, and certainly in the published history of those times, which I have seen, his name no otherwise appears than in the affirmative on the passage of the bill. After the close of his last senatorial term, Judge Smith was appointed the first judge of the county courts, in April 1814, and held the office till February, 1821, when he resigned the place. He died at Fairfield in this county, October 7th, 1836, at the mature age of 67 years; ripe in honors and in the enjoyment of competent wealth, the fruits of a long life devoted to business pursuits. He left a family.

While devoted to the cause and responsibilities of legislation, he was not unmindful of local affairs near home. He aided in the founding and building up the first academy established in the county, and exerted his best efforts, in conjunction with others, in behalf of the medical institution located at Fairfield, some notice of which will be found in another place.

Ephraim Snow

Was a native of the state of Connecticut, and removed from Killingworth into this county, some time before 1800. He was appointed sheriff of the county, in 1806, and held the office only one year. The appointment being an annual one, owing to a political revolution in the appointing power, he of course was not continued or reappointed in 1807. He lived and died at Herkimer village. I place Mr. Snow's nonreappointment to political causes, because, I notice his predecessor, Mr. Cook, whose place he took, was his successor in 1807.

Henry Tillinghast

Was a native of East Greenwich, Kent county, Rhode Island; the son of Benjamin Tillinghast, one of an extensive circle of family connections, known in former times to have exerted a pretty potent influence in that state, and not the least influential of the numerous and wide spread family, was the father of the subject of this notice; and the son emulated the fame of a worthy sire. Henry served an apprenticeship to the tanning business, with Charles Dyer, Bennington county, Vermont. He went to Vermont, in 1789, and in 1792 took up his residence in the town of Norway, when about twenty years of age. In the following year he returned to Vermont, married Miss Sarah Dyer, who at this present writing is his respected surviving widow; and seated himself permanently in the almost unbroken wilds of the Royal grant.

He was an active, thorough, business man; early gave his attention to the business of tanning, an occupation not only useful, in a new country, but very remunerative when the home demand exceeded the supply, as is most usually the case where the population is rapidly increasing, and there is almost a total nonintercourse with the general market, owing to bad roads, and the want of facilities for communication.

But Mr. Tillinghast did not confine himself to this mechanical pursuit alone. Farming early engaged his attention, and the hitherto untouched forest was subdued, and fertile acres were made to yield their annual crops for the sustenance of man. These employments, however, did not content the active energies of this son of the land of Roger Williams. I do not think he was aspiring and ambitious of political distinction, merely for the sake of office, and the emoluments of place. A conscientious conviction that his own cherished political views were the cardinal maxims of good government, prompted Mr. Tillinghast, at an early day, to take the field as a champion of republicanism, against one of the most formidable opponents of that party in the county, Thomas Manly, who had seated himself in Norway, a short time before Mr. Tillinghast.

While I wish to place Mr. Tillinghast's actions on the basis of a love of country, I must not be understood as questioning in any way the motives and objects of Mr. Manly. The contest was long, and attended with varied success. The majority of votes polled by either political party, for several years, was very small, seldom exceeding ten or twelve, often a less number, and one year, each of the assembly candidates received 105 votes in the town. Mr. Manly was then one of the candidates. There was not any personal antagonism indulged by either party, during this long contest for political supremacy. Mr. Tillinghast held various town offices in his town, and performed the duties of them to the general satisfaction of his fellow citizens. In what I have said about Mr. Manly and Mr. Tillinghast, it should not be inferred that there were not other prominent and leading men in the town, of both parties, who participated in the strife for the political mastery, and who exerted a proper share of influence whenever the parties were rallied to the polls.

At the legislative session of 1823, the first convened under the constitution of 1821, Mr. Tillinghast was one the members of assembly from this county. He was elected on the ticket with John Dygert and Abijah Beckwith. The session was an important and interesting one. He was again a member of the assembly in 1835. He was a cautious and prudent legislator, and attentive to his public duties. His practical good sense, sound judgment and clear perception of things, seldom failed him on any emergency.

He held the important office of supervisor of his town nearly thirty years in succession, and that of a magistrate several terms. His devotion to his country, its safety and honor, lay deeper and broader than mere wordy pretensions. He was ready and willing to act in a post of danger, should occasion require it, and with that view organized during the war of 1812, a company of volunteer exempts, of which he was designated the captain, who held themselves ready to serve their country in the field against the common enemy. He was somewhat of a military tactician, and would often, after the weary labors of the day were ended, call his little sons around him and teach them the "manual exercise."

Mr. Tillinghast was born on the 22d of May, 1772, and died suddenly in the harvest field on the 29th of July, 1841, in the full fruition of a well spent life. He left a numerous family the inheritors not only of his justly earned fame, but of an estate, the accumulation of fifty years of frugal industry. I have spoken of Mr. Tillinghast's political opinions as I knew them. He was a republican of the Jeffersonian school, and although ardent in feelings and actions, these were always tempered and controlled by a just regard to the conservative principles of the constitution of his country.

STEPHEN TODD

Was born in Wallingford, Connecticut, December 23d, 1773. His father removed to Salisbury, Herkimer county, in 1792, with his family, and commenced the laborious work of converting a wilderness of forest into fruitful fields. Mr. Todd, the younger, worked with his father on the new farm a few years, when he commenced the study of medicine, obtained a license and commenced practice in Salisbury previous to 1800. Doct. Todd attained a very considerable eminence in his profession, and was justly esteemed for his active, humane and zealous efforts to alleviate the "ills that life is heir to," and highly respected for a sound and vigorous understanding. He continued his professional pursuits in Salisbury till near the close of life. He combined, to some extent, agricultural with his professional pursuits, and

I heard him remark that he was one of the first in the county to adopt the change from grain-growing to grazing, and that he felt it to be a duty to encourage and promote this change as the best and only means of reviving the farming interests of the county. He said it was unwise to continue the competition with the western part of this state, Ohio and Michigan, in raising wheat, under almost any circumstances; but it was especially so while the fly and weevil were cutting off the wheat, and the cold seasons so inauspicious to Indian corn. These remarks were strongly impressed upon my mind at the time in consequence of the question, what are the farmers to do, being much discussed, and made the subject of anxious inquiry.

Doct. Todd was the captain of a company of militia light infantry, in the war of 1812 with Great Britain. Now, although neither the active nor passive sympathies of the doctor were with the general or state administrations of that day, at all times and on all occasions, he obeyed the call of his country with patriotic alacrity. I am enabled to give the following incident in the life of Doct. Todd, the facts having been elicited in the course of a semi-judicial investigation had in my hearing. In 1814, Captain Todd, as I will now call him, and a few members of his company had been detached to join the American forces at Plattsburgh in this state, at the time of the invasion by the British under Sir George Provost. Within a few days of the first call, orders were received from Governor Tompkins for the militia of Montgomery and Herkimer counties, *en masse*, to march immediately to Sackets Harbor to defend that post. Capt. Todd felt himself called upon to perform an extra duty, which does not often fall to the lot of an officer, and, when it does, is not always performed with the same anxious solicitude for the welfare of others. He directed the detached men of his company to repair to the rendezvous at Johnstown and report themselves to the commanding officer, and then started with his company *en route* to Sackets Harbor. After proceeding one or two days' march with the company, and seeing that his men were furnished with all needful equipage and provisions, and leaving them under the charge of his lieutenant, Abraham Marsh, to march to the Harbor, he retraced his steps home to Salisbury, and then made hot pursuit to overtake his command before it reached Plattsburgh.

The mention of Sir George and the invasion, brings to recollection an anecdote connected with that event, related by Sir A. N. McN., who was then an ensign in the British army. This, I know, is not exactly the place for such things, but it is too good to keep, and therefore it must come out somewhere, and may as well appear in company with Capt. Todd, at Plattsburgh, as any other officer. Sir A. tells the story with much good feeling and very spiritedly, and I only wish it could be here repeated with the same amusing action he gives when relating it. After the British army had crossed the line on its march to Plattsburgh, Sir A. and two or three other young officers obtained leave one morning to forage for a breakfast at some of the American farm-houses near the line of march. They looked around and selected a house some distance from the road, where from outside appearances they would be the most likely to obtain what they very much required, a good warm breakfast. The young gentlemen were not slow in reaching the goal of their desires, as they wished not only to be first to occupy the ground, but very much inclined to have the smell and taste of a savory meal. They were kindly received at the house, civilly told in reply to their inquiry, that breakfast would be prepared for them as soon as it possibly could. In due time they were seated round the table and appeasing hunger as fast as they could, momentarily expecting a call to duty. My informant says a bright, active and healthful young woman waited upon them, and brought from an adjoining room the hot cakes prepared for them.

The signal or call to join corps and regiments was heard while the young woman was out of the room; the officers had quit their seats at the table and were about to leave the house, when she came in with another plate full of cakes, and seeing they were ready to start, said to them, "Gentlemen, don't be in a hurry, I have more warm cakes for you, and you had better take them now." The young officers in reply, said they would call for them on their return from Plattsburgh. She rejoined, "Perhaps you may then be in too much haste to stop." Sir A. says they were much more light of foot in returning to, than in coming from Canada; and that on his way back with a party of flankers, he passed near the house where they had breakfasted, and hearing some one call, looked up and saw the same young woman standing in the door, who said to him with a roguish smile, "Halloo, mister, won't you call and get your cakes?"

Doctor Todd's campaign to Plattsburgh closed, I believe, his active military service during the war. I think he was on the frontier in one or both of the previous years of the war, but of this I am not certain.

At the November election, 1821, he was nominated by his political friends as a candidate for the assembly, on a ticket with Simeon Ford and Robert Shoemaker, and received a majority of the popular vote over his competitor, but failed to obtain a certificate of election from the county clerk. Dr. Todd's whole vote in the county was 1941; his highest competitor, Gen. Bellinger, had 1644. The returns of two towns, Russia and Winfield, were rejected, whereby he lost 98 majority; but he yet had 199 more votes than either of his opponents. The returns from Danube were assumed to show 207 votes given for Robert Shoemaker, 211 for Simeon Ford, and 202 for Stephen Tood. I say assumed, for that was the construction of the canvasser on examining the certificate of the town inspectors, sent to the county clerk's office. It was, at the time, supposed to be a remarkable fact, that two of the three candidates running on the same ticket should receive so large a vote, and the third none at all, when the printed ballots used at the election throughout the county were alike. The mistake in the certificate made by the town inspectors, if there was one, must have occurred in writing out the names of the candidates and the top of the first d in Todd so much depressed as to look like an o. At any rate, the rejection of the Danube votes from Todd's column, and placing them to Stephen Tood, after the other rejections above noticed, elected Gen. Bellinger by three majority, and he consequently obtained the certificate. The committee on privileges and elections in the house corrected this matter as soon as it came before them, and the assembly, without hesitation, awarded the contested seat to the rightful occupant. The political parties in the house were so nearly balanced, that it was not clearly known, until the legislature met, whether the democratic majority would be one, or the numbers 64 to 64. Casualties might prevent a full attendance at the opening of the session, but these chances were equally balanced. The political opponents of the county clerk complained of his conduct, in not notifying the Danube inspectors of the mistake in their certificate, and whispered pretty audibly that he was looking to the election of speaker and the council of appointment. A democratic majority of one in the house, after Dr. Todd was admitted, rendered any such precautions needless.

Dr. Todd died at Salisbury in the month and same day of the month of his birth, in the year 1827, aged 54 years. He left a family of several daughters, but I do not know whether any sons survived him to bear his name to posterity. He accumulated a very considerable fortune, by active and judicious application to business; and had attained a standing in his profession which many aspire to, but few achieve.

Abijah Tombling

Was not a native of this county. He came into the town of Norway near the close of the last century or at the commencement of the present, where he pursued his profession as a physician and surgeon with considerable success. He was cotemporary with Dr. Willoughby. I am not able to fix the date of his removal to Herkimer village. He succeeded David Holt as United States collector of internal revenue, and held the office until the repeal of the laws imposing those duties. Dr. Tombling was appointed surrogate of the county in November, 1816, and held the place until April, 1821. He was amiable, unassuming and benevolent. In quitting or rather neglecting his profession, and giving his attention to politics, he was not fortunate. He died at Herkimer more than twenty years ago, regretted by a large circle of friends, and leaving a family to mourn his loss.

Edward Varney

Was born in Armenia, Dutchess county, New York, June 6th, 1778. His father, John Varney, was one of the patriotic men of the revolution. He served his country through a protracted war of seven years, enduring its privations, fatigues and sacrifices, with heroic fortitude. His time and substance were devoted to the service of his country, leaving him little of either for the education of his family. The subject of this notice having, by untiring industry and perseverance, accumulated a small patrimony, emigrated with his family, in 1809, to the then wilds of Herkimer county. He became at once a proprietor and tiller of the soil.

In 1812, he was appointed a justice of the peace, an office which, by repeated appointments and elections, he filled with honor during twenty-five successive years. During the same period, he was for many years clerk of the town, and for five years one of the judges of the county court. His first appointment as county judge was made in February, 1823. He also filled the office of supervisor five years, was master in chancery, commissioner of schools, &c. In 1825, he was elected member of assembly. In 1841, he was elected senator of this state in the fourth senate district.

In all stations in which he was called to act, he showed himself capable, faithful and honest. Elevated in principle and urbane in manners, he secured the respect and confidence of his associates. He was bold as he was frank, honest and undisguised. In all his acts, whether private or public, he yielded to the voice of rectitude and conscience, regardless of consequences. Edmund Varney was a republican of the Jeffersonian school.

An ardent admirer and lover of his country, and believing the welfare of that country could only be secured by the supremacy of the democratic party, Judge Varney, during his long life, seldom failed to attend the polls, and to deposit his vote. He has often remarked to the writer, that "the right of suffrage was sacred, and should be preserved inviolate." A few days previous to his death, speaking of the present political aspects of our country, he expressed a decided opinion against the institution of domestic slavery, the "peculiar institution" of the south, and hoped its limits would, under no circumstances, be extended.

He sustained a long and painful illness, from chronic bronchitis, with Christian resignation and fortitude, believing and hoping, with firm assurance, in the immortality of the soul, and that he had the promise of a happy life in the world to come. He calmly expired at his residence in Russia, December 2, 1847.

I find the above obituary notice published in one of the county papers about the period of Judge Varney's death; and after making a few slight alterations in the original article, cheerfully incorporate it with the biographies of the public men of the county. A long and somewhat intimate acquaintance with Judge Varney, enables me to say, the writer has placed a just estimate upon his character, and has done no injustice to the subject.

Richard Van Horne

Was a native of Sussex county, New Jersey, and was born the 15th of November, 1770. He was a son of Abraham Van Horne, a narrative of whom will be found under the town of Stark.

Mr. Van Horne removed from Fort Plain in 1791, with his father and other members of the family, to the head of the Otsquaga creek, now known as Van Hornesville, and commenced the mercantile business in connection with his brother Daniel. As the country opened and became more populated, they increased and extended their business until they became pretty largely engaged in the purchase of wheat and the manufacture of flour for the Albany market. There being neither turnpikes, plank roads, canals nor rail roads in those days, the waters of the Mohawk were used as the medium of transport from the point of shipment at Fort Plain to Schenectady, and from thence the communication was by teams to Albany.

Mr. Van Horne was elected to the legislature of this state from Montgomery county in 1809, 1810, and again in 1812. His official connection with the people of this county, after the annexation of a portion of Montgomery county to Herkimer in 1817, brings this case within the scope of biographical notices to be embraced in this work.

At the election on the 19th, 20th and 21st June, 1821, Mr. Van Horne was put in nomination as a delegate to the convention to revise the constitution of the state with Simeon Ford and Nathan Smith. Sherman Wooster and Sanders Lansing were the opposing candidates to Messrs. Ford and Smith. I have noticed the reasons in another place why the democratic party adopted Mr. Van Horne, or rather did not nominate a candidate against him, and will not again repeat them. That election presented a somewhat curious result. Van Horne's aggregate vote in the county was 3410; Wooster and Lansing's average was 1935 and Ford and Smith's, 1553; showing Van Horne's vote to be nearly 80 less than the other successful candidates, and the democratic majority was 382 only. When the constitution was submitted for ratification, the vote in Danube, Mr. Van Horne's town, was For it, Yes, 68; Against it, No, 363; majority, No, 295; and the majority in the county for the constitution was only

329. Speculation upon matters of this sort may not be very entertaining but may prove useful.

The vote in Danube on the election of delegates was nearly divided, or rather the majority against the democratic candidates was only fifty-five. The avowed opinions of those gentlemen in favor of the prominent features of amendment or change, were fully known to the electors, and hence there must have been a change of sentiment, or there was an influence exerted on the vote for ratification that was quiescent at the delegate election. Mr. Van Horne did not approve of the constitution of 1821, but this objection may not have been founded on the modified extension of the right of suffrage and the abolition of the councils of appointment and revision, the points on which he was understood to be in accord with the democratic party at the time of the election.

The provision in that instrument which ousted the justices of the then supreme court from office, which gave rise to much elaborate discussion in the convention, and on which the political majority in that body did not agree, encountered his opposition at every step, and in every stage of its progress. He would not be likely to sanction an instrument containing unobjectionable provisions, which carried with them what he judged an unjust act of proscription against his friends.

Although several of the members of the convention, with whom he had usually acted, and who sympathized with him on political questions, finally yielded their assent, his mind seems to have been unalterably fixed on the subject, and he gave one of the eight votes against the constitution, when the final question was taken. The posterity of the men of that day, have passed judgment upon the instrument, and repudiated most of its provisions, but they have not made a very rapid stride towards Mr. Van Horne's notions, of a sound and safe constitution.

Mr. Richard Van Horne died at Van Horneville, in the

town of Stark, March 12th, 1823, aged 72 years, 4 months and 27 days. He left a widow and seven children; the former was living at the writing of this brief notice. I hardly need remind the reader, that Mr. Van H. was of Dutch, and not German descent. His ancestors emigrated from Holland. In the prime of life he was actively engaged in business pursuits, appertaining to merchandise and manufacturing, and when the "sere and yellow leaf" of old age overtook him, he reposed on the comforts of a good farm, and the accumulations of an industrious and well-spent life. It is not strange that such a man should win the regards of his neighbors and fellow citizens, and bear their regrets to his final resting place.

EVANS WHARRY

Filled a prominent space in the early history of the county, at the close of the war in 1783. He was of Irish descent, and born at or near Wallkill, Orange county, in 1749. Left an orphan at the early age of sixteen years, by the death of both his parents, being thrown, by this sad event, upon his own resources, he devoted himself to study, and particularly to mathematics, in order to acquire the theory of navigation; having made up his mind to adopt and pursue a seafaring life. He made several voyages to the West Indies, as supercargo of some of the small vessels then engaged in that trade, but he found a nautical life unsuited to his health and inclinations, abandoned it, and gave his attention to surveying.

The advent of the American revolution found him in the prime of life and vigor of manhood, and probably with no sympathies for the royal cause. If a thought of adhesion to the crown ever crossed his mind, it "must soon have passed away as the idle wind," for we find him in command of a company in Canada, when the American army under Gen. Montgomery approached and assaulted Quebec. Being stationed at or near Montreal, he was ordered to join the provincial forces below, but afterwards hearing of the fall of Montgomery and the defeat of the Americans, he consulted with Dr. Franklin in regard to the expediency of marching to the city, under the altered circumstances. The American sage said to him "it is a good officer that obeys the command of his superiors," and Wharry immediately commenced a forward movement with his men. After a short progress, however, he was directed to return, and he left Canada with the evacuating army.

Mr. Wharry served his country well and faithfully, during the whole of the eventful struggle for provincial emancipation. The theater of his service was mostly in the northern department, under General Schuyler. The routine of duty was that usually performed by a subaltern staff. I am not aware that he performed permanent service in the line of the army after the expedition into Canada. His country acknowledged those services, by the bestowment of the usual gratuity or pension upon him to the close of his life, and after that upon his venerable relict, who survived him nearly twenty years.

He came into this county in 1785-6, purchased a tract of land, and commenced farming. The home place where he died, near the Little Falls, was a part of that purchase. Being a good practical surveyor, and possessing no small share of energy in mind and body, he was much engaged in the business of surveying, the first fifteen or twenty years of his residence in the county, and was often employed on behalf of the state in making surveys of the public lands. He was appointed one of the judges of the common pleas, and a justice of the peace, August 27, 1798, and held those offices until March 18th, 1805, when he was commissioned as first judge, on the resignation of John Meyer. Judge Wharry continued to hold the office and discharge the duties of his last appointment, until he was sixty years old, the constitutional limit. We have made the important discovery, since 1777, that three score years does not unerringly produce mental incapacity, amounting to disqualification to hold judicial office. So long, however, as the incumbent held by the tenure of good behavior, it may have been well to fix some limit when even that qualification should no longer serve him; and if it was found that mental incapacitation commenced at sixty years, with the average of educated men, that was probably a safe period of limitation. It must, however, be acknowledged, that new lights in the science of government have been pouring in upon us the last fifty years with astonishing rapidity and unexampled exuberance. If we can not discover the origin and cause of the Asiatic cholera, nor detect the peculiar miasma which invigorates this most appalling of modern plagues, who will venture to doubt the capacity of man at this time to originate and perfect such municipal rules of government, as, acting upon the mind, and giving it a direction, must inevitably produce a terrestrial millenium.

Judge Wharry was chosen one of the delegates from this county, in 1801, to the convention called under the authority of an act of the state legislature. He had been elected in the spring of 1800 to the assembly, with George Widrig and Nathan Smith, and was consequently a member of that house when the act authorizing the call was passed. He was again chosen member of assembly in the county, at the spring elections of 1803 and 1804, with Samuel Wright and George Widrig, and the legislative session of 1805 ended his career as a representative of the people of the county. Judge Wharry's position during the revolutionary war enabled him to form a personal acquaintance with Washington, Knox, Hamilton, Burr, George Clinton and other distinguished leaders in that mighty effort in the conquest of freedom and assertion of right. He was an active and zealous politician, and the reader may have noticed his intimate connection and association with Matthias B. Tallmadge. They both came from the same part of the state into the county, although not in the same year.

The upper section of the Mohawk valley was growing into importance; it had been partially occupied along the borders of the river, by an indomitable race of men, since 1724, whose opportunities and facilities for schooling had been extremely limited, owing to their insulated frontier situation, and whose theoretical and practical education were circumscribed to their farming pursuits. This was true of the German population generally, at the opening of the last decade of the eighteenth century, but there were exceptions, and even at that early day, a few educated and well-informed men were found among them. The country, outside of the limits occupied by the German population, north and south, was fast filling up with the Anglo-Saxon race and the descendants of the pilgrims, and the crash of the mighty forests, prostrated by the sturdy blows of the New England axman, was echoed from hill to hill, and rumbled through every valley. Here there was opening a wide and fruitful field for the operation of politicians. I have in another place stated, somewhat at large, the reasons which induced me to suppose that the leading men of the anti-federal or republican party in this state took a deep interest in the political affairs of this frontier.

Governor George Clinton was well acquainted with Judge Wharry in Orange county, during the war, and after its close; and he was aware that the judge's occupation as a surveyor would necessarily require him to be much abroad among the inhabitants, running and marking boundary lines in a new country. This, I think, must have led the governor to direct Wharry's attention to this quarter as a desirable field of operations, professionally and politically.

It will be remarked that Judge Wharry was brought into public life soon after he became an inhabitant of the county; and let it be remembered, that he continued an active and prominent politician until after the close of Governor George Clinton's career in this state. I have left unnoticed several of the minor incidents of the judge's life, which would interest the reader, but my purpose is to deal with the public acts of individuals, which are connected with this county. The subject of this notice died at his residence, in the town of

Little Falls, in the month of April, 1831, aged 82 years. His wife, the daughter of Joseph Belknap, of Newburgh, Orange county, whom he married near the close of the war, survived him several years, and died a few years since, at a very advanced age. She was, in many respects, a very remarkable woman. He left several daughters. He had one or two sons, who left the county many years ago. He died on the spot he had converted to a fruitful field from a dense forest, where he had lived to see his country free, prosperous and happy.

George Widrig

Descended from German parents, but was, I believe, born in this country. I have but little information in respect to the incidents of his life and character, and therefore my sketch must be limited. On the development of political parties at the accession of Mr. Jefferson, he appears to have ranged himself with the republicans. He was seven years in succession chosen a member of assembly in this county, and every year with politicians of his own party, with perhaps one or two exceptions. He was first elected in the spring of 1800. His colleagues, during this long period of service, were Nathan Smith, who served two terms, Evans Wharry, three, Samuel Wright, five, Samuel Merray, Jr., Stephen Miller, Eldad Corbit and John Kennedy, each one term. But few public men in this county have enjoyed the confidence and retained the regards of his fellow citizens to such an extent. He resided many years, if not all his life, within the present limits of the town of Frankfort, near the western borders of the county, after Oneida was erected, where he closed a long and well spent life. Being a major-general of militia during the war of 1812, he was desirous that his division should be called into service to defend his country; but failing in this effort, yet resolved to mingle with her patriotic defenders, and there being no other place where he could serve, in consequence of his military rank, he joined the wagon train one campaign, and served as a teamster.

DOCTOR WESSEL WILLOUGHBY,

Who for a time filled a large space in the public regard, was a native of Connecticut, and lived in that state and in Massachusetts until he came into this state, when a young man, and settled upon the highlands in the town of Norway, about the period of the first settlement of the Royal grant by New England emigrants, and commenced the practice of medicine, which he pursued several years, traversing the by-paths of the then dense wilderness on foot, with his saddlebags on his arm. At this time the old town of Norway embraced a portion of the present town of Fairfield, the whole of Newport, and other parts of the northerly part of the county. He subsequently removed to the valley of the West Canada creek, near the present village of Newport, where he established himself, selecting a beautiful spot of ground on the eastern shore of the creek, on which he erected a beautiful mansion for those times, improved his grounds surrounding it, and spent the remainder of his life, to within a few years of his death, in the practice of his profession. Doctor Willoughby was about twenty years professor of midwifery and of the diseases of women and children, in the college of physicians and surgeons in the western district of New York, established at Fairfield, and during a considerable portion of that time was president of the institution. He was highly distinguished in his profession, and a remarkably public spirited and benevolent man. His position and influence while in the prime and vigor of manhood, contributed largely to the support of the college, and he was among the first who exerted themselves to establish that once highly flourishing and useful institution.

Doctor Willoughby was twice chosen member of the assembly with John M. Petrie and Aaron Budlong, at two successive elections in 1807 and 1808. Being elected at the April elections of those years, he did not take his seat until the sessions held the following winter. Although a man of much learning in his profession, I am not aware that he was accustomed to speak often or to any extent in a legislative body. This was at the first election of Governor Tompkins in 1807. At the election in 1808, the federalists obtained a majority in the assembly, but Doctor Willoughby was not one of that majority.

He was appointed one of the judges of the court of common pleas of the county in March, 1805, and was continued in that commission until March, 1821. Doctor Willoughby belonged to the medical staff of the militia of the county during the war of 1812, and was at Sackets Harbor and on the frontier, whenever his country required his services in that direction. He was elected to congress from the district composed of the counties of Madison and Herkimer in 1814, and must have taken his seat the year following, as his congressional term did not commence till the 4th of March, 1815. My information of his public course as a legislator, is too limited to permit me to speak of it with any particularity. From his connection with the dominant political party in the county and state, I suppose he belonged to the republican party of the times. In the division of that party into bucktail and Clintonian sections, he adhered to the latter.

Dr. Willoughby died at Newport, in this county, in the year 1844, aged seventy-five years.

Chauncey Woodruff

Was a resident of Herkimer village, where he was several years engaged in mercantile business. After the erection of Oneida county, Mr. Woodruff was appointed sheriff of this county in the place of William Colbreath, who retained that office in Oneida.

Mr. Woodruff was first appointed March 19th, 1798, and

held the office by reappointment annually till March 17th, 1802. He died at Herkimer, May 10th, 1810, aged 41 years.

SHERMAN WOOSTER,

In several respects, possessed peculiarities of character which are worthy of extended notice. Although cut down at a mature age, he had already achieved, without the adventitious aids of fortuue or family connections, or a popular profession, and laboring under all the disadvantages of a very limited early education, the highest offices in the gift of the people of this county. He had accomplished this, by force of a strong native intellect, cultivated and improved by application and study, in hours of relaxation from work at his trade. He was emphatically a self-made man. His mind was not cast in the mold which gave forth scintillations of wit and fancy, and if it had been, the want of an early polish did not afford any opportunity of bringing them out. His mind was more like that of Roger Sherman, the Connecticut shoemaker, as shadowed forth in the Madison papers, in the debates on the federal constitution, than that of any other public man within my knowledge.

He was a native of Danbury, Connecticut; born the 17th February, 1779, and died suddenly at Newport, in this county, May 21st, 1833, aged 54 years, 3 months and 4 days. He came to Ballston Spa, in 1787, where he was apprenticed to a hatter. In 1801, he removed to Utica, where he remained working at his trade, until 1804; when he finally settled permanently in Newport, in this county. He was married a short time before this removal, and his wife survived him, and is still living. He carried on his mechanical business a few years after he came to the county, but finally devoted his whole time and attention to the discharge of the duties of various public offices and trusts, principally of a local character, at the early stages of his official career. Besides other town offices, he held those of supervisor and justice of the peace, many years. The former being a town elective office, it was seldom, if ever, a candidate could be brought out against him, who could carry a majority of the electors. He was a faithful and diligent magistrate, and his official conduct generally received the public approval. He was appointed, by the governor and senate, one of the judges of the court of common pleas of the county, in April, 1828, and held the place one term only. He declined a reappointment.

Mr. Wooster's name was first presented to the people of the county, for an elective office, in 1821. He was that year chosen a delegate to the convention called to revise the constitution, of 1777. He was known to the people of the county to be firm, but moderate in his political notions, and the use of his name, at that time, aided materially in securing the election of the republican delegates, in the county, which had very recently cast a small majority against the call of the convention.

A particular reference to Mr. Wooster's votes, on the various important and interesting propositions brought before the convention, in settling the principles of the constitution of 1821, do not seem to me to be called for, at this time. He must be ranked with the movement party, in the convention, of which the principal leaders were, Gen. Root, Gov. Tompkins and Col. Young, although he did not always vote with them, on several of the propositions which they advocated. He was in several instances found arrayed against Mr. Van Buren, on votes where that distinguished member of the convention had made able and zealous efforts to carry a majority of the convention with him. On the whole, Mr. Wooster's course in the convention was highly satisfactory to his political friends in the county, and placed him in a prominent position as a public man. He approved of, and voted for the constitution, as framed and submitted to the people, and I make the above qualification because a large minority of the electors in the county voted against that instrument. Mr. Wooster was neither an ambitious nor a turbulent politician. He was cool, deliberative and conscientious, and seldom gave any public measure his approval simply on the ground of public expediency.

At the November election in 1822, he was chosen one of the four state senators elected in the fifth senate district, under the constitution recently adopted. On taking his seat he drew the long term of four years. Although he was elected in an almost political calm, nearly the whole term of his service in the senate, from January 1st, 1823, to January, 1827, was one of the most stormy and exciting periods in the political history of this state that has occurred; and we have not, before or since, been unfrequently visited by political tornadoes, which not only baffle all description, but set at defiance the ingenuity of man to discover or detect the true causes of their origin. Such is the opinion entertained of us in other states. Even an attempted elucidation of problems of this sort would be unsuited to our purpose.

The political agitations preceding the election of Mr. Monroe's successor, did not commence until after Mr. Wooster's election, and he was consequently not subjected to any personal pledges in regard to that subject. He was left free to ascertain the opinions and wishes of his constituents in the best way he could, and act accordingly. In regard to the celebrated electoral law, which has been necessarily mentioned in the preceding pages of this work, he voted for its postponement to a future day, which was beyond the succeeding annual election, and this was therefore considered a virtual rejection of the bill by its friends, and it was so, in fact, in reference to the pending election. Hence his name, associated with others, as one of the famous SEVENTEEN SENATORS, was pasted up in black letter in public barrooms, and had a conspicuous place in most of the newspapers which advocated the passage of the law. Neither Mr. Wooster nor his friends considered him materially damaged by a proceeding of this sort. At any rate, there never was a body of men so resolutely sustained by their friends in subsequent political conflicts, as were these same seventeen senators, and the names of Bronson, Dudley,

Earll, Livingston, Suydam, and Wright, have not been unfamiliar names at the polls of election for more than twenty years. But Mr. Wooster was friendly to Mr. Crawford's elevation to the presidency, and if he supposed the best interests of the country would be promoted by his election, as he no doubt did, was he not fully justifiable in adopting every legitimate expedient to effect his object and defeat the measures of his opponents? I will not repeat what has been elsewhere stated in regard to the choice of electors by the people, but it is impossible to avoid the conclusion which forces itself upon all familiar with the politics of this state for the last half century, that if the contest in 1824 had been confined to two candidates, the selection of the two great political parties, the controversy about the electoral law would have ended where it began, within the walls of the two houses. This was a contest for political power by the adherents of numerous presidential aspirants, and involved no principle of government acting upon the masses of the community beyond one single election, and so long as the legislature so exercised the powers conferred by law as to be the true exponents of the will of the majority of the electors, the political party or politicians, acting in conformity to this idea, risked but little with friends, when their "sober second thoughts" were appealed to. When the parties come to reflect upon what had been done, and the whole ground had been surveyed, the voters in this county by a majority of about six hundred, at the election in November, 1825, reversed the decision of the preceding year, by returning those members of the assembly who had heartily concurred in Mr. Wooster's course on the electoral law question, and thereby directly sanctioned his previous political course in the senate.

He was elected to the assembly of this state in the fall of 1832, with Dudley Burwell and Joseph M. Prendergast, and was consequently a member of the house of assembly when he died. His votes in the house during the session of 1833, on all the important questions which came up for discussion, were in accordance with his preexisting and expressed opinions. He was opposed to all projects of internal improvements, such as the Chenango canal, whose eventualities were the entailment of a certain debt upon the state, without the slightest prospect of reimbursement from income, even to the extent of the ordinary expenses of repairs. He was one of those statesmen who did not esteem it prudent to contract a debt to develop the resources of a section of country, whose trade and business was not sufficient to maintain and superintend the work constructed; and on this question he agreed in opinion, not only with a large majority of the people of the county, but with many distinguished men in the state. This, it is true, is a subject which has afforded, and always will, a wide range of discussion, and even fair-minded men might possibly entertain antagonistic views in regard to particular projects, and even the general proposition as above stated; but that generation on whom the burthen of canceling the debt might be cast, would not be likely to disagree in regard to the wisdom or prudence of measures that submerged their country in debt. It is difficult to limit the powers of commerce, or even to define the extent of taxation or burthen a highly commercial people can bear, without materially affecting the healthful action of trade. Our own experience as a nation shows the paralysing effects and the ruinous consequences of an overshadowing and crushing public and private indebtedness; and it shows, too, that an animated but steady application to industrial pursuits, aided by extensive commercial relations, how soon a people can wipe out and even forget financial embarrassments. We have only to look at a kindred nation, whose annual revenues exceed our own five fold, and whose public debt, set down in figures, would seem ponderous enough "to crush out" seventeen millions of people; yet we see that nation adding millions to the annual burthens of its subjects, and fitting out naval armaments sufficiently extensive to blockade the approaches by sea of a power whose boundaries circumscribe a large portion of two continents, and some portion of a third, and whose ambition reaches to grasp at a fourth, and this mighty effort is sustained by the power of commerce and trade, domestic and foreign, without seeming to disturb in the least the general prosperity of the country. But here we must pause. The people of the most powerful nations on the continent of Europe, with the exception of France, and she is sustained by internal and external trade, are literally groaning under the burthen of taxation, much of it being required to pay the interest on public debt; and so little credit have many of their governments with the *money kings* of the day, that they can not negotiate a loan except at a ruinous discount of fifteen or twenty per cent. The credit of an impoverished country, or whose subjects are ripe for rebellion, will not command a premium with modern money lenders.

Samuel Wright.

There are but few men in the walks of civil life, and especially those whose minds have been embellished with nothing more than a common school education, who burst forth like meteors, blaze for a moment, attract universal attention, and then become as suddenly extinguished and forgotten. This, however, was the brief course of Mr. Wright in this county. He came from Vermont, and settled within the limits of the present town of Russia, about the year 1793, where he engaged in the business of farming, which, in a new country, consists, for the first few years, in opening roads, clearing up lands, and erecting such buildings as may be required for family purposes.

So soon as the country around him had become pretty well filled up with population, he opened a country store, and traded in "West India and dry goods," not neglecting the "cod fish," a very needful article to a full assortment for the country trade in those days. Having made successful progress in farming and merchandising, Mr. Wright next turned his attention to politics, in which he prospered remarkably well for a time. He was elected member of assembly in 1802, and the four following years. He appears to have been the standing candidate of his party, with General Widrig, for a long time, but his popularity could not always last. Dr. Westel Willoughby, Jr., was a townsman of Mr. Wright, all the northern part of the county then being embraced in Norway, a rising man, and competed vigorously with him for popular favor. Notwithstanding his extraordinary native talents and indomitable Yankee perseverance, Mr. Wright was compelled to yield the palm of victory to his rival. At the election, in 1806, his vote was the lowest of three members who obtained certificates of election, and even then was defeated by the popular votes. Willoughby's official canvass was only 43 below Wright's, and this after 63 votes, intended for the former, had been rejected for informality.

In the winter of 1805, the Merchant's Bank, of the city of New York, was chartered, after being strongly opposed, but not without strong suspicions and direct charges of bribery and corruption; and Ebenezer Purdy, a senator, "who introduced in the senate the bill to incorporate the company, finally was compelled to resign his seat, to avoid expulsion for bribery." On the 16th of March, 1805, Luke Metcalf, a member of assembly, made a statement under oath, which was laid before the house, to the effect that Mr. Wright told him, there were fifteen shares of the stock for each member who would favor or vote for the bill incorporating the bank, which would be worth twenty-five per cent on the nominal price of the stock. That Wright afterwards asked Metcalf if he remained opposed to the bank, and being answered in the affirmative, Wright then said, the same provision would be made for those members who would absent themselves, when the vote was taken on the bill, as for those who should be present and vote for it.

Wr. Wright was twice elected to the assembly after his vote on the bank bill, and after this expose; it was not, however, generally known to his constituents, in April, 1805, that he was suspected of improper practices in regard to the incorporation of this bank. His two colleagues in the assembly also voted for the bill, but were not charged with foul conduct, in procuring its passage. The republican party at this time was hostile to the granting of bank charters, the leading men of the party fearing the influence their managers, who were generally federalists, would be able to exert at the elections, by the influence they would give. Governor Lewis, however, favored the incorporation of this bank; and gave an approving vote for it in the council of revision, when it was objected to by Ambrose Spencer, a judge of the supreme court, on the ground that the passage of the bill was procured in both houses by bribery of the members.

CHAPTER XIII.

This chapter has been arranged into nineteen sections, that being the number of towns in the county. I have endeavored to make the annexed table useful as a reference. The reader will remark a loss of population, in eleven of the towns, in a time of prosperity as great and healthful as any during the present century. These losses have not arisen from a depression in any branch of husbandry. The increase of population in the river towns and villages, along the canal and rail road, and in the towns having wild lands to settle, overbalances these losses, and gives a small addition in the aggregate, for the last ten years; but not equal to the percentage of births over deaths, in the same period.

For the amusement of the curious, I will remark that, four of the towns in the county, commemorate the names of revolutionary generals; the names of three, are derived from Germany; four, from New England; one, is called after a state in the union, and another, after a county in this state; one, bears the name of an empire, and another, a kingdom in Europe; three, are descriptive of the localities which are embraced within their limits, and one, seems an emanation of fancy.

The county is now divided into the following towns, which are given, with the dates of organization, and the population of each town, in 1845, and 1855:

	Names of Towns.	When organized.	Population in 1855.	Population in 1845.	Gains in 10 years.	Losses in 10 years.	From what towns setoff, or taken.
1	Columbia,......	1812	1,831	2,126	.....	295	Warren,
2	Danube,........	1817	1,791	1,693	98	.....	Minden, Mont. co.
3	Fairfield,.......	1796	1,493	1,662	.....	169	Norway.
4	Frankfort,......	1796	3,217	3,082	135	.....	German Flats.
5	German Flats,...	1788	3,855	3,237	618		
6	Herkimer,......	1788	2,866	2,379	487		[German Flats.
7	Little Falls,.....	1829	4,930	4,244	686	.....	Herkimer, Fairfield and
8	Litchfield,......	1796	1,582	1,677	.....	95	German Flats.
9	Manheim,......	1797	1,672	1,872	.....	200	Palatine, Mont. co.
10	Newport,.......	1806	2,015	2,112	.....	97	Herkimer, Fairfield and
11	Norway,........	1792	1,059	1,079	.....	20	Herkimer. [Norway.
12	Ohio,...........	1823	1,087	763	324	.....	Norway.
13	Russia,........	1806	2,288	2,439	.....	151	Norway.
14	Salisbury,......	1797	2,306	1,860	446	.....	Palatine, Mont. co.
15	Schuyler,.......	1792	1,690	1,824	.....	134	Herkimer.
16	Stark,..........	1828	1,478	1,775	.....	297	Danube,
17	Warren,.......	1796	1,741	1,952	.....	201	German Flats. [Russia.
18	Wilmurt,.......	1836	268	89	179	.....	West Brunswick and
19	Winfield,.......	1816	1,397	1,559	.....	162	Litchfield, Richfield and [Plainfield.
	Total in 19 towns,......		38,566	37,424	2,973	1,826	
	Population in 1845,.....		37,424				
	Increase in 10 years,....		1,142				
	Total losses in 10 years,..............				1,821		
	Total net gain in 10 years,............				1,142		

§ 1. Columbia

Contains that part of the county bounded easterly by a line beginning at a maple tree, which stands a small distance easterly from the dwelling house heretofore or late of Abraham Lighthall, at the southeasterly corner of Young's patent, and running thence north twenty-eight degrees east, until it strikes the south line of the town of German Flats, at the distance of one hundred chains, easterly of the northwesterly corner of Henderson's patent, on the north line thereof; northerly, by German Flats, southerly, by the bounds of the county, and westerly, by Litchfield and Winfield.

This town contains the whole of Staley's second tract, except one tier and a half of lots on the westerly bounds, it also contains a small triangular piece, from the northwest corner of Henderson's patent, and the whole of the patent, to Conerad Frank and others, except seven lots on the eastern bounds thereof.

Columbia was settled before the revolution, by several German families from the Mohawk river. The heads of the families, who made one of the settlements, were, Conrad Orendorff, Conrad Frank, Conrad Fulmer, Frederick Christman, Timothy Frank, Nicholas Lighthall, Joseph Moyer and Henry Frink. The place where these families were seated was known as "Coonrodstown," before Columbia was organized, in 1812, and is to this day. A few Germans had also seated themselves at a place then and since called Elizabethtown, to commemorate the name of one or more German matrons among the settlers.

When the new town was about to be set off, and the inhabitants were casting about for a name, some of them desired to have it called Conrad. This was rejected, on account of the Coonish sound it had received, by a mispronunciation. Conrad is quite as *euphonious* as Columbia, and a more ancient name, by several hundred years, than Columbus, from which the town derived its name. There may have been some influential inhabitants in the territory, who had emigrated from Columbia county, and exerted an influence on this occasion; and, although feeling inclined to honor their native county, they would not hope the new town should be a political copyist of its then prominent namesake. Columbia is purely an agricultural town. The north line of it is about four miles from the canal; without villages, except

Asahel Alfred settled in this town in 1791. He was a native of Connecticut, a farmer and an honest man, of steady, industrious habits and good morals. He died in June, 1853, aged 93 years, having always resided on the farm on which he first located, and which was occupied by his son Cyrus in the old age of the father.

He was a soldier of the revolution, having entered the service of his country in his fifteenth year. He served more than three years. He was in the battle of Monmouth; taken prisoner at the Cedars, in Canada, after a smart conflict between the Americans and a party of the enemy, consisting of whites and Indians, and as usual in such cases, both parties took their covers of stumps and trees. Alfred was fired at by an Indian, but not hit. A second shot was made at him, and the ball struck the stump behind which he stood. Mr. Alfred discovered the Indian's head exposed while loading the third time, took deliberate aim at him, fired, and was not again molested from that quarter. The Americans were outnumbered and made prisoners, and as soon as they surrendered, the Indians stripped them of all their clothing except their

Cedarville, a portion of which extends into it; it is somewhat elevated; well supplied with water, but the surface can not be called broken. It is slowly losing its population; a strong indication that cheese making engrosses the farmers' attention, although hop and grain growing is not neglected. In former times, one hundred acre farm lots seemed to content our people; now, that extent of domain is quite too limited. Nor does a small diminution of population in our agricultural towns indicate, in the least, a lack of prosperity, or a want of wealth among those who remain. There are often those, who may wish to seek new homes for increasing families, and they soon find neighbors ready and willing to purchase their farms.

§2. Danube

Contains that part of the county bounded northerly by the Mohawk river, easterly by the bounds of the county, southerly by a line commencing at a point in the east bounds of the county, equidistant from the Mohawk river and the south bounds of the county, thence westerly parallel with the south bounds of the county to a line drawn from the easternmost lock of the old canal, on the north side of the Mohawk river, at the Little Falls, to the head waters of Lake Otsego, and westerly by the said last mentioned line.

Small portions of the Fall Hill, Vaughns and L'Hommedieu patents, nearly the whole of Lindsey's, and parts of

shirts and pantaloons. They took his hat, coat, vest, neckkerchief and silver knee and shoe buckles. When on the march to the British post, one of Mr. Alfred's fellow prisoners being feeble, and not able to keep up with the rest, fell behind, and Alfred remained with him to help him along. While making their way as well as they could, an Indian came up, and, putting the muzzle of his gun close to the sick prisoner's head, blew out his brains. Mr. Alfred was not slow to overtake his fellow prisoners. He was at the capture of Burgoyne and the British army.

My informant, who is a most excellent judge of such matters, says he was a good marksman, and a dead shot at fair rifle distance. He would often relate many interesting incidents that happened to the scouting parties he was engaged in. This service suited him much better than the camp. He was very fond of hunting, and while living on his farm, it was not uncommon for him, after game became scarce in his neighborhood, to leave home in the fall of the year, and be absent from it weeks, on hunting excursions.

J. Vroman's, C. Colden's, Van Horne's and Lansing's patents are within the above boundaries.

Indian Castle Church.

This town, although of recent territorial organization, was no doubt one of the earliest settled by Europeans of any in the county, except those portions of it embracing Burnetsfield, or what was formerly known as the German Flats. The date of Lindsey's and Van Horne's patents, one in 1730 and the other in 1731, indicate this. It has been elsewhere stated in this work, that the Canajoharie mentioned in the early colonial history of the state, extended as far west as the foot of the Little Falls, in 1772, and probably farther before the German Flats district was set off. The casual reader of disjointed documents and isolated statements might infer that the Canajoharie mentioned in connection with the Mohawk tribe of Indians, was circumscribed in its limits to the town of that name in Montgomery county. This is clearly not the fact. The site of the upper Mohawk's castle is in this town, and near the present Indian castle church, now so called, and it has borne that name within the memory of the oldest inhabitants now living, and a uniform and unvarying tradition speaks to the same effect.

The French Itinerary, found in vol. I of the Documentary History of the State, fixes Fort Can-nat-ho-cary at the side of the Mohawk river, on the right bank, and four leagues from Fort Kouari (Herkimer). The writer was no doubt a French spy, sent out from Canada, in 1757, to make a topographical survey of the country, from Oswego to Schenectady and Albany, along the water communications from Lake Ontario to Hudson river. He describes the road on the south side of the river, from Fort Herkimer to the Indian castle; and he says, in his description of the road on the north side of the river, that this fort is opposite to the mouth of the Canada creek.

The fort, so called, was one hundred paces on each side, had four bastions of upright pickets, fifteen feet high, about a foot square, and joined together with lintels. It was not surrounded by a ditch, but was constructed with port holes at regular distances, with a platform or stage all around, to fire from. There were some small pieces of cannon at each of the bastions, and a house at each curtain to serve as storehouses and barracks. There were several Indian families at this time living near this fort.

Sir Wm. Johnson, in Oct., 1772, speaks of having built a church, at his own expense, at the Canajoharees, and laments, that it is in a great measure useless, in consequence of not being able to secure the services of a missionary. I have not been able to fix the period, previous to the revolution, when the first church at the Indian Castle was built. The bell however, was highly regarded by the Indians, and they made an effort, during the war, to carry it off. They took it away in the night and secreted it. This, of course, caused excitement among the German population in the neighborhood, when it became known that the church bell had disappeared. How it was carried off, and what had become of it, engrossed the attention of all, and an immediate and careful search was made for the missing bell, in every direction; but the purloiners knew too well how to cover up and secure their trophy, to prevent a discovery. The search was fruitless, and the inhabitants had nearly given up all hope of its recovery when, one dark night, the sound of the bell was heard in the distance, and the population of the neighborhood were soon in hot pursuit, armed with guns, pitchforks and axes. The bell was recovered. The Indians, after they supposed the search was over, returned, and slung the bell upon a pole, and started with it, but did not secure that unruly member, the tongue or clapper; and the bell and clapper having an unequal momentum in the swing, when carried over uneven ground on a bending pole, came in contact, and by the ding dong sounds led to the discovery.

This town attracts considerable attention, in consequence

of its containing the residence of Gen. Nicholas Herkimer; and, if it was not the birth place of the too celebrated Joseph Brant, a considerable number of the early years of his life were spent at the Indian Castle, with the members of his tribe, where an intimate acquaintance was cultivated between him and Gen. Herkimer, when they were young men. This fort must have been built in 1755; early in that year, Sir William Johnson speaks about constructing forts, at the two Indian castles, and notified Governor De Lancy of his having concluded a contract for their erection. These defenses were made to gratify the Mohawk Indians, who were exposed to the hostile incursions of the French and their Indian allies from Canada. I do not find any account of this fort twenty years afterwards, and if it had not entirely gone to decay before the revolution, it was probably used only as a temporary refuge of the inhabitants, to shield them against the hostile attacks of those for whose protection it was first erected.

In 1722, Governor Burnet, on the petition of the Rev. Petrus Van Driesen of Albany, granted a license authorizing Mr. Van Driesen to build a meeting house in the Mohawk country, for the use of the Indians, on any lands belonging to them. In 1737, a patent for 1000 acres of land was issued to the same gentleman, and it will be noticed that this grant covers lands at the mouth of the East Canada creek, and nearly opposite to the Indian Castle church. The mission at Fort Hunter had been established as early as 1712, and probably before that time, so that Mr. Van Driesen's license had no reference to that station.

I do not find any well founded data to change my conclusions that the church at German Flats was the first erection for religious worship in the county.

Fort Hendrick is marked on Sauthier's map of the province of New York, published in 1779, as being on the south side of the Mohawk river, opposite the mouth of East Canada creek. The Cannatjoharies are also marked as being located at this point. This establishes the fact that the site of the upper Mohawk castle was at the place above designated. And the name of the fort was a compliment to old King Hendrik, whose principal residence during the latter period of his life was at this place.

It should be observed that the grant of 4000 acres to Isaac Vrooman, and of 4000 acres to Ezra L'Hommedieu and Nathaniel Platt, in 1786, out of unpatented lands, by the crown, lying in this town and Stark, shows there must have previously existed very strong reasons for not granting these lands, long before the revolutionary war. These reasons are found in the fact, that they were Indian reservations, or rather, that being in the neighborhood of one of the principal seats of the tribe, the Indians would not consent to part with them upon any terms.

The Mohawk Indians having left the country at the commencement of the war, and not returning as did the Senecas, Cayugas and Onondagas and sue for peace, were treated by the state as having abandoned all their rights as original possessors of the soil, and all the vacant lands within the limits formerly claimed by this tribe, were sold by the state without regarding the Indian title.

The only locality in this town called a village, is Newville, about four miles south from the river, on the Nowadaga creek, and at the foot of Ostrander's hill, from the top of which, at an elevation of 800 feet above the river, is a broad and extended view to the east and southeast, including the lower valley, of nearly thirty miles.

§3. Fairfield

Contains that part of the county beginning on the middle line in Glen's purchase, in the west bounds of Manheim, and running thence westerly along the said middle line of Glen's purchase to the southwest corner of lot number seven; thence northerly to the northeast corner of lot number five in said purchase; thence westerly along the line between lots number five and six, and the same continued to the West Canada creek; thence up and along the said creek, to the town of Newport; then along the bounds of Newport to the

southwest corner of Norway; then along the south bounds of Norway, east to the west bounds of Salisbury; and then south along the same, to the place of beginning.

These bounds have been changed. See subdivision 7, Little Falls, erected in 1829.

This town contains within its limits nearly the whole of Glen's purchase lying north of the base or middle line of said purchase, and a portion of the first allotment of the Royal grant.

There was a German settlement in this town before the revolution, upon what has been called in modern times the Top notch, near the Manheim town line, and about four miles north of Little Falls. Among these German families were the Kellers, Windeckers, Pickerts and others, not of the Burnetsfield patentees, but who came up from the lower Mohawk valley, and seated themselves in Glen's purchase, under the patronage of some of its owners. Mr. Cornelius Chatfield arrived within the territory of the present town of Fairfield, with his family, March 24th, 1785, and settled near or at the spot where the village now is. He is supposed to have been the first New Englander who came into the county after the war, for the purpose of settling on the Royal grant. Mr. Abijah Mann, the father of the Hon. Abijah Mann, Jr., arrived in May following, and located a little west of Fairfield village. There was a small Indian orchard upon or near the lands taken up by Mr. Mann, and the Indians, many years after the revolution, would annually cluster around it, as a loved and venerated spot. A visit, perhaps, to the resting place of some distinguished brave, or some relative of the visitants. This duty was performed so long as the Great Spirit required it.

About the year 1770, three families, Maltanner, Goodbread or Goodbrodt, and Shaver or Shaffer, located about half a mile northeast of Fairfield village, in one neighborhood. This place is now called Maltanner's creek or spring. These people were sent there by Sir William Johnson, to make an opening upon his Royal grant. They had never been suspected by the Americans of being friendly to their cause; nor could they be charged with disloyalty to the king. In 1779, a party of Indians came to this little settlement, but one of their number being sick, they kept shy, as an Indian can, about ten days, to allow their comrade to recover, when, with a yell and a whoop, and brandishing their tomahawks, they fell upon Sir John Johnson's tenants, captured two of the Maltanners, father and son, killed a little girl, 16 years old, of the Shaver family, and then burned up all Sir John's houses and buildings in the settlement. The Goodbrodt and Shaver families and some of the Maltanners escaped to tell the sad story of their bereavements and losses to their rebel neighbors. The Maltanners were taken to St. Regis by the Indians, where they remained three years, and returned in 1782. His majesty's officials in Canada might well suppose the two captives, if allowed to return, would not be very hearty and zealous in the royal cause, after such treatment; and therefore concluded to detain them. The elder Maltanner, when he came back, said he met Sir John in Canada, and told him what had happened, whereat the gallant knight was exceedingly wrathful, and fulminated big words and strong language against the d—d savages, for their conduct in killing, taking captive and dispersing his tenants, and burning his houses. He had other tenants on the grant, loyal and true, who might be treated in the same way. Sir John no doubt felt hurt, not because any tender feeling towards his fellow man had been touched, or any law of humanity outraged; but because the same rule of warfare he had applied to others, had been, and might again be, visited upon himself. This was not the first nor the last instance, in that unnatural struggle, in which the Indians made no discrimination in their warfare; and friend and foe alike were made to sink under the hatchet's stunning blow, and feel the knife's keen edge. Kindness and humanity, in conducting that war, might have achieved what hate and cruelty did not. The ancient Roman apothegm, "*Quam Deus vult perdere, prius dementat*," was so strikingly verified in word and sentiment, as to induce one to think, almost, it was a prophetic enunciation of an actual event, already determined in the councils of heaven.

The first New England settlers who came into this town at the close of the war, took up lands southwesterly of Fairfield village, except those before noticed, with one or two exceptions. Josiah, David and Lester Johnson came into the town from Connecticut, in 1786; John Bucklin and Benjamin Bowen, from Rhode Island; John Eaton, Nathaniel and William Brown, from Massachusetts; and Samuel Low, in 1787: David Benseley, from Rhode Island; and Elisha, Wyman and Comfort Eaton, from Massachusetts, in 1788: Jeremiah Ballard, from Massachusetts, in 1789: Wm. Bucklin, the Arnold families, Daniel Venner, Nathan Smith, Nahum Daniels and Amos and James Haile, most of them from Massachusetts, in 1790: the Neelys came in 1792, and Peter and Bela Ward, from Connecticut, in 1791. The Eatons, Browns, Hailes, Arnolds, Bucklins and Wards seated themselves at and near the present village of Eatonsville. Some of these people changed their residences after a short sojourn in this town. Jeremiah Ballard located about two miles northeast of Fairfield village. He left his family the first winter after he came into the town, and returned to Massachusetts, where he remained until spring.

My informant says this family had nothing to subsist on during a long and dreary winter but Indian corn and white rabbits, when any could be caught. There being no mills then in the country, and if there had been they could not be reached except by the use of snow-shoes and carrying the grist on one's back; the Ballard family resorted to what at this day would be considered a novel method of reducing their corn into a state suitable to be converted into rabbit soup. Having no hand nor other mill to crack or break their corn in, a mortar was the only thing they could resort to, and even this they were destitute of; but when did necessity ever fail to suggest some remedy for surmountable inconveniences. The family procured a large hard-wood log, and having no tools suitable to the object, they burned a hole in it, by concentrating the fire to one spot, sufficiently deep to answer their purpose. In this way, my informant says, this great achievment was accomplished. It was an easy task, after this, to make a pestle out of some hard wood, and crack corn to their stomach's content.

By these means the resolved and noble hearted mother carried her family through the winter, while the father was absent, and it should be hoped was detained by sickness at his former home in Massachusetts.

There were but a few English or New England families, north of the Mohawk, and between the East and West Canada creek, in 1786; not more than four or five, if as many. Fairfield village, the ancient seat of learning of the county, is located very nearly in the center of the town, about 800 feet above the level of the Mohawk river. A notice of the Medical college and the Academy will be found in another chapter. Middleville, a small village situated partly in this town and partly in Newport, on the West Canada creek, is at the junction of the plank roads leading from Herkimer and Little Falls to Newport. The census marshal of this town did not, at the late enumeration, designate the population within these villages. This is probably the best grazing town in the county, and has for a series of years produced and sent to market, annually, more of the Herkimer county staple, cheese, than any other town within the limits of the county.

We must not draw any conclusions unfavorable to this town—that its soil is not good—or that its population is wanting in energy and enterprise, or is destitute of wealth, because we find a moderate and steady decrease in the total number of inhabitants. To the successful progress of agriculture and the accumulation of wealth, and to no other cause, is to be attributed this gradual loss of population.

§ 4. Frankfort

Contains that part of the county, beginning at the south side of the Mohawk river, in the middle of the mouth of a small stream which enters the said river a few rods east of the house now or late of William Dygert, which stream is known as Dygert's mill creek, and running from thence south thirty degrees west, until it meets the southern line of a tract of land granted to Coenrad Frank and others; then westerly along the said southern line to the southwest corner of said grant; then westerly with a straight line to the west bounds of the county; then northerly along the same to the Mohawk river; and then along the river to the place of beginning.

A considerable portion of Cosby's manor, and about one and one quarter of a tier of great lots in Bayard's patent, four lots in Burnetsfield, about half a lot in Frank's patent, four and a half lots in Staley's, a part of Colden's patent, are in this town.

There were some German settlements along the river in this town before the revolution. It appears there was a grist mill at the creek next east of Frankfort village, which was burned by the French and Indians in 1757. A sawmill on the next creek below was also burnt by the same party. The ante-revolutionary settlements in this town were confined to Burnetsfield and Colden and Willet's patents.

Frankfort village, at the east end of the long level on the Erie canal, and of easy access to the New York central rail road, contains a population, by the last census, of 1150 souls, and is an active, prosperous business place, where may be found the usual mechanical establishments of country villages.

The New Graefenbergh hydropathic establishment, erected by Dr. Holland, and opened for the reception of patients in October, 1847, is located in the extreme southwest corner of this town, four and a half miles from the city of Utica, on a stage and post route from that city, through Litchfield and Columbia to Richfield Springs. This establishment has been in operation during the last eight years, and more than one thousand patients in that time have been treated there with satisfactory success. The scenery of this locality is varied and beautiful, and will vie with the most delightful in the state.

The institution will accommodate sixty patients; the rooms are pleasant and comfortably furnished. There is a gymnasium and bowling-alley attached to the house for the amusement and exercise of the patients.

§ 5. German Flats

Now contains that part of the county bounded westerly by Frankfort; northerly, by the Mohawk river; easterly, by Danube and Stark; and southerly by a line beginning at the northeast corner of Litchfield, and running thence easterly, along the southern line of the tract of land granted to Conerad Frank, and others, until it meets the southwest corner of a tract of land granted to Guy Johnson; and then easterly, along the southern bounds thereof, to the town of Stark.

The eastern and southern bounds of this town, as above stated, have been changed. See sub. 7, Little Falls.

This town comprises a very considerable portion of Burnetsfield patent; nearly all of Staley's first tract; the whole of Frank's patent, and a part of Guy Johnson's tract.

German Flats Church.

This town when erected, in 1788, comprised all that part of Montgomery county, south of the Mohawk river, bounded easterly by Canajoharie, the westerly bounds of that town being the Susquehanna river, Otsego lake and a line from the head waters of the lake to the Little Falls; south, by the north line of the town of Otsego, running from the head waters of Otsego lake, in the patent granted to George

Croghan and others, along the northerly bounds of that patent, to the northwest corner of it, and extending westerly to the river, then called Tienaderha, and along the northerly line of the Edminston patent, and westerly, by the west line of the town of Herkimer, continued south to the town of Otsego, or in other words, very nearly by the present eastern bounds of Oneida county. These limits not only embrace the present towns of Columbia, Frankfort, Litchfield, Warren and Winfield, a part of Little Falls, but extend considerably into Otsego county.

The town when erected comprehended only that part of the German Flats district of colonial organization, south of the Mohawk, east of the present west line of the county, and north of Otsego, as before noticed. That district extended much farther south and west, until the erection of the Old England district, a short time before the revolution, which seems not to have been regarded as a municipal territorial division during the war.

After the peace of 1783, however, it was recognized, and local officers appointed for the district.

The church in this town, was the first erected in the county for the accommodation of European worshipers, and their descendants. An Indian mission church, at the place long known as the Indian Castle, in Danube, may have been built at an earlier date. It is said, the former was erected under the auspices of Sir William Johnson; this is very doubtful, although there may be no question whatever, that the Mission church was built under his agency, if it was erected subsequent to the church at German Flats. In the first place, Sir William was not in the country at the date of either of the deeds, mentioned below, and he was not appointed general superintendent of Indian affairs, by the crown, until 1757. He had, however, acted as Indian agent under a colonial appointment, from August, 1749; and in the second place, I am not aware that the colonial government were accustomed to build churches, disconnected from the

Indian missions, when the people were able to bear that expense themselves.

On the 24th of September, 1730, Nicholas Wolever made a deed of trust, of a part of lot number 30, in Burnetsfield, to several persons, to hold the same as a church and school lot; and on the 26th of April, 1733, the trustees conveyed the same lot to the church corporation, which had at that time been organized. Nicholas Wolever was one of the original grantees of the patent, and the above lot was awarded to him. I am not aware that there are now in existence, any records showing when the church was erected, on the spot dedicated to that use. Within the church yard, near the south side, there is a head stone with this inscription:

CAPT. JOHN RING,
Independent Company Provincials,
Died September 26, 1755,
aged 30 years.

The church had been erected, and formed a part of the stockaded defense, since called Fort Herkimer, put up by Sir William Johnson, or by his directions, in 1756. At this time, the population of the German Flats, embracing the settlements on both sides of the river, had more than quadrupled in thirty-five years, and were quite wealthy. The inhabitants did not need, and probably did not require government aid to build a church. At any rate, the probabilities are against any such assumption.

The first regularly settled minister, called by the congregation, was a Mr. Rosecrants, a German protestant, and probably a Lutheran. The time of his arrival and death are beyond the memory of any one now living, and there are no records or monuments now extant which show these dates.

One of those cold-blooded and not unusual murders occurred in this town during the revolution, at a farm-house near the site of Rankin's lock on the canal. The heart sickens at the recital of such deeds of horror and the pen becomes wearied in recording them.

Mr. John Eysaman, with his wife, aged people, his son and his wife and an infant child, were living togther in one house on the south side of the river, about two miles directly east of Fort Herkimer, on the Mohawk river.

An alarm gun had been fired at the fort to notify the inhabitants who were at their farms or out on business, that danger was apprehended, or a lurking enemy had been discovered; the family packed up their portable goods, and loaded them into a cart, and were about ready to start for shelter and protection at the fort, when the house was surrounded by a party of Indians and tories. Old Mr. Eysaman and his wife were killed; the wife of the younger Mr. Eysaman, whose name was Stephen, was also killed. Some one of the assailants wrenched the infant from its mother's arms, and holding it by the feet, dashed its head against a tree, and its little limbs quivered in the agonies of death after it was rudely and barbarously thrown upon the ground and

The Rev. ABRAHAM ROSECRANTS succeeded his brother. The year of his arrival from Germany can not now be fixed with certainty. His own records of marriages, births and deaths show that he was here in 1762. We have concurring traditional accounts of him as early as 1754, and that he was the German minister who was in a manner forced by the friendly Indians to cross to Fort Herkimer, when the settlements on the the north side of the river were destroyed by the French and Indians under M. de Belletre in November, 1757. The field of his clerical labors was coextensive with the German settlements along the whole length and breadth of the Mohawk valley. Being a graduate of a German university, he was, of course, a finished scholar in all those branches of learning relating to his profession. I have stated in another place that Mr. Rosecrants was connected with the Herkimer family by marriage. This connection, and his position as the spiritual adviser of a people proverbial for their strong attachments and great respect for the ministerial office, afforded an opportunity for the exertion of a malign influence against the cause of the colonies during the revolution. To what extent any such influence was used is not now very material to inquire, since it is quite evident he committed no overt act of treason or aggression, as he remained unmolested during the whole war, by the provincial authorities, in discharge of his clerical duties, and left his estates to the inheritance of his children.

Mr. Rosecrants died at his residence on Fall hill, in the present town of Little Falls, at the close of the last century, and was interred by the side of his brother, the former minister, within the walls of the church, nearly under the pulpit.

scalped. The mother was compelled to witness this horrid scene; and Stephen, who was doomed to captivity, being pinioned and driven a short distance heard the screams of his wife, struck down by a war club.

The enemy having taken four scalps, were content to spare the wearer of the fifth to grace their triumph on their return to Canada. This event took place on the 9th day of June, and as Mr. Eysaman returned from captivity at the close of the war, after an absence of three years and nine months, 1779 may be fixed as the year. He said on his return, the Indians and tories, among other of his stock driven away, took three horses, one of them a fine stud, often rode on parade by a British officer, who noticed that Eysaman had always regarded the horse when he was mounted, asked him if he had ever seen the horse before. Eysaman said he had, and that the horse was his. The reply was, "Be off, you d—d rebel, you never owned a horse," and this was all he ever had for.him.

Mr. Eysaman married again after his return from captivity, and raised a family of children, one of whom, Mr. Joseph Eysaman, now lives on the farm he inherited from his father, the spot where the murders were committed. Stephen Eysaman died at the age of ninety-four years. A remarkable case of longevity is presented by this family. Stephen had one brother and four sisters, one of whom lived to the age of 97 years; none of them died under the age of 85 years. The aggregate of the lives of these six persons, all of one family, was five hundred and forty-one years.

The destruction of the German settlements, on the south side of the river, in sight of Fort Herkimer, in July, 1782, by a party of about 600 Indians and tories, has not been heretofore noticed by any of the writers upon our border wars, or if it has, my attention has not reached it.

The enemy were first discovered by Peter Wolever, who, with Augustinus Hess, lived about fifty rods from the fort. Both families were aroused, and finally succeeded in reaching the fort without any casualty, except the death of Hess, who was killed just as he was entering the picket gate. There were at this time only a few troops stationed at the fort. The Americans were not strong enough to act offensively. Valentine Starring was taken prisoner in a field, not far from the stockade, and was put to torture with a view of drawing the provincials to his rescue, when they heard, at the fort, his cries for help and lamentations under his tortures; not succeeding in this, poor Starring was tomahawked and scalped. There was a good deal of desultory firing between the assailants and assailed.

The provincials lost four men, two soldiers and two of the inhabitants, killed. It was supposed the enemy's loss in killed and wounded was much greater, as they could not approach the stockade within musket shot, uncovered. All the buildings in the settlement, except George Herkimer's house, were burned by the invaders, and the cattle driven away. This relation was given by Nicholas Wolever, now living, who was at Fort Herkimer at the time, who also says it was reported that Capt. Brant was not in this action. I will here notice, not an isolated case of human endurance and the tenacity of life, although not of frequent occurrence during the revolution. The wife of Mr. Henry Wetherstone, who had incautiously gone into the field for some domestic object, was set upon by a party of Indians, tomahawked, scalped and, as supposed, her dead body left to be looked after and cared for by her friends. She recovered, and lived many years after her long tress of hair had been exhibited as a trophy of Indian courage and inhuman butchery.

The flourishing villages of Mohawk and Ilion are located in this town, about two miles apart, on the canal. Mr. Remington's extensive rifle factory and armory, where thousands and tens of thousands of death-dealing weapons have been fabricated, was first established where Ilion now is. This establishment was the nucleus around which this village took its start, and being favorably located in respect to proximity to the canal and the central rail road; and having roads of easy grade to the southwestern part of this county, and the northwestern portion of Otsego, and the southeastern parts of Madison counties, the village has become the center of a very considerable business and active trade.

§6. Herkimer

Contains all that part of the county bounded southerly by the Mohawk river, westerly by Schuyler, northerly by Newport and Fairfield, and easterly by Manheim.

The easterly bounds have been changed, see sub. 7, Little Falls.

The whole of Winne's and portions of Burnetsfield, Hasenclever's, Colden's and Willett's patents, and some lots of the Royal grant and Glen's purchase, lay in this town.

The Rev. John Spinner emigrated to the United States, from Germany, in 1801, and landed at the city of New York, on the 12th of May, after a long passage of 63 days. He was born at Warback, a market town in the Electorate of Mentz, January 18th, 1768; was early in life dedicated by his parents to the clerical office, and when only 11 years old, entered the gymnasiun at Bishopsheim, where he remained three years, and was then transferred to the university of Mentz; remained in that celebrated institution of learning until 1788. In the term of his six years collegiate probation, he passed through a thorough course of studies, in philosophy, mathematics, history, languages, ancient and modern, divinity, jurisprudence, medicine. He was then admitted to a Romish clerical seminary, and in 1789 was consecrated to holy orders, in the Roman Catholic church. He assisted in celebrating the funeral obsequies of two German emperors, in accordance with the grand and imposing rites of the Romish communion. The emperor, Joseph II, died February 20th, 1790, and Leopold II, March 1st, 1792. He officiated eleven years as priest, confessor, &c., and about the year 1800, he embraced the Protestant faith and form of worship. On the 18th January, 1801, he married Mary Magdale Fedelis Brumante, a native of Loire on the Maine. She accompanied her husband to this country, and is yet living, at the residence long occupied by the venerable and deceased subject of this notice.

Mr. Spinner, soon after he landed at New York, was called to the spiritual charge of the German congregations at Herkimer and German Flats, and commenced his pastoral functions in September, 1801, and his connection with these churches continued about 40 years. He was engaged about 18 months of this period, however, as a teacher in the High school, at Utica. He conformed to the diciplino of the Dutch Reformed church, but the first settlers of

The town of Herkimer, when organized in 1788, contained all that part of the county of Montgomery, bounded northerly by the north bounds of the state, easterly by Palatine, then extending to the west bounds of the present town of Manheim, southerly by the Mohawk river, and westerly by a north and south line running across the Mohawk river, at the fording place, near the house of William Cunningham, leaving the same house to the west of said line. This fixed the west line of the town on the present western limits of the county, north of the Mohawk, and covered the area now embraced in the towns of Fairfield, Little Falls, Newport, Norway, Ohio, Russia, Schuyler and Wilmont, besides a respectable portion of the northern parts of the state, outside the pre-

the valley, and the ancestors of the people, who composed the principal part of his congregations, were German Lutherans.

His services, during the long period of his ministry, were not confined to the two churches, under his special charge; in that time, he preached to congregations in Columbia, Warren, at the Indian Castle, Esquawk, Manheim and Schuyler, in Herkimer county, Deerfield, Oneida county, Manlius, Onondaga county, and Le Ray, Jefferson county, in some of which places, German emigrants had settled, when they first came into the country, and in others, were found the descendants of those Palatines, who had made their first resting place in the Mohawk valley. He was the third minister in permanent succession called to supply these two churches, after their first organization in the German Flats.

His predecessor, Mr. Rosecrants, died a few years before 1801. The interim was probably supplied with the temporary services of clergymen of other congregations, or by those who were engaged only for short periods. He was tall in stature, dignified in deportment, and polished in his manners, accomplishments, not rarely found among the priesthood of the Romish church. He possessed a capacious and vigorous mind, which had been embellished by a thorough and systematic education in German schools, under the instruction of learned and experienced masters. With the ancient, and most of the modern European continental languages, and especially the French, Spanish and Italian, he was quite as familiar as with his own native German, but from the slow progress he made in acquiring an accurate and easy pronunciation of the English tongue, in the course of twenty-five years, he must have been unfamiliar with it when he came into the county. The younger members of his charge, were in a rapid state of transition. The German schoolmaster, abandoned his desk and ferule to the English teacher, whose language was spoken by a majority of the people, and in which the business of the courts was transacted.

sent county line. These limits also comprehended all that portion of the German Flats and Kingsland districts, organized under the colonial governments, north of the Mohawk, and east of the now westerly bounds of the county.

These territorial divisions of Tryon county into districts were made by acts of the colonial legislature, and stood in the place of towns, or townships. It will be observed, they were very extensive, and covered territory now embraced in several counties. The Canajoharie district, as an instance, extended from the Mohawk to the south line of the state, including the settlements at Springfield, Cherry Valley and the Harper settlement. There were, however, subdivisions of them into precincts, when required.

It was apparent this change must take place, and it was expedient not to delay it. Mr. Spinner applied himself with all the ardor of a young and ambitious man, to keep pace with the times; and preached alternately, in the German and English to suit the elder and younger members of the congregations. From long use and by diligent study, aided by a profound knowledge of Latin, he had mastered the English language in all its significance, but, he could not pronounce the words of it accurately, and with facility. His English sermons were often able productions, and sometimes eloquent. The words were well chosen and appropriately applied. I have alluded to this matter, which to strangers may not seem pertinent to the subject in hand, because it was a cause of some disquiet, but not of repining to him while living. Mr. Spinner died at his residence in Herkimer, on the 27th of May, 1848, aged 80 years 4 months and 9 days. He was kind and affectionate as a husband and a parent, and active and zealous in the discharge of his pastoral duties. He exerted a happy influence over the German population of his charge, by whom his memory is cherished with devotion and respect. Within three weeks of his own death, six members of his former charge went to their final rest, the aggregate of whose ages was more than 480 years. An average of 80 years to seven persons dying within the space of 21 days, is an event of no common occurrence.

The Rev. James Murphy was inducted, as associate minister of these two venerable congregations, by many years the oldest in the county, before the Rev. Mr. Spinner's connection was dissolved. Dr. Murphy, I understand, has no longer any ministerial charge of them.

John Adam Hartman.—Well, what of him, it may be asked? What office did he hold, under the colonial or state governments, which entitles his name to be placed in this chapter of notables? Reader, I never knew, nor does

At the election for town officers, in March, 1789, the first held after the town was organized, the following persons were chosen: For supervisor, Henry Staring; town clerk Melger Fols; assessors, Melger Fols, George Smith, Melger Thum; collector, George Fols; constables, George Fols, Adam Bauman; commissioners of highways, Peter F. Bellinger, John Demuth, Jacob N. Weber; overseers of the poor, Henry Staring, George Weber, Jr., Michael Myers; overseers of highways, Marx Demuth, Philip Helmer, Adam Hartman, Hannes Demuth, Peter Weber, Philip Herter, Hannes Hilts, Jr., Hannes Eiseman; pound masters, George Weber, Jr., Peter Barky, Hannes Demuth, Nicholas Hilts, Hannes Schell.

local tradition tell me, he ever held any other than a voluntary, self-elected place of confidence and trust, among the people of the upper Mohawk valley. Perhaps he was not naturalized, and therefore was ineligible to office under the crown, before the revolution, for he was not born a British subject. But if seven years immersion in the toils and blood of that war, could have made any man a native American, in 1783 he was one, although born in Edenkoben, Germany, in September, 1748. Born and educated a peasant in fatherland, he was accustomed to the severe exposures of a roaming woodman's life, and the luxury of wealth had in no degree enervated a frame of great muscular power, and almost gigantic proportions, nor touched, with its alluring fascinations, a mind and a will as firm and unyielding, as he believed the cause he was engaged in, was just and good. He required no commissariat waggon to attend him on his excursions, to supply him with rations, while in pursuit of or watching the stealthy movements of the enemy. Mothers were gladdened when they knew Hans Adam was on the lookout, in the bush near by, and the confident prattle of children might be heard in the door yard; and the husbandman too could visit his fields, and attend to his cattle and crops, being assured, if danger approached, a signal from Hartman's well-tried musket would announce the fact. Such a man could not fail to find a cheerful welcome and abundant fare at every log cabin in the land, nor were his goings forth on his perilous service unattended by sincere and hopeful aspirations to heaven for his safety and success. The detail of the traditional accounts which have come to us, of his services, encounters and escapes during the perilous period of the seven years frontier conflict, familiar to the reader, would extend this notice beyond any reasonable limit. There is, however, one marked event of his life, yet familiar to the descendants of the revolutionary inhabitants of the county, which may well have place on some more permanent record, than the fading memory of man.

Henry Staring got two offices; Melger Fols, two; George Fols, two; George Weber, Jr., two, and Hannes Demuth, two. A complete Native American High Dutch organization, and nearly every man of them a descendant of the Palatine pilgrims. The voters seem to have excluded every other nationality from their ticket. Did they mean any thing by this? In these times such an act might be thought of peculiar significance.

The town records appear to be perfect since the first

Soon after the peace of 1783, which gave safe conduct, not only to the former white inhabitants of the valley, who confided in the promises of princes, but to the late hostile red man of the forest, to return and look after whatever might interest or concern them, Hartman fell in company with an Indian near the present western limits of the town of Herkimer, at a country tavern, and one of them at least, if not both of them, being strongly inclined to cheer the inner-man with the enlivening influences of fire-water, the Indian soon became exhilarated and loquacious. He boasted, as he then supposed he might, with impunity, of his valorous deeds during the war, spoke of the number of rebels he had killed and scalped, and the captives he had taken; mentioned the places he had visited in the state, and the exploits of his tribe. His inebriate mind could shadow nothing but that he was the most distinguished brave of his nation. Hartman heard all this vain boasting with apparent good nature, and believed it would not be prudent, as he was unarmed, to provoke a quarrel with his boon companion; but when the Indian exhibited his tobacco pouch, made of the skin taken from a white child's arm, and tanned or dressed with the nails of the fingers and thumb still hanging to it, and boasted of his trophy, he came to a resolution, and probably soon after executed it, that, drunk or sober, the Indian should no more boast of his deeds of blood, or exhibit his savage inhumanity. He inquired the way the Indian was going, and being told, said he was traveling the same direction. They left the house together, and took a path leading towards Schuyler, through a swamp. The Indian, in addition to his rifle and other weapons, carried a heavy pack. Hartman was unarmed, and being light, told the Indian, on their, way, he would carry his rifle, and it was given to him. The Indian was never seen or heard of alive after he and Hartman entered the swamp. About a year afterwards a human body was found buried in the swamp muck, by the side of a log laying across the path, and a pack near it, stamped into the wet bog. A rifle was also found in a hollow tree not far distant, and other articles, showing pretty clearly that the owner when alive was not a European. Hartman, when asked where the Indian was, or had gone, said "he saw him standing on a log a few rods in advance, and he fell from it as though he had been hurt." Hartman was not always clear and distinct in his admission that he had shot the Indian; no one at the time,

organization, and judging from the known characters of the principal officers elected, there must have been some very hard political contests in the town between the federalists and republicans in olden times. Success depended very much upon the vigilance of the parties, and it was alike important to both to carry the county town. The history of the county from 1725 to the close of the revolution, comprises but few incidents which did not take place in this, or the present town of German Flats. When these two towns

however, or since, doubted the fact, although there might not have been legal evidence to convict of murder. He was arrested and tried for that offense at Johnstown, but acquitted. Whoever killed the Indian was not instigated thereto for the sake of plunder. In all Hartman's after conversation in regard to this affair, he distinctly and minutely described the tobacco pouch made of human skin, and the nails attached to the finger's end. He survived the close of the revolutionary war more than fifty-three years. He may have lived so far secluded from refined society as not to have seen a glove, and he may have been so ignorant as not to know what constituted a covering for delicate and genteel hands; and if he was at fault in this respect, he was not so great a dunce as not to know the skin of the human arm and hand, nor so blind that he could not see a finger nail. Besides, who that is familiar with Indian customs and habiliments, can believe that an Indian would use a common hand glove for a pouch? How and where would he secure it? He could not fasten it to his belt, and in those days these primitive people did not wear pockets in their garments; their pouches served that purpose, and were made sufficiently long to be secured by winding two or three times round the outside waist belt. The assertion, in Stone's Life of Brant, that this pouch "was probably a leather glove, which the Indian had found," seems to be wholly unsupported by fact or the appearance of truth. I have no desire to make any apology for Hartman, or that he should appear different from what he actually was, a plain, unlettered, unpretending man. He was not "very ignorant," unless the term is strictly applied to his school acquirements. He probably never attended school a single day in his life. Other and more imperative calls upon his time and service were in store for him, after he landed upon our western shores. "A very ignorant man, and thought it no harm to kill an Indian at any time." Is this statement borne out by the facts of the relation as here given? If Hartman killed the Indian, and was so "very ignorant" as to think it no harm to kill one at any time, why did he not do it in the face of witnesses? Why did he seek and wait for an opportunity to do the deed when he and his late open enemy were alone? Why, if so "very ignorant," as to be only a lump of stultified humanity, did not the slayer appropriate the goods of his victim, of considerable value, to his own use? Col. Stone was either misinformed in respect to

were erected, Herkimer had been known by no other name for sixty-three years than the German Flats, and it was not intended to make any change, but to give the name of Herkimer to the territory on the south side of the river, where the Herkimer family were first seated, where most of those who remained in the country then lived, and where the general himself was born. The committee, having the matter in charge, not knowing the localities, inquired of some person who did, whether the German Flats lay on the *right* or *left* bank of the river, expecting to be answered according to the known rule of designation, which is to start at the source of the stream and pass down, noting the objects and places on the right hand bank and on the left hand bank. Being told the German Flats was on the *right* bank, the answer misled the committee, and hence arose the mistake and change. The committee acted upon a settled rule of definition, which their informant did not understand.

this case, or his memory very indistinct when he wrote the history of it. I hope his partiality for the hero of his work did not produce an unfavorable bias on his mind towards those who had been America's most ardent and effective, though humble, defenders. Unless more than one Indian was found prowling through the valley soon after the revolution, exhibiting the skin of a human arm and hand for a tobacco pouch, and boasting of the achievement, the truth of history has been falsified in another quarter.

Hartman from some exposure and by personal conflicts with the Indians had become disabled for life so that he could not labor. He was placed on the invalid pension roll, but, shame to my country, the gratuity bestowed was not enough to sustain the shattered remnant of a frame which had been hacked, lacerated and wounded in the service of his adopted country, without additional assistance from the local overseer of the poor. He died at Herkimer and the head stone at the spot where rests his remains, erected in grateful remembrance of his services, is seen in the burial ground surrounding the Brick church at Herkimer, and in full view from the Court house steps, with the inscription cut upon it:

JOHN ADAM HARTMAN,
Born at
Edenkoben in Germany,
A great Patriot in our War for Independence,
Died April 5th, 1836,
Aged 92 years and 7 months.

Fort Dayton was a small stockaded fort, erected in the northerly part of the present village of Herkimer, by Col. Dayton, of the continental service, in the year 1776, for the protection of the inhabitants on the north side of the river; Fort Herkimer, on the south side, being too far off, and too difficult to reach to secure that object as effectively as was desired. A small force of continental troops or state levies, was retained at this post during the war, and it afforded safe protection to the surrounding inhabitants who sought safety within its pickets, against the marauding parties of the enemy. This spot was for many years before and after the revolution the most populous of any in this part of the country; the public buildings of the county have always remained at the village, and for several years it enjoyed a commercial prosperity unrivaled by any locality in the county; but the opening of the Erie canal damaged its pros-

JACOB SMALL.—This zealous partisan of American independence deserves more than the passing notice I can give to his memory. He was a native of Germany, and came to this country when quite young. He was appointed by the governor and council captain in the regiment of Tryon county militia, under the command of Col. Peter Bellinger, on the 25th of June, 1778. He had previously served as subaltern in the militia and was a brave, active and energetic partisan officer. At whatever point between the Little Falls and Forts Herkimer and Dayton an alarm might be given, Capt. Small with such members of his company as could be collected at the moment were afoot and hastening to repel the attack of the enemy and rescue the stockaded post from assault. The beat of his company was on the north side of the Mohawk river and east of the West Canada creek. His duties as a militia officer were so incessant and required him to be absent from his family so much, that he placed them in Fort Herkimer for protection in the fall of 1777, where they remained until the war closed. His son Jacob, who at that time was about six years old, still survives, and retains a distinct recollection of this fact. The successful stratagem practiced by John Christian Shell, in 1781, when his home was assaulted by Donald McDonald at the head of a party of Indians and tories, shows that Capt. Small's name must have been familiar to the assailants, and that they did not like to await his approach within gun shot.

When Capt. Small removed the wounded refugee to Fort Dayton to have his wounds dressed, he performed the act with all the care and humanity he was capable of exerting on that occasion. The welfare of Shell's two little sons carried into captivity by the enemy may have influenced the Americans

perity a good deal. The old church, a wooden structure and a venerable relic of the past, was consumed by fire in January, 1834, when the Court house was burnt. It was soon after replaced by a handsome edifice of brick, which stands on the main street of the village, near the Court house.

Herkimer village is pleasantly situated on a plain near the junction of the Mohawk and West Canada creek, the surrounding country, except in the river and creek valleys, is a little elevated, presenting rich, varied and delightful prospects, not surpassed in the whole Mohawk valley. The large and pretty extended alluvial flat or bottom lands in this town, containing hundreds of acres, have been under cultivation more than 130 years, and still yield abundant crops in requital of the husbandman's toil, and seem to be inexhaustible. The extensive water power of the West Canada creek, which had been long unimproved, was brought into use about the year 1835, by a company of enterprising citizens of the town, and although the results of this experiment may not have fully met the expectation of some of its most sanguine projectors, there can be no doubt of the very beneficial effects to the village, by the construction and operation of mills and machinery and the use of the water power brought out by the company. That the project has not been more remunerative to the proprietors may right-

in their treatment of the disabled foe; but no matter what the motive may have been, the humane conduct of Capt. Small and his party contrasts favorably with that of their relentless and savage enemies.

Although there was but little active warfare on this frontier during the summer and autumn of 1782, and although Capt. Small had more than five successive years taken his life in his hand and gone forth with his men to beat off and chastise the skulking and savage enemy, and escaped unharmed, he was shot in the apple orchard where he and one or two of his neighbors had gone to gather apples, in the fall of 1783, three days after the definitive articles of peace were signed at Paris between the United States and Great Britain. The formal agreement for the cessation of hostilities between the two powers was not signed until January 20th, 1783, but there had been a virtual cessation after the surrender of Cornwallis, except as to the petty warfare carried on by the Indians, who seemed to have but little respect for a power that would acknowledge itself beaten by its rebellious subjects.

fully be attributed to a nonuse of the property, and not to other causes. Why do not the capitalists in the vicinity devote their means to the erection of manufacturing establishments? They have wealth enough for that purpose. Why do the manufacturing towns in the Eastern states spring up as if by magic? By using capital. No greater facilities of transport can be required than they now have.

§7. Little Falls

Contains all that part of the county set off from the towns of Herkimer, Fairfield and German Flats, comprehended within the following boundaries, viz: beginning on the middle or base line of Glen's purchase, at a point where the line between lots number five and six in said purchase unites with said base or middle line, and running thence south along said line to its southern termination; thence on the same course continued to the south bounds of the town of German Flats; thence along the south bounds of said town to the southeast corner thereof; and thence along the eastern bounds of the towns of German Flats and Herkimer, to the southeast corner of the town of Fairfield; and from thence by a straight line to the place of beginning.

The town covers parts of Glen's purchase, Staley's first tract, Guy Johnson's tract, Vaughn's and Fall hill patent, six lots in Burnetsfield, and small triangular pieces of L' Hommedieu's and Lindsey's patents.

Scene at Little Falls.

I have in the general history of the county brought out some facts peculiarly applicable to this town, and the village which bears the same name, and I now refer to them in this connection. There were German inhabitants in nearly every direction around the present village before the revolution, but only one habitable dwelling and a gristmill within the present corporation limits. The present remarks should therefore be taken as a history of the village locality rather than that of the town. The gristmill destroyed during the revolution was located on the river near the bed of the old canal, and was fed by Furnace creek and the river. The dwelling house referred to was occupied by the miller and his assistants, and probably by persons employed at the carrying place. The road or path used for taking boats and their cargoes by the river falls, was located very nearly on the site of the old canal. The red gristmill, to supply the one destroyed, was erected in 1789, and the old yellow house west of Furnace creek, and near the north bank of the old canal, was built a short time before that period. Mr. John Porteous came to this place in 1790, and established himself in mercantile business. He occupied the yellow house, then the only dwelling within the present village limits. Its

Octagon Church, Little Falls. Erected 1796.

venerable walls are yet standing, the spared monuments of a destructive age. And the old Octagon, too, that so often attracted the admiring gaze of the traveler by stage, canal and rail road, was erected and enclosed about the year 1796, though not finished so as to be occupied at all seasons of the year as a house of religious worship, until nearly a quarter of a century afterwards, which is shown by the following memorial deposited in the ball of the steeple:

"This house was erected in the year of our Lord one thousand seven hundred and ninety-six, under the direction of John Porteous, Abraham Neely, Nicholas Thumb and Henry J. Klock, Esqrs., and completed in the year of our Lord one thousand eight hundred and eighteen, under the superintendence of

Doct. JAMES KENNEDY,
WILLIAM GIRVAN and
JOHN DYGERT, Esqrs., } Building Committee.

JOSEPH DORR and
WILLIAM LOVLAND, } Master Builders.

DAN DALE,
JAMES DORR,
BENJAMIN CARR,
SANDFORD PEARCE,
JAMES SANDERS,
MARTIN EASTERBROOKS, } Workmen.

ROBERT WHARRY,
WILLIAM HADDOCK, } Apprentices.

The Revd. HEZEKIAH N. WOODRUFF,
Pastor of the Church and Congregation,

Little Falls, 23d April 1818.

In hand writing of JOSIAH PARSONS."

But where is that old pile of antique device and rustic architecture? Its lofty pulpit, its pews and singing gallery, where are they? Alas! alas! Gone, swept away by the hand of modern improvement. And the venerable Concord society, not always harmonious as its name imported, the trustees of which were seized of the temporalities for the term of their lives, one of which is not yet extinct, what has become of it? Dead by a nonuser of its corporate franchises, and no longer held in remembrance. I am strongly inclined to perpetrate rhyme, or quote a couplet of poetry, but I repress the feeling. History is much too grave a subject to be mixed up with fabulous tales and poetic fictions.

And the long tin horn used by master Case, to summon the playful and unruly school children to their daily tasks; and on more grave occasions, when God's word was to be dispensed at the village school house, by some itinerant missionary of the cross, then were its notes heard through the confined valley, and echo after echo, in the still sabbath morning, notified the hour of meeting, on the day of rest, for prayer and praise: that, too, has been nearly forgotten, and few now remain to repeat from memory, the amusing story of the tin horn, which schoolmaster Case used to blow with great dexterity and varied note. This horn or trumpet

WILLIAM ALEXANDER, was a native of the city of Schenectady, and came to the village with or soon after Mr. Porteous, with whom he was several years connected in business. He was an active, intelligent merchant, and exerted himself to promote the prosperity of the place. He died January 3d, 1813, aged 37 years, of an epidemic fever, which prevailed pretty extensively in the county, and carried off a great many of the adult inhabitants. His loss was long regretted by the people of the village, who survived him.

EBEN and WASHINGTON BRITTON were brothers, and natives of Westmoreland, New Hampshire. Eben settled in the village in 1792, carried on the tanning business many years, and died August 28th, 1832, aged sixty years. He survived his brother more than twenty years.

While strolling through the cemetery, north of the village, taking notes from the memorials of the dead, my attention was arrested by a broad headstone of white marble, tall and erect, and I transcribed the affectionate testimonial of the wife, who had consigned to the grave the loved and cherished companion of her long and varied life. These are the words spoken by the widowed and stricken heart.

"Died, on the 29th of October, 1842, in the 83d year of his age,
EDWARD ARNOLD.
His widow erected this humble
stone, to commemorate his private worth,
but his nobler monuments are the battle
fields of the American revolution, in
letters of blood. These shall perpetuate his
public virtues when this tribute of a wife's
affection shall have crumbled into dust,
and no human hand can point out the
spot where the hero sleeps."

was about four feet long, and there were but few who could blow it.

The old Octagon church was always regarded as one of the curiosities of the place, and was noticed by the Rev. John Taylor, when on a missionary tour through the Mohawk and Black river countries, in 1802. He made a rough sketch of it, which is preserved in the Documentary History of the state. He says, "this parish (Little Falls) contains six or seven hundred inhabitants," and "in this place may be found men of various religious sects. They have a new and beautiful meeting house, standing about forty rods

Yes, venerable and afflicted matron, I will aid thee to keep in remembrance the final resting place of one who served his country with unyielding fidelity, and remarkable bravery, through the whole eventful struggle of the revolution. He entered the army when only seventeen years old, in one of the New England continental regiments of the line, after some desultory service in detached corps of militia, and remained till the close of the war. He was present when Washington assumed the command of the American forces, at Cambridge, and witnessed his departure from New York in December, 1783. He was in nearly all the battles on the seaboard, from Bunker's Hill to Yorktown. He was active when in the prime of life, and well formed. His constitution was vigorous, and until nearly the close of life, he enjoyed excellent health. Let me perform my promise. He was interred in one of the west tiers of burial lots, in the cemetery at the Little Falls—on ground consecrated by the valor of himself and his compeers to the repose of freemen.

WILLIAM FEETER.—Col. Feeter was a native of the territory now embraced in Fulton county. His name, before it became Anglicized, was written Veeder or Vedder; and in 1786, when he was commissioned an ensign in the militia, it was written Father. In 1791, he was appointed a justice of the peace in this county, under the name of William Veeder. Although the name he bore at an early day indicated a low Dutch origin, this was not the fact. His father was a native of Wittenberg, Germany, and at the commencement of the revolution, the family was settled in the neighborhood of Johnstown, and was so much under the influence of the Johnsons, that all of them, except William, then quite a young man, followed the fortunes of Sir John, and went with him to Canada.

The colonel, in his youthful ardor, felt more inclined to give young America a trial, than to follow the cross of St. George into the wilds of Canada; and on all occasions when the invaders came into the Mohawk valley, for the purposes of plunder and slaughter, he was ever among the first and foremost to volunteer his services to drive them away. On one occasion, in 1781,

back on the hill, built in the form of an octagon." His observations, however, convinced him it was not improved. But I will go back a few years. One of the two lots 12 and 13 Burnetsfield, embracing all the water power on the north side of the river, was owned, before the revolution, by one of the Petrie family, who erected the first grist mill on Furnace creek, and was engaged in the carrying business. The following are the names of some of the persons who settled at this place between 1790 and 1800, and who remained here permanently until death: John Porteous, William Alexander, Richard Philips, Thomas Smith, Joel Lankton, Richard Winsor, William Carr, William Moralee, Washington Britton, Alpheus Parkhurst, John Drummond, Eben Britton, Josiah Skinner.

The construction of the old canal and locks, by the Western inland lock navigation company, gave an impetus

when a party of Indians and tories made a descent upon a settlement in the Palatine district, for the purpose of plunder and murder, the subject of this notice took an active part in punishing the lawless intruders. It appeared that the object of the enemy was to plunder and murder a family related to one of the tory invaders, which was not quite agreeable to him; he therefore gave himself up, and disclosed the nefarious intentions of the enemy, who, finding themselves betrayed, made a rapid flight to the woods. Col. Willett did not feel disposed to let them off without a severe chastisement; he therefore ordered Lieutenant Sammons, with twenty-five volunteers, among whom was William Feeter, to go in pursuit, and they moved so rapidly, that they came upon the enemy's burning camp fires early the next morning. Feeter and six other men were directed to keep the trail, and after a rapid pursuit of two miles in the woods, a party of Indians was discovered lying flat on the ground. The latter, when they saw Feeter approach, instantly arose and fired; but one of the enemy being grievously wounded by the return fire of the Americans, the whole gang of Indians and tories fled precipitately, leaving their knapsacks, provisions and some of their arms. The result of this affair was, that three of the enemy were wounded in the running fight kept up by Feeter and his party, and died on their way to Canada; one surrendered himself a prisoner, and the wounded Indian was summarily dispatched by his former tory comrade, who had joined in the pursuit.

Colonel Feeter seated himself upon Glen's purchase, within the present limits of Little Falls, soon after the close of the revolution, and opened a large

to the growth and prosperity of the place, which brought it into notice at an early period; but the paralyzing policy of the proprietor, who was an alien, in limiting his alienations to leases in fee rendering an annual rent, and refusing to make only a few grants of that description, to which he affixed the most stringent conditions and restrictions in the exercise of trade and the improvement of the water power, kept the place nearly stationary, until 1831, excepting that part of the present village on the south side of the river, not subject to the dead weight of nonalienation. Upon the opening of the Erie canal, in 1825, the only erections in that part of the village were a bridge and toll house, at the south end of the bridge; the Bellinger grist mill and a small dwelling, for the miller's residence, and the Vrooman house.

In 1816, there were only two streets, or thoroughfares, in the village. The turnpike, now known as Main street, and

farm, which he cultivated with success more than fifty years. He raised a family of five sons and seven daughters, some of whom still survive, and others have gone with him to their final rest. All of his children, with two exceptions, I believe, settled in this county. Colonel Feeter adhered through life to doctrine and mode of worship of the German Lutheran church, which must lead one to believe he had been early and thoroughly educated in the tenets of the great reformer. He died at Little Falls, May 5, 1844, aged 88 years.

His father, Lucus Feeter, stood high in the confidence of Sir William Johnson and the whole family, and because his rebellious boy would not consent to abandon his native country and follow the fortunes of Sir John, he was driven from the paternal roof, and compelled to seek a shelter and a home where he could. The surrounding neighbors being mostly adherents of the Johnson family, and friendly to the royal cause, the task of finding a kind and sympathizing friend, and one who would advise and counsel him for the best, may have been a difficult matter for young Feeter to surmount. He succeeded, however, in securing a temporary home in the family of Mr. Yauney, a near neighbor of his father. At a proper time, Mr. Yauney presented a musket to his young protege, and told him he would have to rely upon that for defense and protection, until his country's freedom was acknowledged by the British king. The colonel used that musket through the whole war, and it is now preserved as an heir-loom in the family of his youngest son. Col. Feeter was born at Stone Arabia, February 2d, 1756.

the Eastern and Western avenues, which thenextended on the present line no farther than to cross Furnace creek, where it turned down east of the yellow house, thence over the old canal, and along between the old canal and river, to the head of the falls. The Western avenue was not then opened. The other road was what is now called German, Bridge, Ann and Church streets, crossing the river from the south, and leading to Eatonville and Top-notch. There were not over forty dwelling houses in the place at that time. Before Main street was extended west from Ann, the traveled road was down Ann street, across the old canal, and thence along Mill street. At this time, there was one church, the octagon, not finished, the stone school house, two taverns, two blacksmith shops, five or six stores and groceries, and one grist and one saw mill on the north side of the river. This was nearly the state of things until 1828, except the few erections and improvements that had been made on Main and Ann streets, and two or three dwelling houses on Garden street. Ann street, north of Garden, was a pasture. All that part of the village east of Second and south of the lots fronting on Main street, extending to the river, as well as that portion east of the old Salisbury road, was a drear wilderness, thickly covered with white cedar undergrowth.

I now relate the following incident, which shows the cool courage and resolute determination of the man, or I should say, perhaps, of him and his companion. On one occasion, he and Mr. Gray, the father of the Hon. Charles Gray, of Herkimer, had, during the war, been on an expedition up the river, and were returning in a small canoe; when they reached the Little Falls, instead of taking their light craft over the carrying place, or sending it over the falls empty, they pushed into the stream, and safely navigated their frail vessel amid boiling, surging waters, over the rapids. He performed a like feat at another time during the war, when a comrade in another canoe was stranded on the rocks, and barely escaped drowning.

The reader, who knows the locality as it now appears, may think this rather an improbable story. The fact is not only well attested, but we must reflect, that the stream was not then hedged in and confined by dams, arches and artificial structures, and that the flow of water, at an ordinary flood, was much greater than it is at present.

The village charter, granted March 30th, 1811, was amended in 1827, and the corporation authorized to open streets, which had been dedicated to public use, as laid down on a map made by the proprietor, in 1811. The power given was exerted in the first instance, by opening Albany, Garden and Second streets, at the expense of the owners of the adjoining lots. This touched the proprietor's purse, and he consented to sell in fee the lots on those streets. This, however, did not reach the water power, which was not improved, neither would the proprietors on either side of the river consent to sell lots and water rights, but the alien owner adopted the plan of making short leases, by which he anticipated a rich harvest on the falling in of the revisions. The people of the village were not slow to perceive the fatal effects of this policy, and applied to the legislature for the passage of an act to prohibit the alien proprietor from making any grants or leases, except in fee. These were the conditions on which he was authorized to take, hold and convey lands in this state. The act passed the senate at the session of 1831, and was sent to the assembly for concurrence. The agents offered to sell the whole proprietary interest in the village for $50,000, and active negotiations were set on foot by several parties to make the purchase. The act made slow progress in the assembly. The leading citizens of the village were appealed to, and advised to form a company, and make the purchase. The bill was finally acted upon in the house, and rejected. Almost simultaneous with that rejection, the sale was effected to several members of that body and other parties, and the purchasers in a short time realized a net $50,000 on their purchase, or very nearly that sum. Whether there was any connection between the defeat of the bill, which I had some agency in carrying through the senate, and the sale, I never sought to know. The sale accomplished all that we of the village desired, because we believed the purchasers had bought with the intention of elling out, as fast as they could; but the proprietor, Mr.

Ellice, had a large interest at stake ; he was the owner of other considerable tracts of land, not only in this county, but in different parts of the state ; it was important to him, therefore, to get rid of the restrictive provisions of the bill, in respect to his other lands. His agents in this country were well satisfied that the applicants for coercive but just measures would not rest quietly under one defeat, and that his interests would be damaged in proportion to the duration of the controversy.

The new proprietors made immediate arrangements to bring the property into market, and effected large sales by auction and private sale, in the year 1831, and in the course of a few years, what remained of the original purchase, with other lands of Mr. Ellice on the north side of the river, came into the hands of Richard R. Ward and James Munroe Esquires, of the city of New York, not however as joint owners. No sale of the water power, in separate lots or privileges, were made before Mr. Ward became the sole owner of all that portion of the original purchase from Mr. Ellice. When these were brought into market, Gen. Bellinger, the principal owner of the water power, on the south side of the river, supposing a prior appropriation might not tally with his private interests, also came into market, and mills, factories, foundries and other machinery, were soon in operation, giving life, vigor and animation, to this circumscribed spot.

After the opening of the canal in 1825, the little patch of habitable earth in its vicinity, was soon improved, and what had hitherto been a wild, broken cedar thicket, was converted into a habitable spot and active business place, by the art of man. In 1830, the whole population of the town was, 2,539, and about 1,700 of that number, were within the village limits.

It appears by the recent census that the population of the town on the 1st day of June, 1855, was 4,930, and that within the corporation limits, which embraces a small portion of Manheim, the whole population was, 3,972. The progress

Feeter's Block.

of the village in population and industrial pursuits has been slow, but quite as rapid as any of its sister villages in the valley between Utica and Schenectady. It now ranks the first in population and commercial and manufacturing importance.

This village contains two large and commodious brick schoolhouses, with a capacity of seating 600 pupils, which cost about $10,000; two stone, one brick, and two wood framed churches. These structures have all been erected within the last 25 years, and evince a commendable feeling of public spirit and liberality in the population of the village.

It is a singular, and perhaps a remarkable fact, that

The Benton House. Erected in 1847.

although the inhabitants of the village have increased 2272, in the last quarter of a century, there are not now over 300 residents, who were such in 1830; and not over 30 of the inhabitants who were here in 1815, can now be found within the corporation limits. This place, and the country around it, is as healthful, and the climate is as solubrious, as any in the state. It would now be difficult to visit any considerable town or place of business at the west, even in Missouri and Iowa, without meeting some one who had formerly lived at Little Falls.

The Presbyterian Church. This society had its ecclesiastical organization on the 29th of June, 1812. I think this society had not, for many years a statute or lay organization separate from the Concord society, and until the erection of the brick church at the junction of Ann and Albany streets, in 1831, or about that time.

"The First Presbyterian society of the village of Little Falls in the town of Little Falls in the county of Herkimer," was incorporated April 16, 1831, under the statute passed April 5, 1813, and Robert Stewart, David Petrie, Charles Smith, Daniel McIntosh, Hozea Hamilton, John Scullen and William Hammell were elected the first lay trustees, and at the first meting of the trustees after their election, Elisha S. Capron was appointed clerk, William J. Pardee, treasurer, and John Dygert, collector.

This organization has been regularly continued to the present time, the church regularly supplied with a settled clergyman, and is and ever has been one of the most flourishing Protestant denominations in the town in respect to numbers, and the respectability and wealth of its members.

Mr. Daniel Talcott, an aged member of this church, who died several years ago, made a pecuniary bequest by his will which enures to the benefit of this society.

This corporation own a handsome brick parsonage, situate on Ann street, purchased by the generous liberality of its members at the expense of about twenty-two hundred dollars.

The Episcopal Church. The vestry of Emmanuel church, at the village of Little Falls in the town of Herkimer, was duly incorporated February 22d, 1823.

Nathaniel S. Benton and George H. Feeter, church wardens; Oran G. Otis, Lester Green, Solomon Lockwood, Abner Graves, Andrew A. Barton, William G. Borland, Thomas Gould and Daniel H. Eastman, vestrymen.

The Rev. Phineas L. Whipple of Trinity church, Fairfield, was on the third day of January, 1824, called to officiate as rector, according to the rites of the Protestant episcopal church in the United States, one-half the time for the period of one year, at a salary of two hundred dollars.

The present church was consecrated by Bishop Onderdonk in October, 1835. Trinity church, New York, made a liberal donation of $1500, to aid in building the church edifice.

This organization has been regularly continued to this time, and since 1835 rectors have been inducted and settled, and the services of the church administered with but short intermissions. The corporation own a convenient brick rectory, lately built by the corporation, situate at the corner of Albany and William streets, near the church edifice.

The Baptist Society, Little Falls. At a meeting of the persons usually attending worship with the Baptist church in the village of Little Falls, held pursuant to notice at the stone school house, the usual place of worship of said church, on the 21st day of December, 1830, for the purpose of organizing and forming an incorporated society within the provisions of the statute, Alanson Ingham and Calvin G. Carpenter were appointed to preside at the election of trustees.

After unanimously agreeing to organize a society to be known by the name and style of the Baptist society of Little Falls, a ballot was taken and Daniel Rogers, Alanson Ingham,

Parley Eaton, Henry Haman and Stephen W. Brown were elected trustees.

It was thereupon resolved that the aforesaid trustees, and their successors in office, shall forever hereafter be called and known by the name and title of the Trustees of the baptist society of Little Falls.

To all which we, the returning officers do certify; in witness whereof we have set our hands and seals this 22d day of December, 1830. ALANSON INGHAM,

In presence of CALVIN G. CARPENTER.

PARLEY EATON.

Recorded in the clerk's office, Herkimer county, December 22d, 1830.

In 1832 this society erected a handsome stone church on the south side of Albany street at the corner of Mary street, and have kept up their legal organization under the statute to the present time. Its standing, as a religious body, has always been respectable in numbers and the character of its members.

The Methodist Society.—At a meeting of the male members of the Methodist episcopal society in the village of Little Falls, called according to law at the school house in said village on the 19th day of November, 1832, for the purpose of organizing a corporation under the statute, Henry Heath was chosen chairman and Ebenezer S. Edgerton appointed secretary.

Resolved, That this society be called The Methodist episcopal church of the village of Little Falls.

Resolved, That this meeting do elect five members of the society to serve as trustees of the corporation and take charge of the temporalities of the church.

The meeting then proceeded to the election of trustees, Henry Heath and E. S. Edgerton being chosen tellers of the poll, and on ballot the following person were duly elected, viz :

First class, Edmond L. Shephard, Gilbert Robinson.

Second class, George Warcup, Ebenezer S. Edgerton.

Third class, Henry Heath.

Resolved, That the board of trustees be requested to procure a suitable site for building a church as soon as may be convenient.

At a subsequent meeting of the board of trustees, Henry Heath was chosen chairman of the board, and E. S. Edgerton secretary.

The society immediately set about raising the funds to purchase a lot and build a church. A subscription was opened in October, 1836, the last installment of which was payable in January, 1838. After encountering delays and embarrassments incident to a first effort and infant organization, the society completed the church in 1839, which was dedicated that year and opened for public worship.

The church edifice has since been enlarged and beautified to accommodate the wants and meet the tastes of an increasing congregation. This society is now in a flourishing condition and its members have set on foot a project of purchasing a parsonage house or glebe.

The Universalist Society.—This society was incorporated on the 3d day of May, A. D. 1851, by the name of the First universalist society of Little Falls, Herkimer county, New York, by filing a certificate in the usual form under the statute, in the clerk's office of the county. The certificate was recorded on the sixth day of May, A. D. 1851.

The trustees elected by the male members of the congregation at this organization were Messrs. Wm. B. Houghton, M. M. Ransom, O. Benedict, A. Zoller, L. O. Gay, J. K. Chapman, L. W. Gray, A. Fuller and O. Angel.

This society has still a corporate existence and hold divine service according to the rites of the Universalist church at Temperance hall, in the village of Little Falls.

The society has now a settled minister whose ministrations are well and regularly attended by a respectable congregation. If I may speculate upon such a subject, it is not improbable the members of this congregation will before long erect a church for their accommodation.

The Roman Catholic.—The state census returns show that the Roman catholics have a church and 600 members in this town. I am not aware that there is any lay organization attached to this church, or that the temporalties are held or supervised by any corporate body known to the laws of this state. The church or chapel on John street was erected in 1847, under the charge of the Rev. John McMinamia and enlarged I think in 1853. It is a wooden building. A very neat and apparently commodious brick house, adjoining the church, was built in 1854 and finished in 1855, for the use of the priest having charge of the church. There is also a school house attached to the church, built in 1852, in which a school has been kept a portion of the time since it was erected. I speak from personal recollection, I have no other means of information, when I state a Catholic priest has resided here continually more than ten years past in charge of this church. The census marshals must have made a mistake when they returned the whole number of aliens in the town at 623. There are more than 23 and even more than 100 Protestant aliens in the town, and there are not ten, if there is one, native in the town attached to the Roman Catholic church, or should be numbered as such.

The Protestant Methodists.—A society attached to this denomination was organized in Pain's Hollow in this town in 1833, under the provisions of the statute relating to religious incorporations. In 1840, the society built a church, sufficiently capacious for the accommodation of the inhabitants of the vicinage, and have called and settled a pastor who administers the services of religion regularly every sabbath, according to the established rites of this church. A flourishing Sunday school has been organized and is kept up, and the society have a library of more than one hundred volumes.

§ 8. Litchfield

Contains that part of the county, bounded northerly, by Frankfort; westerly, by the bounds of the county; southerly, by Winfield; and easterly, by a line beginning at the southeast corner of Frankfort, and running thence south thirty degrees west, to the northeast corner of Winfield.

A part of Bayard's patent, and small portions of Staley's second tract, and Conrad Frank's patent, lay in this town.

This town was visited by the New Englanders, soon after the close of the revolutionary war, as were most of the other towns in the county, back from the river. None of the German population had fixed themselves within its limits, previous to that period. Elijah Snow, a native of Westbury, Massachusetts, seated on what is now called Whelock's hill, in 1786. This place was formerly known as Snowsbush. William Brewer, of Worcester, Mass., Ezekiel Goodale of Mass., John Andrews, Christopher Rider, from Connecticut, Ebenezer Drewry and John Everett, from New Hampshire, and John and Eleazer Crosby, from Connecticut, came into the town about the year 1787; Mr. Brewer is still living, and is the oldest inhabitant. A son of John Andrews, named after John C. Lake of New York, was the first child born in the town. Samuel Miller, from Connecticut, came into the town in 1788, and James Gage and Nathaniel Ball, from New Hampshire, arrived about the same period. Selah Holcomb, from Simsbury, Connecticut, settled in this town, in February, 1791. He died June 18th, 1854, aged 86 years. I have not been able to obtain any of the particulars relating to the lives of these pioneers, who opened the forests of Bayard's patent, except in respect of Capt. Holcomb. He was a farmer, sustained a good character, and exerted a good deal of influence among his townsmen. By a long life of persevering industry and economy, he accumulated considerable wealth. He was frequently elected to the local town offices. He exhibited all the traits of an excellent New England farmer. Litchfield may properly be called an agricultural town. The iron foundry, formerly established in this town several years ago, carried on for some time a pretty large business, in the manufacture of hollow ware, which in times of monetary pressure, was used in the barter trade of the country, and notes payable in iron ware of the Litchfield furnace were not unfrequent. There is now no necessity of resorting to this mode of traffic.

Cedarville, which is partly located in Columbia, and partly in this town, is the only village of which Litchfield can boast. Wealth and thrift surrounds the population of this town, in an equal degree with our other towns, where the pursuits of the farmer have been directed to grazing and dairying.

§ 9. MANHEIM

Contains that part of the county bounded easterly by the east bounds of the county; southerly, by the Mohawk river; and westerly, and northerly, by a line beginning at the east end of the easternmost lock of the old canal, on the north side of the Mohawk river, at the Little Falls, and running thence north as the needle pointed in 1772, until an east line strikes the northwest corner of a large lot, number fourteen, in a tract of land called Glen's purchase; then easterly to the east corner of Glen's purchase; and then east to the bounds of the county.

Six of the large lots in Glen's purchase, a part of the fourth allotment of the Royal grant; the whole of John Van Driesen's and Snell and Timmerman's patent, and part of Rev. Peter Van Dreisen's; a part of Vrooman's patent, and some other small grants made by the state, are situated in this town.

The grant of 3,600 acres made in 1755, to Jacob Timmerman and Johan Jost Schnell, commonly known as Snell and Timmerman's patent, is near the central part of the town on an east and west line, and south of the Royal grant. Manheim was settled by German emigrants before the revolution, and the date of this patent may be assumed as pretty near the period when that event took place. The Snells and Timmermans, descendants of these patentees, are still quite numerous in the town, owners of the soil through a long line of inheritance, granted to their own persecuted and always patient and toiling ancestors.

Suffrenus, Peter, Joseph and Jacob Snell, four sons of one of the patentees, made a donation of seven acres of land for a church lot and twelve acres for school purposes. But this was not all. They and their neighbors met upon the lands every Saturday afternoon, and worked at the sturdy forest until the lands were cleared and rendered fit for cultivation.

A church was erected on the lot designed for that purpose, and that ancient edifice was replaced by a new one in 1850-1. The school house in the district stands on the donated lot. Eleven and a half acres of the school lot were transferred by an act of the legislature to the church. How could this be done without the consent of the parties interested?

There were nine men of this Snell family, and among them were Peter, Joseph and Jacob, who went under Gen. Herkimer into the Oriskany battle, and only two of them returned, of whom Peter was one; the other seven were killed. An aged and respectable member of this family, now living, states that these three men were very active and

JOHN BEARDSLEE was born in Sharon, Connecticut, in November, 1759, and died in Manheim, October 3d, 1825, where he had resided more than thirty years. His father, John Beardslee, Senior, was a native of Norwalk, Conn., born about the year 1725, and married Deborah Knickerbacker, in 1748, who numbered among her family connections the Hoffmans and Rosevelts, of Dutchess county and New York city. The subject of this notice married Lavinia Pardee, of Sharon, Conn., in 1795, who survived her husband a quarter of a century, and died in Manheim, in 1854, aged 85 years. Miss Pardee was connected with the Brewsters, Goulds, Waldos, Ripleys and Bradfords, of Connecticut and Massachusetts.

Mr. Beardslee left his father's residence in Connecticut, in 1781, not like Cœlebs in search of a wife, but a young New Englander in search of a fortune, which he aimed to accomplish. He was a practical mechanic, architect and civil engineer. He stopped at Sheffield, Mass., worked one year on a farm, and then went to Vermont, commenced working at his trade, and bought and paid for a small farm, but soon lost it by a defect in the title. Soon after he went to Vermont, he spent a fall and winter on Lakes George and Champlain, fishing and hunting, in company with Jonathan Wright, who afterwards came into the north part of this county, and was known as old Jack Wright, the trapper. Mr. Beardslee then turned his face westward, built a bridge at Schaticoke, and a meeting house in Schoharie. In 1787, he went to Whitestown, then being settled by eastern emigrants, and engaged

zealous in urging Gen. Herkimer to a forward movement on the 6th of August, 1777. They had resolved to fight the enemy, and how fatal was the consequence!

Henry Remensneider, or Rhemensnyder, and Johannes Boyer were the first settlers on Glen's purchase, a few miles north of the Little Falls. They came on to the tract several years before the commencement of the revolutionary war. John Boyer was born near New York; his father emigrated from Elsos in Germany. John was in the Oriskany battle and lost his team of horses and wagon in that bloody affray. He was the immediate ancestor of the Boyer families, once so numerous in this town. His youngest son, Henry, now 75 years old, is still living, and several of his descendants are found in the county, although emigration has somewhat diminished their numbers. Among other German settlers who had seated themselves in this town before the revolution, were the Keysers, Van Slykes, Newmans, Sha-

with White & Whitmore to build mills on shares. He afterwards sold his half at a good advance. He remained at Whitestown till 1792, having been employed by the state to build a set of mills for the Oneida Indians. He completed his contract without returning to the white settlements, after he had commenced it. By humoring the Indians, joining in their sports of hunting and fishing, and exciting their curiosity to see the results of his labors, they cheerfully assisted him in his enterprise, which contributed to make the job quite profitable.

At this time there resided in the neighborhood of the Indians, two well educated, gentlemanly Frenchmen, but perfect recluses, the relic of French colonists, and of that splendid colonial French empire, already struck from the French crown, and which had cost so much of blood and treasure to establish and uphold. Between 1790 and 1796, he built the first bridge across the Mohawk river, at Little Falls, the old red grist mill at that place, the first bridge over the gulf, east of the academy, mills for Richard Van Horne, at Van Hornesville. and for Col. Freye, at Canajoharie, a bridge over the West Canada creek, and the court house and jail, which were burned up in 1833 or 1834, a bridge across the Mohawk river, at Fort Plain, and a bridge over the East Canada creek, a grist and saw mill and fulling works, about half a mile north of the present Mohawk turnpike bridge.

The building of this bridge led to his seating himself at Manheim permanently in this wise. The bridge was erected at the expense of Montgomery county, or paid for by it. In order to obtain the necessary timber, he purchased a

vers, Klacks, Adles and Garters, all of whom drank deeply of the bitter cup of the revolutionary struggle.

Palatine, Oppenheim and Manheim, are names significant of the origin of the people who were the first settlers in these towns. Manheim constituted a part of the Palatine district in Tryon county, and the town of that name until 1797, when it was organized into a separate town. The town remains as it was when annexed to the county in the year 1817. The East Canada creek affords a large supply of water at most seasons of the year, and being intersected with many falls has been used to some extent for manufacturing and mechanical purposes. This water power has been brought into use at a village called Ingham's Mills, where there is a tannery, recently erected, and mills and other machinery in operation. The most important village in the town has the post office designation of Brackett's Bridge, and is sometimes known as Wintonville. Mr. D. B. Winton erected a tannery at this place previous to 1840.

one hundred acre lot west of the creek, and adjoining the site of the bridge, for which he paid £300, New York currency, in March, 1794. After the bridge was completed, he erected the mills, which were finished and in operation in 1795. This was at the flood tide of emigration to the Royal grant and Western New York; the mills attracted attention, and population gathered to his place: by the year 1800, quite a little village, dignified by the name of the City, had sprung up, counting two stores, two taverns, a blacksmith shop, nail factory, a cooperage and a brewery, afterwards came the lawyers, doctors, school masters, and the distillery.

It could also boast having one man drink himself to death on a bet, and the presence of a state prison graduate, frequent performances of Punch and the Babes in the Woods, by Sickles, and daily amusements in the way of turkey shooting, pitched battles with fists, clubs and teeth, and launching batteaux, for the Mohawk river service. At this time there was more business done at Beardsley's Mills, than at Little Falls. In 1801 and 1802, the Mohawk turnpike was completed, and being located south half a mile of the little village, by diverting the travel on this then great thoroughfare, completely used up the City, to the serious loss of the founder. With the view of making good his losses, and fixing himself on the line of travel, where business could be done, he purchased, in 1810, 350 acres of land, laying on both sides of the creek, and between his first purchase and the river, for which he paid $11,500,

This establishment was afterwards purchased by an eminent house in the city of New York, engaged in the leather business, by whom it was enlarged and improved, and is now the most extensive manufactory of the kind in the county or in this part of the country. The village is unincorporated. It contains two churches, two stores, several mechanics' shops, also a saw and grist mill, and a stave and barrel manufactory. There are five houses for religious worship in the town, but I am not able to classify the denominations to which they belong.

I should not do justice to the subject in hand, if I omitted all reference to the name of Major Andrew Fink, who settled in this town soon after the close of the war. He was of German descent, and a native of the lower Mohawk valley. He was well educated, and at the commencement of the revolution, although then a young man, had acquired a very considerable knowledge of military science, unusual for a mere provincial of that day.

a high price, it would seem, at that day. The prospects of business on the turnpike justified this purchase. But our increasing commercial difficulties with great Britain and France, followed by the war of 1812, caused him to postpone carrying out his intentions, when this new purchase was made.

When the peace was proclaimed, in 1815, the project of the Erie canal on the south side of the river was brought forward, and finally consummated. The immediate local effect of opening the canal, was a great depreciation of agricultural lands in the Mohawk valley, the almost certain destruction of such small business places as the East Creek, Palatine and Caughnawaga, on the north side of the river, and the building up of villages on the line of the canal. A greater change than that effected by the canal in the Mohawk valley, has seldom been witnessed in any country. Nearly the whole business was transferred from the north to the south side of the river. The turnpike became almost a solitude, and the villages through which it run, as a desert waste of waters.

It has been claimed, and with much apparent reason, that Mr. Beardslee was seriously injured in *consequence* of the construction, by the state, of the Minden dam across the Mohawk, at St. Johnsville. The ordinary flow of the river is from three to five miles an hour. This dam was made and used as an auxiliary to the canal, and the top line was so high as to overcome all the natural descent between it and the mouth of the East creek, about three and a half miles, and hence the river surface was nearly a level the whole dis-

Mr. Fink was appointed first lieutenant of Capt. Christopher P. Yates's company, raised for special service. The warrants bear date July 15th, 1775. This was the commencement of a military career to which he was attached during the whole revolutionary contest. His constitution was firm, resolution indomitable, and courage undoubted. Major Fink died at a pretty advanced age, and the stone that marks his final resting place may be seen upon a rising ground a little north of the Mohawk turnpike, in full view of the spot where rest the remains of the brave and patriotic Herkimer. I should take great pleasure in noting down the particulars of Major Fink's services in the great struggle for colonial rights and Anglo-Saxon freedom, but on inquiring of the surviving members of his family whether he had left any papers, I was told he once had many letters and papers relating to revolutionary transactions, but they were now all gone. The family say, sometimes one person and then another would desire to look them over to ascertain

tance, presenting, as was claimed, an effectual obstruction to the free flow and discharge of the ice from the creek and river above, during the winter and spring floods.

Mr. Beardslee, by strict attention to business, hard hand work and the application of a sound, inventive mind, twenty-seven years, had accumulated a handsome estate, and which, but for the adversities and losses he met with, in no respect attributable to misconduct or want of sound, discriminating judgment, would have been almost princely in this country and in his day.

He was a tall man, free from obesity, with large black eyes, which he inherited from his father, and a fine figure, bestowed on him by his low Dutch mother. Natural and easy in his address, pleasant and companionable in his intercourse with others, generous and hospitable. He used to say, with much satisfaction, that in all the heavy and difficult structures he had raised, or superintended the construction of, not a man in his employment, or of the motley crowds of people collected on such occasions, as was the custom of that early day, was killed or injured in the least. In the decline of life, he indulged himself a good deal in reading, a gratification he did not enjoy in his youthful days. He died of a scirrhous stomach, from which he had suffered many years. This sketch has been considerably elaborated, because it shows, not only how much a young man of indomitable perseverance and firm resolution can achieve, single handed and alone, but what young Americans have heretofore been in the habit of performing.

some fact or indulge an idle curiosity, and in the end all the papers of any consequence were gone before they were fully aware of it.

All that portion of the town lying between the south end of lots number 17, 18 and 19, Glen's purchase, and the southerly bounds of the first allotment, Royal grant, and the river, except the Snell and Timmerman and a small point of the Peter Van Driesen patents, was ungranted by the crown at the revolution. The state sold small parcels of this tract to Isaac Vroomán, John Van Driesen and others, soon after the close of the war. So late as 1777, Capt. Joseph Brant, the Mohawk chief, claimed the lands more recently known as the Christy place, long occupied by Nathan Christy, Esq., and the lands adjacent, which lay nearly opposite to the Indian castle church, on the south side of the river. The Christy place was an improved farm before the revolution, and Brant rented it to a German for one hundred dollars a year. It is not an idle speculation to assume that these lands had never been sold by the Indians, but were held appurtenant to the upper Mohawk castle.

§ 10. Newport

Contains that part of the county lying within the following bounds viz.: beginning at the southeast corner of great lot number eighteen, in Hasenclever's patent, and running thence on the line of said lot, a northerly course to the Steuben road; then on a direct course to the centre of lot number thirteen, in Walton's patent; then through the centre of lot number sixteen, in Walton's patent, to the west bounds of the county; then on a direct line to the southwest corner of lot number twenty-eight, in the third allotment of the Royal grant; then easterly, along the line of lots to the northeast corner of lot number twenty-three, in said allotment; then south, along the line of lots to the southeast corner of lot number forty-two, in the second allotment of said grant; then on a southerly course to the Canada creek, at the bridge, near the house heretofore or late of Obadiah Kniffin; then west, to the middle of the creek; then down the middle of the same, until a west course will meet the place of beginning; and then west to the place of beginning.

As will be noticed in the above boundaries, a part of Hasenclever's and Walton's patents, and portions of the second and third allotments of the Royal grant, are in this town.

No part of the territory of this town was settled before the revolution, and probably not before 1790. I will pause a moment to record again the Indian name of this creek, as laid down on an outline map of the Mohawk river and Wood creek, showing the relative positions of Fort Bull, Fort Williams and German Flats. This is the name, *Teughtaghrarow.* It is marked on Southier's map of the province of New York, published in 1779, Canada river; and it is so called on a map made by Guy Johnson, in 1771. This

CHRISTOPHER HAWKINS, was the first permanent settler of this town and its first supervisor after its erection. In April, 1834, Mr. Hawkins had prepared a sketch of his juvenile adventures, and at his death he left the manuscript with his family. The volume has been recently placed in my hands, and from it I propose to make condensed abstracts of its contents. This I deem no departure from my general plan. I should willingly give all the space required for a literal copy of the narrative touching the escape of Mr. Hawkins from the Jersey prison ship, and his sufferings before he reached home, if I had it.

Referring to the manuscript, young Hawkins, then in the thirteenth year of his age, and an indented apprentice to Aaron Mason of Providence, R. I., in May, 1777, went to New Bedford, Mass., and shipped on board the privateer schooner Eagle, mounting twelve small carriage guns, commanded by Capt. Moury Potter. This small craft was bound on a cruise for such British vessels as could be captured. The Eagle made her offing and as the officers alleged or supposed, cruised in the track of vessels sailing between New York and England. She crossed the broad Atlantic, however, without seeing or speaking with a single vessel. In due time the privateer made the English coast, where she remained a short time when the captain and crew concluded to "bout ship" and return home in no pleasant mood, as they had promised themselves on the start, as many prizes as they could man, on the outward cruise. On the return passage, the Eagle spoke an unarmed schooner which proved to be a French vessel from the West Indies bound to Halifax, when some dispute arose between the officers and crew of the Eagle in regard to the national character of the schooner, the latter insisting that she was English, and could be made a lawful prize. To settle this point the first lieutenant of the privateer, John Paine, boarded the French vessel and examined her papers, who returned and reported her a French vessel loaded with flour. John Ward, the boatswain, and a large majority of the crew were dissatisfied with this report, but their grumblings did not avail any thing; the officers of the Eagle did not deem it prudent to superadd piracy to the crime of rebellion.

The next vessel overhauled by the Eagle was an English merchant brig, deeply laden, bound to New York, and here, according to Hawkins's relation,

stream, at Newport, is quite as much entitled to the respectable appellation of *river* as the Mohawk is, at any point above the junction of the two streams.

William, Ephraim and Benjamin Bowen, of Newport, Rhode Island, purchased the lands where Newport village is now located, of Daniel Campbell of the city of New York, in 1788-9. Mr. Campbell obtained his title from the commissioners of forfeitures, in July, 1786. Christopher Hawkins, Benjamin Bowen and Joseph Benseley, came from Rhode

John Bull completely outwitted and out-manœuvred brother Jonathan, and this was owing to the inefficiency of Capt. Potter, of the privateer. It was quite dark when the Eagle came up with the brig, which kept on her course without apparently paying any attention to the little craft hovering around her. A broadside from the schooner soon produced an inquiry from the brig, "What in God's name do you want of us?" The reply was, "Shorten sail, come under my lee and send your boat on board me." The Englishman now began to excuse himself, said his boat was lashed under his booms and he could not get her out; that if he could have permission to lie by until morning he would then send his boat on board. This was agreed to, but in the morning there was no brig in sight; she being a pretty good sailer had spread her canvas and departed on her course. It was then determined to stand on the course for Sandy Hook, in the hope of overtaking the brig, but a severe gale from the northeast sprung up, which lasted two or three days, the sea making a clear breach over the schooner's deck, her crew had to exert their utmost skill and energies to keep her from foundering. They had then no time to think of making lawful prize of British vessels.

Before the storm had entirely abated, the privateer was captured by the British sloop of war Sphynx, of twenty guns; the schooner was sunk, and the crew taken as prisoners of war to New York, when a new era in the life of Hawkins was opened to him, and new scenes presented to his juvenile contemplation. After reaching New York, Hawkins and most of his companions were placed on board the prison ship Asia, an old transport, then anchored in the East river. At the expiration of three weeks, Hawkins was taken on board the British frigate Maidstone, of twenty-eight guns, to serve as a waiter to one of the under officers of that ship. He was held in the British service about eighteen months, and being a mere boy, and an officer's waiter, found but little difficulty in getting on quite comfortably in all respects, save the yearning wish to see his mother. Having quieted the apprehensions of his officer in respect to his desire to leave him, by saying he had become satisfied with the service, and did not wish to go home; he often had permission, when his ship was in port, to go ashore in the city of New York. Hawkins was not long in improving an opportunity to make his escape, and

Island to Fairfield, about the year 1788. In 1790, a Mr. Lauton made a small clearing in the town, and put up a log cabin which he abandoned. In the fall of 1791, Mr. Hawkins removed into the town, from Fairfield, with a view to a permanent settlement; and in the spring of the following year, he erected a small house for the Bowens on their property, and Benjamin Bowen seated himself there the same year. In 1793, Mr. Bowen built a sawmill, and the next year,

return to North Providence, which he reached late in November, 1778, pretty well satisfied, as he then thought, with a seafaring life. He remained in the service of Obadiah Olney, of Smithfield, between two and three years, when a fit of roaming again came over him, and he went to Providence and shipped on board a privateer brig, of sixteen carriage guns, commanded by Christopher Whipple, Esq. The vessel soon put to sea, and was captured by two British cruisers, on the fifth day after leaving Newport. Hawkins's prospects were again blasted, and his anticipations of enjoying large receipts of prize moneys were changed to a prospect of a long and gloomy imprisonment. The crew of the privateer brig were taken to New York by the captors, and placed on board the Jersey prison-ship. I can not give in detail the contents of the journal before me. The horrors of "that floating hell," as it has often been called, and the cruelties inflicted by the British officers upon the American prisoners, are too familiar to our countrymen, to require repetition now. There can be no doubt that the American prisoners offended against the police regulations of the ship. Starvation, sickness and extreme privations drove them to madness and desperation. These offenses were punished with savage severity.

In the latter part of September, or the beginning of October, 1781, Hawkins and a shipmate, William Waterman, conceived the hazardous project of making their escape from the prison ship, by swimming to Long Island, a distance, as they calculated, of two and a half to three miles, outside of the sentinels posted along the shore. To get clear of the ship was the main difficulty to overcome. It was impossible to leave the upper deck without being discovered. The prisoners were confined, during the night, to the lower deck, where there were no guards, the gun ports of which were secured by iron bars, strongly fastened to the timbers of the ship. Having secured an old ax and crowbar, they went to work during a heavy thunder storm, and removed the bars from one of the port holes of the lower deck, and after replacing them temporarily, to prevent detection, they stowed their wearing apparel, what little money they had, with some other articles, into their knapsacks, which they fastened to their backs, by passing the lashings under their arms, and across the breast. From the description given of the contents of the knapsacks, they must have been very heavy when saturated with

a gristmill, at this place. Joseph Benseley removed from Fairfield to Newport, in 1795; between this time and 1798, William Wakely, Mr. Burton, Stephen Hawkins, George Cook, Nahum Daniels, Edward Coffin, John Nelson, John C. Green, John Churchill, George Fenner and William Whipple, made permanent locations in the town. These families were from Connecticut, Massachusetts, and Rhode Island. Mr. Wakely kept the first tavern, and George Cook opened the

water, and greatly impeded the progress of swimming. Waterman and Hawkins, thus equipped, left the ship, being let down into the water with the aid of their fellow prisoners, by means of an old service rope, which they had obtained.

After reaching the water, Hawkins passed along the side of the ship to the stern, and then struck out for land, being guided by the lights of the vessel and beacon light on shore, one of the extreme points of the line of the enemy's sentinels. Hawkins did not again see Waterman after he left the Jersey, but has no doubt Waterman succeeded in reaching land. After gaining a point out of gun shot distance from the shore, Hawkins was guided by the half hour call of "all's well," by the sentinels on shore, and directed his course to the one on his right, who gave the last call. This he judged would carry him, when he reached the land, to a point of safety. About half an hour before he gained the shore, his knapsack broke loose. He was unwilling to part with it, and endeavored to retain it, by taking it under one arm and then the other; but he lost his course by adopting this expedient, and made slow progress in reaching land. He was finally compelled to abandon his knapsack and the contents, and was left destitute of all covering when he landed, except an old hat. After being nearly three hours in the water, and swimming about three miles, according to his own statement, he reached land cold, stiffened and nearly exhausted. With considerable difficulty he was able to walk, and concluded he would go to the barn that he and Waterman had agreed on as a place of meeting, before they left their prison.

In reaching the barn, he met with several mishaps, tumbled over a pile of stones, and in his nude state he was exposed to and received several severe bruises and scratches, which excited his anger. This he found restored some degree of animal heat, and by the time he had reached the hay in the barn loft, he felt a strong inclination to sleep, although his blankets were not of the finest texture.

Hawkins left his hiding place as soon as it was dark, and wandered all night, he knew not whither, naked and hungry, in a hard storm of rain, and made another barn his refuge and hiding place the next morning. Here he remained until the next day at noon, when he thought it best to issue from his hiding place, and take an observation, with a view of finding out where

first store in the town. Mr. Hawkins derived his title from the commissioners of forfeitures, through Joh's T. Visscher. Coffin, Green, Nelson, Churchill and others, purchased lands on the west side of the creek, in Walton's patent. It will be noticed that this tract of 12,000 acres, was granted by the crown, in 1768, to five brothers by the name of Walton, and seven other persons, who it may be assumed conveyed their interests to the Waltons as soon as the patent was issued, for no one out of that family ever claimed any

he was. This part of Long Island was then infested with tories, and straggling bands of Hessians were prowling about the country. He supposed, by pursuing an easterly course, that he increased the distance between himself and New York. Nothing very material occurred, hunger pressed him very hard, and he went into a potato field to obtain a few potatoes, which he designed to roast when he could find an opportunity, and here he was discovered by a young woman, who had come with a basket to procure some of the vegetable for family use, at a house near by, and seeing a human being with no covering but an old hat, she dropped her basket, and ran screaming towards the house, while Hawkins was quite as nimble footed in reaching a piece of woods in an opposite direction. Here he armed himself with a large club, and directed his course towards a bay or cove in sight, to avoid the tory hounds, which he feared might be put upon his track. He was not, however, molested, and took up his lodging that night in a barn, upon unrotted flax. The next morning, Hawkins arose with the sun, and pursued his journey through the fields, having the road on his right and the bay on his left, observing the farmers at work in the fields, and avoiding them.

Two and a half days of exposure, without food, began to tell pretty severely upon young Hawkins. He saw two young men at work in a garden near a farm-house, and made up his mind that he would speak to them. He approached in a direction so as not to be seen by the people who were at work in the adjoining fields and told them he wanted some old clothes and something to eat. After some explanations one of the young men directed him to sit down where he was and he would go and speak to his mother and see what she had to say about the matter. Hawkins then felt assured that if his case was to be disposed of by a *mother*, he was safe; and so it proved. The young man soon returned to him with a decent pair of trowsers and some food. Hawkins made no unnecessary delay in covering his nakedness and satisfying his hunger. He was then taken to the old lady in an out-house, who asked him various questions, and among others, if he had a father and mother. Hawkins told her he had a mother at Providence, and that his father was then in the American army. She replied, with tears streaming from her eyes, "I wish you were at home." It was arranged between this

interest in these lands, except through the Waltons. At the date of the grant, and even at the outbreak of the revolution, some of the Walton patentees were known to be officers in the army and navy of Great Britain; and all of them living at the commencement of the war, retired to England, except Gerard Walton, who remained in the city of New York during the whole period of its occupation by the British. Now, there is not any question about the Walton title. It is, so far as I know, perfectly good; but how it was preserved and protected from forfeiture and escheat might interest the curious, and elucidate an event connected with our early history.

The first town meeting after this town was erected, took place in 1807; Doct. Westel Willoughby was the moderator; Christopher Hawkins was chosen supervisor and Phineas Sherman, town clerk. Newport village, containing about

kind matron and Hawkins that he should take a shirt and pair of trowsers, then hanging on the fence, and if he was taken up and any question should be asked about them, he was to say he stole them. This kind and patriotic dame then directed young Hawkins where he could find a canoe and oar to take himself across a small bay which lay in his route to Sag Harbor, gave him more food, and sent him on his way home to his mother.

The husband of this lady, and the father of the two young men to whom Hawkins had first addressed himself, had three years anterior to the time now mentioned, been arrested by the British and confined in the Jersey prison-ship, and had died on board that pestilent old hulk, only two or three weeks before Hawkins came to the house. This explains why this kind hearted woman was so cautious and timid. I can not follow the details of the journal any further for want of room.

The only incident worthy of notice in this connection, which occurred to Hawkins on his way to Sag Harbor, happened at Oyster Bay. He was there arrested by a gang of refugees, detained some time, and finally sent on his way back to New York to be again incarcerated in the prison.ship. He met with friendly treatment from one of the citizens at Oyster Bay, after his arrest, who furnished him with clothes and money, and who told him that a boy of his resources and energy could not long be detained in the prison-ship, if his captors succeeded in getting him there. Young Hawkins did not allow himself to be taken back. He escaped from the guard which had him in custody, and finally reached home in safety, pretty well cured of his seafaring propensities. Mr. Hawkins was quite a young man when he came into the county.

700 inhabitants, is a pleasant and healthy location. A gentleman, distinguished by his position; of enlarged and liberal views and accurate observation, and who had several times passed through Newport to Trenton Falls, before the era of rail roads had diverted the travel, told me, he had never seen in this country or in Europe, anything that exceeded in beauty and variety of scenery the valley of the Canada creek, and the route then traveled from the Mohawk to Trenton. He had visited the highlands and lowlands of Scotland, traversed the Alps and the Appenines, navigated the Rhine, and passed through Germany; but had seen nothing that pleased him so much, as the route above mentioned. This village is connected by plank roads, with the canal and Central rail road, at Mohawk and Herkimer, and at Little Falls.

§ 11. Norway

Contains that part of the county beginning at the northeast corner of lot number thirty-seven, in the second allotment of the Royal grant, and running thence east along the tier of lots to the west bounds of Salisbury; then along the same, north, to the south bounds of West Brunswick (now Ohio); then along the same, westerly, to the town of Russia; and then south, along the towns of Russia and Newport, to the place of beginning.

This town contains portions of the second and third allotments of the Royal grant, and not any other original patents or grants from the crown or state.

Fisher Potter, and his father, Jeremiah Potter, with their families, came into the county from Rhode Island, in 1788, and settled about eight miles north of Fairfield village. They opened a small clearing, and built a log hut to shelter them from the snows and frosts of winter. Their whole store of provisions, to carry them through their first long northern winter, was a crop of potatoes, with some salt, and forest game had to supply the residue of a meager subsistence. A gun and suitable ammunition, were indispensable to a frontier forest life, and they were of course provided. A severe tempest had prostrated several acres of the forest, near the place where this family had made their clearing, and this spot in those days was called a *hurricane*, and here were found the white forest rabbit in abundance. The winter set in, and the snow fell in heaps, to the depth of four or five feet, banking up the outside walls of the log hut and rendering it quite comfortable inside, during the whole winter. The men were employed in procuring fuel and hunting game; one cold frosty morning Fisher and his father strapped on their snow-shoes, took their guns and went into the hurricane after rabbits. They had a small dog with them, only useful to start up the small game. While earnestly intent on obtaining something which would render their potatoes and salt a little more savory and palatable, and somewhat more nourishing, they discovered a hole in the snow "nearly as large as a quart cup," extending down to the ground some four or five feet deep. The sides of this hole in the snow were hard, and covered with white frost flakes, showing that there was some heat below, the exhalations from which escaped through this aperture, and kept it open.

Whatever it might be, our pioneers were not backward in finding it out, and Fisher Potter converting his snow-shoes into a shovel, with right good will dug away the snow down to the ground, until he reached a mass of hemlock boughs; and after removing a portion of them, a considerable cavity was observed in the earth below, but nothing more. A question of some importance now presented itself, and that was, whether they should proceed further to uncover the cavity, in order to ascertain its contents, or to resort to other means to find out whether any living animal was still there; finally, the services of the little dog were put in requisition; he was brought to the hole, and after taking two or three scents, barked valorously, but keeping himself ready to make a safe retreat, if needful. This unusual disturbance roused the habitant below from his torpidity, and he gave evident tokens of disquiet. In the mean time, Fisher, believing he had uncovered an animal that would require something heavier than rabbit shot to quiet him, had stepped back a few paces from the hole, charged his gun with a ball, and both were ready for the encounter.

Bruin, not intimidated by the noise, and resolved to punish the intruders upon his dominions with a few heavy squeezes, if he could catch them, presented his comely visage at the hole of his den, when Fisher placing the muzzle of his gun within a few feet of his bearship's head, gave him the whole charge. The bear was killed, and being large and fat, and the meat tender, he was worth more than his weight in white rabbits, to the famishing family. My informant, Mr. A. B. of F., now seventy-four years old, and who possesses a remarkably clear and accurate recollection of the incidents attending the first immigration of the New Englanders into the county, says, he saw old Mr. Potter and his son Fisher, when they first came out of the woods, the spring after the incidents above related. He says Fisher was a tall man, but lean and gaunt when he came out first; his complexion was sallow, and he appeared very much as though he had been nearly starved. Old Mr. Potter said, that killing the bear was a very lucky thing for the family, and probably saved them from starvation, as their other provisions, potatoes and rabbits, when they could kill any, were getting quite short. Mr. Potter lived to a good old age, and died in 1813. Between 1788 and 1790, John, Andrew, and Amos Coe and Capt. Hinman, came into the town from Connecticut; John and David Corp, N. Faning, Thomas Manly and David Underhill, from Vermont; five families by the name of Brayton, from Rensselaer county. The first effort at clearing up farms in this town, was made in 1786, by a Mr. Whipple and Christopher Hawkins, from Rhode Island. They did not prosecute their enterprise. The first grist mill in this town was built by Carpenter Cole, on Du Bois brook; the first saw mill by Capt. David Hinman, northwest of Norway village.

Drs. Willoughby and L. Dewey, and the father of Colonel D. C. Henderson, the latter from Vermont, settled in the town in 1792. Some discrepancy as to dates may exist, growing out of this state of facts. It was often the case, that settlers would come into the town, make a small clearing, put up a log house, and make all the preparations they could in one season, return home in the fall of the year, and bring on their families the next spring. There is no probability that any portion of the Royal grant received any accession of population, after the revolution, until the sale of it was perfected by the commission of forfeitures, and they only sold five of the small lots in the first allotment late in the year 1784.

Norway village lays on the old state road, is located near the centre of the town, and contains about thirty-three dwelling houses and 150 inhabitants. This town must divide the honors with Ohio, in respect to the paternity of Graysville, a small but thriving village on the north bounds of it, and which has grown into importance by the lumber and tanning business. Like all the lands on the Royal grant, those in this town are well adapted to grazing, and butter and cheese constitute its principal agricultural products.

In the year 1842, some members of Mr. Fisk's family, in Norway, in chopping down a maple tree, discovered, near the heart of it, indications of cuts made in the wood with a sharp instrument. The tree being a large one, curiosity was excited, they then chipped off the exterior wood, when they found the plain marks of a blaze, three hacks and a small piece of the edge of an iron or steel hatchet. These wounds appearing to have been made in the tree when it was a small sapling, the parties were induced to make a careful count of the grains of wood that had grown outside of the blaze and hacks, and found three hundred full circular grains of wood formed around the tree. The small piece of the hatchet and a block of wood from the tree were preserved.

A healthy tree makes one new grain or layer of wood a year; these cuts and hacks must, therefore, have been made in 1542, if there was no mistake in counting, and it is said there was none whatever. The inquiry is made, whence came and who bore this instrument, denoting European civilization, more than fifty years before Henry Hudson made his appearance in the bay of New York. Was it obtained from the Spaniards, under Cortes, who first landed in Mexico, in 1509? No permanent settlements were made on the Atlantic coasts of the United States till after the beginning of the seventeenth century, and it is quite certain the hatchet did not come from that quarter. Was it obtained from the French in Canada? No colony was founded there until 1608, by that nation. Whence, then, did it come? It may have been obtained on the sea coast, from the people attached to an European vessel, who had made a temporary landing at some point. But were native Indians accustomed to blaze and notch or hack the forest trees, under any circumstances? Certainly not when on the war path. They never left any such permanent evidences of their whereabouts. The existence of the blaze and hacks inclosed inside of three hundred grains or layers of sound wood, either cast a doubt on what has hitherto been viewed as certain, so far as regards our American forests, or presents an interesting question for antiquarian inquiry.

The extracts given in another chapter, from the journals of two missionaries, sent from Massachusetts, in the early part of the present century, to spy out the nakedness of the land, supply destitute places, and look after the scattered members of their own denomination, descendants of the Pilgrims, will attract some attention to this town. Norway, in 1855, is not what it was in 1801-2. Since then it has been shorn of territory equal to some German principalities, although not quite as productive and populous.

The statistical returns of the late census show there are two Baptist churches in this town, one Episcopal, one Methodist episcopal, and one Presbyterian. I have been kindly furnished with a history of the organization of one of these Baptist churches, to which I cheerfully give a place, premising it with an expression of the deep regret and disappointment I have felt, while penning these sheets, in not being able to do the like with every church organization in the county.

On the 25th of December, 1828, the members of the regular Baptist church, of the town of Newport, then residents of the town of Norway, met at the house of Mr. Dudley Smith, and organized by appointing Mr. Osee Bronson, moderator, and Jefferson Tillinghast, clerk, after the usual religious exercises.

This meeting resolved to petition the "mother church" to be constituted into a church in the town of Norway. The petition was granted May 24th, 1830, and on the 14th of June following the Norway members, 8 males and 15 females, 23 in all, were convened as a conference, a preliminary step to church organization. On the 28th of September, 1830, a council of delegates from the neighboring churches was convened at the Presbyterian meeting house, to consider the subject of organizing a Baptist church in this town. Of this council Samuel Dexter, of Frankfort, was chosen moderator, and the Rev. Willard Judd, of Salisbury, appointed clerk.

The council resolved to fellowship the members of the conference as a church of Jesus Christ. The Rev. Elon Galusha, of Whitesboro, preached on this occasion, and the Rev. William Hogeson, of Stratford, gave the hand of fellowship.

The first pastor of this church was the Rev. R. T. Smith, who commenced his services in January, 1831. He was succeeded by the Rev. W. B. Curtis, C. E. Brown, L. O. Lovel, N. Furgoson, E. D. Towner, Francis Prescott, Mr. S. A. Douglass, a licentiate, and again by the Rev. C. E. Brown, in March, 1853, who is the present pastor of this church. Since its organization, the church has had 294 members connected with it, 170 of whom were added by baptism. The number reported to the association in 1854, was 90. Four members of this church have become ministers of the gospel; and one, a lady, went on a foreign mission to Assam, where she died soon after her arrival. This church has a lay organization, under the statute, which holds the temporalities, the church building and parsonage. The Rev. Mr. Brown promptly furnished the foregoing information. I thank him for it, and have followed his suggestion in another matter.

§ 12. Ohio

Has been recently incorporated or erected. The territory of which this town now comprises a part, was set off from Norway in 1823, and erected into a new town by the name of West Brunswick, since changed to Ohio, in 1836. In 1823, Norway extended to the north bounds of the county, and so did the town of Russia.

Ohio is now bounded on the south by the north bounds of the Royal grant, east by the west bounds of Salisbury, north by the north bounds of Jerseyfield patent, and the same course continued to the east line of Russia, and west by the east bounds of Russia. This town covers a part of Jerseyfield patent, and contains a small triangular part of Remsenburgh patent, lying northwesterly of the West Canada creek, the north bounds of Ohio, and the west bounds of Russia.

Although this town is too recent in its origin to afford any historical events under its present name, worthy of special notice, yet when its present territory formed a part of the Kingsland district during the revolution, it was the theater of one of those cold-blooded and inhuman murders and burnings so often reiterated between 1776 and 1783, as to sicken humanity by the recital of them. Complainings now avail nothing; these astounding crimes were long since perpetrated, and would before this time have been nearly forgotten, but for historical repetition, and the uncertain agency of oral tradition in the localities where the events happened. Does it console us that retributive justice has long since adjudged the case, passed its sentence, and for many years has been and now is executing its dread decree? If it does, let us fold our arms complacently, and await the final execution of the exterminating judgment; but never forget, no, never, the probable cause nor the occasion of these providential visitations, that we may shape our course so as to avoid a similar punishment.

The sufferer's name, Mount, is not found among the ninety-four persons to whom Jerseyfield patent was granted. He planted himself on a handsome plain a few miles north of the south line of the patent, and a little northerly of the usual route taken by the enemy in traversing the wilderness between the Black river and lower Mohawk valley. He probably went there under the patronage of some of the proprietors, and might reasonably expect to end his days in the seclusion that miles of forest afforded him, with nothing "to molest or make him afraid," save the wild beasts of the wilderness. After leaving Black creek on the confines of Norway, passing over a deep clayish soil, some rather stony ground, gently unudulating, and proceeding north a few miles, the traveler will reach the plain where Mr. Mount had seated himself, and if it be in the spring season or at midsummer, he will stop and gaze with admiration at the beautiful prospect before and around him. This is the spot chosen by Mount for his home. Ohio must then be placed in the list of towns in the county settled by whites before the revolution. The West Canada creek crosses the north-west corner of the town.

Ohio City, so called, contains a small collection of houses near the central part of the town, on the road from Utica to Wilmurt and Hamilton county. Graysville, on the south branch of the Black creek, is a small but thriving village, and is situated in the towns of Norway and Ohio. The creek is here the dividing line between the two towns. A triweekly stage now runs from Graysville to Little Falls, and returns the same day. Ohio has increased in population the last five years nearly one-third. The lumbering business is carried on to a considerable extent in this town. Its agricultural statistics do not range as high as some other parts of the county.

A rehearsal of the murder of the two sons of Mr. Mount in Jerseyfield, would be but little more than the naked statement of the fact that the father and mother having gone to the Little Falls with grain to be ground, returned home and found their sons dead in the barn, their scalps taken, and the little negro boy alive anxiously awaiting his master's return. Mr. Mount came from New Jersey. He must have been in Jerseyfield some years when his sons were killed, for he had made considerable improvements, built a house and barn, planted an apple orchard, and gathered around him farm stock and utensils. His secluded position rendered it quite certain, being about twenty miles from the German settlements on the river, that neither he nor his sons participated in the conflict going on between the crown and the colonies, by any aggressive acts against the former, and if he had at any time previously been visited by any of the strolling actors in the bloody drama then being performed, he did not indulge in offensive language, as he seems not to have then been molested.

Mr. Mount's buildings were not at this time destroyed, but they were afterwards burned by some one. A mill on Mill creek, a few miles north of Graysville, was burned when the young Mounts were killed. No one can now fix a time when this affair happened, but some of the men with Col. Willett, stated they dug potatoes at Mount's place when they returned from pursuing Ross in 1782. Mr. Mount, it is said, made all haste to reach a place of safety, and never again returned to Jerseyfield.

Another version has been given me of this Indian murder, by a gentleman who was employed as a surveyor on the tract in 1808, and had gathered his information from persons then living near the Mount farm. From this relation the family consisted of Mr. Mount, his wife, daughter, two sons and a negro boy. Two Indians had been lurking about the place several days, but had not made any hostile demonstrations, as the young men had taken their loaded rifles with them when they left the house, but on the day they were killed and scalped in the barn, they had neglected this precaution. When the report of firearms was heard in the house, the rest of the family fled to the woods and made their way to Little Falls as fast as they could. Mr. Mount did not see his wife and daughter, after leaving his house, until they met at Little Falls. The Indians, my informant says, burned Mount's buildings when they found the family had left the place.

According to this statement the family must have been prodigiously frightened. It is not improbable, nay, it is quite certain, that there were other white families settled in the town near the place called Ohio City, before the revolution.

Mr. David Thorp moved on to the Mount farm soon after the war and lived there many years. His son, David Thorp, was a member of the assembly from the county in 1832.

§ 13. Russia

Contains that part of the county beginning at the southwest corner of lot number twenty-eight, in the third allotment of the Royal grant, and running thence east along the line of lots to the southeast corner of lot number thirty; then north along the line of lots, and the same line continued to the south bounds of the town of Wilmurt; then westerly along the same to the west bounds of the county; and then along the said west bounds to the place of beginning.

This town contains a part of the third allotment of the Royal grant, portions of Jerseyfield, Remsenburgh and Matchin's patents, and the whole of Lush's, Marvin's and Jacobs's patents.

Russia can not boast of anterevolutionary *habitans*, except the wild beasts of the forest, and the roaming Indian in pursuit of game, or on the war path to reach some point of attack, or circumvent a foe. Indeed, no white settlements were made in the town, until after the year 1790. The state road enters the town near the southeast corner of it, runs diagonally across the third allotment, and reaches Boon's

Bridge, on the West creek, a short distance from the northwest corner of the Royal grant. The town is irrigated by several small streams, and among them is Black creek, all of them tributaries of the West Canada, and affording water power for mills and machinery of different descriptions and capacities, and a needful supply for grazing stock. Trenton Falls, the center of the creek, being the boundary line between the two counties at this point, lay partly in this town, and the crossing place where W. N. Butler was killed is pointed out about two miles above the junction of the Black creek with the Canada, so that this town and Ohio must dispute the palm for this locality.

The industrial pursuits of the population are chiefly directed to grazing and cheese and butter making. Utica is the nearest market town of note, and the Utica and Black river rail road now opens the most feasible route to the eastern market, whether by canal or railway, for the products of this town, diverting nearly the whole of its commercial trade to Utica.

Stodard Squires, from Connecticut, was the first settler; he came into the town in the year 1792. The Millington family, from Vermont, and the Smith family, came into the town, and took up lands, within a few years after Squires. Farley Fuller, George Taylor and Roscum Slocum moved into the town about the year 1795, and between that time and 1800 this town settled very fast. John G. Squires, a son of Stodard, was seven years old when his father moved on to the grant. He is now living, and occupies the same farm on which the family located when they came into the town. Mr. Squires is very particular and quite certain as to the locality of the Butler crossing, and his designation of the spot is supported by the declarations of an aged revolutionary veteran, Mr. Williams, who was with the American troops under Willett, and which I have derived from Jeremiah Cory, Esq., late sheriff of the county. Mr. Williams must have visited the spot, giving credence to his own declarations some fifteen or twenty years ago; and Mr.

Squires asserts, that a bayonet and other warlike instruments were found near the place he points out. I have felt very anxious to fix the place of Walter N. Butler's death with reasonable certainty.

It may be assumed then, I think, that the two parties, the pursued and the pursuers, crossed the Canada creek about two miles above the junction of the Black creek with the West Canada, and in the neighborhood of the twin rocks. This place is about twenty-seven miles north of Herkimer village. There is no doubt but the hostile parties crossed the Black creek, and that the American advance and the British rear guards had a pretty smart encounter at that point. I have noticed but one fact in the course of my researches which seems to contradict the position now assumed. The Mount place, at which Willett's party encamped on their return from pursuing the enemy, is several miles nearly due east from this crossing place, and it may not seem probable that Willett, whose object it was to reach the German Flats as soon as possible, with his hungry troops, would have taken that route to reach a point nearly south from this crossing place. But he no doubt had good reasons for retracing his steps upon his recent trail, and this slight deviation from a direct course to Fort Dayton, should not be allowed to overbalance the traditional relations we now have. Ross and Butler, whose object was to reach the Black river, knew the most direct course to reach that point, and they were on it. The destruction of Fort Schuyler "by fire and flood," in May, 1781, and the withdrawal of the troops stationed there to Forts Herkimer and Dayton, render it quite improbable that any of Willett's troops went to the former post in October, 1782. The spot where Butler fell deserves a monument, to point out to unborn Americans where a severe chastisement was inflicted, and where the scourger fell. The mound on the west bank of the creek, formerly pointed out as Butler's grave, has been entirely washed away, and his remains have been scattered over the valleys once desolated by his revengeful arm.

§ 14. Salisbury

Contains all that part of the county, bounded south by Manheim; northerly and easterly, by the bounds of the county; and westerly, by the west bounds of Manheim, continued north to the southerly bounds of a tract called Jersyfield, and then northerly, to the bounds of the county; along a straight line run to the southerly extremity of the division line, between the tracts called Nobleborough and Arthurborough.

A part of Jerseyfield patent, and portions of the first, second and fourth allotments of the Royal grant are in this town.

This town was peopled before the revolution, with several families of tories or persons friendly to the crown, though they may not have committed any overt act of treason against the colonies. Living on the Royal grant, they were, no doubt, the tenants of, or went there under the protection of the Johnson family. They were allowed to remain unmolested by the Indians and tories, during the whole war; but when the commissioners of forfeitures, in 1784, claimed the grant, as the property of the state, they may not have esteemed the protection of their royalist landlords as of much value, or their titles, if they held any, as securing to them "an indefeasable estate of inheritance." One of these people, named Johnson, lived on lot number 154, in the first allotment, Royal grant, on the road between the old Salisbury meeting house and the Four corners. Daniel Lobdell, another of them, lived in the westerly part of the town, about one mile southerly of the old Salisbury meeting house.

These parties were conveniently located, to suit the purposes and accomplish the objects, of those who planted them on the direct route from the Mohawk valley, to the head waters of the Black river. Here the disaffected could congregate in safety, and mature their plans of mischief; and from these points, runners could be dispatched to hover round the out-settlements, collect information, watch the movement of troops in the valley, and even spy out what was going on at the block-houses and stockades, and outside of the principal forts; and here, too, straggling parties of the enemy received aid and comfort, and were seasonably notified of whatever was important for them to know, and within the power of these people to give.

Old Mr. Lobdell had four or five sons, who at an early period of the war went to Canada with a party of Indians, and remained there until after peace was proclaimed. Joe, one of them, was waiter to a British officer, and used to boast after his return, of his sumptuous living while in Canada. He was pensioned by the United States, for revolutionary services. In what way he contrived to convert his menial labor for a British officer, into military service for the colonies, and to make satisfactory proof to the commissioner of pensions, may be best explained by a resort to the records at Washington.

A few New England families may have located in this town, before 1788. Between that time, and 1794, the immigration was pretty rapid. The Salisbury meeting house, since converted into a wagon factory, or an appurtenant to one, was erected during the latter year. Mr. Jabez Ayers put up the first frame building erected in this town. The following names are familiar as being among the early settlers: Avery, Cook, Hackley, Hallett, Todd, Hopson, Burrell and Waterman. The Rev. Caleb Alexander, who visited this town in 1801, as a missionary, says it then contained a population of 1694.

Salisbury Center, is a small village, situate on Spruce creek. Here are several sawmills and other mills and machinery propelled by water, with a large tannery. Salisbury Corners, two or three miles west of the Center, holds a respectable place among the business localities of the town; and Devereaux, at the northeast corner of the grant, has many years been known as a point from which considerable quantities of sawed lumber have been sent to the canal and rail road at Little Falls, for the eastern market. The western section of this town is well adapted to grazing, and the dairy business has been successfully carried on there, for many years. The northern portion is well supplied with hemlock, whence the tanners in that section draw large quantities of bark. The state road passes through the southwest corner of the town.

§ 15. Schuyler

Contains all that part of the county beginning at the Mohawk river, on the line which divides the lands heretofore or late of Eli Spencer and Benjamin Taber in Colden's patent, and running thence in a straight line to the southeast corner of the land now or late of Joel Harvey, on the Steuben road; then to the southwest corner of the town of Newport; then southwesterly along the west bounds of the county to the Mohawk river; and then down the same to the place of beginning.

The whole of Kass's patent and parts of Cosby's manor, and Hasenclever's and Walton's patents are in this town.

This being one of the most ancient towns in the county, as respects the period of settlement, and the most ancient in regard to the crown alienations of title to some of the lands within its territory, "in free and common soccage as of the manor of East Greenwich in the county of Kent," would be looked to for a rich supply of historical incident, and numerous recitals of amusing anecdotes, and thrilling stories of burnings, murders, scalpings, captures and escapes. In this we are disappointed. Several German families had settled within the present limits of the town, before the French war, and among them were the Kasts and Starings; but these were looked upon as outlaying appendages and suburban to the principal Palatine village below. There was a good carriage road in 1757 on the left bank of the river from the crossing where Utica now stands, through Schuyler to the Palatine village, German Flats, which was traversed by M. de Belletre with his French and Indians in 1757. They burned two houses on the Kast patent and every thing in the shape of houses and buildings on the way to the village. The inhabitants soon returned and resumed their occupations, and between this time and 1775 the town had received some additions to its population along the river. There was a store on Cosby's manor in 1766, and John Wolff, Doct. Petry's wife's father, then lived on the manor. The land in Schuyler is generally of good quality, and the river alluvial flats are as strong lands and yield as luxuriantly as any other in the valley. Along the river and about three miles north the surface presents quite a level aspect.

This town, although not the birth place, was many years the residence of Judge Henri Starring, with whose name the reader has become somewhat familiar; and here was concocted the celebrated Yankee pass. There was some additions of German population in this town immediately after the revolution, but the accessions of immigrants from the east and from New England did not take place at an early period after that event. There were formerly several low swampy pieces of ground along the river in this town, in which, if oral tradition speak the truth, more than one unfortunate Indian after the peace of 1783 found an untimely grave. There are no villages in the town. Several efforts have heretofore been made to use the waters of the Mohawk for hydraulic purposes, and considerable sums of money have been expended for that object, but these efforts were unavailing and the money sunk.

This may be properly called a farming town, quite as much so as any in the county; and although the people, for a time, were rather reluctant to change their mode of husbandry, they have now come into the way of getting rich. The loss of population the last five years indicates this result.

§ 16. Stark

Contains all that part of the county bounded northerly by Danube; easterly and southerly by the bounds of the county; and westerly by a line drawn from the easternmost lock of the old canal, on the north side of the Mohawk river at Little Falls, to the head waters of Lake Otsego.

Burr's map of the county shows that parts of Henderson's,

L'Hommedieu's, Vaughn's, McNiel's, J. Vroman's, C. Colden's, Livingston's and Lansing's patents are in this town.

This town, before 1817, constituted a part of Minden, Montgomery county. Before the revolution and at the close of that war, before the organization of towns in this state, this territory lay within the limits of Canajoharie district of Tryon county. All the lands in this town, except a portion of L'Hommedieu's and J. Vroman's patents, which lay within its boundaries, were granted by the colonial government before the revolution. As will be seen by a reference to the table of titles, several of these grants were made about one hundred years ago, and a considerable time before the colonial difficulties comenced with the mother country.

There were two small European settlements near the southerly line of the town, before 1775; one on the Otsquago creek, called the Otsquago settlement, comprising, among others, the Shalls, the Bronners and Fetherlys, whose descendants are yet found enjoying the fruits won by the martyrdom of their ancestors. The other settlement was at the Kyle, so called. This may have been within the limits of Springfield, and a short distance from the east line of the town of Warren. A family by the name of Eckler or Ecklar, had seated themselves at this place on Henderson's patent, or rather, perhaps, Petrie's purchase. Both of these settlements were broken up during the revolution, and the inhabitants compelled to fly for refuge and protection to Fort Plank, where they remained till the close of the war. I visited the Eckler settlement in August, 1854, and found John, one of the sons of Henry Eckler, who was driven off by the Indians and tories, and a younger brother, still on the old homestead which had passed from father to sons, through three generations, and the title yet held by will. No alienations out of the family having taken place, since the first grant, by the patentee. This is an occurrence so unusual, that I have deemed it worthy of particular notice. John Ecklar, at the time I saw him, was 71 years old; he had a brother, Henry, living in Sharon, aged 88 years, the other brother was 68 years of age, a hale and robust man, who evinced a little inquisitiveness about the object of my visit, surmising, perhaps, I might be inquiring into titles to land. The worthy yeoman should have considered his beyond all dispute or impeachment. Emanating from the crown, and sealed with ancestral blood in asserting the just rights of the colonists, followed by a marked possession of an hundred years, who would hazard an inquiry into such a man's right to the soil he cultivated ?

Starkville P. O. and Van Horneville P. O., in this town, situated on the Otsquago creek, are points of some note. A plank road has recently been constructed from Fort Plain through these villages into the northerly part of Otsego county.

Van Horneville affords a very considerable water power, well adapted to manufacturing, milling and mechanical purposes; and it has been appropriated to these objects to a considerable extent, by the enterprising proprietors. Abraham Van Horne, the father of Richard and Daniel Van H., settled here with his family in 1791, opened the wilderness at the head waters of the Otsquago creek, erected houses and built mills. I have been informed that two run of Esopus mill stones for a grist mill, were drawn through the woods by four horses, from the Mohawk river, on a wood-sled. Whether the four stones were taken through the woods as a load, or only one of them, my informant did not state. It was no doubt pretty *hard* sledding, whatever might be the number taken for a load. Mr. Abraham Van Horne emigrated from New Jersey into this state in 1771, and first settled on a farm in the present town of Florida, Montgomery county, and removed from thence in 1783 to Fort Plain. He was a member of the Tryon county committee of safety in June, 1775, from the Mohawk district, and continued a member several consecutive years, firmly attached to the cause of American freedom. He was appointed sheriff of Tryon county, May 22d, 1781, and no man could hold a commission signed by George Clinton, whose devotion and patrotism was doubted in the least. Mr. Van Horne died in March, 1810, at his home place, now called Van Horneville, aged 72 years. The subject of these brief remarks was not, of course, the Abraham Van Horne, one of the patentees of the grant made in 1731, designated by that name; nor was that patentee a member of the Tryon county committee. I have therefore ventured to give Mr. Van Horne the position in the revolutionary contest which family tradition seems to have marked out for him.

The soil of this town appears well adapted to the raising of hops and grain of various descriptions, and agricultural industry seems to have taken that direction to a considerable extent, but grazing and cheese making are not neglected.

According to the census returns, this town contains four churches. One regular Baptist, one Baptist and Lutheran, one Methodist episcopal, one Union. Starkville, in the easterly part of the town, has a population of 110 inhabitants, and Van Hornesville, near the south bounds, has 228. This town appears to have lost 297 in population out of 1775, since 1845, and this within a decade of almost unexampled success and prosperity with the agricultural classes.

§ 17. Warren

Contains all that part of the county bounded westerly by Columbia, southerly by the bounds of the county, easterly by the bounds of the county and the west bounds of Stark, and northerly by German Flats and Little Falls.

It embraces the principal part of Henderson's and Theobald Young's patents.

The reader of these pages has no doubt observed that there were settlements of whites some distance south of the Mohawk river before the revolution. These were principally, if not entirely, composed of Germans from the upper valley. Andrustown, so called, and the settlement at the Little lakes, were within the present limits of the town of Warren.

In March, 1792, Samuel Cleland, from Colchester, Massachusetts, came into this town and settled, with his family. This was the first New England family that immigrated hither. Mr. Cleland had five sons, Norman, Salmon, Jonas, Martin and Moses. Jonas and Moses now survive, the former being 75 years old. Norman died in 1831, aged 62 years, and Salmon went to his final rest at the advanced age of 84 years. Martin died when about 20 years old. The father, Samuel Cleland, died at Warren, October 10th, 1834, aged 90 years, 4 months and 14 days. Danforth Abbot, Hugh Panel and Amos Allen, from Massachusetts, settled in this town about the same time. Elder Phineas Holcome, the first settled minister in that part of the county, came in soon after Mr. Samuel Cleland. This town was organized in 1796, four years after the immigration from the east set in, and must have filled up pretty fast. Jonas Cleland, Esq., informed me that when his father first came into the county, he located himself not far from the German settlement of Andrustown. That he found the bones of a man unburied near the charred ruins of a dwelling, and collected and interred them. The tradition of that day designated these human bones as the remains of a Mr. Bellinger, who escaped to his house when that hamlet was sacked and burned by the tories and Indians, during the revolution, and would not quit it when set on fire. He preferred thus to die, rather than endure the lingering torments of captivity and death, perhaps according to the savage mode of infliction. A man must be bold, resolute and determined, who would so resolve and act. Let it not be said he exhibited a stolid indifference to life. He had seen, perhaps, his wife and children slaughtered, and might expect the same fate when within reach of the tomahawk. His cattle had been collected and driven away, the Indian firebrand had been applied to his barn, stacks and other property, and looking at death as certain, he placed himself on the funeral pyre, and awaited its approach.

Warren is the southernmost town in the county, is nearly eight hundred feet above the level of the Mohawk river, high ground from which the waters descend northerly, easterly and southerly. The surface of the land is considerably undulating, and the soil generally appears quite as well adapted to hop and grain growing as grazing. There are, however, a number of large dairy farms in the town. Owing to the large quantities of manure required to keep the hop fields in good yield, the dairy business has been found a profitable adjunct in the farming line. There is to me a something so homelike and lifelife in the appearance, at midsummer, of large fields of Indian corn, grain of various descriptions and potatoes, I can not resist giving utterance to the reflection, that such a people must abound in wealth, because they are not dependent.

The principal local points in this town are Crain's corners P. O., Jordanville P. O., Page's corners, and the Little lakes, Warren P. O. Andrustown still retains its local name, and here are found descendants of the German Palatines, who first opened the forest on Henderson's patent; the Shoemakers, Bells, Crains, Hoyers, and others. The Little lakes, whose waters discharge into the Otsego, are in the extreme southeast part of the town, three miles east of Richfield springs. The great western turnpike passes through the village located between these two small bodies of water. The white cedar swamp lands in this town are nearly as valuable as any other in it. The timber is used for hop poles.

§ 18. Wilmurt

Is the largest town in the county, and probably in the state, and contains that part of the county commencing at the southwest corner of the town of Morehouse (in Hamilton county), and running westerly on the north line of the Jerseyfield patent, until it strikes the West Canada creek; thence continuing the same course of said Jerseyfield line, until it strikes the west line of Herkimer county; thence northerly, on said line, until it strikes the north boundary line; thence easterly, along the north bounds of said county, until it strikes the northwest corner of the town of Morehouse; thence southerly, on said line, to the place of beginning.

Within these boundaries are all those parts of Remsemburgh and Vroman's patents, Adgate's, Brown's, Nobleborough, Moose river and Watson's tracts, and Totten and Crossfield's purchase, which lie in the county.

This town has trebled its population in five years, to be attributed to the increase of the lumber business, under the direction of the Messrs. Hinckley and others, who are largely engaged in that trade in the north part of the county. The legislature have heretofore appropriated $5000, to remove obstructions from the West Canada creek; obstructions which hindered the floating of logs and unsawed lumber from the sources of the creek, during the spring floods, to an extensive set of mills in operation near Prospect, Oneida county, where many millions of feet of boards, plank and other sawed lumber are cut out annually, and sent to market.

The machinery of these mills, and all the arrangements for booming and securing the logs, bringing them to the ways, where they are to be taken on to the saw carriages, and for removing the plank and boards when sawed, and disposing of the refuse stuff, are spoken of as being equal to any similar establishment in the country. The mineral regions of this town will be approached, if not immediately intersected, by the Saratoga and Sackets Harbor rail road.

In 1792, Alexander Macomb, of New York, purchased of the state 1,920,000 acres of land, at nine pence per acre, lying in the northern part of the state, and the same year John Brown, of Rhode Island, bought of Macomb, or obtained the title to, about two hundred thousand acres of that purchase, which was afterwards divided into eight townships, numbered from one to eight inclusive, and townships number one, two, six and seven were also subdivided into small lots. This tract does not lay on Moose river proper, and only a small triangular point of township number eight extends into Hamilton county. The westerly parts of towns one, two, three and four are in Lewis county. This has been many years called Brown's tract. According to Burr's map of the county, a northerly branch of the Moose river runs through the southern portion of the tract. Mr. Brown visited his lands near the close of the last century, made some improvements in the way of opening roads, building houses and erecting mills, intending and expecting to make sale of them. Mr. Brown died, however, before he realized any of his anticipations, and no doubt a great many more men will die before that wilderness will be seen "to blossom as the rose." In 1846, the commissioners of the land office were offered *five cents* an acre for a considerable portion of townships one and two, but they refused to take less than eight cents an acre.

A son-in-law of Brown, Mr. Charles F. Herreshoff, went on to the tract a few years after the death of Brown, for the purpose of making permanent improvements upon it and bringing the lands into market. This project was quite as visionary, far more expensive, and in the end, more fatal to the projector, than the antecedent one had been to Brown. Herreshoff expended a large sum of money in clearing up the lands, repairing the former mills built by Brown, and erecting new ones, in building houses and opening roads, and at one time had gathered around him some thirty or forty families. He also erected some iron works in township number seven, and actually succeeded, it is reported, in making about one ton of iron. But Herreshoff's outlays were large, and it required something more "to speed the plough" than could be raised on the tract, or from the proceeds of the iron; he therefore resorted to the expedient, which he doubtless had often indulged in before, of drawing on his friends in Providence for the needful means to consummate a dearly cherished object. The draft was returned to him protested; he felt dishonor keenly, and deliberately shot himself through the head with a pistol. He was ardent, ambitious, probably visionary, and could not have had much practical experience of the business he was engaged in; and if he died "as a fool dieth," it was a choice of evils with him. He preferred death, a suicidal exit from the world, to the crushing endurance of mortified feelings, groping his way through life in poverty, and as he thought, covered with dishonor.

After Herreshoff's death the people he had brought there left the settlement, and iron works, mills, barns and houses, with one exception, went rapidly to decay. It is understood that sometimes one and then another family has been found bold and hardy enough to keep watch and ward on the tract since Herreshoff died. A great portion of the tract, if not all of it, has been sold for arrears of taxes and bid in by the state.

In 1815, a Mr. Noble, a venerable patriarch, and nephew of the patentee of Nobleborough patent, had found his way there through the woods, and was enjoying a wilderness life as he best could in a green old age. It will be observed that this large tract was purchased of the state by Arthur Noble in 1787; he made some improvement on these lands as early as 1790, and then erected a sawmill and had some boards sawed out which he took to Ireland. The settlement broke up and another effort to colonize the tract, in 1793, was made with the like success. The remains of a grist and sawmill were seen at this settlement about the year 1811 by Mr. William Bensley of Newport. Mr. Noble must have been influenced by a monomania like that of John Brown's, when he caused a carriage road to be cut and cleared to his lands, over which he passed in his coach. Mr. Noble sojourned for a time at Little Falls while his experiments in the woods were going on, but finally returned to Scotland, where he died many years since. There are large quantities of excellent timber on the lands in this town, of almost every description, except pine, found in our northern latitude. Portions of the surface are broken and stony, and other portions can be brought under cultivation and will make fair grazing lands. The iron mines of this region are spoken of as rich and inexhaustible.

§ 19. Winfield

Contains all that part of the county, beginning in the west bounds of the county, where the same are intersected by a line run due east from the northeast corner of township number twenty of the Twenty townships, so called, and running thence easterly to a bound on the south side of the Utica and Minden turnpike at the southeast corner of the town of Litchfield; and then south thirty degrees west to the bounds of the county; and then along the bounds of the county easterly, southerly and westerly to the place of beginning: comprising within its bounds parts of Bayard's, Lispenard's and Schuyler's patents.

This town was settled by whites before 1800, but at what period I am not able to state; probably between that time and 1790. A small part of it lay within the limits of the Old England district until the municipal organization of the counties in this part of the state into townships took place. Its area is not large, containing only about fifteen thousand acres, as returned by the assessors. The soil is good and highly productive. More attention has been here given to wool growing than any other town in the county. The products of butter and cheese, as given by the census returns, show that this branch of industry has not been forgotten.

Several streams which flow southerly into the Unadilla river, have their rise in this town and Litchfield, and afford very considerable facilities for milling and mechanical pursuits, which have not been left unimproved. The Great Western turnpike passes through the southerly part of the town, which, before the days of canals and rail roads, was a large thoroughfare thronged with stages, carriages, teams and droves of cattle, but now almost a solitude.

The village of West Winfield, whose population is nearly four hundred, is located very near the west bounds of the county. It contains an academy incorporated by the regents of the university. I refer the reader to another chapter for a more particular description of this institution. The locality is pleasant and healthy. A bank organized under the laws of the state has recently been established in this village. The plank road from Ilion on the Mohawk to the Great Western turnpike, a short distance east of this place, has caused a very considerable portion of the trade and travel of the Unadilla country to center at and pass through the village northerly to the canal and Central rail road.

List of Towns in the county and the number of voters in each, and list of Villages and Population in each, in 1855:

	Towns.	Voters.		No. Aliens.	No. School Houses.	Names of Villages.	When Incorporated.	Population in 1855.
		Native	Naturalized.					
1	Columbia,.......	453	3	67	11	Cedarville, ...	....	145
2	Danube,.........	334	42	265	9	Coldbrook, ...	....	218
3	Fairfield,........	314	9	180	12	Frankfort, ...	....	1150
4	Frankfort,........	557	83	345	15	Herkimer,....	April 6, 1807,.	1371
5	German Flats,....	775	107	337	11	Ilion, ...	Nov'r 3, 1852,	812
6	Herkimer,.......	542	56	339	12	Little Falls,...	March 30, 1811	3972
7	Litchfield,.......	307	50	188	10	Mohawk, ...	April 16, 1844,	1355
8	Little Falls,......	856	196	612	11	Jordanville, ..	....	125
9	Manheim, ...	325	39	167	9	Middleville, ..	....	295
10	Newport,........	405	37	196	10	Newport,.....	....	671
11	Norway,.........	224	18	198	10	Salsbry Center	....	319
12	Ohio, ...	188	31	135	7	Poland, ...	....	179
13	Russia,..........	475	38	236	17	VanHonesville	....	228
14	Salisbury,......	457	44	246	14	Starkville,....	....	190
15	Schuyler,........	328	58	217	11	Jacksonburgh,	....	206
16	Stark,...........	358	12	107	9	Brocket's Br.,.	....	389
17	Warren,.........	465	11	69	11	Inghams Mills,	....	132
18	Wilmurt,........	41	9	71	2	Russia,.......	....	140
19	Winfield,........	307	24	80	10	West Winfield	....	381
		7711	867	3955	201			

APPENDIX.

No. 1. *Referred to at page 42.*

[Council Minutes XIII, page 162.]

At a Council held in Albany, the 9th day of September, 1721. Present: His Excellency, William Burnet, Esq., &c.; Capt. Walter; Mr. Cadwallader Colden; Mr. James Alexander.

The petition of several Palatines, in behalf of themselves and others, at Skohere, praying his Excellency's leave to purchase a Tract of Land on the Mohacks River, for their use and settlement, which his Excellency communicated to this Board.

It is the opinion of the Council, that the Palatines have leave to purchase a certain Tract of Land, in the name of his Majesty, upon the Mohacks River, above the fall, about forty miles beyond Fort Hunter, and that the said purchase be made within a year after the date of the Lycense, to be in pursuance hereof, a Patent will be granted to them, their heirs and assigns, under the same Restrictions and Reservations as other vacant lands are granted to his Majesty's Subjects in this Governmt, they taking care the said Land be not granted, Purchased or Patented to any others from the Governmt heretofore.

INDIAN DEED.

To all christian people or Indians to whom these presents shall come at any time, Know ye that we being some of the principal sachems or chiefs of the five Nations of Indians, belonging to the crown of England, do for ourselves, to and with the consent of all other Indians belonging and proprietors of a certain tract, parcell or parcells of land lying and being on both sides of the Mohawks river, beginning at the first carrying place, being the eastermost bounds, called by the natives Astenrogen, running along on both sides of the said river westerly unto Garrendagaraew, or the upper end of it, it being about twenty-four English miles long on both sides of the said river, Together with all the woodland northerly and southerly of the said meadow land as far as the said Palantines or High Dutchmen please to take, containing about in acres we know not, do of our own free will, and for the respect we have for the Government of New York, and likewise we have taken into consideration of the number of Christians that came from England called Palantines or High Dutch men, which now want land to manure to maintain their familys; and we having land enough that cannot use, Do for ourselves, our heirs, executors and administrators, that is our children and children's children for ever, Do give, grant, sell, alien, enfeoffe and confirm, and by these presents Do give and grant, sell, alien, enfeoffe and confirm, all the aforementioned premises, unto John Conradt Wiser Jun., Jacob Kop, John Jose Petres, Conradt Rygerds, Nicholas Fuller, Henry Mayor, Ausorian Smith, Rutles Karring, Peter Spice, Peter Waggoner, Peter Connift Kerne, Jacob Warynoo, &c., with all other High Dutch men or Pallantines in this Government, for a settlement, and we have heard that it is his Excellency's desire, and do grant it for a small consideration of payment, the whole premises above mentioned unto the said Pallantines or High Dutch men now under the crown of England, and to their heirs, executors, administrators and assigns for ever, all and singular the above mentioned premises with the appurtenances thereunto belonging; To have and to hold all the aforesaid lands with the woods, underwoods, pasture ground, meadows, lowlands, uplands, rivers, rivuletts, islands, the grass, the timber, and timber woods and all the appurtenances and privileages in the said bounds belonging or in anywise appertaining unto the aforementioned High Dutch men or Pallantines of this Government under the crown of Great Britain, and to their heirs, executors, admts and assigns for ever, To their sole and only proper use and behoofe for ever. In witness whereof, we the native owners and proprietors of the aforementioned premises, Do set our marks and take of the seale, that our children's children may know from this day, being the ninth of July, annoq Domini 1722, and we do likewise impower and authorize to sign, seale and set the mark belonging to us the five nations, as they are our chief Sachems one, two or three of every nation. FRERYORIS, a Mohawk, his hand mark and seal [L. S.]. KAHYAWGAHROTUN, being the mark of the Undogos, and seal [L. S.] [L. S.]. KANECGARAH, the Senkes mark and seal [L. S.] ODOSSECTOH, the mark and seal of the Onido [L. S.] [L. S.]. The mark and seal of the Cawyogos [L. S.] [L. S.]. Signed and delivered in the presents of us, Interpreter Laurens Clasens, Leo Stevens [L. S.], her mark, Interpreter, Josa Sanderse Glen, Justice; Adam Vrooman, Justice; Jan Wemp, Justice.

[Council Minutes XIV, page 81.]

At a Council held at Fort George, in New York, January ys 17th, 1722-3.

Present: His Excellency William Burnet, Esq., &ca.; Collo. Beekman, Mr. Van Dam, Mr. Barberie, Mr. Harrison, Doctor Colden.

Petition of John Jost Petrie and Conradt Rickert, in behalf of themselves and others, the Palatines, concerned in the Purchasing of Lands of the Indians, setting forth, That in pursuance of his Excellency's Lycence, the 9th of September, 1721, they had purchased of the Indians a tract of land lying above the fall of the Mohacks River, which is about forty miles to the westward of Fort Hunter, and praying that the same may be surveyed according to the Indian purchase now produced to this Board, in order that they may obtain his Maties Letters Patent, was read.

Ordered, that the said petition, together with the Indian purchase, be referred to the Gent. of this Board, or any five of them.

His Excellency withdrawing, the Gent. of this Board Resolved into a Committee.

His Excellency returning to the Council Chamber, took his place at the Board.

Then the Gentlemen of the Committee, to whom was referred the petition of John Jost Petri and Conradt Rickert, Palatines, in behalf of themselves and others, reported that they had considered of the same, and were of opinion that his Excellency may grant to the Petitioner and such other Persons as are now desirous to settle the Limits of the Tract Petitioned for so much of said Land as they shall be willing to take up in the following manner vizt. That every person, Man, Woman and Child be entitled to one hundred acres each, and that before the survey be made, the number and names of all the Persons to be concerned be certified to the Surveyor General or his Deputy before the Survey be made, which Report was approved of by the Board, and this Board does advise and consent that his Excellency may Grant the said Land under such quit rent, Reservations and Restrictions as is and are directed in his Excellency's Instructions from his Majesty.

It is the opinion of this Board, that, considering the number of People for whom this Tract is Petitioned; it will not be contrary to the meaning and design of the said Instructions if the whole Tract should extend in its greatest length upon the Mohacks River, since the Tract to be allotted to any particular Person or Family is not to do so.

Ordered, that this Opinion of the Board be exprest in the Warrant to the Surveyor General.

No. 2. Referred to at page 200.

LIST OF PATENTS OR TRACTS OF LAND

In the County of Herkimer, with the date of the Patent, number of acres therein, and name of Patentee.

Adgate's Patent.—Date, 1798; 43,907 acres; Matthew Adgate, patentee.

Bayard's Patent.—Date, 1771; 50,000 acres; *Wm. Bayard, Robert Bayard,* Joshua Mulloch, Thomas Shipboy, Peter Sylvester, Henry Van Schaack, Robert Adams, Richard Cartwright, James Phyn, *Wm. Kane,* Allen McDougall, George Lindesay, Jacob Brower, John Van Dalsem, Rudolph Sickles, William Benson, James A. Stewart, Alexander Stewart, Jun., Robert Henry, Robert McLallan, John Vernor, William Proctor, Adrian Renaudet, Carden Proctor, Richard Nassau Stevens, Thomas Edwards, John

Constable, Alexander Ellis, John Duncan, Dunlap Adams, Wm. Adams, James Adams, David Edgar, Wm. Edgar, James Rankin, Jane Lyle, John Van Alen, Barent Van Alen, Abm. Schenck, Henry Remsen, Henry Remsen, Jun., John Taylor, Joseph Griswold, Robert Harding, John M. Brelun, Wm. Butler, Frederick W. Hecht, George Ball, John Gregg, Wm. Jones, Thomas Pettit, Robert Ross, Richard Hazard, William Dudley and Thomas Griswold, patentees.

Brown John's Tract.—Date, 1792. This tract is part of the 1,920,000 acres of land granted to Alexander Macomb, by letters patent dated January 10, 1792.

Burnet's Field Patent.—Date, 1725; 9400 acres; John Jost Petri and others (see the names chap. iii, p. 44).

Colden Cadwallader's Patent.—Date, 1738; 3,000 acres; Cadwallader Colden the younger, and Coenradt Ryghtmeyer, patentees.

Cosby's Manor.—Date, 1734; 22,000 acres; Joseph Worrell, William Cosby, John Lyne, Thomas Freeman, Paul Richards, John Felton, Charles Williams, Richard Shuckburgh, Timothy Bagley, James Lyne and Frederick Morris, patentees.

Colden Alexander's Patent.—Date, 1761; 4,000 acres; Alexander Colden, William Willett, Stephen DeLancey and Christopher Blundell, patentees.

Frank Coenradt's Patent (commonly called Staley's 3d Tract).—Date, 1765, 5,000 acres; Coenradt Frank, Frederick Frank, George Herchkeimer, Michael Stigh and Peter Piper, patentees.

Fall Hill Patent.—Date, 1752; 2324 acres; Johan Joost Herkimer and Hendrick Herkimer, patentees.

Freemason's (see *Bayard's*) *Patent.*

Glen's Purchase.—Date, 1739; 1660 acres; Jacob Glen. (It appears that the tract of land called *Glen's Purchase*, in the county of Herkimer, was laid out into thirty-nine lots, and granted to different persons, as follows):

Patrick McClaughry and Andw. McDowell, 1738; 3710 acres; lots 10, 16, 17, 26, 37.

J. DeLancey, J. Lindsay and Abm. Glen, 1738; 5426 acres; lots 3, 5, 7, 11, 19, 20, 29, 34.

Lendert Helmer, 1739; 1970 acres; lots 13, 21, 38.

Jacob Glen, 1739; 1660 acres; lots 15, 25.

Archibald Kennedy, 1739; 1950 acres; lots 12, 22, 30.

John Schuyler, Jr., 1739; 1990 acres; lots 14, 24, 35.

Arent Bradt, 1739; 1907 acres; lots 6, 23, 27.

Philip Schuyler, 1739; 1863 acres; lots 9, 18, 36.

Samuel Auchmuty, 1761; 1090 acres; lots 31, 32, 33.

William Mitchell, 1761; 1910 acres; lots 2, 8, 28.

William Ogilvie, 1761; 2000 acres; lots 1, 4, 39.

Wm. Alexander and Henry Frey, two of the executors of John Porteus, deceased, to Alexander Ellice. Deed dated March 19, 1801, conveying, among others, the following lots of land, viz:

Lot No. 27 in Burnetsfield, south side of the Mohawk river, and lots Nos. 12 and 13, in same Tract, north side of the said river, each containing 100 acres. (Recorded in the Secretary of State's office.)

Hasenclever's Patent.—Date, 1769; 18,000 acres; Peter Hasenclever, David Greame; Mary Croftes, James Crawford, George Jackson, John Elves, Arthur Forest, Richard Willis, John Duval, Thos. Dampier, Wm. Robertson, Wm. Berry, Neal Ward, Mary Lucy Sleech, Hutchinson Mure, Catharine Hasenclever, Mary Elizabeth Hasenclever and Charles Croftes, patentees.

Henderson's Patent.—Date, 1739; 6000 acres; James Henderson, John Kelly and James Henderson, younger, patentees.

Henderson's or Petrie's Purchase.—Date, 1740; 6000 acres; Philip Livingston, John De Peyster and John Jost Petrie. This patent consists of lots 1, 2, 8, 9, 15 and 16, in the Tract called Henderson's or *Petrie's Purchase.*

Johnson Guy's Patent.—Date, 1765; 2000 acres; Guy Johnson, patentee.

Jerseyfield Patent.—Date, 1770; 94,000 acres; Henry Glen, Alexr. Campbell, John Visscher, Jr., Philip Garlock, Harmanus H. Wendell, Alexander Ellis, Cornelius Cuyler, Simon Schermerhorn, John McCrea, Christopher Yates, Nicholas Brando, Petrus Dederick, Wilhelmus Osterhout, Isaac Vrooman, Ryer Wemple, Myndert R. Wemple, Mary Vrooman, John Farril, Jacob S. Vrooman, Tunis Van Vleck, Wm. Lyghtall, Hendrick Brower, Jun., John Baptist Wendell, Frederick Auker, Segar Van Sandford, Myndert Wemple, Volkert Vedder, Omie Le Grange, Jacob Jacobse, Myndert La Grange, James Shuter, Robert Clench, Wm. Peters, Abm. C. Groot, Harmanus Wendell, Lucas Van Vechten, Philip Van Vechten, Cornelius Wendell, Jacob H. Wendell, John H. Wendell, Barent W. Vrooman, Jacob A. Vrooman, John Walker, Jacob Lansing, Samuel Van Slycke, Simon Schermerhorn, Jun., Adam Van Slyck, Harmanus Bradt, Nicholas Van Petten, Hendrick Brower, Arent Van Petten, John Brown, Caleb Beck, Matthew Lyne, John Mynderse, Wm. Hanna, John Duncan, Mary Grant, John Abeel, Garret Abeel, Evert Byvanck, Jun., Gerard Bancker, John Byvanck, Benjamin Stymets, Isaac Sloover, Derick Brinckerhoff, John Baptist Van Eps, Isaac Truax, Jacobus Mynderse, Jacobus Van Eps, Peter Truax, Wm. Phillips, James Cotter, John Tyms, James Mordaunt, Alexander McCullagh, John McIntyre, Alexander Stewart, Edward Laight, John Lamb, John Tayler, Edward Nicoll, Charles Nicoll, Charles Doughty, Wm. Whitehead, Elizabeth Breese, John Van Sice, Volckert P. Douw, James Deas, Samuel Bayard, Sen., Angus McDonald, Samuel Breese, Samuel Doughty and John Visscher, patentees.

Kast Johan Jurgh Patent.—Date, 1724; 1100 acres; Johan Jurgh Kast, Lodowick, Sarah, Dorothy, Margaret, Elizabeth, Mary and Anna Mary, children of said Johan Jurgh Kast, patentees.

L'Hommedieu's Patent.—Date, 1786; 4000 acres; Ezra L'Hommedieu and Nathaniel Platt, patentees.

Lindsay's Patent.—Date, 1730; 3000 acres; John Lindsay and Philip Livingston, patentees.

Livingston's Patent.—Date, 1762; 20,000 acres; Philip Livingston, Rudolph Keller, John Burk, Edward Earl, Samuel Bailey, Wm. Denning, Wm. Livingston, Jeremiah Van Rensselaer, *Peter Dubois*, John Hansen, John James Beekman, Peter Hansen, Roger Townsend, Wm. McCracken, John Cuyler, Myndert Burger, Michael Hugo Frazier, Wm. Bailey, Gerardus Lansingh and Philip Lansingh, patentees.

Lansingh's Patent.—Date, 1753; 6000 acres; Jacob Lansingh, Abm. Lansingh and Jacob Glen, patentees.

Lispenard's Patent.—Date, 1770; 9200 acres; Leonard Lispenard, Leonard Lispenard, Jr., Anthony Lispenard, David Johnston, Stephen De Lancey, John Fitzpatrick, Jordan Cook, Peter Stuyvesant, Tunis Somerndyck, Martin Shier, Geo. Stanton, Henry Stanton, Rose Graham and Mary Graham, patentees.

Macomb's Purchase.—Date, 1792; John Brown's Tract consists of part of 1,920,000 acres of land, granted to Alexander Macomb, Jan. 10, 1792.

McNiel's Patent.—Date, 1761; 4000 acres; John McNeil, Alexander McKey, Alexander Stewart and Oliver Templeton, patentees.

Machin's Patent.—Date, 1786; 1600 acres; Thomas Machin, patentee.

Moose River Tract.—Date, 1847; 13,080 acres; Anson Blake, patentee. Township No. 1 not granted, except 2 lots; township No. 2 not granted; township No. 5 not granted, but one lot.

Nobleborough Patent.—Date, 1787; 40,960 acres; Arthur Noble, patentee.

Royal Grant (or Kingsland), granted to Sir William Johnson by Letter's Patent under the great seal of England. It is not recorded in the secretary of state's office, and neither the date of the patent nor the number of acres granted are known. It was subdivided into four allotments.

Remsenburgh Patent.—Date, 1787; 48,000 acres; Henry Remsen, George Klock, Jacob G. Klock and Dirck Van Ingen, patentees.

Schuyler's Patent.—Date, 1755; 43,000 acres; Abm. Lynsen, David Schuyler, Nicholas Packard, Peter D. Schuyler, Gerardus Stuyvesant, James Livingston, John Willett, Leonard Lispenard, Gualtherus Dubois, Peter P. Schuyler, Nicholas Bayard, Christopher Bancker, Samuel Heath, John Van Cortlandt, Philip Van Cortlandt, Wm. Kelly, David Vanderheyden, Robert Benson, John De Peyster, Jr., John Meyer, Augustine Moore and Conradt Mathyse, patentees.

Snell and Timmerman's Tract.—Date, 1755; 3600 acres; Jacob Timberman and Johan Joost Schnell, patentees.

Staley's Patent, 1st and 2d Tracts.—Date, 1755; 34,000 acres; Rudolph Staley, *Johan Jost Herckheimer, Jun.*, Thomas Schoonmaker, Peter Bellinger, Jun., Frederick Orendorph, Hans Michael Ittig, Jun., Nichs. Woolaver, Hendrick Spone, Augustus Hess, Christopher Fox, Rudolph Schoonmaker, Samuel Broughman, Jacob Ittigh, Jacob Kesslaer, Nichs. Herckheimer, Hans Dederich Staley and Geo. Kesslaer, patentees.

Totten and Crossfield.—Date, 1786; 25,200 acres; Zephaniah Platt, patentee.

Township No. 42 divided into 127 lots; very few lots granted: township No. 45, township No. 50, divided into lots and sold by the state

Van Driesen Petrus' Patent.—Date, 1737; 1,000 acres; Petrus Van Driesen, patentee.

Van Driesen John's Patent.—Date, 1786; 428 acres; John Van Driesen, patentee.

Van Horne's Patent.—Date, 1731; 8,000 acres; Abraham Van Horne, Wm. Provoost, Philip Livingston and Mary Burnet, patentees.

Vaughan's Patent.—Date, 1770; 8,000 acres; John Vaughan, Cornelius Cuyler, *Abm. Cuyler*, Henry Cuyler, Catharine Cuyler, Andrew Meyer, Adam Borger and James Stephenson, patentees.

Vrooman's Patent.—Date, 1790; 9760 acres; Isaac Vrooman, patentee.

Vrooman's Patent.—Date, 1786; 4,000 acres; Isaac Vrooman, patentee.

Vrooman's Patent.—Date, 1790; 433 acres; Isaac Vrooman.

Watson James' Tract.—Date, 1792. This appears to be part of the 1,900,000 acres granted to Alexander Macomb, January 10, 1792.

Winne's Patent.—Date, 1741; 2,000 acres; Peter Winne, patentee. [There is a tract of 4,000 acres in Canajoharie granted to Peter Winne and James Dillon in 1741].

Walton's Patent.—Date, 1768; 12,000 acres; Wm. Walton, Jun., Jacob Walton, Thomas Walton, Gerard Walton, Abm. Walton, Anthony Van Dam, John Van Dam, Robert Ross Waddell, John Keen, Wm. Ross, Robert Hyslop and Christopher Dudley, patentees.

Young's Patent.—Date, 1752; 14,000; Theobald Young, Adam Young, Frederick Young, Andries Young, Gerrit Staats, Henry Douw, Jacob Ten Broeck, Gerardus Groesbeck, Benjamin Nicoll, Henry Holland and Cornelius Ten Broeck, patentees.

No. 3. Referred to at page 201.

[Land Papers, vol. XVI, 45.]

To the Honble. Cadwallader Colden, Esqr., President of His Majesty's Council and Commander in Chief of the Province of New York and the Territories depending thereon in America:

The Petition of Sir William Johnson, Baronet, Ferrall Wade, George F. Cheap, James Rogers, Dennis Madden, John Johnston, William Johnston, Peter Frax, Michael Russell, Wilhelmus Russel, Paul Reiter, Philip H. Klyne, John Spangenbergh, Lucas Veder, Lawrence Eman, Michael Sallenger, Matthias Link, Hanthy Creitz, George Stam, George Stam, Junr., Peter Cooley, John Johnson, Peter Servis, Christopher Servis, Francis Rupert, Adam Rupert, Hannis Wert, Andreas Snyder, Conradt Creitzenbergher, Conradt Smith, Jonathan French, Jacob Pickle, Hannis Wolfe Barlet, Augustus Eikler, Jacob Sefer, Johannis Alt, Bastian Steenmyer, Stephen Kipp, George Kipp and Peter Frederick. Humbly Showeth:

That there is a Tract or Parcel of Vacant Land, situate lying and being in the County of Albany on the North side of the Mohawks River near to the Conajoharie Castle, and beginning at the Northwesterly Corner of the Rear line of a Patent or Tract of land purchased by the late Teady McGin and others and lately surveyed by his Widow Sarah McGin, which Corner or beginning is on the Bank of a Creek or Kill called by the Indians Dekayoharonwe, and about thirteen miles from the Mohawks River, which Creek falls into the said Mohawk River about Two hundred Yards below Fort Hendrick or Conajoharie Castle, thence running from the Said Northwesterly Corner of said McGin's rear line a Westerly Course to the West bank of another Creek or Kill, called by the Indians Deyoshtoraron, by the Christians Canada Kill at Burnetsfield, from thence down along the West side of the said Creek or Kill to the Lands Patented formerly, So down to the Mohawk River then Running round the Several Tracts of Land already Patented within the Above mentioned two Creeks, and taking in all the Vacant Lands between the said two Creeks from the Rear Line Quite to the Mohawks River, Containing about Forty Thousand Acres of Land; which your Petitioners are desirous immediately to settle and improve, being willing to submit to such Restrictions as to the Settlement or Cultivation of the said Tract of Land as shall be judged Reasonable.

Your Petitioners therefore humbly Pray Your Honour will be favourably Pleased to Grant to them Your Honour's Lycense to purchase in his Majesty's Name of the Native Indian Proprietors thereof the Quantity of Forty Thousand Acres of the Tract of Land above described in Order to enable them to obtain his Majesty's Letters Patent for one Thousand Acres to each of the Petitioners, Under the Quit Rent Limitations and Provisoes directed and Appointed in his Majesty's Instructions.

And Your Petitioners as in duty bound shall ever Pray, &c.

Wm. Johnson,
In behalf of himself and his Associates.

New York, 27th March, 1761.

8th July, 1761, Read and referred to a Committee.

[Council Minutes XXIII, 368.]

At a Council held at Fort George in the City of New York, on Wednesday the Eighth day of July, 1761. Present: The Honoble Cadwallader Colden, Esqr., President and Commander In Chief &ca.; Mr. Kennedy, Mr. Horsemanden, Mr. Chambers, Mr. Smith, Mr. Watts, Mr. Walton.

The Petition of Sir William Johnson, Baronet, Ferrall Wade, George F. Cheap, James Rogers, Dennis Madden, John Johnston, William Johnson, Peter Frax, Michael Russell, Wilhelmus Russell, Paul Reiter, Philip H. Klyne, John Spangerburgh, Lucas Veder, Lawrence Eman, Michael Sallenger, Mathias Link, Hanthy Creitz, George Stam, George Stam, Junr., Peter Cooley, John Johnson, Peter Servis, Christopher Servis, Francis Rupert, Adam

Rupert, Hannis Wert, Andreas Snyder, Conradt Creitzenbergher, Conradt Smith, Jonathan French, Jacob Eickle, Hannis Wolf Barlet, Augustus Eikler, Jacob Sefer, Johannis Alt, Bastian Steenmyer, Stephen Kip, George Kip and Peter Frederick was presented to the board and read, setting forth that there is a Tract or parcel of vacant Land situate, Lying and being in the County of Albany, on the North side of the Mohawks River, near to the Conajoharie Castle, and beginning at the Northwesterly Corner of the Rear line of a Patent or Tract of Land purchased by the Late Teady McGin and others, and lately surveyed by his Widow Sarah McGin, which Corner or beginning is on the Bank of a Creek or Kill, called by the Indians Dekayoharonwe, and about Thirteen miles from the Mohawks River, which Creek falls into the said Mohawks River about Two hundred Yards below fort Hendrick or Conajoharie Castle, Thence running from the said Northwesterly Corner of the said McGin's rear Line, a westerly Course to the West bank of another Creek or Kill, called by the Indians Deyoshteraron, by the Christians Canada Kill at Burnets field, from thence down along the West side of the said Creek or Kill, to the Lands patented formerly, so down to the Mohawk River, then Running round the several Tracts of Land already Patented within the above mentioned two Creeks, and taking in all the Vacant Lands between the said Two Creeks from the Rear line Quite to the Mohawks River, Containing about forty thousand acres of Land, which your Petitioners are desirous Immediately to settle and improve, being willing to submit to such Restrictions as to the Settlement and Cultivation of the said Tract of Land, as shall be judged Reasonable; and therefore humbly praying a Lycence to purchase in His Majesty's name, of the Native Indian Proprietors thereof, the Quanty of Forty thousand acres of the said Tract of Land, in order to Enable the Petitioners to Obtain His Majesty's Letters Patent for One Thousand Acres to Each of the Petitioners.

On Reading whereof it is Ordered that the said Petition be Referred to the Gentlemen of the Council or any five of them.

No. 4. *Referred to at page 243.*

MEMBERS OF THE HERKIMER COUNTY MEDICAL SOCIETY, AND DATES OF ADMISSION.

1806. Westel Willoughby, Jr., George Rogers, Andrew Farwell, Amos Haile, Jonathan Sherwood, Rufus Crain, Isaac Sears, Abijah Tombling, David Perry, John Eastman, Samuel Redfield.

1807. Benjamin Hazen, Nathan Harwood, Jacob Abrams, William Frame, James Hadley.

1808. Francis Smiley, James Kennedy, Jacob L. Sherwood.

1809. Asa Flint.

1810. Nathaniel Jacobs, Harvey W. Doolittle, Josiah Noyes.

1812. Roland Sears.

1813. David Dixerson, Seth S. Beck.
1814. William R. Ellis, Nathan S. Willard.
1817. John Warner.
1818. Martin L. Bryan, John Holmes.
1819. Calvin W. Smith, Stephen Todd.
1820. Abel Millington, Benjamin G. Ellis, Bryant Burwell, Elijah Hanchet.
1821. Caleb Budlong, Silas Clark, Jonathan Averill, Thomas Phelon, Sylvanus Dewey, Warren Day.
1822. James Carder, Abel Hannahs.
1823. Abner N. Clark, Hozea Hamilton, Elisha Powell, Lester Green.
1824. Moses Johnson.
1826. John R. Brown, Hubbel Lowrie, James McGee, William Noble.
1827. J. S. Spaulding, Henry Lockwood, William Van Zant.
1828. David Coon, Albert W. Bowen, Francis B. Etheredge, Peter Sherwood.
1829. David Bingham, Peter P. Murphy, Guy Marshal, Bonaparte Philio, Elias Palmer, Daniel Belknap, Jr., Ezra A. Mulford, Z. Waldo Bingham, Professor Allen.
1830. Daniel Harvey, Ira C. Backus, Nelson Isham.
1831. Killhorne Hannahs, Alfred Ladd, Justus H. Vincent, John De Lamater, William Mather, Shadarick N. Vincent, Alfred E. Varney.
1832. Hiram Hadley, Preston Chamberlin, Walter Booth.
1833. James F. Johnson, Meazer Hall, Andrew F. Doolittle.
1834. Al-Frederick Smith, Elisha Powell, Nathan Spencer, David I. Pashall, John Everett.
1835. Brazilla Budlong, Abram Snyder, Simon Goodell.
1836. Leonard Haskins, C. L. Easton, James Wheeler.
1837. Charles Shepard.
1838. James M. Row, Amos Rolan, Abel Green, Alanson White, Calvin A. Griffith.
1839. Dr. Gaylord, Dr. Loomis.
1840. Silas A. Ingham, Ira Smith, W. H. Parkhurst, Milton W. Gray.
1841. Peter Hawn.
1842. John H. Champion, Charles W. Fox.
1843. ——— Coe, ——— Williams.
1844. Harvey Hunt, George Beakley, Horace Day, Stephen Turtelott.
1845. Adam Miller.
1848. S. R. Millington, P. Pruyn.
1850. John Duffin, A. H. Holmes.
1852. Abram Hawn.
1854. James E. Casey.

No. 5. Referred to at page 292.

LIST OF SHERIFFS, SURROGATES, CLERKS AND COUNTY JUDGES OF HERKIMER COUNTY:

SHERIFFS.

William Colbreath,	1791	Stephen Hallett,	1821
Peter Smith,	1795	John Dygert,	1826
William Colbreath,	1796	John Graves,	1829
Chauncey Woodruff,	1798	Fred. P. Bellinger,	1832
William H. Cook,	1802	Francis E. Spinner,	1835
Ephraim Snow,	1806	Stephen W. Brown,	1838
William H. Cook,	1807	William C. Crain,	1841
John Mahon,	1808	Jeremiah Cory,	1844
Philo M. Hackley,	1810	William J. Skinner,	1847
John Mahon,	1811	Daniel Hawn,	1850
Henry Hopkins,	1813	Lorenzo Carryl,	1853
John Mahon,	1815	Peter Countryman,	1856
Robt. Shoemaker,	1817		

SURROGATES.

Moses Dewitt,	1791	Nathl: S. Benton,	1821
Arthur Breese,	1794	Arphaxed Loomis,	1828
Sanford Clark,	1798	C. S. Benton,	1837
Dan Chapman,	1803	Lauren Ford,	1841
Philo M. Hackley,	1807	Ezra Graves,	1845
Dan Chapman,	1808	Robert Earl,	1856
Abijah Tombling,	1816		

CLERKS.

Jonas Platt,	1791	John Mahon,	1821
Joab Griswold,	1798	Jabez Fox,	1823
Elihu Griswold,	1804	Abijah Beckwith,	1826
Peter M. Myers,	1810	Julius C. Nelson,	1832
Elihu Griswold,	1811	John Dygert,	1835
Aaron Hackly, Jr.,	1812	Erwin A. Munson,	1841
Peter M. Myers,	1813	Standish Barry,	1847
Aaron Hackly, Jr.,	1815	Elkenah T. Cleland,	1853
Walter Fish,	1817	Cornelius T. E. Van Horne,	1856

JUDGES.

*Henry Staring,	1791	Abraham Hardenburgh,	1791
Michael Myers,	1791	*Henry Staring,	1794
Hugh White,	1791	Michael Myers	1794

* First Judge.

Hugh White, 1794
Jedediah Sanger, 1794
*John Frank, 1794
James Dean, 1794
*Henry Staring, 1797
Hugh White, 1797
Jedediah Sanger, 1797
John Frank, 1797
James Dean, 1797
*Jedediah Sanger, 1797
Phineas Gates, 1798
John Meyer, 1798
Evans Wharry, 1798
Michael Myers, 1799
John Meyer, 1799
Evans Wharry, 1799
Phineas Gates, 1799
Benjamin Bowen, 1800
*John Meyer, 1800
*Evans Wharry, 1805
Nathan Smith, 1805
George Rosencrantz, 1805
Walter Fish, 1805
Westel Willoughby, Jr., 1805
George Rosencrantz, 1808
Westel Willoughby, Jr., 1808
Walter Fish, 1808
David V. W. Golden, 1810
*David V. W. Golden, 1811
George Rosencrantz, 1811
Walter Fish, 1811
Westel Willoughby, Jr., 1811
*Nathan Smith, 1814
George Rosencrantz, 1814
Walter Fish, 1814
Westel Willoughby, Jr., 1814
Rudolph Devendorff, 1814
George Rosencrantz, 1817
Walter Fish, 1817
Westel Willoughby, 1817
Rudolph Devendorff, 1817
David Holt, 1817
John McCombs, 1817
Rufus Crain, 1817
George Paddock, 1817
Almond Luce, 1817
Daniel Hurlbut, 1817
John Herkimer, 1817
George Rosencrantz, 1820
Westel Willoughby, 1820
David Holt, 1820
John J. Prendergast, 1820
*David Holt, 1821
John Herkimer, 1821
Sanders Lansing, 1821
Almond Luce, 1821
Rufus Crain, 1821
*Henry Brown, 1823
Sanders Lansing, 1823
Rufus Crain, 1823
John Mahon, 1823
Edmond Varney, 1823
*Hiram Nolton, 1825
Rufus Crain, 1828
John Mahon, 1828
Sherman Wooster, 1828
Augustus Beardslee, 1828
*Michael Hoffman, 1830
*Nathaniel S. Benton, 1833
*Arphaxed Loomis, 1835
Jonas Cleland, 1833
John B. Dygert, 1833
Abijah Osborn, 1833
Richard Herendeen, 1834
John B. Dygert, 1838
David R. Currier, 1838
Charles Gray, 1838
Ira Coe, 1840
*Arunah C. H. Smith, 1840
Augustus Beardslee, 1843
John W. Beckwith, 1843
Boughton Everatt, 1843
*Ezra Graves, 1845
Asa Vrickey, 1845

* First Judge.

Attorneys and Counselors.

Peter P. Mesick, Jan. 16, ... 1805
William W. Dougherty, May 26, 1807
Aaron Hackley, Jr., Oct. 7, ... 1807
Artemas Stoel, July 22, ... 1808
Theodore H. Chapin, Oct. 8, ... 1808
Matthew Myers, May 23, ... 1809
William D. Ford, May 23, ... 1809
Benj. Wright, Jan. 19, ... 1810
William J. Dodge, Jan. 3, ... 1811
Geo. H. Feeter, Oct. 1, ... 1811
Henry Brown, Jan. 8, ... 1812
Lauren Ford, Jan. 10, ... 1812
Jabez Fox, Jan. 7, ... 1813
Joseph Mason, Jr., May 5, ... 1813
Gaylord G. Pinney, Oct. 6, ... 1813
Hiram Nolton, Oct. 5, ... 1814
Ralph Waterman, Oct. 5, ... 1815
Daniel Grant, Dec. 12, ... 1815
Michael Hoffman, Dec. 14, ... 1815
James Macauley, Dec. 14, ... 1815
William B. Goff, July 4, ... 1817
Nathaniel S. Benton, July 9, ... 1818
Chas. J. Bartow, April 7, ... 1819
Thos. L. Conkling, April 8, ... 1819
Oran G. Otis, Oct. 6, ... 1819
Jeduthan Steele, April 6, ... 1820
Chas. Gray, May 7, ... 1822
Jared S. Maynard, Dec. 31, ... 1822
Augustus Beardslee, Dec. 27, ... 1824
Arphaxed Loomis, May 2, ... 1825
Abijah Osborn, Jan. 1824
James B. Hunt, Jan. 1824
Herkimer Sternberg, Sept. 5, ... 1825
Dudley Burwell, Sept. 7, ... 1825
James Brown, Dec. 29, ... 1825
E. S. Capron, Feb. 3, ... 1829
Saml. Phillips, Oct. 6, ... 1829
Volney Owen, Oct. 1831
Danl. Tisdale, Oct. 2, ... 1832
John Bartow, June 3, ... 1833
Jarvis N. Lake, June 13, ... 1833
Ezra Graves, Feb. 7, ... 1834
F. J. Littlejohn, Feb. 1, ... 1830
Edward C. Pinney, June 12, ... 1830
Levi Downing, Oct. 9, ... 1830
Hiram Riggs, Feb. 11, ... 1831
A. W. Enos, June 13, ... 1832
Geo. B. Judd, June 1, ... 1829
A. C. H. Smith, June 2, ... 1828
E. P. Hurlbut, June 3, ... 1828
Joseph Hunt, Feb. 5, ... 1828
Henry W. Clarke, Oct. 3, ... 1836
Hugh Henderson, Feb. 1, ... 1836
Rodman L. Joyce, Feb. 1, ... 1836
G. F. Van Vechten, Feb. 8, ... 1837
Daniel Gros, Feb. 6, ... 1837
Almanzor D. Fish, June 6, ... 1837
Geo. B. Wood, June 6, ... 1837
William B. Holmes, Oct. 2, ... 1837
Thos. C. Ripley, Feb. 8, ... 1833
E. B. Talcott, June 5, ... 1838
John C. Underwood, June 4, ... 1835
William Brooks, Jr., June 4, ... 1838
Ely T. Marsh, Feb. 14, ... 1839
William W. Mann, June 5, ... 1839
Wm. R. Anthony, Oct. 8, ... 1839
Jos. Benedict, Feb. 3, ... 1840
Sebeus C. Maine, Feb. 7, ... 1840
I. E. L. Hamilton, Oct. 5, ... 1841
John A. Rasback, Oct. 13, ... 1841
Delos Lake, Feb. 8, ... 1842
Henry H. Cozens, Feb. 9, ... 1842
Wyman Trask, Feb. 9, ... 1842
Geo. N. Middlebrook, June 15, . 1842
E. W. Smith, June 5, ... 1843
D. F. Monk, June 5, ... 1843
John Runyan, Jr., June 6, ... 1843
Huet R. Root, Feb. 5, ... 1844
M. K. Gaines, Feb. 7, ... 1844
A. C. Harris, June 3, ... 1844
Wm. Barrett, June 3, ... 1844
Phocion Hoffman, Oct. 17, ... 1844
A. H. Prescott, Feb. 4, ... 1845
Chas. A. Burton, Feb. 6, ... 1845
Jos. N. Wightman, Feb. 11, ... 1848
Saml. Earl, Oct. 7, ... 1848

Elkenah T. Cleland, Oct. 7,.... 1848	Robert Earl, June 10,.......... 1847
John H. Wooster, Feb. 3,...... 1846	Chas. S. Benton, Feb. 2,....... 1835
Levi Parsons, Feb. 10,......... 1847	Peter L. Fraser, Feb. 5,........ 1835

District Attorneys.

Michael Hoffman,............. 1823	Hiram Nolton,................ 1837
George H. Feeter,............. 1825	Hiram Nolton,................. 1840
Aaron Hackley,............... 1828	Hiram Nolton,................. 1843
Jas. B. Hunt,................. 1833	George B. Judd,.............. 1848
Simeon Ford,................. 1836	Volney Owen,................. 1851
Michael Hoffman,............. 1836	Volney Owen,................. 1854
Dudley Burwell,.............. 1836	

Prior to the above, I find among the old indictments on file that the first District Attorney of this county, was the Hon. Nathan Williams. The next I am able to find was Joseph Kirkland, whose appointment it would seem must have been about the year 1815. The next, Thos. H. Hubbard, who it seems officiated in the years 1817 and 1818, when Simeon Ford was appointed, who held up to the commencement of Mr. Hoffman's first term.

No. 6. *Referred to at page* 292.

[The list of Members elected to Congress is prefaced by an abstract of Congressional Districts.]

1797, March 28, the legislature passed a law forming Montgomery and Herkimer into a congressional district without designation as to number. In 1798, when Oneida county was erected, the former territory of Herkimer set off as Oneida and to Chenango was retained as a congressional district with Montgomery and Herkimer.

In 1802 the counties of Herkimer, Oneida and St. Lawrence composed the 15th congressional district of the state and elected one member. In 1808, Herkimer, Lewis, Jefferson and St. Lawrence composed the 10th district. In 1812, Herkimer and Madison formed the 18th district. This county was constituted the 15th district in 1822. In 1832 Herkimer and Lewis formed the 16th district. In 1842 Herkimer and Montgomery formed the 17th district, and in 1851 St. Lawrence and Herkimer were constituted the 17th congressional district.

This was a most remarkable conjunction. The people of these two counties have as much intercourse with each other, and probably less than those of Jefferson, and Suffolk counties. Although the territory of the two counties joins, there can be no personal communication between the inhabitants except through Jefferson, Lewis and Oneida counties by the western route; or Franklin, Clinton, Essex, Warren, Washington, Saratoga, Schenectady and Montgomery counties by the eastern route; or if preferred the railways will enlarge the circuit by way of the Atlantic Ocean on the east, or Niagara Falls and Lake Ontario on the west, when the steamers are afloat. Any communication by way of the adjoining territory for purposes of business is wholly impracticable.

Names of Electors

Of President and Vice President of the United States, chosen from the county since its organization and the year of election:

Peter Smith,	1796	Henry Ellison,	1836
George Rosencrantz,	1812	Thomas Burch,	1840
Nicholl Fosdick,	1816	Asa Chatfield,	1848
Rufus Crain,	1828	William C. Crain,	1852

Members of Congress.

1802. Gaylord Griswold.
1808. John Nicholson.
1814. Westel Willoughby, Jr.
1818. Aaron Hackley, Jr.
1822. John Herkimer.
1824. Michael Hoffman, who was reelected in 1826, 1828 and 1830.
1832. Abijah Mann, Jr., who was reelected in 1834.
1836. Arphaxed Loomis.
1842. Charles S. Benton, who was reelected in 1844.
1846. George Petrie.
1848. Henry P. Alexander.
1850. Alexander H. Buell, who died at Washington, after a short illness, near the close of his congressional term.
1854. Francis E. Spinner.

Members of Conventions

Called to amend the State Constitution.

1801. Evans Wharry, Mathias B. Tallmadge, George Rosecrants.

This convention was called to consider certain specified subjects named in the act of the legislature, passed April 6th, 1801, in reference to the constitution 1777. The convention sat at Albany and completed its labors October 27th, 1801.

1821. Sanders Lansing, Richard Van Horne, Sherman Wooster.

This convention was assembled pursuant to the recommendations contained in an act of the legislature, passed March 13th, 1821, to revise the constitution of 1777. It was held at Albany, adopted many radical changes in the former constitution and closed its sessions November 10th, 1821. This constitution was ratified by the people at a special election held on the 15th, 16th and 17th days of January, 1822.

1846. Michael Hoffman, Arphaxed Loomis.

Pursuant to the recommendations of the act passed May 13th, 1845, this convention assembled at Albany, and completed its labors October 9th, 1846.

The whole frame work of the fundamental law of 1822, was reconstructed by this body and many radical changes made. The constitution agreed to by this convention was ratified by the people November 3d, 1846.

MEMBERS OF THE STATE SENATE

Elected from Herkimer County from its first organization in 1791 to the present time.

1796. Michael Myers, held four years.
1802. John Meyer, held one year.
1803. Matthias B. Tallmadge, held four years.
1806. Nathan Smith, held two terms.
1815. John J. Prendergast, held one term.
1819. George Rosecrantz, held one term.
1823. Sherman Wooster, held four years.
1828. Nathaniel S. Benton, held his seat three years and three months. Resigned April 14, 1831.
1835. Abijah Beckwith, held one term.
1842. Edmund Varney, held one term.
1848. Thomas Burch, held two years.
1850. George H. Fox, who held until the spring of 1851, when he resigned and John Sanford of Montgomery county was elected in his place for the residue of the senatorial term.

The senatorial terms from the organization of the state government in 1777 to 1846 were four years; and by the ratification of the present constitution, these terms have been reduced to two years. Until 1822 all state elections were held in April of each year, and the legislative term commenced on the first Monday of July following. Since and including 1822, state elections have been held in November of each year, and the legislative term commenced on the first Tuesday of January following. This will explain what might otherwise seem a little incongruous in the years noted.

MEMBERS OF ASSEMBLY

From the erection of the county to this time.

1792. Michael Myers.
1793. Same.
1794. Jedediah Sanger.
1795. Same.
1796. Jonas Platt.
1797. Isaac Brayton, Gaylord Griswold, Joshua Leeland, Henry McNiel, Arthur Breese, Mathew Brown, Jr., Lodowick Campbell.
1798. Gaylord Griswold, Henry McNeil, Nathan Smith, Mathew Brown, Jr., Benjamin Bowen, Lodowick Campbell, Isaac Foot.
1799. Phineas Gates, John Cummins, Jr., Lodowick Compbell.
1800. John Mills, Thomas Manly, John Myer.
1801. Evans Wharry, George Widrig, Nathan Smith.

1802. Nathan Smith, George Widrig, Samuel Merry, Jr.
1803. Samuel Wright, George Widrig, Stephen Miller.
1804. Evans Wharry, Samuel Wright, George Widrig.
1805. Same.
1806. George Widrig, Samuel Wright, Eldad Corbit.
1807. George Widrig, John Kennedy, Samuel Wright.
1808. Westel Willoughby, Jr., John M. Petrie, Aaron Budlong.
1809. Same.
1810. Thomas Manly, Christopher P. Bellinger, Rudolph Devendorff.
1811. Christopher P. Bellinger, Robert Burch, Hosea Nelson.
1812. Robert Burch, Rudolph J. Shoemaker, Samuel Woodworth.
1813. Rudolph I. Shoemaker, Hosea Nelson, John Graves.
1814. Aaron Hackley, Jr., Jonas Cleland, Christopher P. Bellinger.
1815. Aaron Hackley, Jr., Jonas Cleland, John McCombs.
1816. John McCombs, Henry Hopkins, William D. Ford.
1817. Abijah Beckwith, George Rosecrantz, William D. Ford.
1818. Aaron Hackley, Jr., Nichol Fosdick, George Rosecrantz.
1819. Nichol Fosdick, Jonas Cleland, Henry Gros.
1820. James Orton, Jacob Markell, Philo M. Hackley.
1821. Simeon Ford, Thomas Manly, Daniel Van Horn.
1822. Simeon Ford, Stephen Todd, Robert Shoemaker.
1823. John Dygert, Abijah Beckwith, Henry Tillinghast.
1824. Christopher P. Bellinger, John Graves, Caleb Budlong.
1825. Samuel Dexter, Jr., Warner Folts, Jacob Wire.
1826. Jonas Cleland, Nicholas Schuyler, Edmund Varney.
1827. Frederick P. Bellinger, Richard Smith, 2d, Daniel C. Henderson.
1828. David R. Currier, Abijah Mann, Jr., John P. Snell.
1829. Abijah Mann, Jr., John B. Dygert, Cornelius Sloughter.
1830. Frederick P. Bellinger, Abijah Mann, Jr., Russell Hopkins.
1831. Atwater Cook, Jr., Nicholas Lawyer, Olmstead Hough.
1832. William C. Crain, David Thorp, Daniel Dygert.
1833. Sherman Wooster, Dudley Burwell, Joseph M. Prendergast.
1834. Charles Dyer, Augustus Beardslee, Timothy J. Campbell.
1835. Henry Tillinghast, Peter P. Murphy, Charles Gray.
1836. Stephen Ayres, Frederick Bellinger, Thomas Hawks.
1837. Aaron Hackley, Henry L. Easton.
1838. Abijah Mann, Jr., Volney Owen.
1839. Atwater Cook, Jr., Benjamin Carver.
1840. Daniel Bellinger, George Burch.
1841. Michael Hoffman, Arphaxed Loomis.
1842. Same.
1843. John T. Hall, Walter Booth.
1844. Michael Hoffman, Peter H. Warren.
1845. William C. Crain, Alexander H. Buell.
1846. William C. Crain, Henry Eysaman.

1847. Abijah Beckwith, Jefferson Tillinghast.

1848. James Feeter, 1*. Lawrence L. Merry, 2*.

1849. Frederick P. Bellinger, 1*. Asa Wilcox, 2*.

1850. Asa Vickery, 1*. Humphry G. Root, 2*.

1851. John H. Wooster, 1*. Daniel Shall, 2*.

1852. John Hoover, 1*. Charles Delong, 2*.

1853. Arphaxed Loomis, 1*. John Beckwith, 2*.

1854. Gardun Hinkley, 1*. Dean Burgess, 2*.

1855. Edmund G. Chapin, 1*. William Bridenbeeker, 2*.

1856. Samuel Green, 1*. Amos H. Prescott, 2*.

ADDITIONAL NOTE.

In 1777-8, Michael Edic and Abraham Van Horne were Members of Assembly from Tryon county.

In 1778-9, George Henry Bell and Abraham Van Horne.

1781-2, William Petry.

1782-3, William Petry and Andrew Frinck.

1786, Abraham Van Horne was a member from Montgomery county.

1788-9, Henry Staring.

1789-90-91, Michael Myers.

The persons bearing the above names have been noticed in this work. It is therefore proper to append the information contained in this note.

* The numeral figures designate the number of the assembly district.

INDEX.

LIST OF BOOKS

PUBLISHED BY

Joel Munsell, 78 State st.,

ALBANY, N. Y.

Considerable interest being now manifested, among book collectors, in the subject of American Local History, the attention of such is requested to the following list of respectable works in that line, and to all others the suggestion is respectfully made, that a library of American History is at least a suitable appendage to the household of every American citizen.

Retail Prices.

History of Herkimer County, including the Upper Mohawk Valley. By N. S. Benton. 1 vol. 8vo, cloth,........ 2 50

Life and Times of Gen. John Lamb, an Officer of the Revolution, who commanded the post of West Point at the time of Arnold's defection, and his correspondence with Washington, Clinton, Patrick Henry, and other distinguished men of his time. By Isaac Q. Leake. 1 vol. 8vo, 432 pp. Portrait and Maps. Sheep,........ $2 00

This is a valuable contribution to the history of the American Revolution, presenting a mass of new facts in relation to the preliminary movements of the principal actors in that great drama, derived from the papers of Gen. Lamb, and other sources not before investigated.

Notes on the Iroquois, or contributions to American Ethnology, chiefly in relation to the Aboriginal History, Population and Antiquities of Western New York. By Henry R. Schoolcraft, 2 colored Portraits (King Hendrik and Pocahontas). 1 vol. 8vo, cloth,........ 2 50

History of Schoharie County, and Border Wars of New York, By J. R. Simms. 1 vol. 8vo, sheep (scarce),........ 2 50

History of St. Lawrence and Franklin Counties, New York, from the earliest period to the present time. By F. B. Hough. 1 vol. 8vo. Portraits, maps and cuts, cloth,........ 3 00

History of Jefferson County, in the State of New York, from the earliest period to the present time. By F. B. Hough. 1 vol., 8vo, maps, portraits and cuts, cloth,........ 3 00

Burgoyne's Campaign, an original, compiled and corrected account of, and the memorable battle of Bemis's Heights, Sept. 19, and Oct. 7, 1777, from the most authentic sources of information, including many interesting incidents connected with the same; and a map of the Battle Ground. By Charles Neilson. 1 vol. 12mo, morocco,........ 1 50

American Genealogy, being a History of some of the Early Settlers of North America and their Descendants, from their first emigration to the present time, with their intermarriages and collateral branches, including notices of prominent families and distinguished individuals, with anecdotes, traditions, sketches of the founding of cities, villages, manors, and progressive improvements of the country from its wilderness state to the present era, illustrated by genealogical tables. By JEROME B. HOLGATE. 1 vol. 4to, ½ Turkey morocco,.. 5 00

Annals of Albany. By JOEL MUNSELL. 6 vols. 12mo, 6 00

> Its contributions to history and antiquities contain much that is curious and interesting, obtained at no little cost of time and labor. No one has done more to recall the ancient features of the city. Curious in these matters, the author culls and preserves them in their antique forms, and thus rescues them from the oblivion into which the structures, the ways, the customs, and even the names of the olden times would otherwise be liable to pass. The modern names and places, by the side of the ancient annals and things, combine the past and the present in useful and interesting juxtaposition. The curious in these researches will find this book a treasure, and well worth the price. It has fine views of Albany, as it is, and illustrative wood cuts and maps; but its chief interest consists in its portraiture of Albany as it was in the olden time.—*Argus.*

Typographical Miscellany. (Historical and Practical.) By J. MUNSELL. 1 vol. 8vo Cloth,.. 1 00

Trappers of New York, or a Biography of Nicholas Stoner and Nathaniel Foster; together with Anecdotes of other celebrated Hunters, and some account of Sir William Johnson and his Style of Living. By JEPTHA R. SIMMS. 1 vol. 12mo, cloth,.. 1 00

American Biographical Panorama. By WILLIAM HUNT. 1 vol. 8vo, 480 pp. with portraits of all the signers of the Declaration of Independence, ½ sheep,.. 2 00

Memorial of Ambrose Spencer, former Chief Justice of the Supreme Court of the State of New York. 1 vol. 8vo, with portrait,.... 1 50

Map of the City of Albany, colored and bound in cloth, 25

Every Day Book of History and Chronology, embracing the Anniversaries of Memorable Persons and Events in every period and state of the world, from the creation to the present time. By JOEL MUNSELL. 2 vols. 12mo, ½ sheep.. 2 00

> This work discovers great research and good judgment, and especially as a work of reference is deserving of all praise. Its great value consists in its bringing together a multitude of important facts from the four winds and presenting them in a form which renders them at once accessible to every body. To every student this book is a perfect labor-saving machine; and to persons of every description it will be found of great value, as bringing a great amount of valuable matter within very narrow limits.—*Argus.*

American Geology, containing the Principles of the Science and their Application to Mining, etc., by Dr. E. EMMONS, 1 vol. 8vo, illustrated on stone and wood,.. 3 00

Helderbergia: an apotheosis of the Anti-Rent War. Albany, 1855. 54 pp. 8vo, paper,.. 50

Cases of Personal Identity, 1 vol. 8vo, ½ calf,.......... 1 00

American Literary Magazine, by T. DWIGHT SPRAGUE. Albany, 1847. 2 vols. 8vo, ½ sheep, ... 3 00

Transactions of the Albany Institute, 3 vols., 8vo, with illustrations, ... 7 50

Catalogue of the Library of the Albany Institute. 1 vol. 8vo, ½ morocco, 1855, ... 3 00

The Model Pastor: Life, &c., of Rev. Elisha Yale, D. D. By Rev. JEREMIAH WOOD. 1 vol. 12mo, cloth, ... 1 25

Catechism for the use of Evangelical Lutheran Churches, 18mo, paper, ... per hundred, 4 00

Albany Directory. By J. MUNSELL. 12mo, ½ cloth, ... 1 00

Gospel Crown of Life. A System of Philosophical Theology. By THOMAS MITCHELL. 1 vol. 8vo, cloth, ... 1 00

Webster's Calendar, or the Albany Almanac; Astronomical calculations prepared with accuracy and care, and copyrighted by J. MUNSELL. 36 pp., 12mo, paper, ... 06

This is the oldest almanac now published in the United States, having been commenced in 1784. The trade supplied, by the gross or thousand, at short notice, with advertisement on last page if desired, at a liberal discount.

Frequent calls being made for back numbers, considerable pains have been taken to gather them, so that sets may be had, from the year 1844 to the present time, embracing twelve years, in paper covers, price one dollar.

Lucinda, or, the Mountain Mourner, being authentic facts in a series of Letters from MRS. MANVILL, in the state of New York, to her sister in Pennsylvania. 12mo (paper 25 cents), cloth, ... 50

Contributions to the knowledge of the different kinds of Brand in Cereals and Blight in Grain. By A. C. CORDA. Translated from the German by E. Goodrich Smith, of the United States Patent Office. 32 pp. 4to. 3 steel plates, paper 50 cts. (large paper copies), ½ morocco, ... 1 00

Conversations on the Present Age of the World in connection with Prophecy. By JEROME B. HOLGATE. 12 mo, cloth, ... 1 00

The American Magazine and Repository of Useful Literature; devoted to Science, Literature and Arts, and embellished with engravings. By J. S. & B. WOOD, Albany. 2 vols. in 1, 8vo, 1841-2 (complete) ½ cloth, ... 1 00

The American Journal of Agriculture and Science. By Dr. E. EMMONS and A. OSBORN, Albany, 1844-6, 6 vols. 8vo, plates, paper, ... 6 00

American Journal of Agriculture and Science: devoted to the promotion of Agriculture, Horticulture, Science, Arts and Industry. By C. N. BEMENT. Albany, 1848, 1 vol. 8vo, paper, ... 1 50

The last two forming 7 vols. complete—valuable agricultural and scientific works.

Drawings and Tintings. By ALFRED B. STREET. (Comprising *The Grey Forest Eagle*, and other minor poems). 48 pp., 8vo, ½ mor. 50